THE
PRACTICAL
PRODUCE
COOKBOOK

Recipes compiled by
Ray and Elsie Hoover and family

Stratford, WI

1st Printing July, 1997
2nd Printing October, 1997
3rd Printing February, 1998
4th Printing October, 1998
5th Printing September, 1999
6th Printing July, 2000
7th Printing July, 2001

Little Mountain Printing
4A Bordner Road
Richland, PA 17087

ISBN 0-9656842-9-6

Dedicated

to

all who have

discovered the joys

of eating

vegetables.

Table of Contents

Introduction and Acknowledgments.............. iii
Asparagus.. 1
Beans... 9
Beets... 23
Broccoli.. 29
Brussels Sprouts 37
Cabbage.. 43
Carrots.. 55
Cauliflower.. 63
Celery and Celeriac................................. 69
Corn... 77
Cucumbers.. 87
Eggplants.. 95
Greens... 103
Ground Cherries..................................... 111
Kohlrabies... 113
Lettuce and Salad Greens............................ 117
Melons... 129
Okra... 133
Onions... 137
Parsnips... 151
Peas... 157
Peppers.. 165
Potatoes... 173
Pumpkins... 187
Radishes... 197
Rhubarb.. 201

(Continues on the next page.)

Contents (cont.)

Salsify... 211

Spinach... 213

Strawberries.. 221

Summer Squash... 233

Sweet Potatoes... 253

Tomatoes... 263

Turnips and Rutabagas..................................... 285

Winter Squash... 293

Vegetable Canning and Freezing Guide........... 303

Fruit Canning and Freezing Guide.................. 305

Bibliography... 314

Index.. 315

INTRODUCTION and ACKNOWLEDGMENTS

The Practical Produce Cookbook is the result of the combined efforts of our family, Ray and Elsie Hoover with our children Scott, Katrina, William, Kerra, Kelsie and Kristie. The idea for the book was born at the Wausau Farmer's Market, Wausau, WI where we began selling produce the summer of 1996. One day, Scott, after hearing many people ask how to prepare fresh produce, came home from market and suggested we put together a produce cookbook.

This idea merged with one Elsie had been thinking about for some time—a guide to canning and freezing fruits and vegetables. The result was a much larger undertaking than anyone had initially anticipated.

We began in January of 1997, when our home business—Maranatha Market (bulk foods and seasonal produce)—was at its seasonal low. With the icy grip of our Wisconsin winter making it easy to stay indoors, we plunged full speed ahead.

At first our deadline for the manuscript was the beginning of March, then April and finally May. It was completed just in time for spring planting.

Early in March, the project took a new twist when Elsie was diagnosed with invasive breast cancer, resulting in a mastectomy, followed by chemotherapy. Because much of the work had already been done and feeling the Lord had led so far, we decided to continue on, working around and through the physical, emotional and spiritual highs and lows of cancer, surgery and chemotherapy.

In familiarizing ourselves with Elsie's cancer we discovered a confirmation for putting the book together—the health benefits of fresh vegetables. Research results have proven that fresh vegetables decrease the risk for certain types of cancer. Particularly important in cancer prevention are the cole vegetables (broccoli, cauliflower, cabbage, Brussels sprouts and kohlrabi) and tomatoes. Vegetables are also important sources of fiber, vitamins and minerals. Where it is known, we have included nutritional information for individual vegetables on the divider pages.

You will also find scripture verses inserted at the bottom of some of the pages throughout the book. Working in the garden, with seeds, plants and harvests, brings our thoughts many times to our Creator, God. Most of the verses used follow the farming/gardening theme, used so often in Bible illustrations. As a result, we pray this book will be not only a means to enhance physical health, but spiritual health, too.

(continued next page)

Cover and divider page art was done by Elsie. Information on the dividers was written by Ray. Elsie was responsible for selecting, editing and organizing the recipes. Scott (17) learned the art of pizza making every Monday night while we were working on the book. Katrina (14) made supper most of the other evenings during that time. Scott and Katrina both helped in copying recipes and proofreading text. William, Kerra, Kelsie and Kristie were as patient and understanding of the disruptions to our normal routine as 10, 7, 5 and 2 year-olds could be.

A special thanks to our mothers Mrs. David (Miriam) Hoover and Mrs. Isaac (Florence) Kulp who taught us many of the practical aspects of gardening and food preservation.

Thanks too, to those who contributed recipes for the book and to the many who offered encouragement and support while we were working on the project.

Also, thanks to Norman Rohrer of the *Christian Writers Guild,* Plume Lake, CA for his help in editing the divider pages.

Finally, and most importantly, thanks to God who has given us the blessing of gardens and the vegetables they yield. If the book is of help to you for any reason in planting, preparing, picking or preserving your produce— give God the glory.

Ray Hoover
1997

While the earth remaineth, seedtime and harvest, and cold and heat, and summer and winter, and day and night shall not cease.

Genesis 8:22

iv

Asparagus

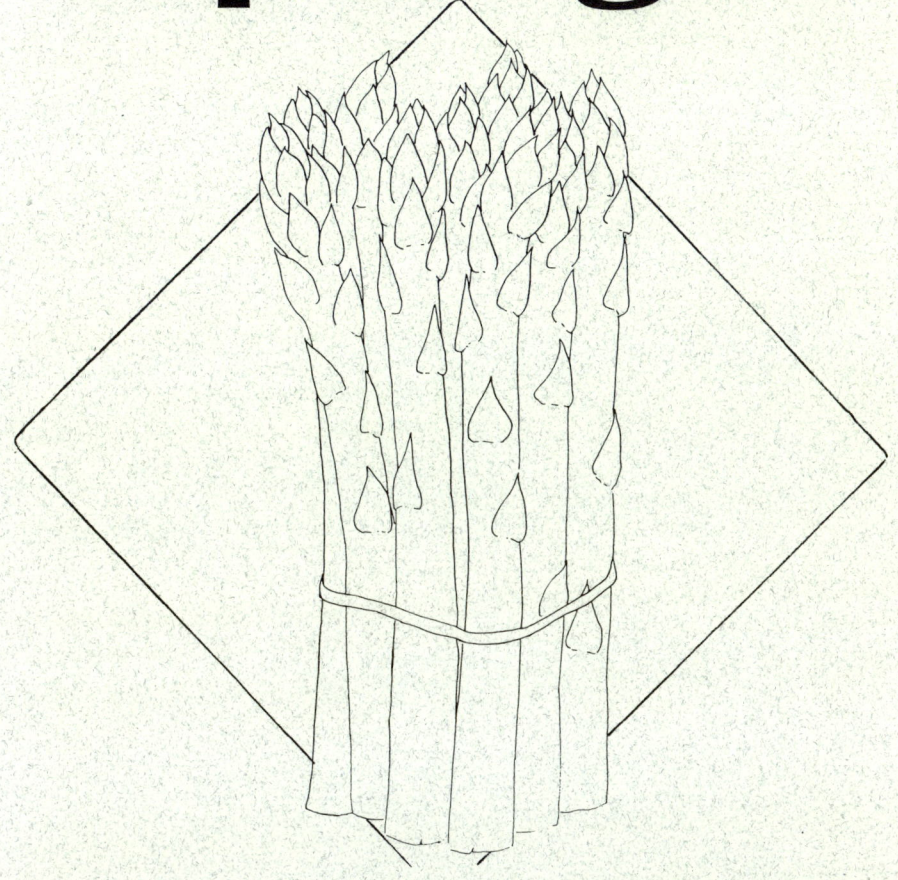

Harbingers of harvests to come, stately asparagus spears are the earliest of all the vegetables you can grow and harvest in your garden. Though asparagus grows well in most areas of the United States, the ideal climate freezes the soil a few inches deep in the winter.

Asparagus beds last many years, so build them with care. Dig deep and add plenty of organic matter to the soil. Asparagus can be started from seed, but root crowns are the method of choice. Plant one or two-year-old crowns in late spring 18 inches apart in trenches 5 feet apart and 8-10 inches deep. Cover the crowns with two inches of soil. Continue to fill in the trench as the asparagus shoots grow until it is completely filled in.

An alternative that can be used successfully in heavy, poorly drained soil is to build a ridge 1 foot high and about 2 feet across. Dig the trench into the ridge and cover as before.

Diligent fertilization of your bed in spring before growth starts and again as soon as harvest is done will encourage more growth and thicker spears.

Perhaps to develop the grace of patience, asparagus can't be picked at all the first year after it's planted and only sparingly the second and third years. After that you can pick to your heart's content for 6-8 weeks.

Asparagus grows quickly. In cool weather you may pick every third day, but as the weather warms you will want to pick every day for the best quality spears.

To harvest, cut or break spears at ground level when they are 5-8 inches high. Use as soon as possible. If you must keep asparagus, put it upright in an inch of water and store it in the refrigerator. Asparagus looses sugar quickly in warm temperatures.

Don't let the woody ends of older spears go to waste. Peel the tough skins by starting at the base and tapering off toward the top. You'll find tender asparagus underneath the thick skin.

Whether you boil, steam or stir fry your asparagus, remember: don't overcook it.

Asparagus is a good source of folate, vitamin A and vitamin C. It is low in calories and high in fiber.

Yield: 1 lb. fresh asparagus = 20 medium spears = 3 cups chopped
1 ¼ lb. = 1 pint frozen asparagus

ASPARAGUS SOUP

2 1/2 - 3 c. 1-inch asparagus
   pieces, cooked
1 c. reserved cooking water
1/2 T. butter

3/4 c. flour
3 1/2 c. milk
1 T. chicken soup base or bouillon
salt, pepper and nutmeg to taste

Set cooking water aside. Melt butter, stir in flour. Add milk a little at a time, stirring constantly until thickened. Dissolve soup base in reserved cooking water and add to white sauce. Add cooked asparagus. Season to taste. Simmer 15-20 minutes on low, stirring frequently.

CREAM OF ASPARAGUS SOUP

2 T. butter
1 1/2 c. chopped onions
6 c. diced asparagus
4 c. chicken broth or water

1 chicken bouillon cube (optional)
1 c. light cream
1/8 tsp. pepper
salt

Melt butter in a large kettle. Sauté onions approximately 4 minutes. Add asparagus, chicken broth and bouillon cube. Simmer until asparagus is tender; 10-15 minutes. Cool slightly then puree in blender. Reheat. Add cream and season to taste.

ASPARAGUS AND CHEDDAR CHEESE SOUP

3 T. butter
1/2 lb. asparagus, trimmed and
   cut into 1/2 inch pieces
1 clove garlic, minced
3 T. flour

4 c. milk
2 c. shredded cheddar cheese
2 tsp. mustard
1/2 tsp. salt
1/8 tsp. white or black pepper

Melt butter in a heavy saucepan. Add asparagus and garlic; sauté about 5 minutes, stirring occasionally. Blend in flour; cook 3-5 minutes, stirring constantly. Reduce heat. Gradually stir in 1 cup of milk and cheddar cheese. Stir constantly for about 5 minutes or until cheese is melted. Stir in remaining milk and rest of ingredients. Gently heat, stirring occasionally, until soup is hot.
Variation: Broccoli florets, green beans or peas can be substituted for the asparagus.

1

ASPARAGUS CHICKEN CHOWDER

3-3 1/2 lb. chicken
3 1/2 quarts water
2 tsp. chicken bouillon granules
2 T. butter
2 medium carrots, chopped
1 medium onion, chopped
1/2 lb. fresh asparagus, cut into
    1/2 inch pieces

2 c. cubed peeled potatoes
2 tsp. salt or to taste
1 1/2 tsp. thyme
1/2 tsp. pepper
1/2 c. flour
1 1/2 c. whipping cream
2 T. chopped fresh parsley

Place chicken, water and bouillon in a large kettle. Cover and bring to a boil; skim fat. Reduce heat; cover and simmer for 1 to 1 ½ hours or until chicken is tender. Remove chicken; cool. Remove 1 cup broth and set aside. Sauté carrots, onion and asparagus in butter over medium heat until tender crisp. Add to kettle along with potatoes, salt, thyme and pepper; return to a boil. Reduce heat; cover and simmer for 20 minutes or until potatoes are tender. Combine flour and reserved broth; stir into soup. Bring to a boil; cook and stir for 2 minutes. Debone chicken and cut into thin strips; add to soup along with cream and parsley. Heat through (do not boil).

ASPARAGUS–SALADS

ASPARAGUS VINAIGRETTE

2 lb. cooked chilled asparagus
1/4 tsp. salt
1/2 tsp. Dijon mustard

2 T. lemon juice
1/2 c. olive or vegetable oil
2 T. chopped shallots or onions

Whisk together all but asparagus. Pour over asparagus. Serve chilled.

ASPARAGUS RADISH CUCUMBER SALAD

1 c. cooked asparagus tips
1 c. sliced radishes
1 c. sliced cucumber
2 c. shredded lettuce

1/4 c. chopped green pepper
6 green onions, chopped fine
1 T. finely chopped parsley
1/2 c. grated cheddar cheese

Toss all ingredients together with your favorite dressing, or pass dressing separately.

HOW TO COOK ASPARAGUS

Fill a skillet large enough to lay asparagus spears in with ½ inch of water. Bring water to boil and add 20 large spears or 3-4 cups cut asparagus and 1/2-1 tsp. salt. Return to a boil then reduce heat and cook 5-7 minutes or until tender crisp. Drain.

Serve with butter or browned butter or sprinkle with hard boiled egg yolks, cheese, or grated parmesan cheese. Broil until cheese is golden brown if desired.

MOCK HOLLANDAISE

3/4 c. mayonnaise or salad dressing	1 T. lemon juice
1/2 c. milk	1/2 tsp. salt
	1/8 tsp. pepper

Combine everything in small sauce pan. Heat slowly, stirring constantly, just until hot. Serve hot over cooked asparagus.

FRIED ASPARAGUS

asparagus spears	butter
flour	salt

Wash and trim asparagus. Cut thick spears in half lengthwise. Dip in flour. Fry in butter until golden brown; turning once. Sprinkle with salt.

FANCY ASPARAGUS

1 lb. asparagus	4 oz. can mushrooms, drained
1 T. vegetable oil	1/2 tsp. salt
2 T. water	1/8 tsp. pepper
1/4 c. minced onion	2 T. cream

Wash asparagus thoroughly and slice diagonally into 1 ½ inch pieces. Combine oil and water in skillet. Bring to a boil. Add asparagus, onion, mushrooms, salt and pepper. Cook, covered for 5-7 minutes, or until tender crisp, stirring occasionally. Drain well then add cream and heat through.

ASPARAGUS STIR FRY

1/3 c. chicken broth or water
2 T. soy sauce
2 tsp. cornstarch
1 tsp. sugar
1/4 tsp. ground ginger
3 T. vegetable oil

3 c. 1 inch diagonally cut
   asparagus pieces
1 medium carrot, thinly sliced
1 medium zucchini, thinly sliced
1 medium onion, sliced ¼ inch
   thick, separated into rings

Stir together first 5 ingredients. Set aside. Heat oil over high heat in a large skillet. Add vegetables. Stir constantly until vegetables are tender; about 5 minutes. Add soy sauce mixture, stirring constantly until mixture boils and thickens.

Variation: Remove vegetables from skillet. Stir fry ½ lb. thin strips of raw chicken, beef or pork in 2 T. oil for approximately 5 min. Add some minced garlic or soy sauce for extra flavor. Add vegetables and heat through.

QUICK ASPARAGUS STIR FRY

1 1/2 T. oil
3 c. asparagus cut diagonally into
   1-inch pieces
1/4 c. chicken broth or water

1/4 tsp. salt
1/4 tsp. pepper
soy sauce

Heat oil in a wok or large skillet. Add asparagus. Stir fry one minute. Add broth. Cover. Lower heat; cook until tender, 3-5 minutes. Season with salt, pepper and soy sauce.

Hearken; Behold, there went out a sower to sow; and it came to pass, as he sowed, some fell by the wayside, and the fowls of the air came and devoured it up. And some fell on stony ground, where it had not much earth; and immediately it sprang up, because it had no depth of earth: But when the sun was up, it was scorched; and because it had no root, it withered away. And some fell among thorns, and the thorns grew up, and choked it, and it yielded no fruit. And other fell on good ground, and did yield fruit that sprang up and increased; and brought forth, some thirty, and some sixty, and some an hundred. And he said unto them, He that hath ears to hear, let him hear.

Mark 4:3-9

CHICKEN ASPARAGUS STIR FRY WITH SPAGHETTI

2 T. butter
2 T. flour
1/4 tsp. pepper
1 1/2 tsp. salt, divided
2 c. milk
1 cube chicken bouillon
1/4 c. grated parmesan cheese
4-5 c. 1-inch diagonally cut
   asparagus
1 medium carrot, thinly sliced

1 medium zucchini, sliced 1/4 inch
   thick
1 medium onion, sliced 1/4 inch
   thick, separated into rings
4 T. vegetable oil, divided
4 chicken breasts cut into thin
   strips
1 lb. spaghetti, cooked and
   drained

Melt butter, stir in flour, pepper and 1/2 tsp. salt. Gradually stir in milk; add bouillon. Stir constantly until sauce thickens and boils. Remove from heat and stir in cheese. Keep sauce warm. Sauté asparagus, carrot, zucchini and onion in 2 T. vegetable oil in a large skillet. Add 1/2 tsp. salt. Cook, stirring frequently, until vegetables are tender crisp—about 5 minutes. Remove vegetables. Add 2 more T. oil and 1/2 tsp. salt to skillet. Stir fry chicken until tender—about 5 minutes. Return vegetables to skillet. Heat through. Add vegetable mixture and sauce to cooked spaghetti and mix well.

ASPARAGUS PARMESAN

1 1/2 lb. asparagus, washed and
   trimmed
1/2 c. butter

1/2 c. grated Parmesan cheese
1/2 tsp. salt
1/4 tsp. pepper

Cook asparagus 5-7 minutes or until tender crisp. Melt butter in a casserole. Place drained asparagus in the melted butter. Combine remaining ingredients and sprinkle on asparagus. Bake at 450 degrees, 5-10 minutes or until Parmesan cheese is melted.

While the earth remaineth, seedtime and harvest, and cold and heat, and summer and winter, and day and night shall not cease.

Genesis 8:22

ASPARAGUS AU GRATIN

4 cups cooked asparagus
3 T. butter
3 T. flour
1/2 tsp. salt or to taste

2 c. milk
1 c. grated Swiss or cheddar
    cheese
buttered bread crumbs

Place cooked asparagus in a buttered baking dish and set aside. Melt butter in sauce pan and add flour and salt; stir until smooth. Add milk and stir well. Bring to a boil then simmer slowly at least 5 minutes. Stir in cheese. Pour over asparagus and sprinkle with bread crumbs. Bake at 425 degrees for 15-20 minutes.

ASPARAGUS QUICHE

1 unbaked 9 inch pie shell with
    fluted edges
1/2 lb. slivered, boiled ham
3 c. 2 inch asparagus pieces,
    cooked
3/4 c. grated Swiss cheese

2 T. minced onion
3 eggs, beaten
1 c. light cream
1/2 tsp. salt
1/4 tsp. nutmeg

Place ham in pie shell. Top with cooked asparagus. Sprinkle with cheese and onion. Beat remaining ingredients together and pour on onions. Sprinkle with more cheese if desired. Bake at 350 degrees for 25-30 minutes.

ASPARAGUS SOUFFLÉ

5 eggs, separated
1/4 c. butter
1/4 c. flour
1 1/3 c. milk
1 tsp. salt
dash pepper

1 T. minced onion
1/4 c. grated sharp cheddar
    cheese
1 1/4 c. finely chopped fresh
    asparagus

In large bowl let egg whites warm to room temperature—1 hour. Melt butter in medium saucepan. Blend in flour. Stir in milk slowly; cook over low heat, stirring until thickened and smooth. Add salt, pepper, onion and cheese; stir until blended. Set aside to cool. Grease well a 1 1/2 quart dish or casserole. Add asparagus to cooled sauce. With mixer at high speed, beat egg whites until stiff peaks form when mixer is slowly raised. In separate bowl, beat yolks until thick and light. Blend in sauce. Fold asparagus mixture into egg whites. Turn into prepared dish. Set in pan containing about 1 inch hot water; then bake at 350 degrees for one hour.

6

BAKED ASPARAGUS WITH EGGS

2 c. buttered bread crumbs	1/8 tsp. pepper
15-20 cooked asparagus tips	1/4 c. butter
5 hard boiled eggs chopped	1/4 c. flour
1 tsp. salt	1 1/2 c. milk

Brown bread crumbs. Place half of the crumbs in the bottom of a baking dish. Add asparagus and eggs in alternate layers. Add salt and pepper then cover with remaining crumbs. Melt butter in saucepan and add flour; stir well. Gradually add milk, stirring constantly. Bring to a boil and boil several minutes. Pour on top of bread crumbs. Bake at 350 degrees for 45 minute

ASPARAGUS LOAF

1 c. coarse cracker crumbs	1/4 tsp. pepper
1/4 c. butter	2 eggs
1/4 c. finely chopped onion	2 c. hot milk
1 T. chopped parsley	4 c. 1-inch asparagus pieces
1/2 tsp. salt	

Sauté cracker crumbs in butter with onion, parsley, salt and pepper approximately 5 minutes. Beat eggs lightly. Stir hot milk into eggs. Add asparagus and crumbs. Put mixture in a buttered 5x9 loaf pan. Bake at 375 degrees for 30 minutes or until set. Can be served with white sauce flavored with chives and/or Parmesan cheese.

ASPARAGUS BRUNCH CASSEROLE

1/4 c. butter	8 eggs
1/2 lb. 1-inch asparagus pieces	2 1/2 c. milk
1 onion, cut in thin wedges	1/2 tsp. marjoram
8 c. French bread cubes	1/2 tsp. salt
2 c. shredded Cheddar cheese	1/8 tsp. pepper
1 c. cubed cooked ham (optional)	

Melt butter. Add vegetables and cook, stirring until tender crisp—about 3-5 minutes. Combine bread cubes, 1 c. cheese, ham and vegetable mixture; mix well. Put in a buttered 13 x 9 pan. Combine eggs, milk and seasonings; mix well. Pour evenly over bread mixture. Cover and refrigerate 12-24 hours. Bake, uncovered, at 350° until golden brown and puffed—about 45-50 minutes. Sprinkle remaining cheese evenly over top, and bake until the cheese is melted—about 1 minute.

ASPARAGUS—CANNING AND FREEZING

HOW TO CAN ASPARAGUS[1]

Raw pack: Wash, trim and cut into 1-inch pieces. Pack tightly without crushing. Add 1/2 teaspoon salt to pints and 1 teaspoon to quarts. Iodized or plain table salt may be used. If desired, salt may be reduced or eliminated.

Hot pack: Prepare as for raw pack. Boil in water 2 to 3 minutes. Pack hot and fill with hot cooking liquid, leaving 1 inch head space. Add salt as for raw pack.

Process in a pressure canner; pints 30 minutes and quarts 40 minutes. Process at 10 lb. of pressure for elevations up to 1000 ft. above sea level; 15 lb. of pressure for elevations over 1000 ft. above sea level. Dial gauges should be at 11 lb. of pressure up to 2000 ft. above sea level.

HOW TO FREEZE ASPARAGUS[2]

Cut or break off tough ends. Wash thoroughly. Sort according to thickness of stalks. Leave whole or cut into 1 to 2-inch lengths. Water blanch small stalks 1 1/2 to 2 minutes, medium stalks 2 to 3 minutes and large stalks 3 to 4 minutes.

The sower soweth the word. And these are they by the way side, where the word is sown; but when they have heard, Satan cometh immediately, and taketh away the word that was sown in their hearts. And these are they, likewise which are sown on stony ground; who, when they have heard the word, immediately receive it with gladness; and have no root in themselves, and so endure but for a time: afterward, when affliction or persecution ariseth for the word's sake, immediately they are offended. And these are they which are sown among thorns; such as hear the word, and the cares of this world, and the deceitfulness of riches, and the lusts of other things entering in, choke the word, and it becometh unfruitful. And these are they which are sown on good ground; such as hear the word, and receive it, and bring forth fruit, some thrirtyfold, some sixty, and some an hundred.

Mark 4:14-20

Beans

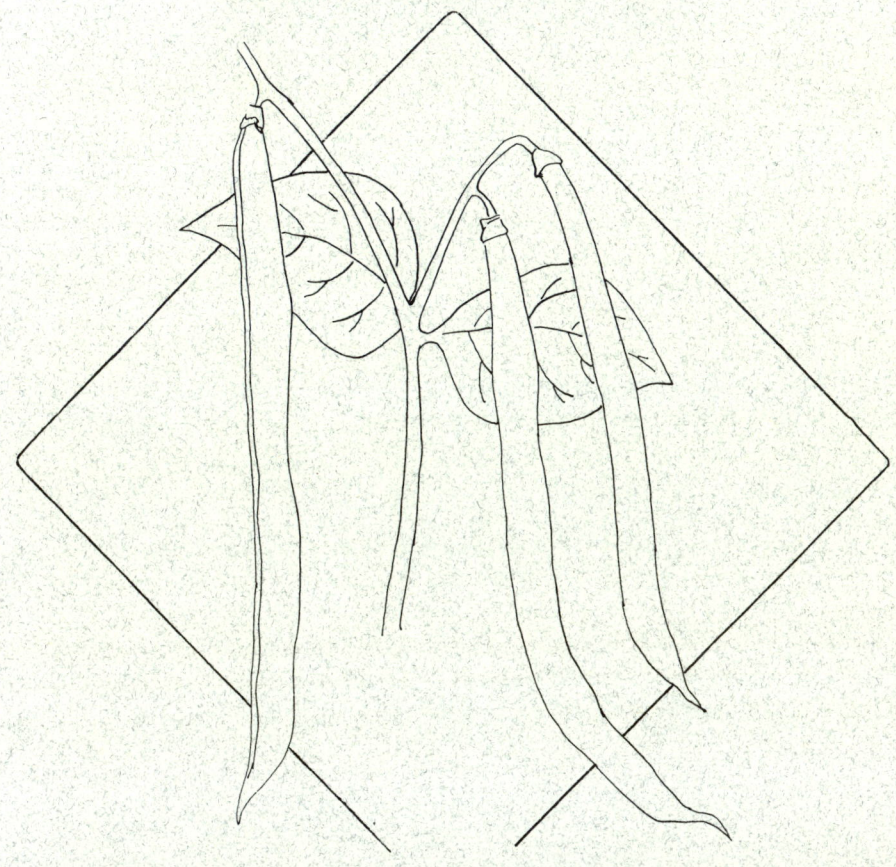

Snap beans, delicious and easy to grow, come in three colors: green, yellow and purple. The yellow beans are known as wax beans.

Plant snap beans when the soil is warm and the danger of frost is past. Do not plant your beans too early. Most beans do not germinate until the soil reaches 60 degrees.

Sow seeds 1 inch deep in heavy soil and 1½-inches deep in sandy soil. Plant 3-5 inches apart. Flat, podded beans such as limas need more space. Bush snap beans produce for about three weeks. For a continuous supply, plant successive sowings every 2-3 weeks through midsummer.

Pick beans when plants are dry to avoid spreading disease from plant to plant. Beans are subject to diseases that survive in soil so be sure to rotate your bean patch on a three year basis. Snap beans are best when picked the size of a pencil or a little thinner. If you let old pods hang on your plants you greatly decrease the growth of younger pods.

Green beans can be stored in the refrigerator for about one week. Place unwashed in a sealed plastic bag or container. Rejuvenate limp beans by soaking them in ice water for up to 30 minutes.

Shell beans are snap beans that matured in the pod. Shell beans left in the pod to dry are—logically enough—called dry beans. All beans, if allowed to grow long enough, will go from a snap, to a shell, to a dry bean. However, not all beans are good in all stages.

Limas, favas, horticultural beans, and soy beans are all eaten as shell beans. They can also be dried.

Soybean pods ripen all at one time. When pods begin to lose their bright green color, clip the plants near the base. To shell, strip off pods, rinse and boil for 5 minutes. Cool, then shell by popping the beans out of the pods.

Pick shell beans when the seeds are tender but well formed and the pods are lumpy and plump. Pick dry beans late in the season when the plants are dead and the beans are beginning to get hard.

Fresh shell beans can be substituted in recipes calling for dried beans. Just remember to use at least twice as many shell beans. Shell beans will not expand as dry beans do. Two cups uncooked dry beans equal four cups cooked beans; two cups uncooked shell beans equal two cups cooked beans.

Dry beans are an excellent source of protein. Green beans are rich in folate, vitamin A and vitamin C.

Yield:

green beans and wax beans—1 lb. = 4 cups chopped beans
1 bushel = 30 lb. = 30-45 pints
lima beans—1 lb. shelled = 4 cups
1 bushel (unshelled) = 32 lb. = 12-16 pint

GREEN BEAN SOUP

1 c. chopped onion	1 c. uncooked macaroni
2 T. butter	2 qt. water or broth
2 c. cut green beans	1 tsp. salt or to taste
1 1/2 c. diced potatoes	1 tsp. basil
1 c. sliced carrots	1/4 tsp. pepper

Sauté onion in butter in a large kettle. When onion starts to brown add remaining ingredients. Bring to a boil then simmer approximately 45 minutes.
Variation: Slice in smoked sausage.

SHELL BEAN SOUP

1 c. chopped celery	1 c. sliced carrots
1 c. chopped onions	2 qt. broth (chicken or beef)
3 T. oil	2 c. finely sliced cabbage
4 c. fresh shell beans, shelled	1/2 tsp. salt or to taste
1 tsp. thyme	pepper

In large sauce pan—sauté celery and onions in hot oil for 5 minutes. Add beans, thyme, carrots and broth. Bring to a boil, skim, then reduce heat and simmer partially covered for 20 minutes or until beans are tender. Add cabbage and simmer 10 minutes longer or until cabbage is tender. Season with salt and pepper to taste.

LIMA BEAN SOUP

6 c. chicken broth	2 medium potatoes, diced
4 c. lima beans	1 medium onion, chopped
2 c. corn	1 tsp. oregano
1 c. cooked, diced chicken	1/2 tsp. basil
1/2 c. sliced carrots	salt and pepper to taste

Combine all ingredients. Bring to a boil. Reduce heat, cover and simmer 30-35 minutes.
Variation: Add 1/4 c. butter while cooking and 1 c. light cream at the end.

LIMA BEAN CHOWDER

2 T. butter
1 large onion, chopped
1 medium, potato, peeled and
    diced
3 c. water
2 c. fresh lima beans
2 tsp. salt

1/4 tsp. pepper
2 c. fresh corn
1 c. shredded cabbage
13 oz can evaporated milk or
    1 1/2 c. cream
1 c. shredded cheddar cheese

Melt butter in a 3 quart saucepan. Add onions; cook until tender. Stir in potato, water, limas, salt and pepper. Bring to a boil then reduce heat, cover and simmer 10 minutes or until vegetables are tender. Gradually stir in milk and cheese. Cook, stirring constantly for 3 minutes.

NAVY BEAN SOUP

1 1/2 c. dry navy beans
2 qt. water
1 tsp. salt or to taste
3/4 c. celery, diced

3/4 c. carrots, diced
1 medium onion, chopped
1 meaty ham bone (optional)
1/4 tsp. pepper

Wash and sort beans. Combine beans, water and salt in large saucepan. Let stand overnight. Add remaining ingredients. Cover and bring to a boil. Reduce heat and simmer 2 to 4 hours or until beans reach desired tenderness. Add additional water if necessary.
Variation: Omit celery and carrots.

OLD-FASHIONED NAVY BEAN SOUP

1 1/2 c. dry navy beans
1 tsp. salt or to taste
pepper

2 qt. milk
3 T. butter
1/4 c. cream (optional)

Bring beans to a boil. Boil for 2 minutes and remove from heat. Let stand one hour, still covered with water. Then cook until soft—2 to 4 hours. Add milk, butter, salt and pepper. Bring almost to a boil. Add cream if desired.

In the morning sow thy seed, and in the evening withhold not thine hand: for thou knowest not whether shall prosper, either this or that, or whether they shall be both alike good.

Ecclesiastes 12:6

GREEN BEAN SALAD

6-8 c. cut green beans	2 tsp. sugar
1 thinly sliced onion	2 T. horseradish
1 c. sour cream	1/4 tsp. salt
2 T. vinegar	pepper to taste

Cook beans 3 minutes, rinse in cold water and drain well. Add remaining ingredients to cooled beans. Marinate overnight in refrigerator.

RAW GREEN BEAN SALAD

2 c. chopped young green beans	1 small cucumber, diced
1/2 cup chopped green pepper	salt and pepper to taste
1/4 c. radishes, chopped	dressing of your choice, enough to
1/2 medium onion, diced	hold salad together

Combine vegetables and mix well. Add dressing of your choice. Chill and serve.

GREEN BEAN AND TOMATO SALAD

2 lb. green beans	5 T. olive oil
2 lb. ripe tomatoes	1 T. wine vinegar
salt and pepper to taste	1 T. Worcestershire sauce

Cook the beans in salted water until tender but still crisp, leaving them whole if they are young and slim. Chill. Scald the tomatoes in boiling water 1 minute. Peel and cut them in eighth, removing seeds and pulp. Sprinkle with salt and pat dry with paper towels. Put the oil, vinegar and Worcestershire sauce in a salad bowl. Mix well and add salt and pepper to taste. Add the beans and tomatoes and mix again. Refrigerate for 1 hour.

He that tilleth his land shall be satisfied with bread: but he that followeth vain persons is void of understanding.

Proverbs 12:11

THREE BEAN SALAD

1 1/2 c. 1 inch green bean pieces,
    cooked
1 1/2 c. 1 inch wax bean pieces,
    cooked
1 1/2 c. fresh shell beans, cooked
1 c. chopped green peppers
3/4 c. thinly sliced red onions

1 clove garlic, minced
2/3 c. vinegar
1/3 c. sugar
1/4 c. olive or vegetable oil
1/2 tsp. Worcestershire sauce
1 tsp. salt
1/8 tsp. pepper

Cool cooked beans. Combine with peppers, onions, and garlic. Place remaining ingredients in a jar and shake well. Toss with vegetables until well coated.

GREEN BEEN SALAD WITH LIMAS

2 1/2 c. cooked green beans
2 1/2 c. cooked lima beans
1 c. mayonnaise

1 head lettuce
2 sliced hard boiled eggs

Mix beans with 1/2 of the mayonnaise. Arrange lettuce leaves in salad bowl. Put in beans and top with remaining mayonnaise. Garnish with egg slices.
Variation: Use French dressing instead of mayonnaise.

BEAN AND BACON SALAD

4 c. cooked kidney beans
1 c. diced green peppers
1 c. diced celery

1/2 c. thinly sliced green onions
1 lb. bacon
1 large head ice berg lettuce

Combine beans, peppers, celery and onions. Chill. Cut bacon into 1 inch pieces, fry and drain on a paper towel. Break lettuce into bite size pieces. Toss everything together. Serve with your favorite dressing.

For the earth which drinketh in the rain that cometh oft upon it, and bringeth forth herbs meet for them by whom it is dressed, receiveth blessing from God.

Hebrews 6:7

HOW TO COOK GREEN BEANS

Bring 1 inch of water to boil in a 2 qt. saucepan. Add 4 cups cut green beans and 1 tsp. salt or to taste. Return to a boil. Reduce heat. Cover and simmer 5-10 minutes or until tender crisp. Drain. Add butter.

Variations: Brown chopped onion in butter, add to cooked beans and toss lightly. Sprinkle buttered beans with pieces of crumbled bacon or with Parmesan cheese. Brown slivered almonds in butter. Mix lightly with beans.

STIR FRIED GREEN BEANS

3 T. vegetable oil
4 c. 1-inch diagonally cut green beans
2 ribs celery, cut diagonally
1/4 lb. mushrooms, sliced into 1/4 inch slices

1/2 c. beef broth or water
2 T. soy sauce
1 T. corn starch
1/4 tsp. ginger

Heat oil. Add green beans. Cook, stirring frequently, about 5 minutes. Add celery; cook 2 minutes. Add mushrooms; cook 3 minutes or until beans and celery are tender crisp. Combine remaining ingredients until well blended and stir into skillet. Stir constantly until mixture boils and thickens.

WAX BEANS AND TOMATOES

4 c. wax beans, cut into 1 inch pieces
2 T. vegetable oil
2 tomatoes, peeled, seeded and chopped

1 tsp. sugar
1 tsp. salt
1/8 tsp. pepper
2 T. water
2 T. chopped parsley (optional)

Sauté beans in hot oil for 5 minutes. Stir in all but parsley, Cover and simmer until beans are tender crisp. Sprinkle with parsley and serve.

13

GREEN BEANS WITH HARD BOILED EGGS

3 hard boiled eggs
2 T. butter
2 T. flour
1/2 tsp. salt
1/4 tsp. dry mustard

1/8 tsp. pepper
1 c. milk
6 c. chopped, cooked and drained
    green beans

Remove yolks from eggs and press through a sieve; set aside. Chop whites and set aside. Melt butter; stir in flour, salt, mustard and pepper. Gradually stir in milk. Cook, stirring constantly, until mixture boils and thickens. Stir in egg whites. Spoon over hot green beans and sprinkle with egg yolks.

GREEN BEAN POTATO PANCAKES

1 1/2 c. finely diced green beans
2 c. grated potatoes
1/4 c. chopped onions

2 large eggs, lightly beaten
1/2 tsp. salt or to taste
1/8 tsp. pepper

Combine ingredients and fry in vegetable oil or a mixture of butter and oil.

GREEN BEANS WITH SOUR CREAM AND BACON

4 c. 1-inch green bean pieces
1 T. butter
1 small onion, finely chopped
1 T. flour
1 T. sugar
1 tsp. parsley

3/4 tsp. salt
1/2 c. milk
1 T. vinegar
1/2 c. dairy sour cream
4 slices bacon, diced, cooked and
    drained.

Bring 1 inch of water to a boil in a 2 quart saucepan and add beans. Reduce heat. Cover and cook 7-9 minutes or until beans are tender crisp. Melt butter in a skillet; add onion and cook until tender. Stir in flour, sugar, parsley and salt. Gradually stir in milk. Cook until mixture boils and thickens. Reduce heat and stir in vinegar. Stir some of the hot mixture into the sour cream, then stir sour cream into hot mixture. Add green beans. Heat through but do not boil. Sprinkle bacon on top.

And Jesus said unto him, no man having put his hand to the plough, and looking back, is fit for the kingdom of God.

Luke 9:62

14

GREEN BEANS WITH POTATOES AND HOT DOGS

4 c. green beans broken into short
    pieces
12-15 small new potatoes,
    unpeeled, cut in half
1/4 c. chopped onion

1 tsp. salt or to taste
1/4 tsp. pepper
5-10 hot dogs, cut into 1/2 inch
    pieces
1-2 T. butter

Bring one inch of water to a boil in a saucepan. Add all ingredients but butter. Cook until potatoes are fork tender. Add butter.

GREEN BEAN BAKE

8 c. 1-inch green bean pieces
1/4 c. finely chopped onion
2 T. vegetable oil
1 T. vinegar
1 1/2 tsp. salt

1/8 tsp. pepper
2 T. dry bread crumbs
2 T. grated Parmesan cheese
1 T. melted butter

Cook beans in water about 5 minutes. Drain. Toss with onion, oil, vinegar, salt and pepper. Pour into a 2 qt. casserole. Combine remaining ingredients and sprinkle over beans. Bake, uncovered, at 350° for 20-25 minutes.

GREEN BEAN HAM POTATO CASSEROLE

3/8 c. butter
3/8 c. flour
3 c. milk
1 1/2 c. grated cheddar or
    American cheese

4 c. green beans, cooked
4 medium potatoes, cooked and
    diced
3 c. cooked, diced ham

Melt butter and stir in flour. Add milk, stirring constantly until thickened. Remove from heat. Add cheese and stir until melted. Arrange potatoes in a buttered casserole. Cover with green beans. Pour 1/2 of cheese sauce over green beans. Add ham and remaining cheese sauce. Top with buttered bread crumbs if desired. Bake at 350 degrees approximately 30 minutes.

HOW TO COOK SHELL BEANS

Place shell beans in 1 inch of water. Add herbs if desired. Bring to a boil, then lower heat and simmer. Cook until tender, 10-25 minutes, depending on the size of the bean. Drain. Season with 1 tsp. salt to 4 c. beans or to taste. Add butter if desired. A little milk can be added.

LIMA BEANS AND CORN (SUCCOTASH)

2 c. lima beans	1 tsp. salt
2 c. corn	1 c. water
2 T. chopped onion (optional)	2 T. butter

Put everything but butter into a saucepan. Bring to a boil. Reduce heat and simmer approximately 25 minutes. Drain and add butter.

HERBED FAVA BEANS

4 lb. fava beans (Italian broad beans)	salt and pepper to taste
	1 T. chopped parsley (or 1 tsp. dry)
6 T. olive or vegetable oil	
1 T. butter	1 T. chopped fresh basil (or 1 tsp. dry)
2 cloves garlic, minced	
1/2 c. onion, minced	

Shell the beans and cook in boiling water until just tender. Drain. Heat the oil and butter, add the garlic, onion, salt and pepper and cook 3 minutes. Add the beans and toss well. Add the parsley and basil, toss again and serve at once.

SHELL BEAN CASSEROLE

1 1/2 lb. ground meat	3 medium potatoes, diced
1 small onion, chopped fine	2 c. shell beans
1/2 tsp. salt	1 pt. tomato juice
1/2 tsp. pepper	2 beef bouillon cubes
1/4 tsp. garlic powder	

Mix first 5 ingredients. Form into 20 small balls; put into cake pan and bake 15 minutes at 350 degrees. Mix remaining ingredients in a large saucepan. Stir in meatballs and bring to a boil. Put into baking dish. Cover. Bake at 350 degrees for 30 minutes. Stir, then continue baking until vegetables are done.

KIDNEY BEAN CASSEROLE

4 c. cooked kidney beans	2 T. vinegar
1 medium onion, chopped	2 tsp. mustard
1/2 c. ketchup	1 tsp. salt
3 T. brown sugar	4 strips bacon

Combine beans and onions. Stir together all but the bacon and add to the beans. Put beans in a casserole and lay bacon on top. Bake at 375 degrees for 45 minutes.

BARBECUED LIMA BEANS

5-6 c. shelled lima beans
4 slices bacon, diced
2 ribs celery, chopped
1 onion, sliced
1 green pepper, chopped
1 clove garlic, minced
2 c. tomato juice

1/4 c. brown sugar
1/4 c. vinegar
1 T. mustard
2 tsp. Worcestershire sauce
1 tsp. chili powder
1/2 tsp. salt

Cook limas in one inch of water approximately 20 minutes. Drain well. Brown bacon in same saucepan. Drain. Combine all ingredients with bacon drippings then put in a casserole. Cover and bake at 350 degrees for 1 hour.

POT ROAST WITH LIMA BEANS

2-3 lb. beef roast
2 c. water
4 medium carrots, quartered
4 medium potatoes, quartered
2 stalks celery, quartered

4 small onions
2 T. minced fresh parsley
salt and pepper to taste
4 c. chopped red tomatoes
1 1/2 c. cooked lima beans

Heat a large heavy saucepan and sear roast on all sides. Add water. Lower heat and cook for two hours. Add all but lima beans. Cover and cook until vegetables are tender. Add cooked lima beans and heat through.

HORTICULTURAL BAKED BEANS

4 c. shelled horticultural beans
2 slices bacon
1 c. chopped onion
1/4 c. molasses

1 T. mustard
1 bay leaf
2 tsp. salt

Cover beans with 4 c. water and bring to a boil. Skim top and add remaining ingredients. Reduce heat, cover and simmer 4 hours.

Be not deceived; God is not mocked: for whatsoever a man soweth, that shall he also reap. For he that soweth to his flesh shall of the flesh reap corruption; but he that soweth to the Spirit shall of the Spirit reap life everlasting.

Galations 6:7,8

HOW TO COOK DRY BEANS

2 c. dry beans   **6 c. water**

Bring to a boil. Boil for two minutes; remove from heat. Let stand one hour, still covered with water, then cook until tender. You may need to add more water. Add a tsp. of salt per 4 c. of cooked beans. Add other seasonings as desired.

Presoaked navy beans, peas, small red beans and small white beans take approximately 3-3 1/2 hours. Or cook for 10 minutes in a pressure cooker.

Presoaked kidney beans and pinto beans take 2-2 1/2 hours in a regular soup pot or 5-7 minutes in a pressure cooker. Great Northern beans take just a little longer.

BOSTON BAKED BEANS

2 c. dry navy or soy beans   **1/4 c. firmly packed brown sugar**
1 c. chopped onion   **1 tsp. salt**
1/2 c. molasses   **1/4 lb. salt pork or bacon, diced**
1/2 tsp. dry mustard

Soak beans overnight or cover with water, bring to a boil, boil 2 minutes. Skim off loose bean skins if using soy beans. Remove from heat and let stand one hour. After soaking put beans and onion in a large kettle and cover with water. Bring to a boil then simmer 1 to 1 1/2 hours. Drain liquid into a small bowl. Combine 1 cup of liquid with molasses, mustard, brown sugar and salt. Place half of the salt pork or bacon in the bottom of a 2 qt. casserole. Place beans on top and pour molasses mixture over the beans. Add more of reserved liquid to cover beans if necessary. Top with remaining salt pork or bacon. Cover and bake at 350 degrees for 3 hours. After 2 hours of baking add more liquid if too dry. Uncover and bake 30 minutes longer or until beans are the desired consistency.

REFRIED BEANS

1 1/4 c. dry pinto beans   **1/2 tsp. salt**
2 c. water   **2 tsp. chili powder**
1 c. chopped onion   **1 tsp. cumin (optional)**
2 T. vegetable oil

Combine beans, water and onion in a saucepan. Cover and heat to boiling. Boil for 2 minutes. Remove from heat and let stand 1 hour. Add enough water to cover and heat to boiling. Cover and boil gently until beans are tender, about 1 1/2 hours. Add more water if needed. Mash beans. Stir in remaining ingredients.
Variation: Add 1 c. peeled and chopped tomatoes or 1/2 c. shredded cheddar cheese.

KIDNEY BEANS AND SAUSAGE OVER RICE

1 lb. dry red kidney beans	1/2 c. chopped celery
2 tsp. garlic salt	3 garlic cloves minced
1 tsp. Worcestershire sauce	1 c. peeled, seeded, chopped
1/4 tsp. hot pepper or hot pepper	tomatoes
sauce	2 bay leaves
1 qt. water	1/4 cup minced fresh parsley
1 lb. fully cooked smoked	1/2 tsp. salt
sausage, diced	1/2 tsp. pepper
1 c. chopped onion	hot cooked rice

Place beans in a large kettle; add water to cover by 2 inches. Bring to boil; boil for 2 minutes. Remove from heat; cover and let stand for 1 hour. Drain beans and discard liquid. Add garlic salt, Worcestershire sauce, hot pepper and water; bring to a boil. Reduce heat; cover and simmer for 1-1 1/2 hours. Meanwhile, in a skillet, sauté sausage until lightly browned. Remove with a slotted spoon to bean mixture. Sauté onion, celery and garlic in drippings until tender; add to the bean mixture. Stir in tomatoes and bay leaves. Cover and simmer for 30 minutes or until beans are tender. Discard bay leaves. Stir in parsley, salt and pepper. Serve over rice.

BEANS – CANNING AND FREEZING

HOW TO CAN GREEN, WAX AND ITALIAN BEANS[1]

Raw Pack: Wash and trim. Cut into 1 or 2-inch pieces. Pack tightly. Add 1/2 tsp. salt to pints and 1 tsp. to quarts. Iodized or plain table salt may be used. If desired, salt may be reduced or eliminated. Cover with boiling water, leaving 1 inch headspace.

Hot Pack: Wash, trim and cut as above. Cover with boiling water; boil 5 minutes. Pack hot beans into jar. Add salt as for raw pack. Cover with boiling cooking liquid, leaving 1 inch headspace.

Process in a pressure canner; pints 20 minutes and quarts 25 minutes.

Process at 10 lb. of pressure for elevations up to 1000 feet above sea level. Process at 15 lb. pressure for elevations above 1000 feet above sea level. Dial gauges should be at 11 lb. up to 2000 ft. above sea level.

THREE BEAN SALAD TO CAN

1-1/2 c. green or yellow beans
1-1/2 c. canned, drained red
    kidney beans
1 c. canned, drained garbanzo
    beans
1/2 c. trimmed and thinly sliced
    onion
1/2 c. trimmed and thinly sliced
    celery

1/2 c. sliced green pepper
1/2 c. vinegar
1/4 c. lemon juice
3/4 c. sugar
1-1/4 c. water
1/4 c. oil
1/2 tsp. canning salt

Snap off ends of beans. Cut or snap into 1 to 2 inch pieces. Blanch 3 minutes and cool immediately. Rinse kidney beans with water and drain again. Prepare and measure all other vegetables.

Combine vinegar, lemon juice, sugar and water and bring to a boil. Remove from heat. Add oil and salt and mix well. Add beans, onions, celery and green pepper to solution and bring to a simmer.

Marinate 12 to 14 hours in refrigerator, then heat entire mixture to a boil. Fill jars with solids. Add hot liquid, leaving 1/2-inch headspace. Process 10 minutes in boiling water canner.

DILLY BEANS

4 qt. whole green or wax beans
1/4 tsp. cayenne pepper or 1 small
    dried hot pepper per jar
1/2 head fresh dill or 1-1/2 tsp. dill
    seed or weed per jar
1 clove garlic per jar

1/2 tsp. whole mustard seed
    per jar
5 c. distilled vinegar
5 c. water
1/2 c. canning salt

Wash beans thoroughly; drain and cut into lengths to fit pint jars. Place pepper, mustard seed, dill and garlic in each jar. Pack beans vertically in jars. Combine vinegar, water and salt; heat to boiling. Pour boiling hot solution over beans, filling to 1/2 inch of top of jar. Process in boiling water canner for 10 minutes.

Neither is there salvation in any other: for there is none other name under heaven given among men, whereby we must be saved.

Acts 4:12

HOW TO CAN FRESH LIMA BEANS[1]

Raw Pack: Shell and wash. Pack into jars and cover with boiling water. For small beans, leave 1 inch headspace in pints, 1 1/2 inches in quarts.

Large beans: Leave 1 inch headspace in pints, 1 1/4 inches in quarts. Do not pack down. Add 1/2 tsp. salt to pints and 1 tsp. to quarts. Iodized or plain table salt may be used.

Hot Pack: Shell; cover with boiling water; bring to boil. Pack loosely to 1 inch of top. Add salt as for raw pack. Cover with boiling cooking water, leaving 1 inch headspace.

Process pints for 40 minutes and quarts 50 minutes. Process in a pressure canner at 10 lb. of pressure for elevations up to 1000 feet above sea level. Process at 15 lb. for elevations above 1000 feet above sea level. Dial gauges should be at 11 lb. of pressure up to 2000 ft. above sea level.

HOW TO CAN GREEN SOYBEANS[1]

Hot Pack: Shell and wash green soybeans. Cover shelled beans with boiling water and boil 5 minutes. Pack hot and cover with boiling water, leaving 1-inch headspace. Add 1/2 tsp. salt to pints and 1 tsp. to quarts. Iodized or plain table salt may be used. If desired, add 1/2 to 1 T. sugar.

Process in a pressure canner; pints 60 minutes and quarts 70 minutes. Process at 10 lb. of pressure for elevations up to 1000 feet above sea level and 15 lb. for elevations over 1000 feet above sea level. Dial gauges should be at 11 lb. of pressure up to 2000 feet above sea level.

HOW TO CAN DRY BEANS[1]

Use kidney, navy, soybeans, great northern, or any other dry bean or pea. Soak beans 12-18 hours in cold water or boil 2 minutes and soak for 1 hour. Drain. Cover with fresh water and boil 30 minutes. Pack hot, leaving 1-inch headspace. Add 1 tsp. salt to quarts and 1/2 tsp. salt to pints. Cover with boiling water, leaving 1-inch headspace.

Process in a pressure canner; pints 75 minutes and quarts 90 minutes. Process at 10 lb. of pressure if you live up to 1000 feet above sea level. Process at 15 lb. of pressure if you live above 1000 feet above sea level. Dial gauges should be at 11 lb. of pressure up to 2000 feet above sea level.

HOW TO CAN BAKED BEANS USING DRY BEANS[1]

Soak and boil beans until tender. Bake according to regular recipe, adding water as needed. Pack hot beans, leaving 1-inch of headspace. Be sure there is sauce to cover the beans.

Process in a pressure canner; pints 65 minutes and quarts 75 minutes. Process at 10 lb. of pressure if you live up to 1000 feet above sea level. Process at 15 lb. of pressure if you live above 1000 feet above sea level. Dial gauges should be at 11 lb. of pressure up to 2000 feet above sea level.

HOW TO CAN DRY BEANS WITH MOLASSES OR TOMATO SAUCE[1]

Soak beans overnight or cover with water and boil 2 minutes; remove from heat and soak 1 hour. Drain. Cover with fresh water and heat to boiling; drain and save liquid for sauce. Fill jars 3/4 full of hot beans and cover with boiling sauce, leaving 1-inch headspace. Add a 1-inch cube of pork, ham or bacon to each jar if desired.

Molasses Sauce: Mix 1 qt. cooking liquid, 3 T. molasses or sorghum, 1 T. vinegar, 2 tsp. salt and 3/4 tsp. dry mustard. Heat to boiling and pour over hot beans. Make as much as you need to fill your jars.

Tomato Sauce: Mix 1 qt. tomato juice, 1 c. catsup, 3 T. sugar, 2 tsp. salt, 1 T. chopped onion and 1/4 tsp. ground cloves. Heat to boiling. Process according to baked bean instructions.

HOW TO FREEZE GREEN BEANS

Select young tender beans. Sort and snip ends. Wash. Leave whole, cut into uniform lengths or slice lengthwise into strips for French style. Cut Italian beans into 1-1/2 inch lengths.[2]

Blanch for 3 minutes, cool immediately in cold water; drain and package into containers.

HOW TO FREEZE GREEN BEANS – UNBLANCHED

Snap off ends of ends of green beans and snip or break into desired lengths. Wash and allow to dry completely. When beans are dry, put into freezer bags or boxes. Beans will keep approximately 6 months with this process.

HOW TO FREEZE LIMA BEANS

Select well-filled pods with beans ready for table use. Shell, wash and sort according to size. Discard immature, old or split beans. Blanch small beans 1 minute, medium beans 2 minutes and large beans 3-4 minutes. Cool immediately in cold water; drain and put in containers.

Beets

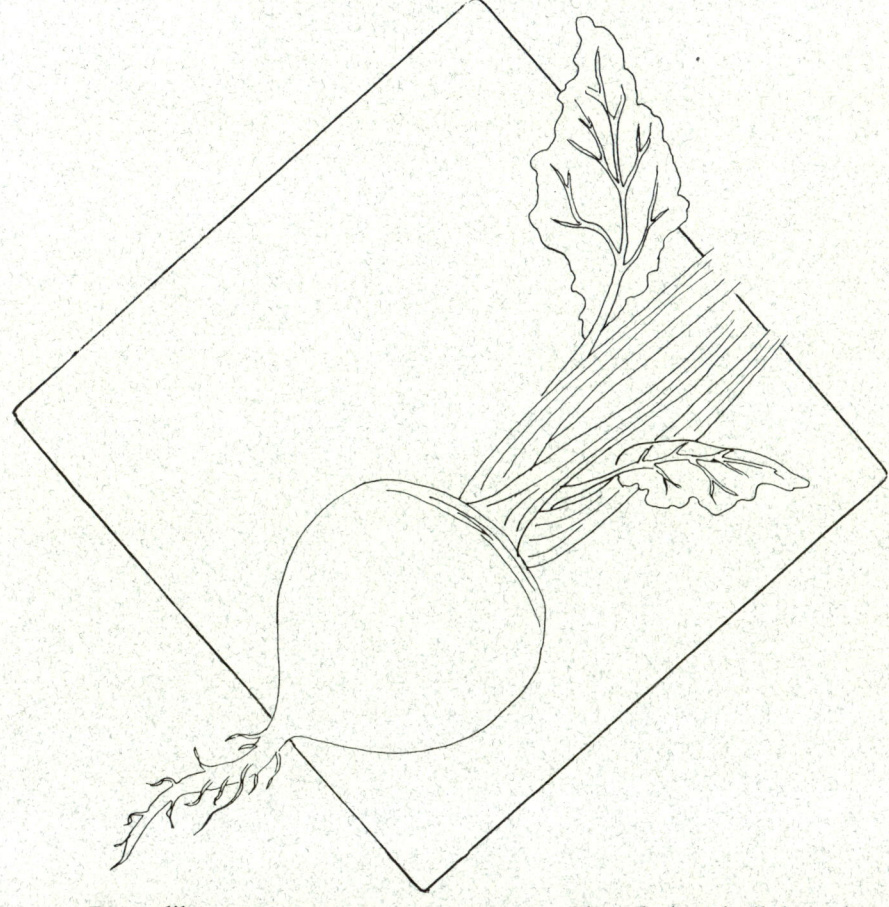

Beets, like carrots, are very easy to grow. They do best in light or loamy soil. Although often called "red beets", beets also come white and yellow. Beets are a root crop, but young beet tops are highly edible as greens, too.

Beets prefer cool weather and can withstand light frost, so plant beets directly into the soil as soon as the ground can be worked in the spring. Plant ½ inch deep, about 1 inch apart. Thin beats at least twice, once at 2 weeks and again at 4 weeks. A garden rake works well for the first thinning. Use the tender tops from later thinnings as greens. Final spacing should be from 2 to 4 inches.

Beets have a high moisture content and need plenty of water while growing. The most common problem with growing beets is overplanting and/or underthinning. Crowded beets may be tough and stringy from lack of moisture. Beets are one of the most pest-free and disease-free of all vegetables.

Harvest beets at 1 ½ -3 inches across. Big beets can be sliced into finger-size sticks and eaten raw with dip. Grated raw beets are a colorful addition to a salad as well. Leave the tap root and one inch of stem on unpeeled beets for cooking so they don't bleed as much. If beets are to be mixed with other ingredients, add them just before serving so the rest of the ingredients don't turn red.

Beets are rich in folate and vitamin C. Beet greens are high in potassium, calcium, iron, beta carotene and vitamin C.

To store beets, layer them in sand and keep in a cool, moist place with temperature below 45 degrees.

Yield: 1 lb. fresh beets = 4 cups chopped
1 bushel (without greens) = 52 lb. = 35-42 pints
1 bushel greens = 12 lb. = 8-12 pints

BORSCHT

1 lb. stewing beef cut into bite-
    size pieces
8-10 c. water
3 c. diced raw beets
1 1/2 c. diced onion
4 c. peeled, chopped tomatoes
3 c. finely chopped cabbage

salt to taste
1/4 tsp. pepper
1 tsp. celery seed
3/4 tsp. dried thyme
2 bay leaves, crumbled
3-4 T. lemon juice
1 T. sugar

Place beef in large soup pot with water. Bring to a boil, skim off scum, reduce heat and simmer until beef is almost tender. Add beets and onions and simmer for 30 minutes or until vegetables are tender. Add tomatoes, cabbage, seasonings, lemon juice and sugar. Cook 25 more minutes.

BEETS–SALADS

RAW BEET SALAD

1/4 c. vinegar
1/3 c. vegetable or olive oil
1 tsp. sugar
1/2 tsp.

1/8 tsp. pepper
2 c. coarsely shredded raw beets
4 c. shredded lettuce
1 T. finely chopped chives

Combine first 3 ingredients. Add salt and pepper to. Mix with beets and marinate at least 30 minutes. Add lettuce just before serving. Toss, then sprinkle with chives.

BEET AND APPLE SALAD

2 c. cooked beets, diced
2 c. diced apples
1/3 c. oil
1 1/2 T. lemon juice

1 T. white vinegar
1/8 c. honey
1/4 tsp. salt
1/8 tsp. pepper

Combine beets and apples. Whisk remaining ingredients together and pour over beets and apples.

BEET MACARONI SALAD

1 3/4 c. dry macaroni, cooked and
    drained
4 c. cooked, diced beets
1 c. lightly cooked peas

1/2 c. chopped onion
1/2 c. chopped celery
1 c. mayonnaise or salad dressing

Combine macaroni with well drained beets and peas. Add remaining ingredients. Chill several hours or overnight.

BEET AND EGG SALAD

2 c. cooked diced beets
2 diced hard boiled eggs

2 T. chopped onion

Combine cold beets with eggs and onion. Chill. Serve with dressing.

BEETS – SIDE AND MAIN DISHES

HOW TO COOK BEETS

Wash beets and trim all but 1-inch of the stem off. Leave tap root on beets. Place in a 2 quart saucepan with 1-inch of salted water. Bring to a boil. Reduce heat and simmer gently, partially covered, until beets are tender. Medium to small beets take 30 minutes. Drain and cool; trim stem and root; peel. Reheat in melted butter. Season to taste.
Variation: Chilled whole beets can be hollowed out and filled with egg salad.

HOW TO COOK BEET GREENS

Wash carefully. Steam, sauté or stir fry 3-4 minutes, or boil in salted water until barely tender. Season to taste. Toss with butter or buttered bread crumbs. Sprinkle with hard-boiled egg if desired.

ROASTED BEETS

5 medium beets, washed and
    trimmed
2 T. olive or vegetable oil

1 T. vinegar
1 T. chopped fresh dill
1/4 tsp. salt or to taste

Wrap each beat in foil and place on a cookie sheet. Bake in a preheated 400 degree oven for 1 hour or until beets feel tender when pressed. When beets are cool enough to handle, peel skins. Quarter beets. Combine oil, vinegar, dill and salt. Add beets; toss to coat.

ORANGE GLAZED BEETS

3 c. cooked beets, diced
2 T. butter
2 tsp. flour

2 T. brown sugar
1/2 c. orange juice

Melt butter. Blend in flour. Add brown sugar and orange juice, stirring constantly until thickened. Drain beets; add sauce to beets.

BABY BEETS IN SOUR CREAM

1/4 c. sour cream
1 T. vinegar
1 T. minced green onion
3/4 tsp. sugar

1/2 tsp. salt
dash cayenne pepper
2 1/2 c. halved cooked beets,
    drained

Combine ingredients, except beets; mix well. Add sauce to beets; heat slowly, stirring to coat.

HARVARD BEETS

3 c. sliced, cooked beets
3 T. corn starch
1/3 c. sugar
3/4 tsp. salt

1 1/2 c. beet liquid (or beet liquid
    plus water)
2 T. vinegar
1 1/2 T. butter

Mix cornstarch, sugar and salt. Blend in beet liquid, vinegar and butter. Cook over moderate heat, stirring constantly, until thickened. Add beets to sauce. Let stand 10 minutes to blend flavors. Heat to serving temperature.

PICKLED RED BEET EGGS

1 can pickled beets

hard boiled eggs, peeled

Place beets, juice and whole peeled eggs in a large glass jar. Be sure eggs are covered. Store in the refrigerator for 2-3 days before eating. Serve with the pickled beets.

BEETS – CANNING AND FREEZING

HOW TO CAN BEETS[1]

Remove tops, leaving 1 inch stem and tap root. Wash. Cover with boiling water until skins slip easily. Can small beets whole; cut larger ones into uniform slices or dice them. Pack hot. Cover with boiling water, leaving 1 inch headspace. Add 1/2 tsp. salt to pints and 1 tsp. to quarts. Iodized or plain table salt may be used.

Process in a pressure canner; pints 30 minutes and quarts 35 minutes. Process at 10 lb. pressure for elevations up to 1000 feet above sea level. Process at 15 lb. of pressure for elevations over 1000 feet above sea level. Dial gauges should be at 11 lb. of pressure up to 2000 feet above sea level.

PICKLED BEETS

1 gal. beets	1 T. whole cloves
2 qt. vinegar	3 sticks cinnamon
2 c. water	2 T. salt
6 c. sugar	

Choose smaller beets if they are to be left whole. Wash beets, leaving 1-inch of stem and the roots intact. Cook, unpeeled, until skins can be easily slipped off. Mix other ingredients and bring to a boil; simmer 15 minutes. Pack hot peeled beets into jars. Pour hot pickling solution over beets and cover with lids. Process in boiling water canner for 30 minutes
Yield: 7 to 8 pints

RED BEET SALAD TO CAN

12 red beets	3 c. vinegar
1/2 bunch celery	1 1/2 c. red beet juice
1 small head of cabbage, shredded	4 c. sugar
6 peppers, chopped	pepper to taste
3 onions, chopped	

Cook whole red beets approximately 40 minutes; peel and grate. Cook celery 3 to 4 minutes. Prepare the vegetables and combine them in a large kettle with remaining ingredients. Boil until the vegetables are tender. Pack hot into jars. Adjust lids and rings; process in boiling water canner for 15 minutes.
Yield: approximately 10 pints.

HOW TO FREEZE BEETS[1]

Remove tops, leaving 1/2-inch stem. Wash; cook until tender: small, 25-30 minutes; medium, 45-50 minutes. Cool, peel, slice or cube.

HOW TO FREEZE BEET GREENS

Pick young, tender, leaves. Wash thoroughly, cutting off woody stems. Blanch 2 minutes; avoid matting of leaves. Cool immediately in cold water, drain, package and freeze.

And the LORD God planted a garden eastward in Eden; and there he put the man whom he had formed. And out of the ground made the LORD God to grow every tree that is pleasant to the sight, and good for food; the tree of life also in the midst of the garden, and the tree of knowledge of good and evil. And a river went out of Eden to water the garden; and from thence it was parted, and became into four heads. And the LORD God took the man, and put him into the garden of Eden to dress it and to keep it.

Genesis 2:8-10,15

NOTES

Broccoli

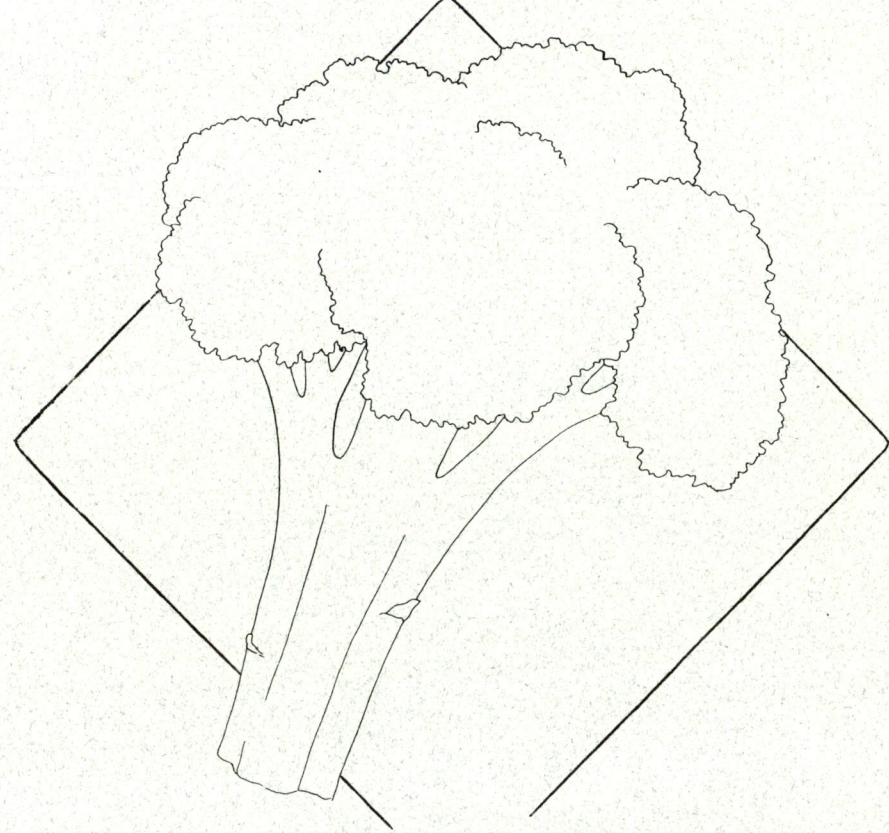

Broccoli is one of the most popular of the cole family of vegetables. The family also includes cabbage, cauliflower, brussels sprouts, Chinese cabbage, collards, kale and kohlrabi.

All of the cole vegetables contain bioflavonoids that help reduce the risk of cancer of the colon, breast, cervix, lung, prostate, esophagus, larynx and bladder. While all the vegetables in this family contain bioflavonoids, broccoli seems to be one of the best in cancer prevention.

Broccoli can be either seeded directly into the ground or transplanted. Sow seeds ½-1 inch deep, 6 inches apart, in rows 2-3 feet apart. Thin to a final spacing of 18-24 inches. Broccoli is a cool weather plant, so plant as soon as your soil can be worked in the spring. Mid-summer plantings for fall harvests work well, too.

Transplants should have 4 or 5 true leaves when set out. If the stems are crooked, plant up to the first leaves so the plant is not floppy. Broccoli grows best when temperatures are below 80 degrees. It is frost hardy. Broccoli requires fertile soil with good moisture-holding capacity or irrigation.

Broccoli takes from 60-80 days to mature from transplants. Harvest the main head while buds are still closed tight. Cut about 3 inches of the stalk off with the head.

Most varieties of broccoli will produce smaller side shoots from the main stem if side shoots are kept cut. Side shoots must be harvested every few days to keep them from flowering. Once yellow flowers appear, broccoli is tough and bitter.

If broccoli has not been sprayed for cabbage worms, soak in ice cold salt water for 30 minutes before cooking. Most of the worms will float to the top, but it's still a good idea to examine each head carefully for stubborn worms.

Do not overcook broccoli. It is bright green, not olive green when tender crisp. Broccoli is delicious raw with dips and in salads as well.

In addition to its known ability to help prevent cancer, broccoli is also a good source of vitamin C, vitamin A and folate along with calcium, iron and other minerals.

Broccoli will keep for up to a week if kept unwashed in the refrigerator.

Yield: 1 lb. = 5 cups florets

1 lb. = 1 pint

BROCCOLI – SOUPS

CREAM OF BROCCOLI SOUP

2 1/2 c. finely chopped broccoli
    (peel thick stems)
1/4 c. butter
1/4 c. chopped onion
1/3 c. flour

2 c. milk
2 chicken bouillon cubes
1/8 tsp. nutmeg (opt.)
1/2 tsp. salt
1 c. process cheese (e.g. Velvetta)

Cook broccoli until tender. Reserve liquid. Melt butter in a skillet. Sauté onion in butter then blend in flour. Slowly stir in milk. Add bouillon cubes, nutmeg, salt and cheese. Cook and stir until thickened. Boil 1 minute. Add 1 c. of reserved liquid to white sauce. Add broccoli and heat through.
Variation: Put cooked broccoli and onion in the blender.

BROCCOLI AND HAM SOUP

6-8 c. chopped broccoli
3-4 c. chicken broth
1 c. light cream or whole milk
2 c. cooked, diced ham

1 tsp. salt
1/4 tsp. pepper
2 T. butter
1/2 lb. Swiss cheese, shredded

Cook broccoli and broth in a large covered saucepan for 7-8 minutes. Remove broccoli. Add cream, ham, seasonings and butter to broth. Bring to a boil and simmer 5 minutes. Stir in cheese and broccoli. Heat but do not boil.

BROCCOLI – SALADS

BROCCOLI SALAD

2 bunches broccoli, broken into
    florets
1/4 c. chopped onion
10 strips bacon, fried and
    crumbled

1 c. mayonnaise
1/3 c. grated parmesan cheese
1/4 c. sugar
2 T. vinegar

Combine broccoli, onion and bacon. Mix remaining ingredients together. Toss lightly with salad.
Variations: Add 1 c. cubed cheddar cheese, 2 chopped hard boiled eggs or 1 c. salted sunflower seeds. Omit Parmesan cheese from dressing if desired.

BROCCOLI PASTA SALAD

8 oz. uncooked spiral pasta
1 1/2 c. broccoli florets
1/2 c. cubed mozzarella cheese
1/2 c. halved cherry tomatoes

1/2 c. chopped red bell pepper
1/3 c. sliced, pitted ripe olives
(optional)
1 c. Italian dressing

Cook pasta according to package directions; drain and rinse with cold water until cooled. Combine remaining ingredients except dressing. Add dressing; toss well. Serve chilled. If preparing a day ahead, refrigerate, then stir in 1/4 c. additional dressing before serving.

BROCCOLI CAULIFLOWER SALAD

1 bunch broccoli
1 head cauliflower
1/2 lb. bacon, fried and crumbled
1 c. shredded cheese

1 chopped onion
1 c. mayonnaise
1/4 c. sugar
1 T. vinegar

Cut broccoli and cauliflower into bite size pieces. Add bacon, cheese and onion. Combine remaining ingredients and toss with salad just before serving. Add 2 hard boiled eggs if desired.

MARINATED BROCCOLI AND CAULIFLOWER

2 bunches broccoli
2 heads cauliflower
1 c. cider vinegar
1 T. sugar
1 T. dried dill weed

1 T. salt
1 tsp. pepper
1 clove garlic, minced
1 1/2 c. vegetable oil

Separate broccoli and cauliflower into small florets. Combine remaining ingredients and pour over broccoli and cauliflower. Cover and refrigerate for 24 hours basting occasionally. When ready to serve drain and arrange on a serving tray.

To everything there is a season, and a time to every purpose under the heaven: a time to be born, and a time to die; a time to plant, and a time to pluck up that which is planted.
Ecclesiastes 3:1, 2

BROCCOLI – SIDE AND MAIN DISHES

HOW TO COOK BROCCOLI

Bring 1-inch of water to a boil in a large kettle. Add 4 c. broccoli florets and peeled, sliced, stems and 1/2-1 tsp. salt. Return to a boil. Reduce heat, cover and simmer 7-10 minutes or until tender crisp. Drain. Serve plain, buttered or with a sauce.

Variations: Sprinkle buttered broccoli with Parmesan cheese, or bacon or crumbled blue cheese. Or melt 1/4 c. butter and add 1 c. dry bread crumbs. Sauté until crumbs are lightly browned and then sprinkle on broccoli.

SOUR CREAM SAUCE

1 c. sour cream	1/4 tsp. salt
1 T. chopped fresh chives or	3 drops Worcestershire sauce
green onion tops	white pepper to taste

Combine all ingredients thoroughly at least 2 hours before serving. Refrigerate. Serve with cooked broccoli. Also good on baked potatoes.

OVEN FRIED BROCCOLI FLORETS

1 1/2 c. sour cream	1 bunch broccoli cut into florets
1 tsp. Worcestershire sauce	with 1-inch stems
1/2 tsp. garlic salt	1/2 c. crushed cornflakes

Stir together sour cream, Worcestershire sauce and garlic salt. Dip broccoli into sour cream mixture, then roll in crushed cornflakes to coat. Place on greased baking sheet. Bake at 400 degrees approximately 20 minutes. Serve warm.

BROCCOLI CELERY STIR FRY

3 T. vegetable oil	3 T. soy sauce
6 c. 1/2-inch broccoli slices	1/2 tsp. ground ginger
2 c. chopped celery	

Heat oil in large skillet. Stir in broccoli and celery. Stir fry 5-7 minutes. Add soy sauce and ground ginger.

Verily, verily, I say unto thee, Except a man be born again, he cannot see the kingdom of God.

John 3:3

BROCCOLI CARROT STIR FRY

2 T. vegetable oil
1 1/2 c. small broccoli pieces
1 c. thinly sliced carrots
1 small onion, sliced and
    separated into rings

3/4 c. chicken broth or hot water
1/2 tsp. salt
1 T. cornstarch
1 T. cold water
1 tsp. soy sauce

Heat oil in wok or large skillet. Add broccoli, carrots and onions. Stir fry one minute. Add broth and salt. Cover and cook until carrots are tender crisp—about 3 minutes. Mix cornstarch, water and soy sauce. Add the vegetables and stir until thickened.

BROCCOLI CHICKEN STIR FRY

3 T. vegetable oil, divided
1 lb. skinless, boneless chicken
    breasts, cut into thin strips
1 1/2 c. broccoli florets
1 c. thinly sliced carrots
1/2 c. green and red pepper strips

10 3/4 oz. can cream of
    mushroom soup
1/4 c. water
1 T. soy sauce
4 c. cooked rice, hot

Heat 1 T. oil in a large skillet. Stir fry chicken in two batches until browned, adding another T. of oil for the second batch. Remove chicken. Add remaining oil and vegetables. Stir fry until tender crisp. Stir in soup, water and soy sauce. Heat to a boil. Return chicken to pan. Heat through. Serve over hot rice.

BROCCOLI PASTA STIR FRY WITH CHEESE

2 c. broccoli florets
1 c. carrot slices
1/4 c. butter
2 c. summer squash slices
1 1/2 c. 1-inch asparagus pieces

1/2 lb. process cheese spread,
    (e.g. Velvetta) cubed
3/4 c. light cream
1/4 lb. pepperoni, chopped (opt.)
4 oz. pasta, cooked and drained
1/3 c. grated Parmesan cheese

Stir fry broccoli and carrots in butter for 3 minutes. Add squash and asparagus; stir fry until tender crisp. Reduce heat. Add cheese spread and cream. Stir until cheese spread is melted. Add cooked pasta and mix lightly.

BROCCOLI QUICHE

1 unbaked pie shell with fluted
   edge
2 c. chopped broccoli, cooked and
   drained
1 c. cooked, diced chicken
6 oz. Swiss cheese (cubed)

3 eggs
1 c. whipping cream
2 T. lemon juice
1 tsp. salt
1/8 tsp. pepper
chopped chives

Sprinkle broccoli in the bottom of the pie shell. Top with chicken, then cheese. In a small bowl using a wire whisk, beat eggs, cream, lemon juice, salt and pepper until blended, but not frothy. Pour over cheese. Sprinkle with chives. Bake at 375 degrees for 35-40 minutes. Let stand 10 minutes before cutting.

BROCCOLI SOUFFLÉ

6 T. butter
1/3 c. flour
3/4 tsp. salt
1/4 tsp. ground nutmeg
1/8 tsp. pepper

1 1/2 c. milk
6 eggs, separated
1 1/2 c. chopped broccoli, cooked
1/4 tsp. cream of tarter
1 c. shredded Swiss cheese

Melt butter, stir in flour, salt, nutmeg and pepper until smooth. Stir milk in gradually. Cook until mixture boils or thickens. Remove from heat. In a small bowl beat egg yolks with a fork. Stir some of the hot mixture into the eggs, then pour eggs back into hot mixture. Cook over low heat, stirring constantly, for one minute. Remove from heat and stir in broccoli. Beat egg whites and cream of tarter until stiff. Fold broccoli mixture and Swiss cheese into the egg whites. Pour into 2 quart soufflé dish and place on lowest rack in oven. Bake at 375 degrees for 45 minutes or until top is puffy and brown.

QUICK BROCCOLI CHICKEN NOODLE DINNER

1 T. vegetable oil
3/4 lb. boneless skinless chicken
   breast, cut into 1-inch pieces
1/2 tsp. garlic powder

1 3/4 c. chicken broth
6 oz. wide egg noodles, uncooked
2 c. chopped broccoli
1 c. shredded cheddar cheese

Heat oil in a large kettle. Sprinkle chicken with garlic powder; cook in oil until no longer pink, about 5 minutes, turning occasionally. Add broth; heat to boiling. Add uncooked noodles and broccoli, stirring to coat noodles with liquid. Heat to boiling; reduce heat. Cover; simmer 10 minutes or until noodles are tender, stirring every two minutes. Remove from heat; stir in cheese until melted.

BROCCOLI CHICKEN CASSEROLE

6 c. chopped broccoli, cooked
2 c. diced cooked chicken
4 T. butter
2 T. chopped onion
4 T. flour

2 c. milk
1/2 c. shredded cheese
2 tsp. mustard
1 tsp. salt

Peel any tough stems before cooking broccoli. Place cooked broccoli in a casserole. Sprinkle chicken over broccoli. Melt butter in a skillet. Sauté onion until tender. Blend in flour. Gradually add milk stirring constantly until sauce thickens and boils. Add remaining ingredients. Stir until cheese melts. Pour over chicken. Bake at 400 degrees for 25 to 30 minutes.
Variation: Replace chicken with cooked ham.

BROCCOLI HAM BAKE

3 c. hot cooked rice
6 c. chopped, cooked broccoli
1/4 c. butter
1 c. chopped onion
3 T. flour

1 tsp. salt
1/4 tsp. pepper
3 c. milk
3 c. cubed cooked ham
1/2 lb. sliced American cheese.

Spoon cooked rice into a buttered 13x9 pan. Drain broccoli and place in a single layer over rice. Melt butter and sauté onion until soft. Stir in flour, salt and pepper. Add milk and stir until sauce thickens and boils, 3 minutes. Stir in ham. Heat through then pour over broccoli. Place cheese slices on top. Top with buttered bread crumbs if desired. Bake at 350 degrees for 45 minutes.

BROCCOLI TUNA CASSEROLE

6 c. chopped broccoli
10-1/2 oz. can mushroom soup
1/4 c. milk

2 small cans tuna, drained
2 T. butter
1/2 c. bread crumbs

Peel tough stems before cooking broccoli, drain. Combine milk and soup. Place broccoli in a shallow baking dish. Top with tuna. Pour sauce over tuna. Melt butter. Mix with bread crumbs and sprinkle on top of the casserole. Bake uncovered at 350 degrees approximately 20 minutes.

BROCCOLI–FREEZING

HOW TO FREEZE BROCCOLI

Wash; soak heads down1/2 hour in salted water (1/4 cup salt per gallon water) to drive out insects. Rinse in fresh water and drain. For uniformity in blanching, split stalks lengthwise, leaving heads about 1 to 1 1/2-inches in diameter. Blanch in water for 3 minutes.²

Cool immediately in cold water; drain and put in freezer containers.

Another parable put he forth unto them, saying, the kingdom of heaven is likened unto a man which sowed good seed in his field: but while men slept, his enemy came and sowed tares among the wheat, and went his way. But when the blade was sprung up, and brought forth fruit, then appeared the tares also. So the servants of the householder came and said unto him, Sir, didst not thou sow good seed in thy field? from whence then hath it tares? He said unto them, An enemy hath done this. The servants said unto him, Wilt thou then that we go and gather them up? But he said, Nay; lest while ye gather up the tares, ye root up also the wheat with them. Let both grow together until the harvest; and in the time of harvest I will say to the reapers, Gather ye together first the tares, and bind them in bundles to burn them: but gather the wheat into my barn.

And his disciples came unto him, saying, Declare unto us the parable of the tares of the field. He answered and said unto them, He that soweth the good seed is the Son of man; the field is the world; the good seed are the children of the kingdom; but the tares are the children of the wicked one; the enemy that sowed them is the devil; the harvest is the end of the world; and the reapers are the angels. As therefore the tares are gathered and burned in the fire; so shall it be in the end of this world. The Son of man shall send forth his angels, and they shall gather out of his kingdom all things that offend, and them which do iniquity; and shall cast them into a furnace of fire: there shall be wailing and gnashing of teeth. Then shall the righteous shine forth as the sun in the kingdom of their Father. Who hath ears to hear, let him hear.

Matthew 13:24-30, 36-43

NOTES

Brussels Sprouts

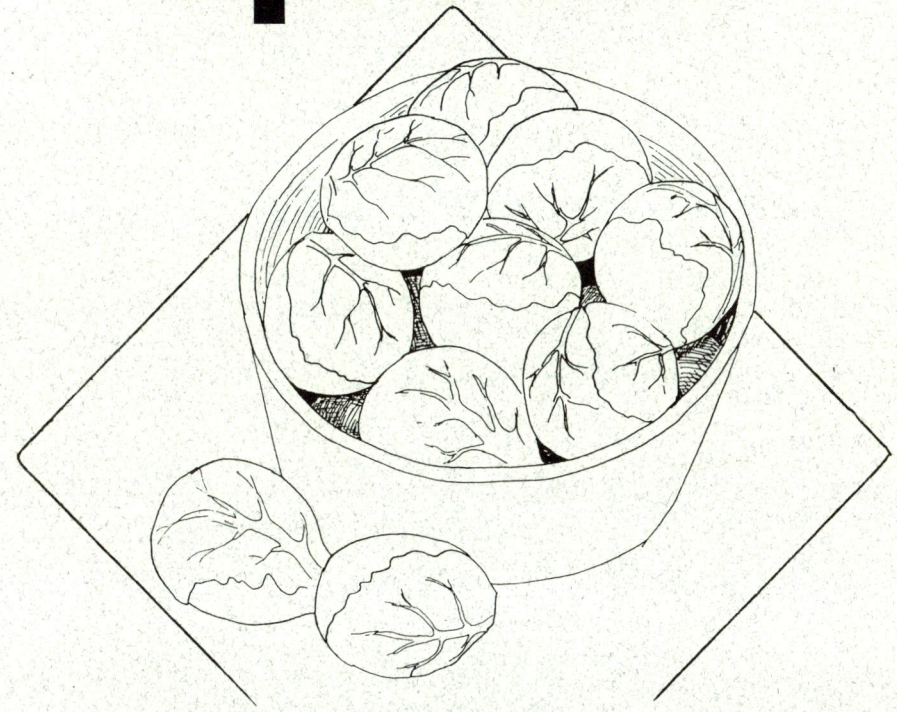

This cool-weather member of the cole family grows miniature cabbages or sprouts on tall, straight stalks that reach up to 20 inches in height. Named after the capital of Belgium, the final 's' in Brussels is an essential part of the spelling.

Brussels sprouts do best grown in cool, moist weather. Plants should be started indoors 4-6 weeks before planting outside. Transplant in full sun 18-24 inches apart in rows 30 inches apart. For direct seeding, sow about four months before expected fall frost date. Sow seeds every 6 inches, ¼- ½ inch deep. Thin to a final spacing of 18 inches.

Brussels sprouts' flavor is enhanced by frost, however they can be harvested as they develop from the ground up. Five to seven days before harvest, remove the leaves from the lower 6-8 inches of the stalk. This diverts energy to the sprout that would otherwise be lost to the leaves. As the sprouts mature, continue to strip the leaves ahead of the sprouts you harvest.

A second method—whole stalk harvesting—is done by pinching the growth point at the top of the plant once the lower sprouts are ½ to ¾ inch in size. This prevents new sprouts from setting, allowing you to harvest a whole stalk of uniform sprouts about 4 weeks after pinching the central bud. This method works especially well for short-season areas where the upper sprouts may not mature anyway.

Whole stalks can be stored for 4 to 6 weeks in a cold cellar. Storage after cutting from the stalk is not recommended for more than 1-2 days because they soon develop a strong flavor.

Brussels sprouts can be eaten raw. Slice them in half and include them on your vegetable trays with dip. As a cooked vegetable, sprouts are good blanched, steamed sautéed or stir-fried.

Cut an x in the base of each sprout before cooking so they will cook evenly. Cook to tender crisp. Over-cooked sprouts lose their bright green color, become mushy and are strong flavored.

Like other vegetables in the cole family Brussels sprouts contain bioflavonoids that help prevent cancer. In addition, Brussels sprouts have high levels of vitamin C and good levels of folate, vitamin A, iron and potassium.

Yield: 1 lb. fresh Brussels sprouts = 4 cups quartered or 3 ½ cups whole
1 lb. = 1 pint

BRUSSELS SPROUTS – SALAD

BRUSSELS CHEF SALAD

3 c. cut, cooked chicken
1 1/2 c. cut, cooked ham
1 c. diced Swiss cheese
3 c. small Brussels sprouts,
    cooked, drained, cooled
1/2 c. cut celery
3 c. broken salad greens

1/4 c. vinegar
1/2 c. salad oil
3/4 tsp. paprika
1 tsp. salt
1/4 tsp. pepper
2 T. sugar

Combine first 6 ingredients. Combine remaining ingredients; pour over chicken-ham mixture and toss gently. Serve immediately.

BRUSSELS SPROUTS – SIDE AND MAIN DISHES

HOW TO COOK BRUSSELS SPROUTS

Trim off outer leaves. Cut an X on the stem end to help sprouts cook more evenly. Bring one inch of water to a boil in a 2 qt. kettle. Add 3 1/2 to 4 cups sprouts and 1/2-1 tsp. salt. Cover and return water to a boil. Reduce heat. Simmer small sprouts 4-5 minutes, medium sprouts 5-8 minutes and large sprouts 8-12 minutes. (Over cooking will cause sprouts to become soggy and strong flavored.) Drain. Add butter and serve. Use leftovers sliced into omelets, salads or stir frys.

LEMON BUTTER SAUCE

1/4 c. melted butter
3/4 tsp. salt
3/4 tsp. paprika

1 T. lemon juice
2 tsp. prepared horseradish

Mix all ingredients well. Serve hot over Brussels sprouts, other vegetables or fish.

Now in the place where he was crucified there was a garden; and in the garden a new sepulchre, wherein was never man yet laid. There laid they Jesus ...

John 19:41, 42a

BRUSSELS SPROUTS WITH BACON

4 c. Brussels sprouts
1/4 lb. bacon
1/2 c. finely chopped onions

2 T. butter
1/2 tsp. salt or to taste
1/8 tsp. pepper

Cook sprouts until barely tender. Fry bacon until crisp. Remove bacon and all but 2 T. of drippings. Add onions and cook until lightly browned. Add sprouts and butter. Reheat. Toss with bacon. Add salt and pepper.

CREAMED BRUSSELS SPROUTS

6 c. Brussels sprouts
1/4 c. butter
1/4 c. flour
1/8 tsp. pepper

2 tsp. instant chicken broth or 1
    bouillon cube
2 c. milk

Trim sprouts, cutting any large ones in half. Cook, covered in boiling salted water 10 minutes or until tender. Drain and return to saucepan. Melt butter; add flour and seasonings. Stir until bubbly. Add milk, stirring constantly until sauce thickens and bubbles 3 minutes. Pour over sprouts and heat slowly just until hot. **Variation:** Add 1/2 cup grated cheese to the sauce.

BAKED BRUSSELS SPROUTS WITH CREAM

4 c. sprouts
cream

1/2-1 tsp. salt
1/8 tsp. pepper

Cut big sprouts in half. Place sprouts in a baking dish. Add enough cream so it is 1/2-inch deep. Season to taste. Cover. Bake at 350 degrees approximately 30 minutes.

For our sakes, no doubt, this is written: that he that ploweth should plow in hope; and that he that thresheth in hope should be partaker of his hope.

I Corinthians 9:10b

BRUSSELS SPROUTS WITH SOUR CREAM

4 c. Brussels sprouts
3 T. butter
2 tsp. lemon juice
3/4 c. sour cream

1/2 tsp. salt
1/2 tsp. sugar
1/8 tsp. pepper

Cut an X in the stem of smaller sprouts. Cut larger sprouts in half. Melt butter. Add sprouts and lemon juice. Cover and cook, for 10 minutes or until fork tender. Shake skillet occasionally while cooking. Stir together sour cream and remaining ingredients. Slowly stir into sprouts. Heat through but do not boil.
Variation: Serve without sour cream.

BRUSSELS SPROUTS AND CHICKEN STIR FRY

2 T. vegetable oil, divided
2 garlic cloves, minced
4 c. quartered Brussels sprouts
1/2 c. chicken broth

1 1/2 c. sweet red pepper strips
2 boneless chicken breasts, diced
1/2 c. sliced onions
1/2 tsp. ground ginger

Heat 1 T. oil in a wok or large skillet. Add garlic and sprouts; stir to coat. Add broth and peppers and stir fry for 2 minutes. Cover and steam for 1 minute. Remove vegetables. Heat the other T. of oil and stir the chicken until it's almost cooked. Add onions and ginger and continue to stir fry until chicken is done. Return vegetables to skillet just long enough to heat through. Serve over hot rice.

BEEFY SPROUT SURPRISES

30 Brussels sprouts
2 lb. ground beef
1 1/2 c. uncooked instant rice
1 medium onion, chopped
2 eggs, slightly beaten
1 tsp. salt

1/2 tsp. garlic salt
1/4 tsp. pepper
2 cans (15 oz. each) tomato sauce
1 c. water
1 tsp. thyme

Cook sprouts 5 minutes. Drain. Combine beef, rice, onion, eggs, salt, garlic salt and pepper. Wrap a scant 1/4 cup of meat around each sprout to form a meat ball. Place in a large flat baking dish. Combine remaining ingredients and pour over meat balls. Cover and bake at 350 degrees for 1 hour or until meatballs are cooked through.
Variation: Use your own meat loaf recipe to wrap sprouts in or use 1 qt. of spaghetti sauce instead of the tomato sauce.

BRUSSELS SPROUTS – CANNING AND FREEZING

SWEET PICKLED BRUSSELS SPROUTS

3 qt. small Brussels sprouts
4 qt. water
4 tsp. canning salt
1 qt. vinegar
2 c. sugar
2 c. thinly sliced onions

1 c. diced sweet red peppers
2 T. mustard seed
1 T. celery seed
1 tsp. turmeric
1 tsp. hot red pepper flakes

Wash sprouts. Remove stems and blemished outer leaves. Boil in 4 qt. of water to which 4 tsp. of canning salt was added for 4 minutes. Drain and pack into pint jars. Combine vinegar, sugar, onion, diced red pepper and spices in a saucepan. Bring to a boil and simmer 5 minutes. Divide onion and diced pepper among jars. Fill jars with pickling solution, leaving 1/2-inch headspace. Adjust lids. Process 10 minutes in a boiling water canner.
Yield: 5 or 6 pints

DILLED BRUSSELS SPROUTS

3 qt. Brussels sprouts
6 c. water
2 c. vinegar
garlic cloves, optional

1/2 c. canning salt
1 1/2 tsp. dill weed or 1 small
    head dill per pint jar

Wash Brussels sprouts. Blanch for 4 minutes in boiling, lightly salted water. Drain and pack into clean, hot pint jars. Combine water, vinegar and salt, bring to a boil. Pour boiling hot solution over sprouts, filling to within 1/2 inch of top of jar. Add 1 tsp. dill weed to each jar. (If using fresh dill, place in jar first.) Adjust lids. Place filled jars in actively boiling water in a canner. Process for 10 minutes. Sprouts may develop a pinkish color due to naturally occurring red pigment.
Yield: 6 pints.
Variation: Use 2 medium heads of cauliflower broken into uniform pieces instead of Brussels sprouts. Blanch for 3 minutes.

HOW TO FREEZE BRUSSELS SPROUTS

Discard discolored heads. Remove coarse outer leaves. Wash; soak sprouts 1/2 hour in salt brine (1/4 c. salt per gallon water) to drive out insects. Rinse, drain. Sort into small, medium and large sizes. Water blanch small sprouts for 3 minutes, medium 4 minutes and large 5 minutes.[2]

Cool immediately in cold water; drain, package and freeze.

Sow to yourselves in righteousness, reap in mercy; break up your fallow ground: for it is time to seek the Lord, till he come and rain righteousness upon you. Ye have plowed wickedness, ye have reaped iniquity; ye have eaten the fruit of lies: because thou didst trust in thy way, in the multitude of thy mighty men.

Hosea 10:12-13

NOTES

Cabbage

Cabbage comes in 4 types: green cabbage with smooth leaves, red with purplish-red leaves, Savoy cabbage with crinkled leaves and Chinese cabbage with tall leaves. Savoy and Chinese cabbage heads are not packed as tightly as the red and green types. Chinese cabbage is sometimes called celery cabbage because it looks like a celery plant.

Like all cole crops, cabbage can be direct seeded, but it's usually started from transplants. Start seeds indoors 4-6 weeks before planting out. Set early cabbage 12-18 inches apart and late cabbage 18-30 inches apart. Rows should be 30-36 inches apart. Cabbage likes fertile soil with plenty of moisture and full sun.

Cabbage can be used as soon as the heads have a solid feel. If you have many cabbages ripening at the same time, root prune some of them by twisting the stem about ¼ turn. This keeps the plant from taking in as much water, slows maturity and prevents heads from cracking.

Green cabbage is good fixed any way—raw, in salads, cooked, steamed, braised or fried. Red cabbage has a sharper flavor and coarser texture so it needs to be cooked longer. Savoy cabbage has a more delicate (some say superior) flavor than red or green.

Overcooking cabbage gives it a strong flavor and odor—watch cooking times carefully. Cooking celery with cabbage helps cut the strong cooking odor of cabbage.

Solid heads can be stored for 3-4 months in cold storage with high humidity, although the flavor gets stronger in stored cabbage.

Chinese cabbage is more closely related to mustard than to cabbage. It is often used in quick stir-fries or eaten raw in salads.

Chinese cabbage does not transplant well. Sow seeds thinly in rows 24-30 inches apart. Thin seedlings to 18 inches apart. Chinese cabbage matures in 75-85 days. If it freezes before heads form, you can still eat the greens.

Cabbage is an excellent source of vitamin C and bioflavonoids.

Chinese cabbage keeps for a week in the refrigerator.

Yield: 1 lb. = 4-5 cups chopped

CREAM OF CABBAGE SOUP

2 c. finely chopped cabbage
1 1/2 c. water
1/2 tsp. sugar
1 tsp. salt
1/8 tsp. pepper

1 qt. milk
2 T. flour
2 T. butter
3 T. sour cream
paprika

Combine cabbage, water, sugar and seasonings; simmer 20 minutes. Add milk and bring to a boil. Cream together flour and butter. Add to soup and stir until it thickens. Add sour cream just before serving. Sprinkle with paprika.

CHINESE CABBAGE WITH CHICKEN

2 T. vegetable oil
1/2 lb. thin strips of chicken or
   pork
1 1/2 c. thinly sliced Chinese
   cabbage
1/2 c. finely chopped green onion
1/2 c. finely diced celery
1 garlic clove, minced

1/4 tsp. ground ginger
2 T. soy sauce
1/2 tsp. salt
2 qt. chicken broth
1 c. finely sliced spinach
1/2 c. thinly sliced mushrooms
   (optional)

Heat oil in a large kettle and sauté chicken about 5 minutes. Remove chicken. Sauté green onions, celery, cabbage, and garlic about 2 minutes. Add seasonings and broth. Return chicken to the soup and simmer 5 minutes. Add spinach and mushrooms and simmer 2 minutes more.

For my thoughts are not your thoughts, neither are your ways my ways, saith the Lord. For as the heavens are higher than the earth, so are my ways higher than your ways, and my thoughts than your thoughts. For as the rain cometh down, and the snow from heaven, and returneth not thither, but watereth the earth, and maketh it bring forth and bud, that it may give seed to the sower, and bread to the eater: So shall my word be that goeth forth out of my mouth: it shall not return unto me void, but it shall accomplish that which I please, and it shall prosper in the thing whereto I sent it.

Isaiah 55:8-11

TURKEY MINESTRONE WITH CABBAGE

1 lb. ground turkey
2 c. shredded cabbage
1 c. sliced carrots
1 c. cut green beans
1/2 c. chopped onion
1 1/2 tsp. basil

1 tsp. salt
1/4 tsp. garlic powder
1/4 tsp. pepper
6 c. chicken or beef broth
2 c. peeled and chunked tomatoes
1 medium zucchini, diced

Brown turkey in a large kettle. Add everything but zucchini and bring to a boil. Reduce heat and cook 10 minutes, stirring occasionally. Add zucchini and cook 10 more minutes or until vegetables are tender. Sprinkle with chopped fresh parsley if desired.

CABBAGE–SANDWICHES

CABBAGE SANDWICH SPREAD

1/4 c. chopped cabbage
3 T. chopped apple
3 T. chopped carrot
3 T. chopped celery

3 T. chopped green pepper
1 T. chopped onion
1/4 c. mayonnaise

Combine ingredients and spread on bread.

CABBAGE—SALADS

CABBAGE SLAW

1 c. vinegar
1 c. sugar
3/4 tsp. mustard seed
3/4 tsp. celery seed

1/2 tsp. salt
8 c. shredded cabbage
1 green pepper, chopped
1 onion, chopped

Bring vinegar, sugar, mustard seed, celery seed, and salt to a boil, stirring occasionally. Remove from heat. Cool. Pour dressing over remaining ingredients and toss. Best if refrigerated overnight to blend flavors.

CREAMY CABBAGE SLAW

1 c. mayonnaise
3 T. lemon juice or vinegar
2 T. sugar
1 tsp. salt

6 c. shredded cabbage
1 c. shredded carrots
1/2 c. thinly sliced green pepper

Combine first 4 ingredients. Stir in remaining ingredients. Cover, chill.

VEGETABLE CABBAGE SLAW

2 c. shredded cabbage
1 c. chopped celery
1 carrot, shredded
1 green pepper, chopped
1 cucumber, sliced
1 small onion, chopped fine

4-6 radishes sliced thin
1/4 c. sugar
1 tsp. salt
1/2 tsp. dry mustard
1/4 c. cream
3 T. vinegar or lemon juice

Combine vegetables, mix well. Mix together remaining ingredients and gently stir into the vegetables. Chill before serving.

CABBAGE APPLE SALAD

3 c. shredded cabbage
1 c. diced unpeeled apples
1/2 c. finely chopped celery
1/2 c. chopped salted peanuts

1/2 c. mayonnaise
1/4 c. peanut butter
1/4 c. honey

Toss cabbage, apples, celery and peanuts. Blend remaining ingredients and combine with salad.
Variation: Add 1 c. pineapple tidbits to salad and use the following dressing:

1/2 c. mayonnaise
1 T. pineapple juice

1 T. honey or sugar
2 tsp. lemon juice

Mix well and toss with salad.

HOT CABBAGE SALAD

4-5 c. shredded cabbage
8 strips bacon
vinegar

2 T. sugar
1/2 tsp. salt

Place cabbage in bowl. Fry bacon until crisp; crumble over cabbage. In same skillet, combine drippings and an equal amount of vinegar; add sugar and salt. Heat to boiling pour over cabbage. Toss lightly. Serve warm.

HOT CHINESE CABBAGE SALAD

1 T. vegetable or peanut oil
3 c. thinly sliced celery
2 c. cut green beans
4 c. coarsely chopped Chinese
    cabbage

2 c. coarsely chopped spinach
1 tsp. salt
1/4 tsp. pepper
1/4 c. water

Heat oil in large skillet. Stir in celery and beans; sauté, stirring constantly, 2-3 minutes. Add cabbage and spinach; mixing well. Sprinkle with salt and pepper; pour in water and cover. Cook 10 minutes or just until vegetables are tender crisp.

CABBAGE GELATIN SALAD

3 oz. pkg. lime gelatin
3 oz. pkg. lemon gelatin
2 c. boiling water
1 c. marshmallows
1 c. pineapple juice

1 c. crushed pineapple
1 c. mayonnaise
1 1/2 c. shredded cabbage
1 c. cream, whipped
1 c. chopped nuts

Dissolve gelatin in boiling water. Add marshmallows and stir until dissolved. Drain crushed pineapple and add juice. Cool until it starts to set, then stir in remaining ingredients.

CABBAGE – SIDE AND MAIN DISHES

HOW TO COOK CABBAGE

Bring one inch of water to a boil in a large kettle. Add 5 c. chopped cabbage and 1/2-1 tsp. salt. Return to a boil. Reduce heat and cook, covered, approximately 5 minutes or until tender crisp.

HOW TO COOK CABBAGE WEDGES

Bring 1-inch water to a boil. Add 4 cabbage wedges and 1/2-1 tsp. salt. Return to a boil. Reduce heat and simmer, covered, approximately 10 minutes or until tender crisp. Serve with butter.

SWEET SOUR RED CABBAGE

2 T. vegetable oil or bacon
   drippings
2 T. chopped onion
6 c. shredded red cabbage
1 unpeeled tart apple, diced

1/4 c. brown sugar, packed
1/2 tsp. salt
1/2 c. water
1/4 c. vinegar

Heat oil in a large kettle. Add onion and sauté until tender. Add remaining ingredients. Cook covered, over low heat, stirring occasionally. Cook approximately 15 minutes.

CABBAGE AND NOODLES

1/2 c. onion, chopped
1/4 c. butter
4 c. shredded cabbage
1/2 tsp. salt

1/8 tsp. pepper
8 oz. noodles, cooked and drained
1/2 c. sour cream

Sauté onion in butter. Add cabbage; sauté until tender crisp, about 5 minutes. Sprinkle with salt and pepper. Stir hot noodles into cabbage; add sour cream. Heat through.

CABBAGE AU GRATIN

1 T. vegetable oil
6 c. shredded cabbage
1 onion, diced
6 T. butter
6 T. flour

1 tsp. salt
1/2 tsp. pepper
3 c. milk
1 1/2 c. grated cheese
bread crumbs

Heat oil. Sauté cabbage and onion for 5 minutes. Melt butter; add flour and seasonings. Blend thoroughly. Stir milk in gradually. Cook until thick, then add grated cheese. Stir until melted. Mix cheese sauce with cabbage. Put in baking dish. Top with buttered bread crumbs. Bake at 350° for 30 minutes.

47

STIR FRIED CABBAGE

1 T. vegetable oil	1 c. red or green pepper strips
1 T. butter	1 onion, sliced
3 c. shredded cabbage	1 tsp. salt
1 c. diagonally sliced celery	1/4 tsp. pepper

Heat oil and butter in a skillet. Add remaining ingredients. Cook, stirring frequently, 5 to 7 minutes or until tender crisp.

Variation: Omit salt and pepper and season with 2 T. soy sauce. Add sauce toward the end of cooking time.

STIR FRIED CHINESE CABBAGE WITH CHICKEN

3 T. vegetable oil, divided	1/2 tsp. ginger
3 T. sliced almonds	2 T. soy sauce
2 c. boneless chicken breast cut into thin strips	1/2 c. water
	1/2 c. thinly sliced white onion
1 T. cornstarch	1/4 lb. snow peas
1/2 tsp. sugar	1 1/2 lb. Chinese cabbage

Heat 1 T. oil in a large skillet or wok. Add sliced almonds and sauté until lightly browned. Remove and drain. Add another T. oil and chicken. Stir fry until lightly brown, remove from heat. Blend together cornstarch, sugar, ginger, 1 T. vegetable oil, soy sauce and water. Trim ends from peas. Cut cabbage into 1-inch pieces. Heat last T. of oil in skillet. Add vegetables. Sauté 2 minutes. Add chicken. Pour cornstarch mixture over vegetables and chicken. Cover and cook about 3 minutes. Serve over rice. Sprinkle with almonds.

STOVE TOP CABBAGE ROLLS

1 lb. ground beef	boiling water
1/4 c. chopped onion	2 c. peeled, seeded and chopped
1 tsp. salt	tomatoes
1/4 tsp. pepper	garlic salt
1 c. cooked rice	2 T. cider vinegar
10 large green cabbage leaves	2 T. sugar

Mix beef, onion, salt, pepper and rice. Cover cabbage leaves with boiling water and allow to stand about 3 minutes to make leaves pliable; drain. Roll a portion of meat mixture in each leaf; fasten with toothpicks. Heat remaining ingredients to boiling point in a covered skillet. Add cabbage bundles and simmer, covered, until tender—1 to 1 1/2 hours.

BAKED CABBAGE ROLLS

2-2 1/2 lb. green cabbage	1 1/2 tsp. salt, divided
1 tsp. salt	dash pepper
1/4 c. butter	1/4 c. butter
1 c. chopped onion	1/4 c. flour
1 clove garlic, chopped	6 oz. can tomato paste
1 lb. ground beef or pork	1/2 tsp. salt
1 1/2 c. cooked white rice	dash pepper
3 hard boiled eggs, chopped	1/4 tsp. allspice

Bring 6 c. water to a boil in a large kettle. Add cabbage and salt; simmer 5 minutes. Drain, reserving 2 c. liquid. Remove 12 outer leaves from cabbage. Melt butter in large skillet. Add onion and garlic and sauté until golden brown. Add rest of butter, along with garlic. Sauté, stirring occasionally, about 4 minutes. Add beef, rice, eggs, 1 tsp. salt and pepper. Cook, uncovered, about 5 minutes or until meat is no longer red. Melt remaining butter in a saucepan; remove from heat. Stir in flour until smooth; then gradually stir in 2 c. reserved cabbage liquid. Bring mixture to a boil, stirring constantly. Remove from heat; stir in tomato paste, 1/2 tsp. salt, pepper and allspice. Fill center of each cabbage leaf with 1/2 c. meat mixture. Fold two sides over stuffing; roll up from end. Arrange rolls, seam side down, in greased 3 qt. casserole. Pour tomato sauce over all. Bake at 350°, uncovered, 30 minutes.

CABBAGE ROLLS WITH CORN SYRUP

2-2 1/2 lb. green cabbage, cored	1 c. milk
2 qt. water	1 egg, slightly beaten
1 tsp. salt	1 tsp. salt
1/2 c. butter, divided	1/2 tsp. ground allspice
1 c. finely chopped onion	1/4 tsp. pepper
1 lb. lean ground beef	1/2 c. dark corn syrup
1 c. cooked rice	

Remove 12 large leaves from cabbage. Cook leaves and remainder of head in boiling salted water 6 minutes. Drain and cool. Reserve separated leaves. Chop remaining head of cabbage to yield 2 c. Melt 1/4 c. butter in skillet. Add onion; sauté until golden brown. Remove from heat. Stir in ground beef, chopped cabbage, rice, milk, egg, salt, allspice and pepper. Place about 1/3 c. meat mixture in center of each cabbage leaf. Wrap leaf around filling and tuck under ends. Place seam side down in 13 x 9 baking dish. Brush rolls with remaining butter, melted. Pour corn syrup over rolls. Bake at 400° for 1 hour, turning once. Reduce heat to 350° and turn rolls seam side down. Continue baking 30 minutes or until well glazed.

BAKED PORK CHOPS WITH CABBAGE

4 pork chops, 1/2-inch thick
2 T. vegetable oil
1/4 c. diced onion
1 c. cream of celery soup
1/2 c. milk

3 medium potatoes, peeled, sliced
5 c. shredded cabbage
1/4 c. flour
1 1/2 tsp. salt
1/8 tsp. pepper

Brown chops in hot oil; remove from skillet. Add onion, soup and milk to oil in skillet. Blend; set aside. Starting with potatoes, put alternate layers of potatoes and cabbage into a 2-qt. casserole; sprinkle each layer with flour, salt and pepper; pour soup sauce over each layer. Place chops on top; cover casserole. Bake at 350° for 1 1/4 hours.

CABBAGE AND GROUND BEEF CASSEROLE

1 1/2 lb. ground beef
1/2 c. chopped green pepper
1 onion, chopped
3 celery ribs, chopped
2 c. seeded, chopped tomatoes
1 tsp. vinegar

1/4 c. sugar
1 1/2 tsp. salt or to taste
1/4 tsp. pepper
8 c. shredded cabbage
1 1/2 c. cooked rice
grated cheese

Brown meat then add green pepper, onion, celery, tomatoes, vinegar, sugar, salt and pepper. Cook until almost done. Add cabbage and rice. Mix well. Put into a casserole and top with grated cheese. Bake at 350° for 30 minutes.

If my people, which are called by my name, shall humble themselves, and pray, and seek my face, and turn from their wicked ways; then will I hear from heaven, and will forgive their sin, and will heal their land.

II Chronicles 7:14

TURKEY BREAST WITH CABBAGE AND VEGETABLE STUFFING

1/4 c. butter
2 1/2 c. thinly sliced cabbage
1 c. sliced celery
2 medium zucchini or carrots cut
    into thin strips
1 red or green bell pepper, cut
    into thin strips
1 T. finely chopped fresh thyme
    leaves (or 1/2 tsp. dry)
1/2 tsp. salt
3 c. bread cubes

3 T. butter
1 T. oil
1 T. finely chopped fresh basil
    leaves (or 1/2 tsp. dry)
1 T. finely chopped fresh parsley
    (or 1/2 tsp. dry)
1 T. finely chopped rosemary
    leaves (or 1/2 tsp. dry)
2 lb. boneless turkey breast

Melt 1/4 c. butter in a large skillet. Add cabbage, celery, onion, zucchini, red pepper, thyme leaves and salt; mix well. Cook and stir 5 minutes. Remove from heat. Stir in bread cubes. Spoon into 13 x 9 baking pan. In small pan, melt 3 T. butter over medium heat. Add remaining ingredients; stir gently. Cook 1 minute. remove from heat. Place turkey breast on top of stuffing. Brush turkey with half of sauce. Cover loosely with foil. Roast at 350° for 1 hour. Remove foil. Baste again with remaining sauce. Roast an additional 30 to 45 minutes. Let turkey stand 10 minutes before slicing. Serve vegetable stuffing with turkey.

CABBAGE AND CORNED BEEF

3 lb. corned beef
1 bay leaf
6 whole cloves
1/4 tsp. pepper

8 small new potatoes
8 small whole onions
8 small carrots
1/2 head cabbage, quartered

Rinse beef. Place beef into 6-qt. kettle. Add bay leaf, whole cloves and pepper. Cover with hot water and bring to a boil, covered. Reduce heat and simmer, covered, about 3 hours or until beef is almost tender. Skim if necessary. Forty minutes before beef is done, place potatoes, onions and carrots around meat and cabbage on top. Increase heat to high until steam escapes from cover, reduce heat to low and cook until vegetables are tender, about 30-40 minutes. Place meat on platter and arrange vegetables around it.

For he shall grow up before him as a tender plant, and as a root out of a dry ground: he hath no form nor comeliness; and when we shall see him, there is no beauty that we should desire him.

Isaiah 53:2

REFRIGERATOR SWEET SOUR VEGETABLES WITH CABBAGE

1/2 c. sugar
1 c. white vinegar
1/2 c. water
1/2 tsp. salt

1 tsp. crushed red pepper
1 1/2 lb. green cabbage
2 medium carrots
2 broccoli stalks

Place sugar, vinegar, water, salt and red pepper in a saucepan and bring to a boil. Remove from heat and cool. While syrup cools tear cabbage into bite size pieces. Peel carrots and broccoli stems (save florets for other uses) and slice them thin on the diagonal. Bring 2 qt. of water to a boil in a large saucepan. Add all vegetables at once. Blanch 2 minutes. Drain. Pack vegetables into a quart jar and fill to the top with syrup. Cover and refrigerate at least one week before using. Will keep 2-3 months in the refrigerator.

Therefore we are buried with him by baptism into death: that like as Christ was raised up from the dead by the glory of the Father, even so we also should walk in newness of life. For if we have been planted together in the likeness of his death, we shall be also in the likeness of his resurrection.

Romans 6:4,5

HOW TO MAKE SAUERKRAUT

Remove defective and coarse outer leaves from the cabbage. This will also get rid of any residual insecticide spray or dust. Cut away any spoiled or damaged spots. Rinse heads in cold water to remove dust or visible dirt particles. The bacteria needed to ferment the cabbage are found on the cabbage leaves.

Cut heads into halves or quarters and slice or shred the cabbage so that the shred is as long and thin as possible. If you use a food processor, you may not get this characteristically desirable shred, but it will not affect the fermentation.

Weigh the cabbage. Place it in the container [crock or food grade plastic pail]. For every 5 lb. of cabbage, sprinkle with 3 T. pure canning/pickling salt (use a non-iodized salt because iodine will prevent the bacterial fermentation necessary to change cabbage into sauerkraut). Mix well to distribute the salt uniformly. Allow the salted cabbage to stand a few minutes to wilt slightly. Then pound the cabbage firmly with a wooden tamper until enough juices are drawn out to cover the cabbage. Repeat this procedure, layer by layer, until the container is filled to the desired depth and the cabbage is completely covered with juice. Leave at least 4 or 5 inches between the cabbage and the top of the container.

A water-filled plastic bag is one of the easiest and best ways to both cover and weight down the cabbage. Be sure that you use a heavy-duty, watertight plastic bag that is intended for food use and is not colored. Fill the bag with water to a depth of 3 to 4 inches, allow the bag to completely cover the cabbage and tie securely.

As an alternative method, cover the cabbage with a clean cloth or clear plastic, fitting the covering snugly against the sides of the container. Then cover it with a wooden, china or other nonmetallic disc and place a weight on top. It is absolutely essential that you cover the cabbage and liquid to exclude air, since the fermentation process requires anaerobic conditions (without air).

Place the container of cabbage in a well-ventilated place with a relatively constant temperature. If kept at room temperature (68 to 72° F.), the draut should be ready in three to four weeks. At higher temperatures, fermentation will proceed more rapidly and the kraut will be ready sooner. Similarly, if kept at temperatures lower than 68° F., a slow fermentation will occur, but may be incomplete if the temperature drops below 60° F. It is desirable to provide 68 to 72 degree F. temperature during the first several days in order to begin production of the acid which will preserve the cabbage. Then, if desired, the container could be stored in a cooler area (basement, unheated garage, etc.) if you want a slower fermentation. If the temperature drops below freezing, fermentation will stop, but will start again when the temperature rises into a favorable range.

Check the container daily. During the fermentation, film yeasts or molds may form on the surface of the liquid. If they appear, skim them off. If any discoloration appears within the top inch of kraut, remove it. If you are using a cloth covering, rinse or replace it each time you remove scum or spoiled cabbage.[3]

HOW TO CAN SAUERKRAUT

Heat well-fermented sauerkraut and liquid to simmering (185 to 200° F.). Do not boil. Pack hot kraut into clean, hot canning jars to within 1/2 inch of the top of the jar. Cover with hot juice, leaving 1/2 inch headspace. (If there is insufficient sauerkraut juice to cover all the kraut in the jars, use a boiling hot, weak brine that contains 2 T. salt for each quart of water.) Process in boiling water bath canner 15 minutes for pints and 20 minutes for quarts. Start to count processing time as soon as the hot jars are placed in actively boiling water.[3]

HOW TO FREEZE SAUERKRAUT

Pack kraut and juice in rigid plastic moisture-vapor proof freezer containers, glass freezer jars (leaving at least 1 1/2 inches headspace), or in heavy, tightly sealed plastic freezer bags. Freeze.[3]

COLE SLAW TO FREEZE

8-10 c. shredded cabbage	1 c. vinegar
1 carrot, grated	1/4 c. water
2 tsp. salt	1 tsp. celery seed
2 c. sugar	1 tsp. mustard seed (optional)

Mix cabbage, carrot and salt. Let set 1 hour, then drain well. Combine remaining ingredients and bring to boil. Boil 1 minute. Cool. Stir into cabbage. Let set 1/2 hour. Mix well then put into freezer containers.

HOW TO FREEZE CABBAGE

Frozen cabbage or Chinese cabbage are suitable for use only as a cooked vegetable. Cut into medium to coarse shreds or thin wedges or separate head into leaves. Blanch in water for 1 to 1 1/2 minutes.[2]

Cool immediately in cold water, drain, package and freeze.

54

Carrots

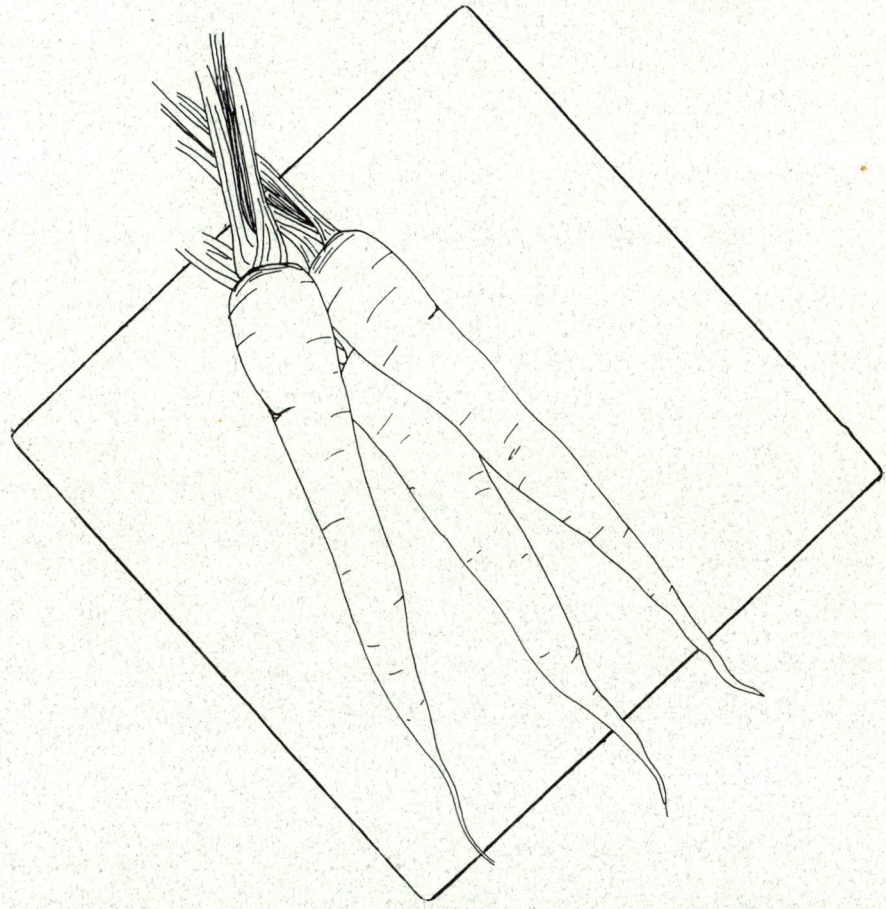

Called by some the king of root crops, carrots are hardy, popular and easy to grow—in the right kind of soil. Given rich, loose, well-drained soil, carrots will grow almost any where in the United States. Deeply worked soil produces the smoothest, best shaped roots. If your soil is heavy and poorly drained, consider building a 12 inch high ridge. Flatten the top of the ridge with the flat side of a hoe or shovel and plant the seed on top of the ridge. Your carrots will have plenty of room to develop long roots, well above the ground level.

Carrots tolerate hot weather quite well, so they can be seeded from early spring as soon as your soil can be worked, until mid-summer. Sow seeds ¼- ½ inch deep in rows 12-18 inches apart. Carrot seed is slow to germinate, taking anywhere from 1-3 weeks, depending on the temperature and moisture. To keep the soil moist and crust-free, place a board or burlap cloth over the row until the seeds start coming up.

When carrot seedlings show above the ground, thin plants to one inch apart. Thin to a final spacing of 2-3 inches 3 or 4 weeks later. Carrots mature in 60-85 days, but can be harvested as soon as they have a good bright orange (not pale) color.

Carrots need plenty of water. Dry soil will cause them to split.

Plant carrots intended for winter storage about 100 days before first expected frost. Dig the carrots after the first frost but before the ground freezes. Store carrots washed or unwashed. Leave 1-2 inches of tops on the root. Layer carrots in moist sand or put in large plastic bags with air holes in them. Carrots stored in near freezing, humid conditions can keep up to six months.

Enjoy carrots raw, cooked, stewed, steamed, baked or dipped in batter and deep fried. They are also good in carrot bread and carrot cake. Try substituting carrots for parsnips in recipes.

Carrots contain high levels of beta carotene the precursor for vitamin A. They are also a good source of potassium.

Yield: 1 lb. fresh carrots = 3 cups diced
1 bushel = 50 lb. = 32-40 pints

CHEESY CARROT SOUP

3 T. butter
2 carrots, peeled and chopped
1 onion, chopped
1/2 c. finely chopped celery
1/4 c. flour
1/2 tsp. salt

1/8 tsp. pepper
1 qt. chicken broth
1/2 lb. cheddar cheese, grated
2 c. milk
1 tsp. parsley

Melt butter and sauté carrots, onions and celery until tender. Add flour, salt and pepper and stir. Gradually stir in chicken broth. Stir in cheese. When melted add milk. Heat but do not boil after adding milk. Sprinkle parsley on top.

TURKEY CARROT PEA SOUP

1/4 c. butter
1 large onion, chopped
1/4 c. finely chopped celery
1/4 c. flour
1 tsp. salt
1/2 tsp. parsley flakes

1/4 tsp. pepper
1 1/2 c. milk
4 c. cubed cooked turkey
5 medium carrots, sliced thin
1 1/2 c. turkey broth
1 1/2 c. peas

Melt butter in a large kettle. Sauté onion and celery until tender. Stir in flour and seasonings. Gradually add milk, stirring until thickened. Add turkey, carrots, and broth. Bring to boil, then cover and simmer 10 minutes. Add peas and simmer approximately 10 more minutes.

CARROTS – SALADS AND SANDWICHES

GRATED CARROT SALAD

1 1/2 lb. peeled, grated carrots
1/2 c. finely chopped green onion
2 T. finely chopped dill
1 tsp. grated lemon rind
3 T. lemon juice

2 T. olive oil
1/2 tsp. sugar
1/2 tsp. salt
1/4 tsp. pepper

Combine carrots, onions, dill and lemon rind. Whisk together remaining ingredients. Toss and serve.

CARROT AND ZUCCHINI SALAD

2 large carrots, diagonally sliced
2 medium zucchini, sliced
1/2 c. vegetable oil
1/4 c. cider vinegar
3/4 tsp. salt

1/4 tsp. pepper
1/4 tsp. tarragon
1/4 tsp. basil leaves
1/4 tsp. oregano
lettuce

Cook carrots 3 minutes in 1 c. boiling salted water. Add zucchini; cook 2 minutes. Drain. Combine remaining ingredients. Pour over hot vegetables. Cover. Chill several hours. Drain, reserving dressing. Serve vegetables on lettuce leaves with dressing.

PINEAPPLE CARROT SALAD

3 oz. package lemon gelatin
1 c. boiling water
10 1/2 oz. can crushed pineapple,
    drained

1 c. pineapple juice
1 1/2 c. grated carrots
1/2 c. chopped nuts

Dissolve gelatin in hot water. Drain juice from crushed pineapple. (Add water if needed.) Add pineapple juice to gelatin. Chill. When mixture begins to thicken add pineapple, carrots and nuts. Pour into a 1-qt. mold or bowl. Serve on lettuce with mayonnaise if desired.

CARROT SANDWICH SPREAD

3/4 c. grated carrots
1/2 c. finely chopped celery
2 T. grated cheese
2 T. salad dressing

1 T. finely chopped green pepper
1 T. chili sauce
1/4 tsp. salt

Combine ingredients and spread on bread.

CARROTS – SIDE AND MAIN DISHES

HOW TO COOK CARROTS

Bring 1 inch of water to a boil. Add 4 c. sliced carrots and 1 tsp. salt. Return to a boil and simmer, covered, approximately 10 minutes. Simmer whole carrots 20 minutes or until tender crisp. Serve with butter if desired.

GLAZED CARROTS

2 T. butter	3 c. cooked carrots, drained, cut
1/4 c. brown sugar	in strips

Blend butter and sugar, in a heavy skillet over low heat. Add carrots. Cook over low heat 5 minutes, turning carrots to coat all sides with syrup.

DILLED CARROTS

3 c. carrots cut into 1-inch pieces	1 tsp. sugar
1/2 c. water	1/2 tsp. salt
2 T. butter	1/2 tsp. dill weed

Combine all ingredients in a saucepan. Cover. Bring to boil then cook gently for approximately 10 minutes or until carrots are tender crisp.

CARROT AND CELERY STIR FRY

1 c. diagonally cut carrot slices	1/4 tsp. salt
1 c. diagonally cut celery slices	1/8 tsp. pepper
1/2 c. green pepper strips	1/4 lb. process cheese, cubed
2 T. butter	2 T. milk

Stir fry vegetables in butter until tender crisp. Add salt and pepper; mix lightly. Stir in process cheese and milk; continue cooking over low heat until cheese is melted.
Variation: Delete cheese and milk.

BAKED CARROT RING WITH CHEESE

4 c. sliced carrots	1/2 tsp. salt
1/2 tsp. salt	1/8 tsp. pepper
1/4 c. butter	3 eggs, separated
2 T. flour	1 qt. peas, cooked

Bring 1 inch of water to a boil; add carrots and 1/2 tsp. salt. Cook 15 minutes or until soft. Cool. Melt butter; add flour and seasonings; mix well. Add slightly beaten egg yolks and mix. Add cooled mashed carrots and mix well. Fold in stiffly beaten egg whites. Pour mixture into a well-buttered 1 1/2 qt. ring mold. Set mold in a pan of water. Bake at 350° for approximately 30 minutes. Invert on a large platter. Fill center and surround with cooked buttered peas.

CARROTS BAKED IN CHEESE SAUCE

12 medium carrots, sliced
1 onion, minced
1/4 c. butter
1/4 c. flour
1 tsp. salt

1/4 tsp. dry mustard
1/2 tsp. pepper
2 c. milk
1/2 lb. American cheese, shredded
2 c. buttered bread crumbs

Cook carrots until tender, drain and put into a 2 qt. casserole. Sauté onion in butter. Blend in flour, salt, mustard and pepper. Add milk and stir until sauce thickens and boils. Add cheese and stir until melted. Pour cheese sauce over carrots and place bread crumbs on top. Bake uncovered at 350° for 25 minutes.

SEVEN LAYER CASSEROLE WITH CARROTS

2 c. raw potatoes, sliced
1 onion, sliced
2 c. raw carrots, sliced
1/2 c. rice, uncooked
2 c. peas

1/2 green pepper, chopped
1 1/2 lb. ground beef
1 can cream of mushroom or
  tomato soup
salt and pepper

Place ingredients in a buttered casserole starting with the potatoes on the bottom and ending with the soup on top. Sprinkle potatoes, carrots, peas and ground beef with salt and pepper. Bake at 375° for 1 1/2 hours.

BEEF STEW WITH CARROTS

1/3 c. flour
1 1/2 tsp. salt
1/8 tsp. pepper
1 1/2 lb. boneless stew beef, cut in
  1-inch cubes
2 T. vegetable oil
3 c. water

5 medium carrots, peeled and
  quartered
4 medium potatoes, peeled and
  cubed
2 onions, sliced
2 ribs celery cut into pieces
1/4 c. water

Combine flour, salt, and pepper, coat meat with seasoned flour. Save remaining flour. Brown meat in oil in a large kettle. Add water and cover. Simmer for 1 hour until meat is tender. Add carrots, potatoes, onions and celery. Return to a boil, reduce heat, cover and simmer 25 minutes. Blend 1/4 c. water with remaining flour. Add to stew, stirring gently; cook until thickened.
Variation: To make Irish stew use lean lamb instead of beef. Add 1 turnip, diced, with carrots and potatoes.

CHICKEN AND DUMPLINGS WITH CARROTS

2-3 lb. frying chicken, cut up	1/4 c. flour
3 c. water	1/2 c. cold water
1 onion, chopped	2 c. flour
2 ribs celery, chopped fine	4 tsp. baking powder
2 tsp. salt	1 tsp. salt
1/4 tsp. pepper	2 eggs, beaten
6 carrots, quartered	1/2 c. milk (or more)
5 small onions	1 tsp. dried parsley

Place chicken pieces in a large kettle. Add 3 c. water, onion, celery, salt and pepper. Bring to a boil then reduce heat and simmer, covered, for 45 minutes. Add carrots and onions; bring to a boil, reduce heat and simmer for 15 minutes. Mix flour with 1/2 c. cold water. Add 1/4 c. broth from the kettle. Stir until smooth then, with heat on high, stir flour mixture into the kettle. Cook, stirring constantly until thickened. To make dumplings, combine dry ingredients. Place beaten eggs into 1 cup measure. Add enough milk to make 1 c. Beat thoroughly. Add eggs and parsley to flour mixture and stir until smooth but do not over beat. Drop dumplings by spoonsful over hot chicken. Cover. Cook over low heat for 10 minutes. Do not lift cover. To serve, pour gravy over chicken and dumplings.

CARROTS – BAKED GOODS

CARROT BRAN MUFFINS

3 c. flour	4 eggs
1 tsp. baking soda	1 1/2 c. vegetable oil
1 1/2 T. baking powder	1 1/4 c. dark brown sugar
1/2 tsp. salt	1/4 c. molasses
1 T. cinnamon	3 c. finely grated carrots
2 c. bran	1 c. raisins

Combine flour, soda, baking powder, salt and cinnamon. Add bran; set aside. Beat eggs; add oil, sugar and molasses. Add carrots, flour mixture and raisins. Fill 24 greased muffin tins 3/4 full. Bake at 350° for 25 minutes. Makes 24 large muffins.

CARROT COOKIES

1 c. butter
3/4 c. sugar
1 1/2 c. grated raw carrots
1 egg, beaten

1 tsp. vanilla
2 1/4 c. flour
2 tsp. baking powder
1/2 tsp. salt

Cream together butter and sugar. Beat in carrots, egg and vanilla. Mix in dry ingredients. Drop by teaspoonfuls onto greased cookie sheet. Bake at 375° for 10-12 minutes. Frost or glaze if desired.

CARROT GINGER COOKIES

2 1/4 c. flour
2 tsp. baking soda
1 1/2 tsp. ginger
1 tsp. cinnamon
1/4 tsp. ground cloves
1/4 tsp. salt

1 c. brown sugar
3/4 c. shortening
1/4 c. molasses
1 egg
1 c. tightly packed, shredded
    carrots

Combine first 6 ingredients. In another bowl, beat brown sugar and shortening until fluffy. Beat in molasses and egg. Add dry ingredients then fold in carrots. Cover and refrigerate until firm. Drop by rounded teaspoons 2 inches apart on greased cookie sheet. Bake at 375° approximately 12 minutes.

CARROT BARS WITH ORANGE GLAZE

2 c. flour
2 tsp. baking powder
1/2 tsp. salt
1/2 tsp. nutmeg
3/4 c. softened butter
1 c. sugar

2 eggs
1 tsp. vanilla
1/3 c. orange juice
2 tsp. grated orange rind
1 c. cooked, mashed carrots

Combine dry ingredients. Cream butter and sugar. Add eggs and vanilla. Add flour mixture alternately with the orange juice and rind. Fold in carrots. Pour into a buttered 13x9 cake pan. Bake at 350° for 30-35 minutes.
Orange Glaze:
1/2 c. orange juice
1 tsp. grated orange rind

1 1/2 c. powdered sugar

Combine ingredients and spread on bars.

CARROT CAKE

4 eggs	3/4 c. nuts, chopped fine
2 c. sugar	2 c. flour
1 1/4 c. vegetable oil	2 tsp. cinnamon
1 tsp. vanilla	2 tsp. baking powder
3 c. raw grated carrots	1 tsp. soda

Combine eggs, sugar, vegetable oil and vanilla. Mix in carrots and nuts. Add dry ingredients. Put into 2, 9-inch cake pans. Bake at 350° for 45 to 60 minutes. Frost with cream cheese frosting.

Variation: Bake in a tube pan at 350° for 50-60 minutes.

Cream Cheese Frosting:

8 oz. cream cheese	1 tsp. vanilla
1/2 c. butter, softened	1 c. chopped walnuts (optional)
4 c. powdered sugar	

Beat cream cheese butter and sugar until creamy. Add vanilla and nuts. Spread between layers and on top.

CARROT BREAD WITH LEMON GLAZE

1 c. shredded raw carrots	1 tsp. soda
1 c. sugar	1 tsp. cinnamon
1/2 c. vegetable oil	1/2 tsp. salt
2 eggs	1/4 c. chopped nuts
1 1/2 c. flour	1/2 c. raisins (optional)

Beat carrots, sugar, oil and eggs 1 minute. Add flour, soda, cinnamon and salt; beat another minute. Stir in nuts and raisins. Pour into a greased 9x15 inch loaf pan. Bake at 350° for 50 to 60 minutes.

Variation: Replace grated carrots with mashed carrots. Leftover carrots are fine.

Lemon Glaze:

1/2 c. powdered sugar	1 T. lemon juice
1 tsp. grated lemon peel	

Blend until smooth. Drizzle over loaf.

61

CARROTS – CANNING AND FREEZING

CARROT MARMALADE

4 carrots
4 lemons
2 oranges

6 c. sugar
3 oz. fruit pectin

Shred carrots. Grate lemon and orange peels and remove white part. Slice lemons and oranges very thin. Bring carrots and fruit to a rolling boil and boil 2 minutes. Stir in pectin and boil 2 more minutes, stirring constantly. Fill and seal 1 c. jars. Process 5 minutes in a boiling water canner.

HOW TO CAN CARROTS[1]

Raw Pack: Wash and peel carrots. Leave small carrots whole; slice or dice larger carrots. Fill jars tightly, leaving 1-inch headspace. Add 1 tsp. salt to quarts and 1/2 tsp. to pints. Cover with boiling water, leaving 1-inch headspace.
Hot Pack: Prepare as for raw pack. Cover with boiling water; boil 5 minutes. Fill jars with hot carrots to within 1-inch of top. Add 1 tsp. salt to quarts and 1/2 tsp. to pints. Fill to within 1-inch of top with boiling cooking liquid.

Process in a pressure canner; pints 25 minutes and quarts 30 minutes. Process at 10 lb. of pressure if you live below 1000 feet above sea level. Process at 15 lb. of pressure if you live at or above 1000 feet above sea level.

HOW TO FREEZE CARROTS

Select tender, smaller carrots. Remove tops, wash and scrape. Slice lengthwise, crosswise or dice. Small carrots may be left whole. Water blanch cut carrots 2 minutes; small whole carrots 5 minutes.[2]

Cool immediately in cold water; drain, package and freeze.

Say not ye, There are yet four months, and then cometh harvest? behold, I say unto you, Lift up your eyes, and look on the fields; for they are white already to harvest.

John 4:35

Cauliflower

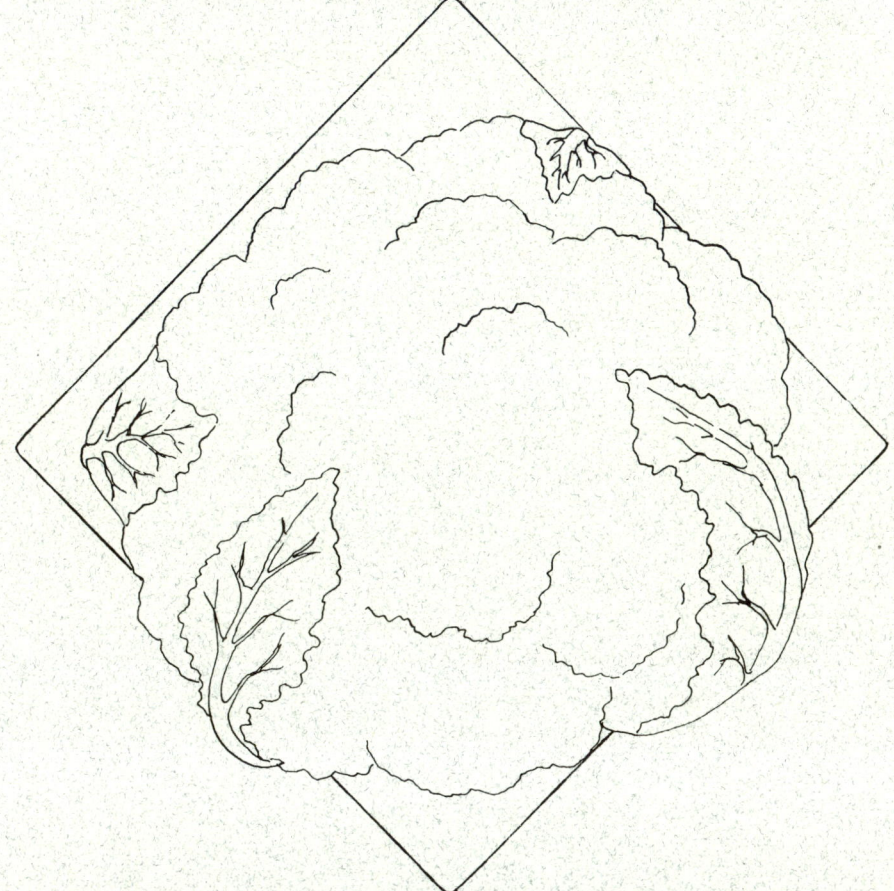

    Don't let the cauliflower-is-hard-to-grow mentality discourage you from enjoying this delightful member of the cole family. While cauliflower is finicky about its cool-temperature requirements to form heads, this can be circumvented with early spring plantings or mid-summer plantings for fall crops.

    Cauliflower is usually grown from transplants that are 4-6 weeks old. Plants that are old and root bound, or stunted from heat stress should be avoided because they will form small heads prematurely. Direct seeding can also be used, especially for fall crops. Sow seeds ½ inch deep every six inches, thinning to a final spacing of 18-24 inches. Allow 3 feet between rows.

    As soon as the white curd can be seen, the outer leaves of the plant should be tied over the developing heads with string or rubber band. This will keep the cauliflower nice and white. Some self-blanching varieties and the new purple and green broccoflowers (cauliflower crossed with broccoli) do not need to be tied.

The edible part of the cauliflower is actually immature, tightly clustered, flower buds. Harvest while the buds are tight and compact. Most varieties will be 5-10 inches across at maturity. Cut the stalk about 3 inches below the head to harvest.

Cauliflower is exceptional raw with dips or in salads. It can also be steamed, blanched or baked in casseroles.

Cauliflower keeps for 2-4 days if refrigerated in a perforated plastic bag.

Cauliflower is and excellent source of vitamin C, folate and potassium. It also provides bioflavonoids and other substances that help prevent cancer.

Yield: 1 lb. (1 medium head) = 4 cups florets

1-1 ¼ lb. = 1 pint

CAULIFLOWER – SOUPS

CREAMY CAULIFLOWER SOUP

2 T. butter	1/2 c. whipping cream
1 1/2 c. diced onion	1 c. milk
6 c. finely chopped cauliflower	1 tsp. salt
4 c. chicken broth	pepper to taste

Melt butter in a large kettle and sauté onions 3-5 minutes. Add cauliflower and broth. Simmer approximately 20 minutes. Add cream, milk, salt and pepper. Heat through.
Variation: Puree cauliflower in the blender for cream of cauliflower soup.

CAULIFLOWER SOUP WITH SMOKED SAUSAGE

4 c. cauliflower florets	1/3 c. flour
1 c. thinly sliced carrots	3/4 tsp. salt
2 c. water	1/8 tsp. pepper
1 lb. fully cooked smoked	2 c. milk
sausage, cubed	8 oz. American cheese, cubed
1/2 c. chopped onion	

Cook cauliflower and carrots in water until tender; set aside (do not drain). Brown the sausage and onion; drain. Add flour, salt and pepper. Gradually add the milk; bring to boil. Cook and stir for 2 minutes. Add cauliflower, carrots and cooking liquid; heat through. Stir in the cheese until melted.

CAULIFLOWER – SALADS

CAULIFLOWER SALAD

1 head cauliflower cut up	2 c. mayonnaise
1 head lettuce cut into bite size	2 T. sugar
pieces	1/3 c. Parmesan cheese
1 onion, chopped	1 lb. bacon, fried and crumbled

Combine cauliflower, lettuce and onion. Cover with mayonnaise mixed with sugar. Sprinkle with cheese and bacon. Refrigerate. Toss 1/2 hour before serving.
Hint: Cook cauliflower with 1 T. of lemon juice for really white cauliflower.

CAULIFLOWER VEGETABLE SALAD

1/2 head cauliflower, thinly sliced
1/2 head lettuce, torn into bite size
    pieces

2 carrots, thinly sliced
2 tomatoes, cut in wedges
1/4 c. green peppers chopped

Toss together lightly and serve with dressing.
Variation: Delete tomato and add 1 small head broccoli, 1/2 c. chopped celery and 1/2 c. chopped onions.

CAULIFLOWER – SIDE AND MAIN DISHES

HOW TO COOK CAULIFLOWER

Bring one inch of water to a boil. Add 4 c. cauliflower florets. Add 1/2-1 tsp. salt. Return to a boil then reduce heat and simmer 5-8 minutes. Drain. Cooking a whole trimmed head takes 10-15 minutes. Serve plain, buttered or with the following butters or cheese sauce.

LEMON BUTTER

1/4 c. melted butter
2 T. lemon juice

1/2 tsp. grated lemon rind

Mix ingredients and toss with 4-6 c. cooked cauliflower just before serving. Also good on carrots, broccoli, green beans, squash, spinach and other greens. Vegetables can be sautéed briefly in lemon butter if desired.

PARMESAN BUTTER

1/4 c. butter

2 tsp. Parmesan cheese

Melt butter. Add cheese. Serve over cooked cauliflower. Also good on asparagus and broccoli.

CHEESE SAUCE

2 T. butter
2 T. flour
1 c. milk

1 c. grated cheddar cheese
1/4 tsp. salt
1/8 tsp. pepper

Melt butter. Blend in flour. Gradually add milk, stirring constantly. Add cheese and stir until melted. Add salt and pepper. Serve over cauliflower or other vegetables.

FRIED CAULIFLOWER

1/2 c. flour
1/4 c. cornstarch
1/2 tsp. salt
1/2 c. ice water

1/4 c. lemon juice
vegetable oil
cauliflower florets, cooked 3-4 minutes

Combine all but oil and cauliflower to make batter. Heat enough vegetable oil to come 1/3 of the way up the pan. Dip cauliflower in batter and fry until golden brown. Turn and brown the other side. Drain well and sprinkle with salt.

CAULIFLOWER WITH CABBAGE

4 c. finely shredded green
    cabbage
1 tsp. salt
1/4 tsp. dry mustard

2 c. small cauliflower florets
1/3 c. minced green pepper
1 T. butter

Half cover cabbage with boiling water, add salt and boil rapidly approximately 7 minutes. Stir in mustard. Add cauliflower and green pepper; continue to cook 5 minutes longer. Drain any excess liquid. Season with butter.

CAULIFLOWER PEA CASSEROLE

1 c. chopped mushrooms
1/4 c. finely chopped onion
4 T. butter
2 T. flour
1 c. milk
1/2 tsp. salt
1/4 tsp. pepper

1 tsp. parsley
1 head cauliflower, separated into
    florets, cooked 3 minutes
1-2 c. cooked peas
1/2 c. Parmesan cheese or
    buttered bread crumbs

Sauté mushrooms and onion in butter about 5 minutes. Remove mushrooms and onions. Stir flour into remaining butter. Gradually add milk. Stir until mixture thickens and boils. Add salt, pepper and parsley. Place cauliflower florets in a casserole. Sprinkle with mushrooms, onions and peas. Pour white sauce over all and sprinkle with Parmesan cheese or bread crumbs. Bake at 400° for 30 minutes.

Hint: Pour boiling water over cauliflower and let set 10 minutes for less crunchy cauliflower salads.

CAULIFLOWER AU GRATIN

1 head cauliflower (cut into
    florets)
4 T. butter
1/4 c. onion
4 T. flour
2 c. milk
1 c. grated cheddar cheese

salt and pepper to taste
1 tsp. Worcestershire sauce
1 tsp. mustard
2 T. Parmesan cheese
1 T. dried bread crumbs
1 T. melted butter

Cook cauliflower in salt water just until tender, drain. Sauté onion in butter, add flour, blend in milk and bring to a boil. Simmer for 2 minutes, remove from heat and add cheddar cheese (reserve 1/4 c.),salt, pepper, Worcestershire sauce and mustard. Stir until cheese is melted. Place cauliflower in a casserole, pour sauce on and sprinkle with reserved cheese and Parmesan cheese, bread crumbs and melted butter. Bake at 350° for 25-30 minutes.

VEGETABLE PIZZA WITH CAULIFLOWER

12 inch pizza crust, baked
2 c. shredded mozzarella cheese
4 c. mixed vegetables
    (cauliflower, broccoli and

red pepper), parboiled 3
    minutes
3/4 tsp. dried basil
3 T. grated parmesan cheese

Sprinkle cheese on pizza crust. Top with well drained vegetables. Sprinkle with Parmesan cheese and basil. Bake at 450° for 12-15 minutes until vegetables are hot and mozzarella bubbles.

CAULIFLOWER BEEF STIR FRY

2 T. soy sauce
1 T. corn starch
1 T. water
1/4 tsp. salt
1/2 lb. 1/8-inch beef strips (cut
    while partially frozen)
2 T. vegetable oil

3/4 c. beef broth or bouillon
3 c. cauliflower florets, halved
2 c. diagonally sliced celery pieces
1 medium onion, sliced
1 c. thinly sliced carrots
1 tsp. salt
1/8 tsp. pepper

Combine first 4 ingredients. Add meat and let stand while preparing vegetables. Heat oil in a large skillet. Add meat and stir fry until it loses its pink color. Add broth slowly, stir until it boils. Add vegetables and mix well. Cover and simmer 7-9 minutes or until vegetables are tender crisp.

CAULIFLOWER – CANNING AND FREEZING

SWEET PICKLED CAULIFLOWER

3 qt. 1 to 2-inch cauliflower
    florets
1 qt. vinegar
2 c. sugar
2 c. thinly sliced onions

1 c. diced sweet red peppers
2 T. mustard seed
1 T. celery seed
1 tsp. turmeric
1 tsp. hot-pepper flakes

Wash cauliflower florets and boil in salt water (4 tsp. canning salt per gallon of water) for 3 minutes. Drain and pack into hot pint jars. Combine vinegar, sugar, onion, diced red pepper, and spices in large saucepan. Bring to a boil and simmer 5 minutes. Distribute onion and diced pepper among jars. Fill jars with pieces and pickling solution, leaving 1/2-inch headspace. Adjust lids. Process 10 minutes in boiling water canner. Yields 5 or 6 pints.

HOT MIXED PICKLE

1 medium head cauliflower,
    separated into florets
1 red sweet pepper, cut in strips
1 1/2 c. celery, cut in 1-inch pieces
2 c. carrots, sliced
2 medium onions, quartered
5 or 6 red chili peppers

1 qt water
1/4 c. canning salt
5 c. vinegar
1 c. water
1/2 c. sugar
1 clove garlic, crushed

Soak vegetables in a solution made from the water and salt for one hour. Combine vinegar, 1 c. water, sugar and crushed garlic clove. Simmer for 15 minutes. Drain vegetables and pack into pint jars. Place one hot pepper in each jar. Pour boiling hot pickling solution over vegetables in the jars, leaving 1/2-inch headspace. Cover with lids. Process in boiling water canner for 10 minutes. Yields 5 to 6 pints.

HOW TO FREEZE CAULIFLOWER

Break heads into small florets about 1-inch in diameter. If insects are present, soak pieces 1/2 hour in salt brine (1/4 c. salt per gallon water). Rinse; drain. Blanch in salted water or add 1 tsp. ascorbic-citric acid mixture per gallon of water to inhibit color changes. Blanch 2-3 minutes depending on size of florets.[2] Cool immediately in cold water; drain, package and freeze.

67

NOTES

68

Celeriac

and

Celery

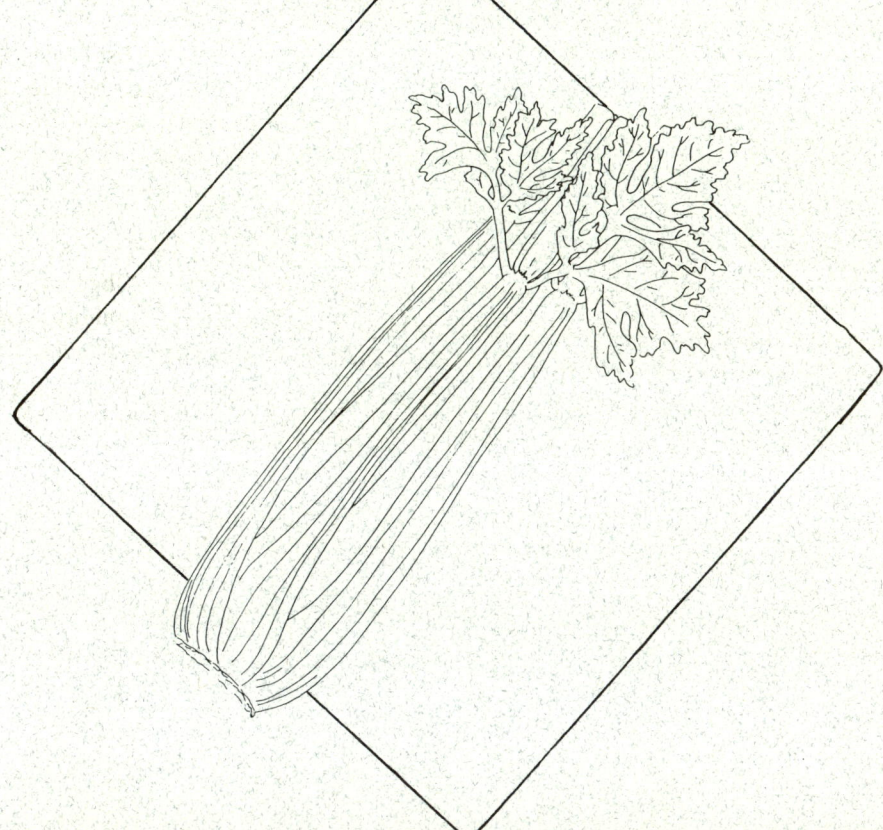

Celeriac (celery root) is a root crop in the same family as the more common, above ground, stalk celery. Don't let the rather hairy, knobby, unkempt appearance of unpeeled celeriac deter you from using this fine, celery-flavored vegetable.

Celery and celeriac require a long, cool growing season. Best results are from transplants instead of direct seeding. Start plants 10-12 weeks before planting outdoors. Celery will bolt if temperatures drop below 55 degrees for 10 days or more, so wait to plant out after temperatures reach 65-70 degrees.

Celery especially, requires a steady water supply throughout the summer. Hot, dry conditions that check plant growth cause celery to get tough and bitter. Both celery and celeriac need fertile, well-drained soil for optimum results.

Many gardeners prefer to blanch their celery before harvesting, although this procedure is not widely recommended anymore because it decreases flavor and nutrients in the celery. To blanch, either wrap the stalk in paper, leaving the top leaves exposed or stake planks on either side of the row, leaving the top leaves exposed. Start blanching about 4 weeks before harvest.

You don't need to wait for the traditional fall crop to use your celery. Go ahead and rob stalks from the plants throughout the summer for flavoring in salads and soups. The plant will keep right on growing.

Harvest celeriac when the roots are 2-4 inches across. It must be peeled to use. Begin by cutting off the leaf and root ends and then cut down the sides from top to bottom. A one pound celeriac root yields about ½ pound usable flesh. To keep the flesh white place it in vinegar water until you're ready to use it.

Both celery and celeriac can be eaten raw or used raw in salads. They're also good in soups, stews and Asian dishes. Try them boiled, braised or steamed for a cooked vegetable.

Celery and celeriac are both high in potassium and provide fiber.

Celery keeps for 2-3 months at 32-35 degrees and 95% humidity. Under normal refrigeration, celery looses moisture and becomes limp within 1-2 weeks. To rejuvenate, soak in ice water before using.

Store celeriac by layering untrimmed roots (remove all but the center tuft of leaves) in moist sand in a pail and placing in a cool cellar.

Yield: 1 lb. celery = 4 cups chopped
       1 lb. celeriac root = ½ peeled root

CELERY SOUP

3 T. butter
4 c. diced celery and leaves
1 c. diced leeks or onions
1/2 tsp. basil
4 c. chicken broth or bouillon

2 T. butter
2 T. flour
1 c. milk
1/2 tsp. salt or to taste
1/8 tsp. pepper

Sauté celery and leeks in 3 T. butter for 5-8 minutes in a 3 qt. kettle. Add basil and broth and simmer 10-15 minutes. Melt 2 T. butter in a small saucepan. Blend in flour, salt and pepper. Gradually add milk, stirring constantly until sauce thickens. Add sauce to soup, mixing well.

CELERY POTATO SOUP

1 c. diced celery
1 c. diced potatoes
1 c. water
1 qt. milk

2 T. butter
1 tsp. salt or to taste
1/8 tsp. pepper

Cook celery and potatoes together in water until soft. Add milk, butter, salt and pepper. Heat but do not boil.

CHICKEN NOODLE SOUP WITH CELERY AND CARROTS

2 1/2 lb. chicken, cut up
1 qt. water
2 c. chopped celery
2 c. chopped carrots
2 tsp. salt or to taste

1 tsp. sugar
1/4 tsp. pepper
2 chicken bouillon cubes
2 c. thin noodles, uncooked

Bring all but noodles to a boil in a large kettle. Cover and simmer until chicken is done, about 45-60 minutes. Skim fat if necessary. Remove chicken and debone. Cook noodles according to directions. Add noodles and chicken to soup. Heat through.

CHICKEN SALAD WITH CELERY

3 c. diced cooked chicken
2 c. chopped celery
4 hard boiled eggs
1/4 c. pickle relish
1/4 c. chopped fresh parsley

2 tsp. fresh chives
1 c. mayonnaise
1 T. lemon juice
1 T. vinegar
salt and pepper to taste

Combine first six ingredients. Mix mayonnaise with lemon juice, vinegar, salt and pepper. Add to chicken and mix.

STUFFED CELERY

3 oz. pkg. cream cheese, softened
1 tsp. lemon juice (optional)
1/2 tsp. Worcestershire sauce

1/4 tsp. garlic salt, onion salt or
seasoned salt
2-3 ribs of celery

Combine everything but celery. Stuff celery then cut each rib into 1 to 3-inch pieces. If desired, garnish with chopped green onions, chopped nuts or sliced olives, or sprinkle with seasoned salt or paprika.
Variations: Stuff 1-inch pieces of celery with cottage cheese and garnish with radish slices cut in half and inserted with the red side up. Or stuff celery with peanut butter and top with raisins.

CELERY – SIDE AND MAIN DISHES

HOW TO COOK CELERY

Bring 1-inch of water to a boil in a large skillet. Add 4 c. sliced celery and 1/2-1 tsp. salt. Return to a boil. Reduce heat, cover and simmer approximately 5 minutes or until tender crisp. Drain.

SAUTÉED CELERY

2 T. butter
2 T. vegetable oil
6 c. sliced celery
1/2 c. sliced scallions or onions

3/4 c. sliced almonds
1/4 tsp. dry basil
salt and pepper to taste

Heat butter and oil in a large skillet. Sauté all ingredients but salt and pepper for 5-10 minutes or until celery is tender crisp. Season to taste.

CREAMED CELERY

4 c. sliced celery
1/4 c. sliced green onions
1/4 c. butter
2 T. flour
1 c. chicken broth

1/8 tsp. pepper
1/2 tsp. Worcestershire sauce
1/2 c. light cream
1/4 c. toasted slivered almonds
(optional)

Sauté celery and onions in butter 5-10 minutes or until tender crisp. Blend flour into vegetables then add broth. Cook, stirring constantly, until sauce thickens and bubbles for 3 minutes. Stir in all but almonds and heat through. Sprinkle with almonds just before serving if desired.

CHEESY CELERY

1 onion
1 T. butter
1 T. flour
1/4 tsp. salt
1/8 tsp. pepper

1 c. milk
1 c. shredded American cheese
1 tsp. dry mustard
4 c. lightly cooked celery pieces

Sauté onion in butter until tender. Stir in flour, salt and pepper. Cook over low heat, stirring constantly until mixture is bubbly. Gradually stir in milk. Boil and stir 1 minute. Add cheese and mustard, stirring until cheese is melted. Stir in celery and heat through.

BEEF AND CELERY STIR FRY

1/4 c. butter
4 c. 1/4 inch diagonally sliced
　　celery
1 medium onion
1/2 tsp. salt or to taste
1/8 tsp. pepper

1 1/2 c. hot water
2 c. cooked beef strips
2 T. cold water
2 T. cornstarch
2 tsp. soy sauce
1 tsp. sugar

Heat butter in a large skillet or wok. Add celery and onion. Stir rapidly. Add salt and pepper and continue stirring 2-3 minutes. Add hot water and beef strips. Cover and cook 2-3 minutes more. Combine cold water, cornstarch, soy sauce and sugar; stir into skillet. Cook 1 minute. Serve over hot rice or chow mien noodles. **Variation:** Add 1 c. mushrooms and 2 c. bean sprouts.

BRAISED CHICKEN WITH CELERY, CARROTS AND ONIONS

1/2 c. flour	1/2 tsp. salt
1 tsp. salt	3 c. sliced celery
1/4 tsp. pepper	1 1/2 c. sliced carrots
3 lb. frying chicken, cut up	3/4 c. finely chopped onion
3 T. vegetable oil	3/4 c. chopped green pepper
3/4 c. hot water	

Combine flour, 1 tsp. salt and pepper; coat chicken pieces with mixture. Brown chicken in hot oil in large skillet. Drain excess oil from pan. Add water and 1/2 tsp. salt. Cover tightly and simmer about 1 hour. Add vegetables and cook approximately 10 minutes longer or until vegetables are tender crisp. Serve over rice if desired.

CURRIED TURKEY AND CELERY

4 T. butter	3 c. milk
2 c. diagonally sliced celery	4 c. diced, cooked turkey or
1 c. chopped onion	chicken
3 T. flour	1 c. halved, pitted ripe olives
2 tsp. salt	(optional)
1 tsp. curry powder	cooked rice
2 chicken bouillon cubes	

Melt 2 T. butter in large skillet and sauté celery and onion about 10 minutes. Melt remaining butter in saucepan; add flour, salt, curry and bouillon cubes and blend well. Add milk gradually. Stir and cook until thickened. Add milk mixture, turkey and olives to celery mixture and heat. Serve on rice.

Come unto me, all ye that labour and are heavy laden, and I will give you rest. Take my yoke upon you, and learn of me; for I am meek and lowly in heart: and ye shall find rest unto your souls. For my yoke is easy, and my burden is light.

Matthew 11:28-30

72

TURKEY PATTIES WITH CELERY

1 lb. ground turkey	1 T. sugar
1/3 c. dry bread crumbs	2 tsp. cornstarch
1/4 tsp. salt	1/8 tsp. ground ginger
1/4 tsp. garlic powder	1 c. chicken broth or bouillon
1 egg	3 T. soy sauce
1 T. vegetable oil	2 tsp. vinegar
1 c. sliced celery	2 medium tomatoes, cut into
1 medium green bell pepper (3/4-inch pieces)	wedges

Combine ground turkey, bread crumbs, salt, garlic powder and egg; blend well. Form into five 1/2-inch thick patties. Heat oil in large skillet until oil sizzles. Add turkey patties. Cook 3 to 5 minutes on each side or until browned and no longer pink in center. Add celery and green pepper. In small bowl, combine sugar, cornstarch, ginger, chicken broth, soy sauce and vinegar; blend well. Add cornstarch mixture to skillet; bring to a boil. Reduce heat to low; simmer 5 minutes or until vegetables are tender crisp, stirring occasionally. Stir in tomatoes; simmer an additional 2 minutes or until thoroughly heated. Serve over rice or noodles.

BAKED WHOLE FISH WITH CELERY STUFFING

1/4 c. corn oil	2 T. hot water
1/3 c. finely chopped onion	1/2 tsp. salt
3 c. bread cubes (about 5 slices)	1/4 tsp. pepper
1 c. chopped celery	3 to 5-lb. whole fish, dressed
1/4 c. chopped parsley	corn oil
1 T. lemon juice	

Heat 1/4 c. oil in 8-inch skillet over medium heat. Add onion and cook, stirring constantly, until transparent. Add bread cubes and stir until coated with oil. Remove from heat. Add celery, parsley, lemon juice, water, salt and pepper; mix well. Place fish on greased baking sheet. Stuff cavity with dressing. Close opening loosely with wooden picks. Brush fish with oil. Bake at 500° for 5 minutes. Reduce heat and continue baking at 400° about 4o to 65 minutes, allowing 12 minutes per pound, or until easily flaked with fork.

Then saith he unto his disciples, The harvest truly is plenteous, but the labourers are few;
Pray ye therefore the Lord of the harvest, that he will send forth labourers into his harvest.
Matthew 9:37,38

73

SAUSAGE AND CELERY STUFFING

1/2 lb. bulk sausage
8 slices slightly dry bread, cubed
2 T. milk
1 c. diced celery

1/4 c. chopped onion
1/2 tsp. salt
2 tsp. poultry seasoning
1/8 tsp. pepper

Brown sausage in skillet. When browned remove with slotted spoon and place in a bowl with bread cubes. Drizzle with milk. Stir celery and onion into drippings in skillet and sauté until soft. Stir in seasonings. Pour over bread mixture and toss lightly. Enough to stuff an 8 lb. turkey.

CELERIAC – SOUPS

CREAM OF CELERIAC AND CARROT SOUP

3 lb. celeriac, peeled and chunked
3 medium carrots, peeled and
chunked
1 1/2 c. chopped onions

8 c. chicken broth
1 c. light cream
salt and pepper

Put vegetables in a large kettle and add 6 c. of the broth. Cover, reduce heat and simmer 15-20 minutes. Puree vegetables in a blender in several batches. Return to soup pot and add remaining broth. Reheat; add cream and seasonings to taste. Heat through but do not boil.

Variation: Use celery instead of celeriac or leeks instead of onions.

CELERIAC – SALADS

CELERIAC SALAD

1 T. lemon juice
3 c. water
2 c. 1/8-inch thick celeriac strips
2 green onion, finely chopped
1/4 c. chopped fresh parsley

1/4 T. olive or vegetable oil
1 T. vinegar
2 tsp. prepared horseradish
1/2 tsp. salt
1/4 tsp. pepper

Combine lemon juice and water. Place celeriac strips into lemon water as soon as cut. Combine remaining ingredients for dressing. Drain celeriac. Toss with dressing and refrigerate at least 2 hours.

CELERIAC AND CABBAGE SALAD

1 c. mayonnaise
1/4 c. mustard
2 T. vinegar
1/2 tsp. salt or to taste

1/8 tsp. pepper
2 1/2 c. 1/8-inch thick celeriac
   strips
2 c. shredded cabbage

Combine all but celeriac and cabbage to make dressing. Cut celeriac into strips, stirring them into the dressing as soon as they are cut to prevent darkening. Add shredded cabbage. Refrigerate at least 2 hours before serving.

CELERIAC GRAPE PINEAPPLE SALAD

1/2 c. water
2 tsp. lemon juice
1/2 tsp. celery salt
1/8 tsp. pepper
1 c. 1/2-inch celeriac cubes
1/4 c. French dressing

8 1/4 oz. can pineapple chunks
1 c. seedless grapes, chilled
1/4 c. toasted almonds
1/4 c. mayonnaise or salad
   dressing
lettuce

Bring water, lemon juice, celery, salt and pepper to a boil. Add celeriac and simmer, uncovered, 5 minutes. Drain and pour French dressing over celeriac. Refrigerate at least 2 hours, stirring occasionally. Drain just before serving. Stir in pineapple, grapes and almonds. Add mayonnaise; toss. Serve on lettuce.
Variation: Use celery instead of celeriac.

CELERIAC – SIDE AND MAIN DISHES

HOW TO COOK CELERIAC

Unpeeled: Bring 1-inch of water to a boil. Add whole, one pound, unpeeled celeriac and 1/2 tsp. salt or to taste. Return to a boil. Reduce heat and simmer 45-50 minutes. If celeriac is less than 1 pound, reduce cooking time. Cool, peel and slice.
Peeled: Peel and slice. Immediately place slices in a mixture of 3 c. water and 1 T. vinegar to prevent darkening. Drain and place in 1-inch boiling water. Return to a boil; reduce heat and simmer 1/2-inch cubes 5-8 minutes. Increase cooking time for larger slices. A little lemon juice can be added to cooking water instead of vinegar to prevent darkening.
Serving Suggestions: Sauté boiled and drained celeriac cubes in butter until lightly brown—4 to 5 minutes. Season with salt and pepper. Sprinkle with parsley.

CELERIAC WITH CHEESE SAUCE

1 1/2 T. butter
1 1/2 T. flour
1/4 tsp. salt
1/8 tsp. pepper

3/4 c. milk
1/2 c. cubed American cheese
1 lb. celeriac slices, cut into 1-inch
cubes, cooked

Melt butter. Add flour and seasonings and blend well. Add milk gradually, stirring constantly until sauce thickens. Add cheese and stir until melted. Serve cheese sauce over hot celeriac cubes.

CELERY – CANNING AND FREEZING

HOW TO CAN CELERY

Hot Pack: Wash; slice or cut into 1-inch pieces. Cover with boiling water; boil 3 minutes. Fill jar with hot celery to within 1-inch of top. Add 1 tsp. salt for quarts or 1/2 tsp. salt for pints. Fill with boiling cooking water, leaving 1-inch headspace. Process in a pressure canner; pints 30 minutes and quarts 35 minutes. Process at 10 lb. pressure if you live up to 1000 feet above sea level. Process at 15 lb. of pressure if you live above 1000 feet above sea level. Dial gauges should be at 11 lb. of pressure up to 2000 feet above sea level.[1]

CHICKEN MIX WITH CELERY CARROTS AND ONIONS

8-10 lb. chicken, cut in pieces
1 T. salt
1/2 tsp. pepper
1 T. chopped parsley

2 c. celery
2 c. carrots, peeled and sliced
thinly
1 c. onion, chopped

Place chicken, salt, pepper and parsley in a large kettle. Cover with water and bring to a boil. Simmer until chicken can be removed from the bones. Skin and debone chicken. Add onion, celery and carrots to broth and bring to a boil. Stir in chicken pieces. Fill jars with hot chicken/vegetable mixture, leaving 1-inch headspace. Cover with boiling broth, leaving 1-inch headspace. Wipe jar rims and adjust lids. Process in a pressure canner 75 minutes for pints; 90 minutes for quarts. Use for stews, soups, Chicken a la King or casseroles. Add cornstarch or flour to the liquid to thicken just before serving. Yields 7-8 pints.

HOW TO FREEZE CELERY

Trim; discard tough and blemished stalks. Wash, dice or cut into 1-inch pieces. Blanch in water for 1 to 2 minutes.[2] Cool immediately in cold water. Drain; pack into freezer containers and freeze. Use only in cooked foods.

Corn

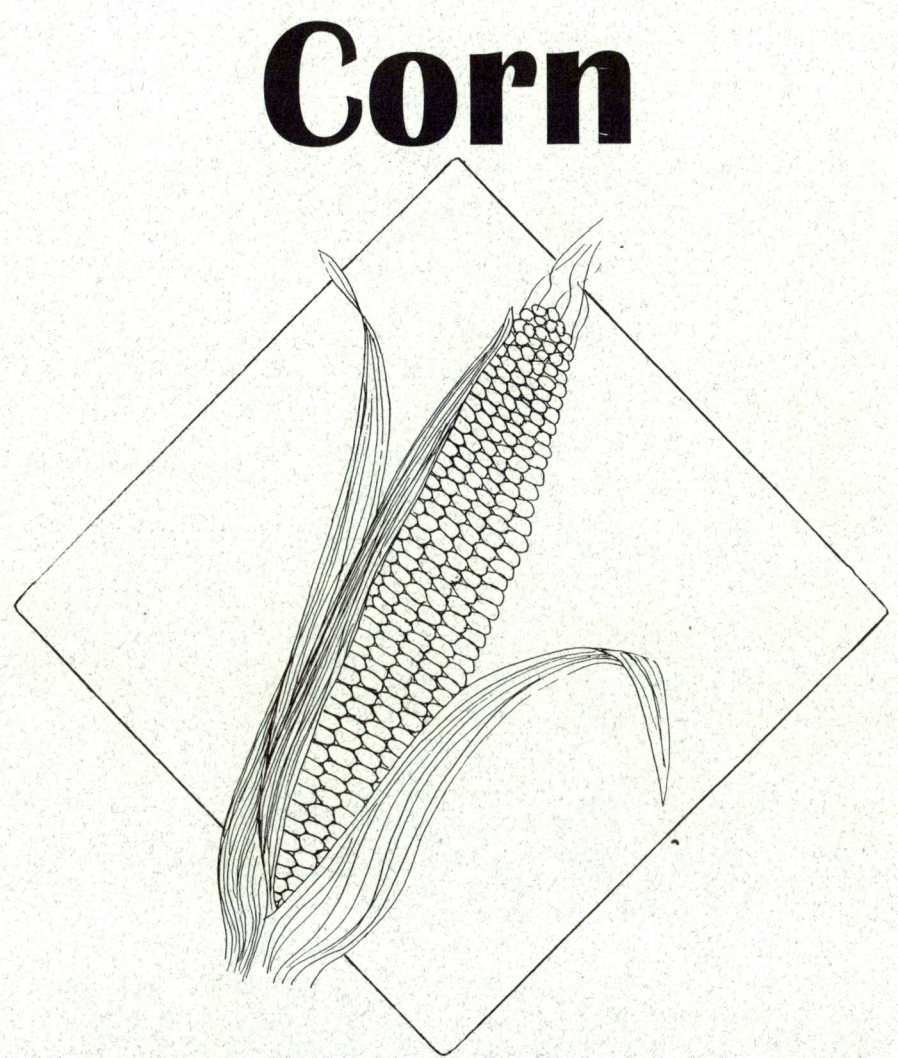

Native to the Americas, corn was first used by the American Indians. Sweet corn as we know it, didn't become popular until about 100 years ago. Today there are four different genetic types of sweet corn available relating to the sugar content in the kernel. The confusion this may cause the beginning gardener is more than compensated by the increased quality and after harvest shelf life of the newer hybrids.

Normal sugary (*su*) varieties are sweet with good flavor. For many years su hybrids were the standard for sweet corn and the only ones available. The old—have your water boiling before you go to pick your corn—adage was a good one because the sugar in su hybrids converts to starch very quickly after harvest and the flavor converts very quickly to blah.

Sugary enhanced—heterozygous (*se-he*) sweet corn is sweeter and more tender than (*su*) types. In addition, the conversion of sugar to starch is slowed increasing the shelf life considerably after harvest. Anywhere from 25-50% of the kernels on an (*se-he*) cob are sugary enhanced.

Sugary enhanced—homozygous (*se-ho*) hybrids are sweeter than se-he because all the kernels on the cob are sugary enhanced.

Shrunken (*sh2*)—named for the shrunken appearance of the seeds— varieties are known as the super sweet hybrids. They have the highest sugar content and the longest after-harvest shelf life. *Sh2* corn needs to be isolated from all other corn varieties by a distance of at least 100 feet or have a difference of at least 10 days in its days to maturity to get the super sweet affect. Cross pollination with other corn results in tough, starchy kernels in both types. Isolation is less critical for su and se hybrids.

Another advantage of the *se* and *sh2* hybrids is the extended harvest— often 1-2 weeks—you can enjoy with these varieties. The su corns tend to get ready and need to be used all at once.

Yellow, white and bicolor sweet corn is available in all the categories.

Plant sweet corn in fertile, well-drained soil every 4-5 inches. Thin to a final spacing of 10-14 inches. If soil moisture is adequate seeds should be planted ¾-1 inch deep. Planting shallow is especially critical for early spring plantings when soil temperature may be marginal. *Su* hybrids will germinate at soil temperatures of 50-55 degrees, *se-ho* and *se-he* hybrids 60 degrees and *sh2* hybrids 70 degrees.

In general, the more shrunken and wrinkled the seed, the warmer the soil temperature needed for germination. *Se* and *sh2* varieties planted in cool spring soils result in disappointing stands.

Sweet corn is ready to harvest approximately 21 days after silk is visible on ½ of the stalks. Ears ready to pick have dried, brown silks and a blunt, full, hard feel at the tip of the ear as opposed to the soft pointed feel of under ripe corn. Keep in mind that the days to maturity given with a particular variety of corn are minimums under ideal conditions. The actual days required can be up to 20 days longer than the given time, depending on weather conditions and how early you planted in the spring.

Sweet corn is best picked fresh and eaten immediately. The new sweeter hybrids can be kept for several days if refrigerated. Leave the husks on until you are ready to use it. To get the best flavor and longest shelf life, pick your corn early in the morning while it is still cool.

Corn is an excellent source of thiamine and folate it also provides some vitamin A and C, potassium and iron.

Yield: 5-6 ears = 3 cups kernels
1 bushel = 35 lb. = 14-17 pints

CREAMY CORN SOUP

1/2 c. chopped celery
1/4 c. chopped onion
1 T. butter
3 c. chicken broth

2 c. corn
1/2 c. sliced carrots
1 c. light cream

Cook celery and onion in butter until onion is tender but not brown. Add broth, corn and carrots. Bring to a boil; reduce heat. Simmer covered for 10-12 minutes. Stir in cream and heat through.

CHICKEN CORN CHOWDER

1 bone-in chicken breast
2 c. water
1 rib celery, cut up
1 bay leaf
1/2 tsp. salt
2 c. milk
2 T. butter
1/2 c. diced onion

1 c. diced celery
2 T. flour
2 c. potatoes, peeled and cut into
1/2-inch pieces
2 c. corn
1/4 tsp. salt
1/8 tsp. pepper

Combine chicken, water, celery, bay leaf and salt in 3 quart saucepan. Bring to boil. Reduce heat and simmer, covered, until chicken is tender. Remove chicken from broth, debone and dice. Set aside. Strain broth. Add milk. Set aside. In 3 quart saucepan, sauté diced onion and celery in butter (3-4 minutes). Blend in flour. Gradually stir in milk mixture. Add potatoes, simmer until tender (15-20 minutes). Stir in chicken, corn, salt and pepper. Heat through. Garnish with minced chives or parsley if desired.
Variation: Delete chicken.

CORN AND HAM SOUP

6 1/2 c. chicken broth
1 pt. corn
1 c. diced ham

1/3 c. chopped onion
1/3 c. chopped green pepper
1 c. light cream

Combine all but cream. Bring to a boil; reduce heat. Cover and simmer 15 minutes. Stir in cream and heat through.

CHICKEN CORN NOODLE SOUP

6 c. chicken broth or part
    bouillon
1/2 tsp. parsley
1 tsp. onion powder
1/8 tsp. pepper
2 T. fresh celery leaves

4 oz. dry noodles
1 1/2 c. corn
15 oz. canned chicken
5 drops yellow food coloring
    (optional)
salt to taste

Bring first five ingredients to a boil. Put in noodles and cook until almost done. Add remaining ingredients and boil 5 minutes.
Variation: Add finely shredded carrots with the celery leaves.

CORN–SALADS

CORN SALAD

3 c. corn kernels
1 c. diced celery
1/2 c. diced red or green pepper
1/4 c. sliced green onion

1/2 c. cider vinegar
1/2 c. sugar
1/4 tsp. dry mustard

Blanch corn in boiling water 3-4 minutes, put in a sieve and run under cold water to cool; drain. (Leftover corn can be used.) Put vegetables in a bowl. Combine vinegar, sugar and mustard. Bring to a boil then pour over vegetables. Chill at least 2 hours before serving or refrigerate overnight.

CORN AND RADISH SALAD

4 c. corn kernels
1 c. sliced radishes
1/4 c. chopped fresh parsley

1/2 c. mayonnaise
1 T. lemon juice
1/2 tsp. salt

Blanch the corn 3-4 minutes. Drain; run under cold water and drain again. Combine corn, radishes and parsley. Stir remaining ingredients together then mix with corn, radishes and parsley. Serve in a lettuce lined bowl.

CORN – SIDE AND MAIN DISHES

HOW TO COOK CORN

Cut Corn: Bring one inch of water to a boil. Add 4 c. fresh corn kernels and 1 tsp. salt or to taste. Return to a boil, reduce heat and simmer 5-8 minutes or until tender.

Corn on the Cob: Place cobs in a kettle of boiling water. Return to a boil. Boil 3-5 minutes.

SAUTÉED CORN

1/3 c. chopped green pepper	3 c. fresh cut corn
1/3 c. chopped onion	3/4 tsp. salt
3 T. butter	1/4 tsp. pepper

Sauté pepper and onion in butter until soft. Stir in corn and seasonings. Cover and cook 8-10 minutes, stirring once or twice.

Variation: Fry 4-6 slices bacon. Remove bacon and reserve 3 T. drippings. Sauté vegetables in drippings. Add less salt. Sprinkle with crumbled bacon before serving.

CREAMED CORN

6 ears corn	1/2 tsp. salt
2 T. butter	1/8 tsp. pepper
1/2 c. whipping cream	

Cut corn off cobs. Melt butter in a skillet. Add corn and cook 1 minute. Gradually add cream, stirring constantly. Cook, uncovered, over medium heat about 10 minutes, or until liquid is absorbed. Stir in salt and pepper.

CORN CURRY

3 T. butter	1/4 to 1/2 tsp. curry powder
2 c. fresh cut corn	1/2 c. sour cream
2 T. chopped green pepper	salt and pepper
2 T. chopped onion	

Melt butter in skillet. Add vegetables and curry. Cover; cook over low heat until vegetables are just tender—8-10 minutes. Stir in sour cream; season to taste. Heat, stirring constantly.

CORN FRITTERS

2 eggs
1/4 c. flour
1/2 tsp. salt
1/8 tsp. pepper
1 tsp. baking powder

2 T. milk or cream
2 c. fresh cut corn (or leftover
corn on the cob)
4 T. vegetable oil (or use 1/2 oil
and 1/2 butter)

Beat eggs and add dry ingredients. Blend in cream and corn. Drop by spoonsful into hot oil in skillet and fry until brown, turning once. Serve with butter and syrup.
Variation: Use only eggs, corn, salt and pepper.

CORN PANCAKES

2 c. flour
2 tsp. baking powder
1 tsp. salt
2 large eggs

3/4 c. milk
2 T. melted butter
2 c. corn

Mix together dry ingredients in one bowl and eggs, milk, butter and corn in another. Combine the two carefully, stirring only until moistened. Cook on a hot oiled griddle, turning once.

SCALLOPED CORN

2 eggs
1 c. milk
2/3 c. cracker crumbs
2 c. cooked corn

1 T. finely chopped onion
3 T. melted butter
1/2 tsp. salt
1/8 tsp. pepper

Beat the eggs and add milk and crumbs. Add remaining ingredients. Mix well and pour into a buttered casserole. Bake at 350° for 40 minutes.

EASY CORN PUDDING

2 c. cut and scraped corn
1 T. flour
2/3 c. whipping cream

1/2 tsp. salt or to taste
1/8 tsp. pepper
1 T. butter

Combine all but butter and mix well. Pour into a buttered 1 quart casserole. Dot with butter. Bake at 325° for 50-60 minutes.

CORN PUDDING

1/4 c. butter
1 1/2 c. cut and scraped corn
1/2 c. chopped onion
1/4 c. flour
1 tsp. salt

1/4 tsp. pepper
2 c. milk
1 c. grated cheddar cheese
3 eggs, slightly beaten

Melt butter in a large skillet. Sauté corn and onion, stirring, 2 minutes. Reduce heat; cook, covered, 10 minutes or until tender. Remove skillet from heat; stir in flour, salt and pepper to combine well. Gradually stir in milk. Bring to a boil, stirring. Reduce heat. Add cheese; cook, stirring until cheese is melted and sauce is slightly thickened. Remove from heat. Stir a little of cheese mixture into eggs then pour back into rest of cheese, mixing well. Turn into a buttered casserole. Set casserole in pan containing 1-inch hot water; bake at 350° for 50 minutes or until sharp knife inserted in center comes out clean. Serve hot.
Variation: Add 1/2 c. chopped green or red peppers with corn and onions.

CORN CASSEROLE

1 1/2 c. fresh corn
1/2 c. chopped onion
1/2 c. green pepper strips
1/2 c. water
1 c. chopped yellow squash or
    zucchini
1 c. chopped tomato

1 c. shredded cheddar cheese
2/3 c. cornmeal
1/2 c. milk
2 beaten eggs
3/4 tsp. salt
1/4 tsp. pepper

Bring corn, onion, peppers and water to a boil; reduce heat. Cover and simmer 5 minutes or until vegetables are tender crisp. Do not drain. Combine remaining ingredients in a large bowl, saving 1/4 c. cheddar cheese. Add undrained vegetables and mix well. Put in a 1 1/2 quart casserole. Bake uncovered at 350° for 45 to 50 minutes. Top with remaining cheese. Garnish with a tomato and pepper slice if desired.

They that sow in tears shall reap in joy. He that goeth forth and weepeth, bearing precious seed, shall doubtless come again with rejoicing, bringing his sheaves with him.

Psalm 126:5,6

CORN QUICHE

1 unbaked 9-inch fluted pie shell
5 slices bacon, cooked, drained
   and crumbled
2 c. corn, cut and scraped
1 c. shredded Swiss cheese

1/2 c. finely chopped onion
1 c. light cream
1/2 tsp. salt
1/8 tsp. pepper
4 eggs

Refrigerate pie shell. Toss together bacon, corn, cheese and onion; sprinkle on pie shell. With a wire whisk beat together remaining ingredients. Pour over corn mixture. Can be sprinkled with paprika if desired. Bake at 400° for 25 minutes then reduce heat to 325° and bake 20 more minutes or until knife inserted in the center comes out clean. Let stand 10 minutes before cutting.

CORNY BRUNSWICK STEW

1 frying chicken, cut up
1/2 c. flour
1/4 c. vegetable oil
1 c. chopped onion
2 c. peeled and diced tomatoes
2 tsp. salt

1/4 tsp. pepper
1 T. Worcestershire sauce
2 c. corn
2 c. fresh lima beans
2 medium potatoes peeled and
   cubed

Coat chicken with flour. In a large heavy kettle heat oil and brown chicken on both sides. Add onion and sauté until lightly browned. Add remaining ingredients. Bring to a boil; reduce heat and simmer 40 minutes or until chicken is tender.

Variation: Bring chicken to a boil in a cup of water. Reduce heat and simmer 1 1/2-2 hours. Debone and cube chicken. Return chicken and broth to the kettle and add remaining ingredients. Bring to a boil; reduce heat and simmer 30-40 minutes or until vegetables are tender.

CORN TOMATO GROUND BEEF PIE

1 lb. ground beef
1/4 lb. pork sausage
1 onion, chopped
1 clove garlic, finely chopped
2 c. corn
2 c. peeled and chopped tomatoes
20 pitted black olives (optional)

1 T. chili powder
1 1/2 tsp. salt
1 c. corn meal
1 c. milk
2 eggs, well beaten
1 c. shredded cheddar cheese

Brown meat, onion and garlic; drain. Stir in corn, tomatoes, olives, chili powder and salt. Pour into an ungreased 9 x 9 dish or 2-quart casserole. Mix corn meal, milk and eggs. Pour over meat mixture. Sprinkle cheese on top. Bake at 350° for 40-50 minutes.

CORNY CORNBREAD

1 c. cornmeal	1 c. milk
1 c. flour	2 eggs
2 T. sugar	1/4 c. vegetable oil
4 tsp. baking powder	1 1/2 c. corn (leftovers are fine)
1/2 tsp. salt	

Mix dry ingredients together. Beat together milk, eggs and oil. Add corn then add to dry ingredients, mixing just until well blended. Pour into a buttered 9x9 pan. Bake at 425° approximately 25-30 minutes.

Variation: Add 1 c. grated cheddar cheese, 2 jalapeno peppers seeded and chopped fine along with the corn.

RAISED CORN MUFFINS

2 c. milk	1 T. (1 pkg.) yeast
1 1/2 c. corn meal	1/4 c. warm water
1/2 c. shortening	2 eggs
1/2 c. sugar	4 3/4 c. flour
1 tsp. salt	1 1/2 c. cooked corn

Scald milk and pour into large bowl. Stir in corn meal, shortening, sugar and salt. Cool to lukewarm. Dissolve yeast in warm water and add to cornmeal mixture with eggs and 2 c. flour. Beat 2 minutes. Stir in remaining flour and corn with a spoon. Cover, and let rise until double in size—approximately 45 minutes. Stir down batter and spoon into 36 greased muffin-pan cups. Let rise, uncovered, until double in size, about 45 minutes. Bake at 400° approximately 15 minutes.

And let us not be weary in well doing: for in due season we shall reap, if we faint not.

Galatians 6:9

CORN – CANNING AND FREEZING

HOW TO CAN WHOLE KERNEL CORN[1]

Raw Pack: Husk, remove silks and wash. Cut kernels from cob 2/3 the depth of the kernels. Fill corn to 1-inch of top of jar; do not shake or pack down. Add 1 tsp. salt for quarts or 1/2 tsp. salt for pints. Iodized or plain table salt may be used. Fill with boiling water, leaving 1 inch headspace.

Hot Pack: Prepare as raw pack. To each quart of corn add 1 c. boiling water. Heat to boiling; simmer 5 minutes; pack hot to 1-inch of top and cover with boiling cooking liquid, leaving 1-inch headspace. Add salt as for raw pack.

Process in a pressure canner; pints 55 minutes and quarts 85 minutes. Process at 10 lb. of pressure if you live up to 1000 feet above sea level. Process at 15 lb. if you live above 1000 feet above sea level. Dial gauges should be at 11 lb. of pressure up to 2000 feet above sea level.

HOW TO CAN CREAM-STYLE CORN[1]

Raw Pack: Husk, remove silks and wash. Cut raw corn from cob at about center of kernel and then scrape cobs. Use pint jars only. Fill corn to 1-inch of top, without pressing down. Add 1/2 tsp. salt to each pint. Fill with boiling water, leaving 1-inch headspace.

Hot Pack: Husk, remove silks and wash. Cut corn from cob at center of kernel and then scrape cobs. For each quart of corn add 1 pint boiling water. Heat to boiling. Use pint jars only. Fill jars with hot corn and liquid to within 1-inch of top. Add 1/2 tsp. salt to each pint.

Process in a pressure canner; pints 95 minutes for raw pack and 85 minutes for hot pack. Quarts UNSAFE. Process at 10 lb. of pressure if you live up to 1000 feet above sea level. Process at 15 lb. if you live above 1000 feet above sea level. Dial gauges should be at 11 lb. of pressure up to 2000 feet above sea level.

Abide in me, and I in you. As the branch cannot bear fruit of itself, except it abide in the vine; no more can ye, except ye abide in me. I am the vine, ye are the branches. He that abideth in me, and I in him, the same bringeth forth much fruit: for without me ye can do nothing. If a man abide not in me, he is cast forth as a branch, and is withered; and men gather them, and cast them into the fire, and they are burned.

John 15:4-6

CORN RELISH

16 to 20 ears fresh corn
2 c. chopped onions
1 c. chopped sweet green peppers
3/4 c. chopped sweet red peppers
1 1/2 c. sugar

1 qt. vinegar
2 T. dry mustard
1 T. mustard seed
2 T. canning salt

Cut corn from ears, but do not scrape. Measure 2 to 2 1/2 qt. cut corn. Combine corn with onions and remaining ingredients in a kettle. Bring to a boil. Cover and simmer 20 minutes, stirring occasionally, to prevent scorching. Pack hot into jars, leaving 1/2-inch headspace. Cover and put lids on. Process in boiling water canner for 20 minutes. Yields 6 to 7 pints.

HOW TO FREEZE CORN

Use only freshly picked corn. For best quality, do 2 or 3 small batches instead of one big batch.

Whole kernel: Do not delay after harvest. Work with a small amount of freshly picked corn at a time. Husk, remove silks and trim ends. Blanch [for 4 minutes]; chill [immediately in cold water]. Corn not thoroughly chilled may become mushy. Cut corn from the cob about 2/3 the depth of the kernel.[2] Put in freezer containers and freeze.

Corn on the Cob: Husk, remove silks. Blanch [for 6-8 minutes]; chill [immediately in cold water] very thoroughly. Pat ears dry. Package whole ears individually, then into a second package. If steam forms in wrap, ears have not completely chilled.[2]

Creamstyle: Husk, remove silks. Blanch [for 4 minutes]; chill [immediately in cold water]. Cut corn in center of kernel; scrape cobs to remove juice.[2] Put in freezer containers and freeze.

Even as I have seen, they that plow iniquity, and sow wickedness, reap the same.

Job 4:8

NOTES

Cucumbers

Cucumbers can be grown and enjoyed fresh just about anywhere in North America. They are in a family of vegetables known as *cucurbits* that also includes melons, squash, pumpkins and gourds. Because they share diseases, members of this family should be rotated on a 3 year basis with non-cucurbit plants.

Cucumbers are classed as either slicers or picklers. Pickling cucumbers have thin, lighter skin than slicers. They can be used for pickling or fresh for anything the slicing cucumbers would be used for. Slicing cucumbers are larger (6-8 inches) with dark green skin. Because the peelings are thicker in slicers, they are usually not suitable for pickling.

Generally, slicing cucumbers are peeled before using, although that is more a matter of preference than necessity. Use pickling cucumbers unpeeled.

When you see a pickle variety described as *gynoecious* it means that the plants are bred to produce mostly female flowers and therefore will have increased yields. They require male pollinator plants that will be included with the seed.

Plant cucumbers after the soil is warm and danger of frost is past. Plant no more than ½ inch deep, 6 inches apart. Thin to a final spacing of 12-18 inches. If space is a concern, try a bush type plant or train the vines onto a trellis.

When seeds fail to germinate it is most likely from planting in cool, wet soil causing the seed to rot before germination. You can circumvent this problem by planting seedlings instead of seeds. We often have requests in our greenhouse for cucumber plants toward the end of June because, "Mine never came up."

By that time the greenhouse plants are gone or over-grown and the individual ends up buying cucumbers instead of picking his own.

We plant our cucumber transplants in black plastic mulch. The plastic mulch keeps weeds down in the row, warms the soil, preserves moisture and speeds plant growth. Transplants should be started in individual pots, 4-6 weeks before setting out. By that time they will have one or two true leaves.

Cucumbers are best tasting and most crisp when picked in the morning with the dew still on the vines and the overnight cool still in the cucumber. Most of a cucumber's weight is water, which is why they don't stay crisp long after they're picked. Shipped cucumbers are waxed by the grower to prevent dehydration and to increase shelf life. The more mature the cucumbers are, the longer they will stay firm after picking.

To keep new fruit setting on your plants all summer long, cucumbers should be picked frequently and watered during dry periods.

Cucumbers are enjoyable as a snack right in the garden. Include them on vegetable trays with dip, in salads or soups, or served as a cooked vegetable. Pickling is the preferred method of preservation.

Cucumbers are a low calorie vegetable that supply fiber to the diet. They also have some vitamin C and folate.

Yield: 1 lb. fresh cucumbers = 4 cups cubed or sliced
1 bushel pickling cucumbers = 50-55 lb. = 40 pints pickles

CUCUMBER SOUP

3 large cucumbers	1/8 tsp. pepper
2 T. butter	1 c. milk
3 T. flour	1/4 c. chopped onion
3 c. chicken broth	1/2 c. cream
1/2 tsp. salt or to taste	2 egg yolks, slightly beaten

Peel cucumbers and cut in half lengthwise; remove seeds; chop pulp and drain. Melt butter in a 3 quart saucepan; add cucumbers and cook 10 minutes. Stir in flour. Gradually add chicken broth and seasonings; set aside. Combine milk and onion and cook 2 to 4 minutes. Combine mixtures and blend in a blender. Bring mixture to a boil. Gradually add 1 cup of mixture to cream and then to egg yolks. Combine mixtures. Heat but do not boil. Serve warm or cold.

CREAMY CUCUMBER SOUP

6 c. peeled, seeded and chopped cucumbers	1/2 c. chopped onions
	2-3 T. lemon juice
2 c. buttermilk	1 tsp. salt
1 c. sour cream	2 T. minced fresh dill

Combine ingredients. Process in a blender until smooth. Chill and serve.

CUCUMBER SALAD

3-4 medium cucumbers	1 tsp. salt
1/2 c. finely diced green pepper	1 c. vinegar
1/2 c. thinly sliced onion rings	1/2 c. white sugar
1/2 T. celery seed	

Wash cucumbers; slice thinly, but do not peel. Combine with peppers, onions and seasonings. Mix together vinegar and sugar, stirring until sugar dissolves. Pour over cucumber mixture. Cover and refrigerate at least 24 hours before serving.

CUCUMBER AND TOMATO SALAD

1/2 c. salad dressing or
    mayonnaise
2 T. vinegar or lemon juice
1/4 tsp. salt or garlic salt

1/4 tsp. leaf oregano
2 or 3 tomatoes, diced
1 large cucumber, diced

In medium bowl, combine first 4 ingredients. Add tomatoes and cucumbers; toss lightly. Refrigerate until serving time.

DILLED CUCUMBERS

2 T. olive or cooking oil
1 T. vinegar

1/2 tsp. dried dill weed
1 cucumber scored and sliced

In small bowl, blend first three ingredients; pour over cucumber slices. Cover and chill.

CUCUMBERS IN SOUR CREAM

2 large cucumbers, sliced
1 tsp. salt
1 c. sour cream
1/4 c. chopped onion

2 T. sugar
2 T. vinegar
Pepper

Slice cucumbers into shallow bowl. Sprinkle with salt and let stand about 20 minutes. Drain. Add remaining ingredients and toss lightly. Chill before serving.

CUCUMBERS IN VINEGAR AND OIL

1/4 c. cooking oil
1/2 c. vinegar
2 T. sugar
1/2 tsp. salt

dash pepper
1 cucumber, thinly sliced
1 small onion, thinly sliced
lettuce

In bowl, combine all ingredients except lettuce. Cucumber can be scored with a fork before slicing. Cover and chill 1 to 2 hours. (Cucumbers may be refrigerated in vinegar dressing for several days.) Drain, reserving dressing. Serve on lettuce leaves or toss with lettuce pieces, using oil and vinegar mixture as dressing.

MOLDED CUCUMBER SALAD

3 oz. pkg. lime gelatin
3/4 c. boiling water
1/4 c. cold water
2 T. lemon juice
1 1/2 c. finely chopped, peeled,
    seeded cucumbers

1 c. sour cream
1/2 c. finely chopped celery
2 T. minced green onion
1/2 tsp. dried dill weed

Combine gelatin and boiling water, stirring until dissolved. Stir in cold water and lemon juice. Refrigerate, stirring occasionally, until uniformly thickened. Fold in cucumbers, sour cream, celery, onion and dill. Spoon into a 4 cup mold.

CUCUMBERS – SANDWICHES

CUCUMBER SANDWICH SPREAD

1 1/2 c. finely chopped cucumber
1/2 c. chopped celery
3 oz. pkg. cream cheese
1/2 c. mayonnaise or salad
    dressing

1 T. minced onion
1/4 tsp. salt
1/8 tsp. pepper
1 tsp. chopped parsley

Partially peel and remove seeds from cucumber before chopping. Drain well by squeezing between two layers of a clean cloth. Combine cucumber with remaining ingredients. Mix well. Spread on buttered bread.

CUCUMBERS – SIDE AND MAIN DISHES

SAUTÉED CUCUMBERS

3 T. butter
4 c. quartered, sliced cucumbers

1 T. chopped fresh chives or dill
salt and pepper

Melt butter in a skillet. Sauté cucumbers and chives 2-5 minutes, or until tender crisp. Season with salt and pepper.

STIR FRIED CUCUMBERS

3-4 T. vegetable oil
2 c. thinly sliced cucumbers
4 green onions, sliced
1 sweet red pepper, seeded and
  thinly sliced

2 small tomatoes, cut into thin
  wedges
1/2 tsp. salt or to taste
1/8 tsp. pepper

In a large wok or skillet heat one T. oil. Stir fry cucumbers about 2 minutes and remove from wok. Add more oil if necessary. Stir fry green onions and red pepper for 3 minutes. Remove from wok. Add more oil. Stir fry tomatoes one minute then add cucumbers, peppers and onions. Mix well and heat through. Season.

CUCUMBERS – CANNING AND FREEZING

REFRIGERATOR PICKLES

1 qt. vinegar
1 qt. sugar
1/3 c. salt
1 1/2 tsp. celery seed

1 1/2 tsp. mustard seed
1 1/2 tsp. turmeric
cucumbers
onions

Mix all but cucumbers and onions together until sugar is dissolved. This mixture does not have to be heated. Fill quart jars with thinly sliced unpeeled cucumbers. Slice one onion into each jar. Fill jars with syrup mixture; cover with lid and store in refrigerator. Keep refrigerated. Can be stored for several months.

REFRIGERATOR DILLS

3 gallons small or medium
  pickling cucumbers
5 or 6 heads of dill
1 1/2 c. salt

2 gallons water
5 garlic cloves, sliced
2 T. mixed pickling spice

Wash cucumbers removing any blossoms. Place in a stone crock, food-grade plastic bucket or stainless steel container. Distribute the dill heads evenly throughout the container. Make a brine of the remaining ingredients. Pour over cucumbers and weigh down with a plate to keep the cucumbers submerged. Cover and allow to ferment at room temperature for 1 week. After 1 week, pack the pickles into jars and refrigerate to halt fermentation. Keep refrigerated until used; do not heat process. Yields 10 to 12 quarts.

FRESH PACK DILL PICKLES

(Use this recipe to make a few quarts or dozens of quarts of pickles. Keep proportions of vinegar, water and salt constant as you increase the amount of pickling solution.)

pickling cucumbers, 2 to 6 inches
    long
dill heads (or 1 T. dill seed, dill
    weed or dill juice = 1 head
    fresh dill)

onion slices, 1/4-inch thick
garlic cloves, peeled

Pickling Solution:

1 qt. vinegar
3 qt. water

1 c. canning/pickling salt

Wash the cucumbers carefully. Cut a tiny slice off the stem and blossom ends to facilitate absorption of pickling solution. Place 1 or 2 garlic cloves, slice of onion and a head of dill into the bottom of a hot canning jar. Pack the cucumbers into the jar, making sure that they are below the threaded neck of the jar. Cover cucumbers with boiling pickling solution to within 1/2-inch of the top of the jar. Put lids on and place jars in actively boiling water in a boiling water canner. Process pints or quarts in boiling water canner for 10 minutes. Start to count processing time as soon the jars are placed in the boiling water.

BREAD AND BUTTER PICKLES

2 gallons thinly sliced cucumbers
1 qt. sliced onions
1/2 c. salt
2 qt. water

2 qt. vinegar
4 c. sugar
1 tsp. turmeric
1/4 c. whole mustard seed

Cover sliced cucumbers and onions with brine made by mixing salt and water. Let stand 3 hours; drain. Mix remaining ingredients and pour over cucumbers and onions in a kettle. Place on low heat and heat just to boiling. Pack in jars, leaving 1/2-inch headspace. Process in boiling water canner for 10 minutes.

Hint: If dill is ready before cucumbers store it in the freezer. Wash if necessary, shake off excess moisture and allow to air dry for an hour. Put it in a plastic bag and shut it. Or dill heads can be put in a jar with vinegar. Cover the jar and keep it in a cool dry place. Use vinegar along with dill heads in pickle recipes.

FOUR DAY SWEET GHERKINS OR CHUNK PICKLES

5 qt. (7 lb.) whole cucumbers 1 1/2
    to 3 inches long or
7-8 to lb. medium cucumbers
1/2 c. canning salt
8 c. sugar

6 c. vinegar
3/4 tsp. turmeric
2 tsp. celery seed
2 T. mixed pickling spice
4 sticks cinnamon

Day 1: Morning: Wash cucumbers thoroughly; drain. Place in large container and cover with boiling water.

    Afternoon: (6 to 8 hours later) Drain; cover with fresh boiling water.

Day 2: Morning: Drain; cover with fresh boiling water.

    Afternoon: Add salt; cover with fresh boiling water.

Day 3: Morning: Drain. For gherkins prick cucumbers in several places with table fork. Cut large cucumbers in chunks or slices 1/2-inch thick. Make a syrup of 3 c. sugar and 3 c. vinegar; add turmeric and other spices. Heat to boiling and pour over cucumbers. (Cucumbers may be only partially covered at this point.)

    Afternoon: Drain syrup into pan; add 2 c. sugar and 2 c. vinegar to the syrup. Heat to boiling and pour over pickles.

Day 4: Morning: Drain syrup into pan; add 2 c. sugar and 1 c. vinegar to syrup. Heat to boiling and pour over pickles.

    Afternoon: Drain syrup into pan; add remaining 1 c. sugar to syrup; heat to boiling. Pack pickles into clean, hot jars and cover with boiling syrup to within 1/2-inch of top of jar. Cover and process for 10 minutes in boiling water canner. Yields 9 to 10 pints.

PICKLE RELISH

12 large unpeeled cucumbers
8 large onions
4 red sweet peppers
4 green sweet peppers

1/2 c. salt
1 qt. vinegar
4 c. sugar
2 T. mixed pickling spices

Chop fine or grind the vegetables; mix with salt and let stand 12 hours or overnight. Drain well. Combine vinegar, sugar and then add spices tied in a bag. Bring to a boil and add vegetables. Simmer 30 minutes. Remove spice bag. Quickly pack into prepared pint jars, leaving 1/2-inch headspace. Put lids and rings on. Process in a boiling water canner for 10 minutes.

Serve on hotdogs or hamburgers or mix with mayonnaise to make tarter sauce.

CHOW CHOW

1 pt. sliced cucumbers	1 pt. sliced carrots
1 pt. chopped sweet peppers	2 T. celery seed
1 pt. chopped cabbage	4 T. mustard seed
1 pt. sliced onions	1 qt. vinegar
1 pt. chopped green tomatoes	2 c. water
1 pt. chopped celery	4 c. sugar
1 pt. lima beans	4 tsp. turmeric
1 pt. cut green beans	

Soak cucumbers, peppers, cabbage, onions and tomatoes in salt water overnight (1 1/2 cups salt to 2 qt. water). Drain. Cook lima beans, green beans and carrots until tender. Drain. Mix soaked and cooked vegetables with remaining ingredients and boil 10 minutes. Pack hot into pint jars. Process in boiling water canner for 10 minutes. Yields 6-8 pints.

FREEZER CUCUMBER PICKLES

4 lb. pickling cucumbers, sliced	3/4 c. water
8 c. thinly sliced onions	4 c. sugar
1/4 c. salt	2 c. vinegar

Combine cucumbers, onions, salt and water in two large bowls. Let stand at room temperature for 2 hours. Add sugar and vinegar; stir until sugar dissolves. Pack into 1-pint freezer containers, leaving 1-inch headspace. Cover and freeze for up to 6 weeks. Thaw at room temperature for 4 hours before serving. Yields 10 pints.

FREEZER SWEET DILL PICKLES

1 lb. 3-inch cucumbers	1 c. sugar
3/4 lb. small yellow onions	1/2 c. cider vinegar
4 tsp. salt	1 tsp. dried dill weed or to taste
2 T. water	

Thinly slice cucumbers and onions. Mix cucumbers, onion, salt and water in a non-aluminum bowl and let stand about 2 hours. Drain, but do not rinse. Return vegetables to the bowl and add sugar, vinegar and dill. Let stand, stirring occasionally until sugar is dissolved completely and liquid covers the vegetables. Pack into freezer containers and freeze. Defrost before using.
Variation: Omit dill weed.

NOTES

Eggplants

Eggplant is a close relative of tomatoes, peppers and potatoes. These smooth skinned, oval to elongated vegetables range in color from white, to black, to purple, to neon pink.

Eggplant is a hot weather plant, but some short day varieties (such as dusky) do quite well in northern gardens.

Plants should be started 8-10 weeks before your expected frost free date. Wait to set eggplants out until daytime temperatures are 70 degrees or above. Cool weather can stunt eggplant growth and cause unsatisfactory fruit development. Set plants 2 feet apart with 2-3 feet between the rows. Rotate eggplant on a three year basis to prevent disease and pests. (Don't rotate with tomatoes, peppers or potatoes since they share similar diseases.)

Eggplant is ready to use when you can press your thumb into the flesh and make a dent which springs back when you remove your thumb. Immature fruit is hard and can't be dented. Over-ripe fruit dents but doesn't spring back when you remove your thumb. The skin should be smooth and glossy. When cut in half, the best eggplant will have white seeds. If the seeds are brown, the flesh is past its prime. The easiest way to harvest eggplant is with a pruning shears. Leave the cap and part of the stem on the eggplant.

Once plants have set 6 fruits, terminal buds can be pinched to enhance growth and maturity in the remaining fruit.

Eggplant is good steamed, baked, fried, boiled, sautéed or stuffed. Skin can be left on with young, tender fruit. Tougher skins should be peeled off.

In certain preparations it is helpful to slice and salt eggplant then drain in a colander for 30 minutes. Lightly squeeze out moisture and pat dry. This removes excess moisture, decreases oil absorption while cooking in oil and helps remove any bitterness the eggplant may have. Bitterness is not usually a problem, but can be with over-ripe eggplants.

Because of its high water content, eggplant loses moisture fast after harvest and becomes wrinkled and soft. It will keep for about one week at 40-50 degrees and 85% humidity.

Eggplants are nutritionally challenged but are valued in vegetarian dishes for their meaty flavor and texture. They are low in calories, unless fried in oil.

Yield: 1 lb. fresh eggplant = 12-16 slices or 6 cups cubed

EGGPLANT SALAD

2 medium eggplants
1 tsp. lemon juice
1 T. finely chopped onion
1 c. diced celery
1/2 c. chopped walnuts

1/4 c. French dressing
Romaine, Bibb or other lettuce
hard boiled eggs
olives
mayonnaise

Peel and cube eggplants. Cook in salted water with lemon juice. When eggplant is tender, drain and cool. Mix with onion, celery, walnuts and French dressing. Chill. Serve on lettuce. Garnish with quartered hard boiled eggs and olives and top each serving with a spoonful of mayonnaise.

ROASTED EGGPLANT SALAD

1 medium eggplant
2-3 cucumbers, chopped
2 tomatoes, chopped
1 green bell pepper, diced
1 large onion

2-3 cloves garlic, minced
3 T. olive or vegetable oil
juice of one lemon
salt and pepper to taste

Prick eggplant in 2 to 3 locations. Place on cookie sheet and roast at 375° for 30-35 minutes. Cool, peel and chop. Seed cucumbers if necessary and chop, add to chopped tomatoes, peppers, onion and garlic. Toss all ingredients. Blend olive oil and lemon juice, salt and pepper. Pour over chopped vegetables and refrigerate overnight. Serve on lettuce leaves.

EGGPLANT CHEESE SANDWICHES

4 1/2-inch slices eggplant
salt
1 egg, beaten

seasoned bread crumbs
oil
2 slices mozzarella cheese

Salt eggplant and let drain for 30 minutes. Pat dry, dip in egg then in crumbs. Heat oil in a skillet. Brown eggplant slices on one side. Turn 2 slices and top with cheese. Put the remaining eggplant slices on the cheese with uncooked side facing up. Cook until the bottom is brown then turn and brown the top.

EGGPLANTS – SIDE AND MAIN DISHES

HOW TO COOK EGGPLANTS

Bring 1-inch of water to a boil. Add an eggplant, cut into 1-inch cubes and 1/4 tsp. salt. Return to a boil; reduce heat, cover and simmer 3 to 5 minutes or until tender. Drain.

SAUTÉED EGGPLANT

2 lb. eggplants	**1/2-3/4 c. olive or vegetable oil**
salt	**salt and pepper**

Cut peeled eggplants into 3/4-inch cubes. Sprinkle with salt, let drain for 30 minutes then pat dry. Heat oil, 1/4 c. at a time. Add some eggplant cubes, leaving space between cubes. Sauté 6-8 minutes or until cubes are browned on all sides and tender. Stir constantly (or shake the pan) so the eggplant doesn't burn. Finish cooking eggplant in batches. Season with salt and pepper.
Variation: Add minced fresh herbs, onions or garlic while sautéing eggplant.

GRILLED EGGPLANT

2 large eggplants, cut into 1/2-inch slices	**olive oil**
salt	**pepper**

Sprinkle egg plant slices lightly with salt. Place in colander or strainer and let stand one hour. Wipe excess salt off egg plant. Brush with olive oil and sprinkle with pepper. Grill, broil or sauté on both sides until golden brown (approximately 5-8 minutes).

The wicked worketh a deceitful work: but to him that soweth righteousness shall be a sure reward.

Proverbs 11:18

DEEP FRIED EGGPLANT

1 1/2 c. flour
1/2 c. cornstarch
1 tsp. baking powder
cold water

vegetable oil for deep frying
eggplants cut into rounds or thin
    slices

Mix flour, cornstarch and baking powder with enough cold water to form the consistency of heavy cream. Make sure there are no lumps. Refrigerate until thoroughly chilled. In a wok or deep fryer heat oil to 350-375°. Dip eggplant slices into batter. Allow excess to drip off before placing it in the hot oil. Do not crowd wok or deep fryer. Remove with a slotted spoon and drain on paper towels. Serve immediately with dipping sauce. (See following recipe.)
Variation: Use carrots, zucchini, mushrooms or radishes.

DIPPING SAUCE

1/4 c. sugar
1/4 c. ketchup
1/4 c. cider vinegar
1/4 c. pineapple juice

soy sauce to taste
4 tsp. cornstarch
4 tsp. water

Bring sugar, ketchup, vinegar and pineapple juice to a boil. Add enough soy sauce to color the mixture lightly. Mix cornstarch with water and add to mixture. Return to a boil and cook until thickened.

BAKED EGGPLANT SLICES

1 medium eggplant
salt
1/2 c. mayonnaise

1/2 c. minced green onion
1 c. cracker crumbs
1/2 c. grated Parmesan cheese

Peel eggplant and cut into 1/2-inch thick slices. Sprinkle with salt, let drain 30 minutes then pat dry. Combine mayonnaise and onion. Spread on both sides of eggplant slices. Mix crumbs with cheese. Dip coated eggplant into crumb mixture. Place on a baking sheet. Bake at 375° approximately 20 minutes.

MASHED EGGPLANT PATTIES

1 medium eggplant, peeled and
    cut into 1/4-inch slices
1 small onion, chopped
1 c. water
1 tsp. salt, divided

1/8 tsp. pepper
1 c. cracker crumbs
1/2 c. yellow corn meal
1/2 c. vegetable oil

Bring eggplant, onion, water, 1/2 tsp. salt and pepper to a boil. Reduce heat and simmer until tender. Drain well and cool. When cool, place mixture in a bowl and mash with a fork. Stir in cracker crumbs. Place corn meal on a piece of waxed paper and drop eggplant, by rounded T. onto it. Roll in corn meal until well coated. Pat into 3-inch patties. Heat 2 T. oil in skillet, fry four patties at a time, turning once at 4-5 minutes. Add additional oil as needed.

EGGPLANT PIZZAS

2 medium eggplants, unpeeled, cut
    into 1/2-inch slices
1/2 c. olive or vegetable oil
    (reserve 1 T.)

1 small onion, diced
2 cloves garlic, minced
2 c. pizza sauce
1 c. grated mozzarella cheese

Place the eggplant slices on a baking sheet. Brush each slice with oil and broil until the eggplant is golden brown. Turn the slices over, brush with oil, broil until golden. In a large saucepan, heat 1 T. oil and sauté onion and garlic. Add pizza sauce and bring to a boil. Remove from heat and carefully spread on eggplant slices. Sprinkle with cheese and broil for 5 minutes or until the cheese is bubbly and the eggplant heated through.

EGGPLANT CASSEROLE

2 c. peeled, cubed eggplant
2 T. finely chopped onion
1/4 c. water
2 eggs, slightly beaten
2 slices soft bread, torn in small
    pieces

1/2 c. milk
1/2 tsp. salt
pepper to taste
1 1/4 c. shredded cheddar cheese

Cook eggplant and onion in unsalted water approximately 5 minutes; drain well. Combine all ingredients except 1/4 c. cheese; mix well. Pour into a greased 1-quart casserole. Bake uncovered at 350° for 25 minutes. Sprinkle with remaining cheese and bake 5 minutes longer.

EGGPLANT ONION AND TOMATOES

1 large eggplant	1/2 tsp. salt
salt	1 tsp. oregano
1/2 c. chopped onion	1/4 tsp. pepper
1/4 c. butter	1/2 c. sour cream
2 medium tomatoes, peeled and	2 T. chopped parsley
sliced	

Peel the eggplant and cut into 1-inch cubes. Sprinkle cubes with salt and let drain 30 minutes. Pat dry. Sauté eggplant and onion in butter in a large skillet approximately 8 minutes or until tender crisp. Stir in tomatoes, salt, oregano and pepper. Cover and cook slowly for another 10 minutes. Remove from heat. Stir in sour cream and parsley and serve.

EGGPLANT PARMESAN

2 small eggplants	1 tsp. oregano or basil
salt	1 tsp. parsley
2 T. olive or vegetable oil	1/4 tsp. pepper
1/4 c. minced onion	1/2 c. flour
2 cloves minced garlic	2 T. olive or vegetable oil
4 c. peeled and sliced tomatoes	1 c. mozzarella cheese
2 tsp. sugar	1/2 c. grated Parmesan cheese
1 tsp. salt	

Cut eggplants crosswise into 1/2-inch slices. Sprinkle with salt and let drain at least 30 minutes. Meanwhile heat oil in a large skillet. Sauté onion and garlic 3 minutes. Add tomatoes, sugar, salt, herbs and pepper. Bring to a boil, reduce heat and simmer 30 minutes. Pat eggplants dry. Dust with flour. Heat 2 T. oil in a skillet and lightly brown eggplants on both sides. Place half of the slices in a 13x9 pan. Cover with half of the tomato sauce and half of the mozzarella cheese. Repeat the layers and sprinkle Parmesan cheese on top. Bake at 350° for 30 minutes.

Variation: Use spaghetti sauce instead of making tomato sauce.

Hint: Salting cut eggplant and allowing to drain for 30 minutes greatly reduces eggplants tendency to absorb oil while cooking. Salting also helps eliminate any bitter taste in over-ripe eggplant. Salt an eggplant by peeling and slicing or cubing, then sprinkling it with salt. Let drain 30 minutes. Rinse if desired, then pat dry or pat dry without rinsing. Adjust salt in the recipe if not rinsed. An alternative to salting eggplants is blanching for 2 minutes. Blanching results in some loss of flavor.

STUFFED EGGPLANTS

2 medium eggplants
salt
oil
salt and pepper
1 c. chopped onion
4 T. olive or vegetable oil
1 lb. ground beef

1 T. fresh chopped parsley
1 c. peeled, seeded and chopped
   tomatoes
1 c. cooked rice
3/4 tsp. salt
Parmesan cheese (optional)

Cut eggplants in half lengthwise.   Make several cuts on the exposed flesh. Sprinkle with salt and drain 30 minutes, flesh side down.   Squeeze and pat dry. Brush with oil.   Put a little water into a baking pan and bake eggplants at 400°, cut side up, 15-20 minutes.   Scoop out flesh leaving 1/2-inch of flesh on shells. Sprinkle eggplants with salt and pepper. Chop flesh. Sauté onions in oil several minutes then add eggplant flesh and sauté until golden brown.   Remove from skillet and brown beef.   When beef is browned add eggplant mixture, parsley, tomatoes, rice and salt.   Mix well; fill eggplant shells and place in a baking dish. Sprinkle with Parmesan cheese if desired. Bake at 400° approximately 20 minutes.

VEGETARIAN STUFFED EGGPLANT

2 medium eggplants
1 c. chopped onion
3 T. butter
chopped eggplant flesh
1 1/2 c. dry bread crumbs
1 T. chopped parsley

1/2 tsp. salt
1/2 tsp. pepper
2 eggs
1 c. grated Swiss or cheddar
   cheese
1/4 c. grated Parmesan cheese

Prepare eggplants as instructed in Stuffed Eggplants. Sauté onion in butter for 3 minutes.   Add chopped eggplant flesh and sauté until lightly browned. Remove from heat and add bread crumbs, parsley, salt and pepper. Beat and add eggs. Add cheese. If mixture is too stiff, add a little milk or cream. Fill eggplant shells with the mixture and sprinkle Parmesan cheese on top. Bake at 400° approximately 20 minutes.

Hint: Peel tough-skinned eggplants.   Tender skinned young eggplants can be eaten with or without peeling.

EGGPLANT BEEF SKILLET

1 small eggplant cut into 1/2-inch
    slices
salt
1 lb. ground beef
1/4 c. chopped onion
1 T. flour
1 8-oz can (1 c.) tomato sauce

3/4 c. water
1/4 c. chopped green pepper
1 tsp. oregano
1 tsp. chili powder
1/2 tsp. salt
1 c. shredded process cheese

Sprinkle eggplant slices with salt. Let drain 30 minutes. Pat dry. Brown beef and onion in a skillet. Spoon off excess fat. Sprinkle flour over meat; stir. Add tomato sauce, water, green pepper, oregano, chili powder and salt. Mix well. Sprinkle eggplant lightly with salt and pepper; arrange slices over meat. Cover; simmer until eggplant is tender—10-15 minutes. Top with shredded cheese.

HOT DOG AND EGGPLANT CASSEROLE

1 medium eggplant (1 1/4 lb.)
salt
flour
1/3 c. olive or salad oil
1/2 c. chopped onion
1 1/2 tsp. salt

1/4 tsp. pepper
1/4 tsp. basil
1 small clove garlic, crushed
1 lb. hot dogs, cut in 1-inch pieces
4 c. peeled chopped tomatoes
cooked white rice

Peel eggplant. Cut into 1-inch cubes. Sprinkle cubes with salt and let drain 30 minutes. Pat dry. Toss cubes with flour to coat lightly. In hot oil in large skillet sauté onions until tender—about 5 minutes. Add eggplant, salt, pepper, basil and garlic. Cook, stirring occasionally, until eggplant is browned. Add hot dogs and tomatoes, mixing well. Bring to a boil; reduce heat and simmer, covered, 10 minutes, stirring occasionally. Serve over rice.

Hint: Eggplant and summer squash can be used interchangeably in many recipes.

EGGPLANT AND BEEF PIE

1 unbaked 9-inch pie shell	1 T. chopped parsley
1 small eggplant (about 1 lb.)	1/4 c. chopped celery
salt	1 tsp. Worcestershire sauce
4 T. butter, divided	1 tsp. salt
1/2 c. finely chopped onion	dash pepper
1 clove garlic, crushed	1/8 tsp. nutmeg
3/4 lb. ground chuck	8 oz. (1 c.) tomato sauce

Refrigerate pie crust until ready to use. Cut unpeeled eggplant into 1/2-inch cubes; measure 2 cups. Sprinkle with salt and let drain 30 minutes. Pat dry. Melt 2 T. hot butter in a saucepan. Cook eggplant, covered, 5 minutes; drain. Melt rest of butter in a skillet. Sauté onion and garlic until onion is tender—about 5 minutes. Add ground chuck and rest of ingredients to skillet; mix well. Cook, over medium heat, 5 minutes, stirring occasionally. Add eggplant to meat mixture, turn into pie shell. Bake at 375°, 45 to 60 minutes, or until crust is golden. Serve hot.

EGGPLANTS–FREEZING

HOW TO FREEZE EGGPLANT[2]

Peel [tender eggplant] and cut into slices 1/3-inch thick. To preserve natural color, soak 5 minutes in a solution of 4 T. salt per gallon water or 1/2 tsp. ascorbic acid in one quart water. Blanch for 2 minutes in steam. [Cool immediately in cold water.] Package in layers with each slice separated with two pieces of wrap.

He that soweth iniquity shall reap vanity: and the rod of his anger shall fail.

Proverbs 22:8

Greens

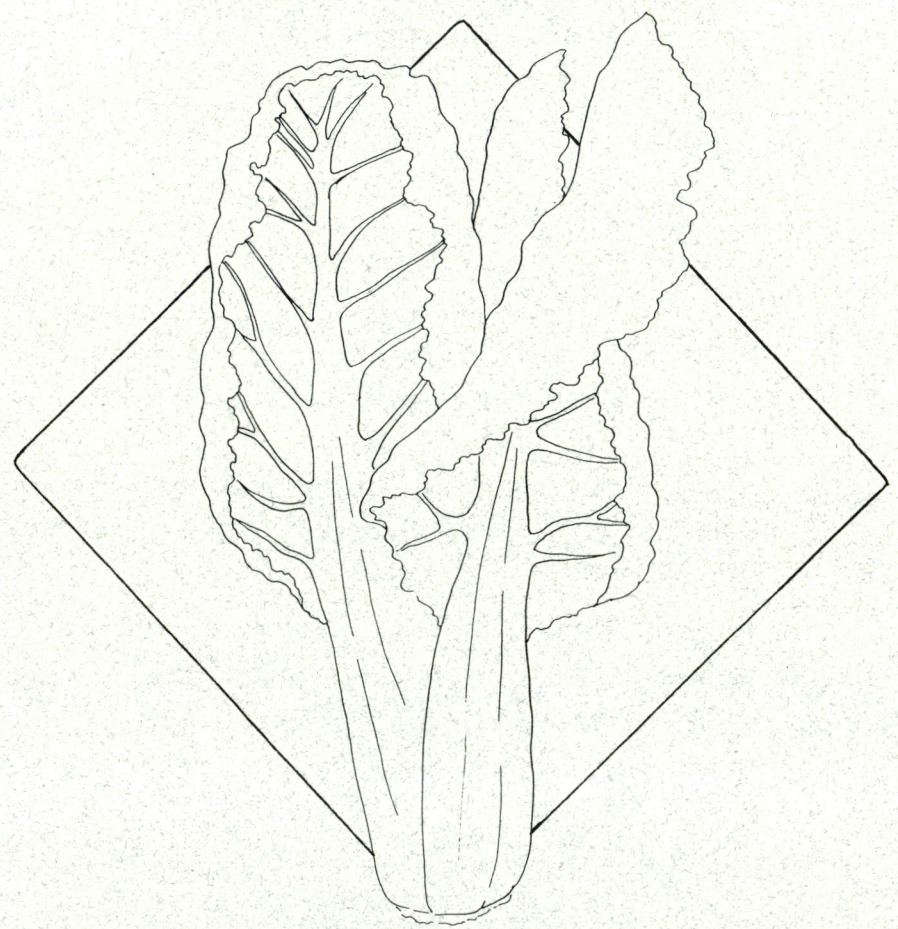

"Greens" refers to any vegetable that is used for its green (surprise!) leaves. Included in the category are collards, turnip greens, beet greens, *broccoli raab*, mustard greens, dandelion, kale, spinach and Swiss chard. Although greens have distinctive flavors that lend them to a particular preparation, they can be used interchangeably in recipes. Use whatever's available.

In general, greens do best in cool weather, so sow seeds direct as soon as your ground can be worked in the spring. Sow 1/2-inch deep, thinning to a final spacing of 6-inches. Tender thinnings can be used in salads or sautéed. Midsummer plantings for fall crops work well, too. A good choice for fall and winter harvest is kale. Kale is extremely hardy, with a better flavor after a hard frost. In milder areas it can be picked through most of the winter.

One of the easiest greens to grow, Swiss chard (or chard) is hardy in cold weather and tolerant to hot weather. Most areas of the country are suitable for growing Swiss chard.

Chard comes with either white or red stalks. Red chard is sometimes called rhubarb or ruby chard. Use the two types interchangeably in recipes. Chard is in the beet family, but doesn't develop any root bulbs.

To keep greens growing fast, supply plenty of water. If the soil dries out, or with hot weather, greens soon get bitter and unusable. (Swiss chard is the exception; it does well throughout the summer.)

Begin harvesting greens before they're mature—they will be milder and less bitter than full sized leaves. Greens continue to grow as you cut the larger leaves on the outside of the plant.

Many people prefer to cook greens in bouillon to soften their sometimes sharp edge. However you choose to cook them, the cardinal rule is don't *overcook*. It doesn't take long to turn a tasty cooked green into a watery, limp, grayish, unappealing mass.

Unwashed greens placed in a perforated plastic bag will keep for about one week in the refrigerator.

Kale contains high levels of beta carotene, vitamin A and E. It also provides some folate, calcium, iron and potassium. Like other cole crops, kale is rich in bioflavonoids that help protect against cancer. All greens are high in fiber and low in calories.

Yield: 1 lb. fresh greens = 1 ½ - 2 cups cooked
1 bushel = 12 lb. (kale 18 lb.) = 8 -12 pints (kale 12 -18 pints)

CREAM OF GREENS SOUP

2 T. butter
1 c. diced onions
1 garlic clove, minced
1/2 tsp. thyme
12 c. chopped greens

2 c. peeled, diced potatoes
4 c. water or chicken broth
1 c. cream or whole milk
1 tsp. salt or to taste
pepper

Heat butter in a large kettle. Sauté onion, garlic and thyme about 5 minutes. Add potatoes, greens and water and simmer for 15 minutes. Let cool slightly then puree in a blender. Return to kettle; add cream, salt and pepper and heat through.

CHARD SOUP

8 c. chard, finely chopped
1 c. sliced celery
1 c. chopped onion
2 T. olive or vegetable oil
2 T. butter

2 large potatoes, peeled and diced
5 c. broth or water
1 tsp. salt or to taste
pepper

Separate chard stems from leaves. String any tough stems and slice thin. In a large kettle sauté the sliced stems, celery and onions in hot oil and butter for 5 minutes. Add potatoes and broth. Bring to a boil. Reduce heat and simmer 15 to 20 minutes. Stir in the chard leaves and cook 4-5 minutes. Season to taste.

KALE AND CHICKEN SOUP

3 leeks, thinly sliced
2 T. olive or vegetable oil
2 medium potatoes, peeled and
    cubed
5 c. chicken broth

4 c. diced, cooked chicken
1 tsp. thyme
1/8 tsp. pepper
2 bunches kale, stemmed and
    chopped

Saute leeks in oil 2 minutes. Add potatoes and broth. Bring to a boil. Reduce heat and simmer 15 minutes or until potatoes are tender. Add chicken, thyme and pepper. Continue to simmer. Add kale; cook 5 minutes or until kale is soft.

DANDELION SALAD

6-8 c. young dandelion leaves, chopped	1/4 c. vinegar
4 slices bacon	2 tsp. sugar
1/4 c. chopped green onion	1/4 tsp. salt
	2 hard boiled eggs, chopped

Wash dandelion well before chopping. Fry bacon and drain on paper towel. Add onion, vinegar and sugar to hot drippings in skillet. Pour hot dressing over dandelion. Add bacon and toss. Top with chopped eggs and serve at once.

DANDELION POTATO SALAD

1 qt. young dandelion greens	1 onion chopped
2 c. diced, cooked potatoes	1/2 c. French dressing
3 hard boiled eggs	

Combine all ingredients and serve on lettuce leaves

CHARD SALAD

1 lb. coarsely chopped chard	1/4 c. lemon juice
1/2 c. thinly sliced celery	1/2 tsp. dry mustard
1/2 c. thinly sliced radishes	1/4 tsp. celery seed
1/4 c. sliced onions	salt and pepper to taste
1/4 c. olive oil	

Steam chard 3-5 minutes; drain. Rinse under cold water to cool. Drain well. Combine chard, celery, radishes and onions; toss. Put remaining ingredients in a jar with a tight lid and shake well. Pour over salad. Toss to coat. Season to taste and serve.

Hint: Use tender greens raw in salads.

GREENS – SIDE AND MAIN DISHES

HOW TO COOK GREENS

Bring a large kettle 2/3 full of salted water, bouillon or broth to a boil. Add greens. Start timing when you put the greens in. Boil:

Beet Greens	3-4 minutes
Broccoli Raab	3 minutes
Collards	10-20 minutes
Dandelion	1-3 minutes
Kale	5-10 minutes
Mustard Greens	2-5 minutes
Swiss Chard	1-2 minutes
Turnip Greens	4 minutes

These times are for the leafy parts. Trim larger stems and place in boiling water one or two minutes before leaves.

Variation: Bring 1/4-inch of salted water to a boil and add a pound of greens. Return to a boil, reduce heat and simmer until tender. Or simply steam greens in the water that clings to them after washing.

SAUTÉED CHARD

5-6 c. chopped chard
2 T. butter

1 T. oil
salt and pepper to taste

Cut stems off chard. Heat butter and oil in a skillet. Add stems and sauté for one minute. Add leaves, toss to coat, then cover and simmer 3-4 minutes or more.

KALE OR MUSTARD GREENS WITH GARLIC

1 lb. kale or mustard greens
1 T. olive oil
1 T. minced garlic

1/4 c. water
salt and black pepper

Wash greens thoroughly. Discard the tough stems; tear the leaves into bite-size pieces. Heat oil in a large kettle and sauté garlic for about 1 minute. Add water and bring mixture to a boil. Add greens and salt and pepper. Toss to mix. Cover, reduce heat and steam kale for 5-7 minutes or until it is tender, but still bright green. Cook mustard greens 3-5 minutes.

KALE AND ONIONS

2 lb. small white onions, peeled
1 tsp. salt, divided
1 1/2 lb. kale, washed, trimmed
    and coarsely chopped
2 T. butter

2 T. flour
3/4 tsp. rosemary leaves
1/8 tsp. pepper
1 c. milk
3/4 tsp. Worcestershire sauce

Bring 1-inch of water to a boil in a large kettle; add onions and 1/2 tsp. salt. Reduce heat, cover and simmer 10 minutes. Add kale. Cover; cook 5 minutes. Drain. Melt butter in smaller sauce pan. Stir in flour, rosemary, pepper and 1/2 tsp. salt. Cook until smooth. Gradually stir in milk and Worcestershire sauce. Stir constantly until mixture boils and thickens. To serve, place kale and onions on a serving platter and spoon sauce on top.

KALE WITH SOUR CREAM

3 lb. kale
1 T. butter
1 tsp. salt

1/4 tsp. pepper
1/8 tsp. nutmeg
1 c. sour cream

Wash the kale in cold water and remove heavy stems. Put in a saucepan with boiling salted water to cover. Simmer, covered, for 5-10 minutes or until kale is tender. Drain and chop fine. Return chopped kale to saucepan and stir in the butter, salt, pepper and nutmeg. Heat through. Stir in sour cream gradually. Heat through, but do not boil.

COLLARDS WITH CANADIAN BACON

1 T. chopped onion
1/2 c. diced Canadian bacon
2 T. vegetable oil

1 1/2 lb. collard greens, chopped
salt and pepper to taste

Sauté onions and bacon in hot oil for 5 minutes. Add greens and toss to coat. Cover and reduce heat. Simmer 10-15 minutes, stirring frequently. Season to taste.
Variation: Omit Canadian bacon.

Hint: In older chard, separate stems from leaves and cook stems longer.

GREENS WITH RED PEPPER

1 bunch tender greens (turnips,
   mustard, collards or kale)
1/4 c. butter
1 medium red sweet pepper, cut
   into 1/2-inch pieces

2 cloves garlic, minced
1/2 tsp. salt
1/8 tsp. pepper

Wash greens well. Trim tough stems. Chop coarsely. Bring 1/4-inch water to boil in a 10-inch skillet. Add greens. Cover and cook one minute or until greens are wilted. Drain and set aside. Melt butter in same skillet. Add red pepper and garlic; cook until tender. Stir in greens, salt and pepper. Cover and cook 3-5 minutes.

MIXED GREENS AND POTATOES

1/2 lb. kale
1/2 lb. turnip greens
1/2 lb. spinach
2 T. bacon drippings
2 c. diced potatoes
1/4 c. boiling water

1 1/2 tsp. salt
1/2 tsp. sugar
1/4 tsp. pepper
dash cayenne pepper
6 strips crisp bacon

Wash greens in warm water. Rinse 3 times in cold water. Put bacon drippings into 3-quart saucepan. Add potatoes, boiling water, salt and sugar. Cover; cook 15 minutes. Add kale and cook 5 minutes. Add spinach and turnip greens and cook 4-5 minutes longer. Add pepper and cayenne. Toss lightly. Top with crisp bacon. Serve with creamy mayonnaise sauce. (See following recipe.)

CREAMY MAYONNAISE SAUCE

9 T. butter
3/4 c. flour
1 tsp. salt
1/4 tsp. pepper

1 1/2 c. milk
1/2 c. mayonnaise
1/2 T. lemon juice
1/2 T. chives

Melt butter and stir in flour and seasonings. Gradually add milk, stirring constantly. Boil several minutes. Remove from heat and add remaining ingredients. Pass with greens.

CHARD WITH RICE

1 1/2 c. uncooked rice
3 c. water or broth
1/2 c. chopped onion
1 clove garlic

1/4 c. butter
6 c. finely chopped chard
1 tsp. parsley or basil
salt and pepper to taste

Cook rice in salted water or broth until liquid is absorbed and rice tender. Meanwhile sauté onion and garlic in hot butter 4-5 minutes in a large skillet. Add chard and sauté 4-5 minutes. Stir in parsley and cooked rice. Heat through and season to taste.

CHARD CASSEROLE

2 lb. chard
1 tsp. salt, divided
5 T. butter, divided
3 T. flour

2 c. milk
1/4 c. shredded Swiss cheese
1/4 c. grated parmesan cheese
1/4 c. soft bread crumbs

Wash chard well; drain. Cut off stalks and cut into 1-inch pieces. Coarsely chop leaves. Bring 1-inch water to a boil in a large kettle. Add chard stalks and 1/2 tsp. salt. Reduce heat. cover and cook 3 minutes. Stir in chard leaves and cook 2 minutes. Drain well. Melt 3 T. butter. Stir in flour and 1/2 tsp. salt. Gradually stir in milk until smooth. Stir constantly until mixture boils and thickens. Remove from heat and stir in chard and cheese. Turn into a 2-quart casserole. Top with bread crumbs and remaining butter. Bake at 425° approximately 20 minutes.

BEEF STEW WITH KALE

2 lb. stew meat
water
1/2 c. barley
1 c. chopped onions
1 rib celery, chopped
1 bay leaf

2 tsp. salt
2 c. diced potatoes
1 1/2 c. sliced carrots
8 c. sliced kale
1 T. Worcestershire sauce
1/4 tsp. pepper

Cover meat with water; add barley, onions, celery, bay leaf and salt. Bring to a boil, skim scum and reduce heat. Cover and simmer 1 hour or until beef is tender. Add potatoes and carrots, cover and cook 15 minutes longer. Add kale and cook uncovered for 10 minutes more. Add Worcestershire sauce, pepper and more salt if desired.

HOW TO FREEZE GREENS[2]

Cut off large, tough stems; discard all damaged leaves. Wash thoroughly several times. Blanch 1 lb. greens in 2 gallons water. Blanching times are as follows:

Beet Greens	2 minutes
Kale	2 minutes
Chard	2 minutes
Mustard Greens	2 minutes
Turnip Greens	2 minutes
Collards	3 minutes
Tender spinach	1 1/2-2 minutes

[Cool immediately in cold water, drain, package and freeze.]

Hint: Mature greens benefit from simmering in water, broth or bouillon. Young greens can be sautéed.

Hint: Greens cook down to one fourth, or less, of their precooked volume.

NOTES

Ground Cherries

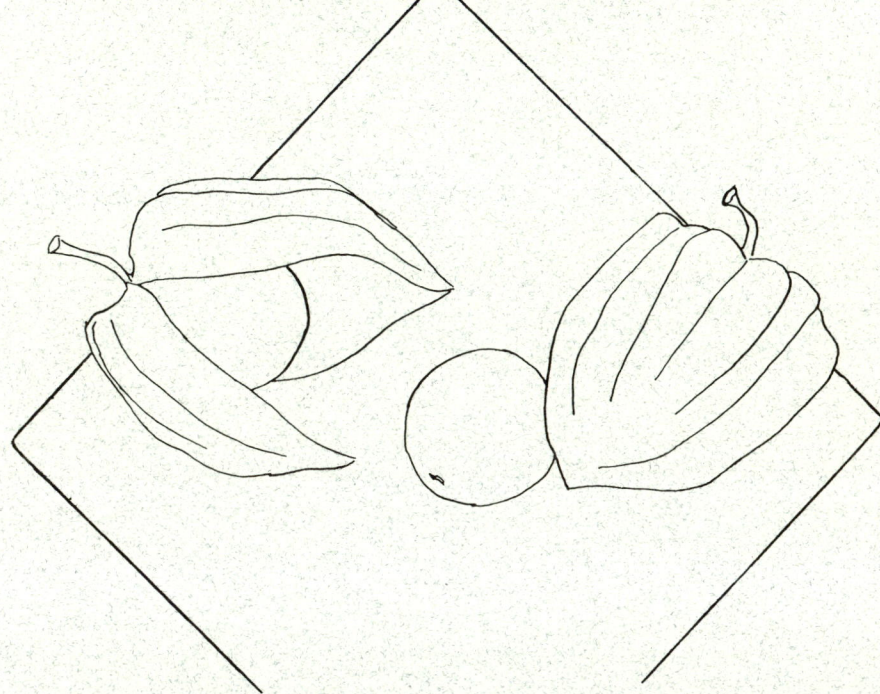

These delectable members of the tomato family are also called husk tomatoes, husk cherries, cape gooseberries and strawberry tomatoes. Growth requirements are similar to those for tomatoes, although ground cherries tolerate a slightly cooler climate.

Ground cherries are usually grown from plants started 6-7 weeks before transplanting. Set plants out after danger of frost. Plant three feet apart in rows three feet apart.

I never remember my mother planting ground cherries. She took advantage of all the volunteer plants that came up in her garden where ground cherries were growing the previous year. That worked fine in Indiana where summers were long enough to get a good crop of ground cherries from volunteer plants. Here in central Wisconsin we get lots of volunteers, but alas, they don't get ready before our fall frost freezes them off.

Ground cherries are ripe when the fruit turns a deep yellow and the husks are papery dry and tan colored. They usually drop to the ground when they're ripe.

I grew up thinking that ground cherries and pie were synonymous. Since then I've learned they can also be enjoyed raw, made into jam or dried in sugar and used as raisins.

Left in the husks in a dry place, ground cherries will keep for several weeks.

GROUND CHERRIES – PIES

GROUND CHERRY PIE

2 9-inch pie crusts	2/3 c. brown sugar
1/3 c. sugar	1 T. lemon juice
1/3 c. flour	2 T. butter
3 1/2 c. ground cherries	

Put one crust in the pie plate. Combine sugar and flour and put in the crust. Fill with the ground cherries. Sprinkle with brown sugar and lemon juice. Dot with butter. Put the top crust on and seal the edges. Bake at 400° for 15 minutes then at 350° for 40 minutes or until done.

Variation: To top with crumbs instead of a crust, combine 3 T. flour, 3 T. sugar and 2 T. butter.

GROUND CHERRY PIE WITH MERINGUE

2 eggs, separated	1 T. butter
1 c. sugar	6 T. water
2 T. flour	1 baked pie shell
2 c. ground cherries	

Beat egg yolks. Add sugar, flour, ground cherries, butter and water. Boil until thick. Pour into a baked pie shell. Beat egg whites until stiff for meringue. Put meringue on top of pie filling and brown slightly.

GROUND CHERRIES – CANNING AND FREEZING

HOW TO CAN GROUND CHERRIES

Raw Pack: Fill jars with washed berries, shaking gently to get a full pack. Cover with boiling syrup (4 c. water for 2 c. sugar) or water, leaving 1/2-inch headspace. Process in boiling water canner; pints 15 minutes, quarts 20 minutes.

Hot Pack: Place 1/2 to 3/4 c. water in pan and add berries. Heat for 1 minute. Pack hot, adding boiling syrup as for raw pack, leaving 1/2-inch headspace. Process in boiling water canner, pints or quarts, 15 minutes.

GROUND CHERRY JAM

2 lb. ground cherries (3 3/4 c. prepared)	6 c. sugar
	1 box fruit pectin
1/2 c. lemon juice	1/4 tsp. butter

Prepare ground cherries by grinding them in food processor. Measure 3 3/4 c. Add lemon juice. Measure sugar and set aside. Mix fruit pectin into fruit and add butter. Bring to a full rolling boil over high heat, stirring constantly. Immediately add all of the sugar. Bring back to a full rolling boil and boil exactly 4 minutes, stirring constantly. Ladle quickly into prepared jars. Process for 10 minutes in a boiling water canner.

HOW TO FREEZE GROUND CHERRIES

Husk and wash ground cherries. Scald for 2 minutes, chill in cold water and drain. Pack in syrup (4 c. water for 2 c. sugar) and freeze.

You can also freeze unwashed ground cherries by removing the husk and freezing without blanching. When ready to use, wash the frozen ground cherries before they thaw and use in recipes.

The Lord is my shepherd; I shall not want. He maketh me to lie down in green pastures: he leadeth me beside the still waters. He restoreth my soul: he leadeth me in the paths of righteousness for his name's sake. Yea, though I walk through the valley of the shadow of death, I will fear no evil: for thou art with me; thy rod and thy staff they comfort me. Thou preparest a table before me in the presence of mine enemies: thou annointest my head with oil; my cup runneth over. Surely goodness and mercy shall follow me all the days of my life: and I will dwell in the house of the Lord for ever.

Psalm 23

Kohlrabi

To the Germans, the name says it all—*kohl* (cabbage) *rabi* (turnip). Indeed, kohlrabi looks like an above-ground turnip. Not too surprisingly, since the plant was developed by crossing a cabbage with a turnip.

The edible part of the plant is an enlarged section of the stem that develops just above the ground.

Kohlrabies like cool weather with plenty of moisture, so they do best planted in early spring or midsummer for a fall crop. Direct seed as soon as the soil can be worked in the spring. Sow seeds ½ inch deep every 1-2 inches. Thin to a final spacing of 4-6 inches between plants. If you prefer plants, start indoors 4-6 weeks before setting outside.

Begin using kohlrabies when the bulbs are 1 inch across. Don't let them get much bigger than 2 inches. Larger bulbs get tough and woody.

Young kohlrabi leaves can be used in recipes for greens. Remove the tough stems from the leaves by folding the leaf lengthwise, grasping the stem in one hand and pulling while holding the leaf in the other hand.

Kohlrabies are excellent raw. Just cut off the root and leaf ends and peel the outer skin off. Cut in slices or wedges and serve as is or with dips. Kohlrabies can also be boiled or steamed for a cooked vegetable.

Kohlrabies are an excellent source of vitamin C and potassium. Like other cole vegetables, kohlrabi contains cancer-preventing bioflavonoids.

KOHLRABIES – SALADS

KOHLRABI RADISH SALAD

3 c. grated, raw kohlrabi	2 T. vinegar
1 c. sliced, red radishes	2 tsp. sugar
1/3 c. olive or vegetable oil	1/4 tsp. salt
1 T. lemon juice	1/8 tsp. pepper

Combine kohlrabi and radishes. Whisk together remaining ingredients. Pour over salad, toss and serve.

KOHLRABI VEGETABLE SALAD

1 c. 1/2-inch kohlrabi cubes	1/4 c. vegetable oil
1 c. 1/2-inch green bean pieces	2 T. vinegar
1 c. 1/2-inch carrot cubes	1 tsp. salt
1 c. peas	1/2 tsp. paprika
1 c. small cauliflower florets	

Combine all ingredients and let stand in a cool place at least one hour. Top with mayonnaise if desired.

KOHLRABIES – SIDE AND MAIN DISHES

HOW TO COOK KOHLRABIES

To cook sliced bulbs bring 1-inch of water to a boil. Add one pound (7-9 bulbs) of peeled, sliced bulbs and 1/2 tsp. salt or to taste. Return to a boil; reduce heat and simmer 20 minutes or until tender crisp.

To cook whole bulbs, add unpeeled bulbs to boiling water. Return to a boil and simmer until tender (approximately 30 minutes). After cooking peel skin. Bulbs can be peeled before cooking but will lose some flavor. Serve cooked kohlrabi with butter or sour cream. Sprinkle with parsley or dill.

To cook kohlrabi tops, bring 1-inch of water to a boil. Add chopped tops. Return to a boil; reduce heat and simmer 5-10 minutes. Season to taste.

Hint: Kohlrabi bulbs can be substituted for turnips in recipes.

113

SAUTÉED KOHLRABIES

2 T. vegetable oil
4 c. diced kohlrabi
2 cloves garlic

1 T. chopped onions
1 tsp. basil

Heat oil in a large skillet. Add remaining ingredients and sauté 8-10 minutes or until kohlrabi is tender.

MUSTARD KOHLRABIES

4-6 medium kohlrabies, sliced
2 T. butter

1 T. mustard
1/2 tsp. salt

Cook kohlrabies until just tender. Heat butter in a skillet; stir in mustard and salt. Add drained kohlrabies and toss. Cook, turning slices, until golden brown.

CREAMED KOHLRABIES

3 medium kohlrabies
1/2 tsp. salt
3/4 c. cottage cheese

1/2 c. milk
1/4 tsp. salt
1/8 tsp. pepper

Remove leaves, wash and quarter kohlrabies. Drop into boiling water and add salt. Cook 18-20 minutes. Drain. Peel and put into blender. Add remaining ingredients. Blend 2 minutes or until smooth. Reheat.

KOHLRABIES WITH TOMATOES AND PEPPERS

4 c. diced kohlrabies
2 T. butter
1 clove garlic, minced
1 small onion, chopped
1 small green pepper, chopped

2 tomatoes, peeled, seeded and
    chopped
1 tsp. parsley
salt and pepper to taste

Cook kohlrabies approximately 5 minutes. Drain and set aside. Melt butter in a large skillet. Sauté garlic, onion and green pepper 2 minutes. Add tomatoes and parsley; cook 2 more minutes. Add kohlrabies and sauté another 2 minutes. Season to taste with salt and pepper.

Hint: Peeled, raw kohlrabies are great with dips or sliced into salads

CHICKEN STEW WITH KOHLRABIES

3-4 lb. chicken
2 lb. kohlrabies
1/4 c. butter
2 c. sliced onions
1 c. peeled, seeded and chopped
    tomatoes

2 tsp. salt
1 tsp. parsley
1/2 tsp. pepper
4 c. chicken broth or water
2 c. 1/2-inch carrot pieces

Cut chicken into serving size pieces. Trim and peel kohlrabies and cut into 1-inch chunks. Heat butter in a large kettle and sauté onions, tomatoes, salt, parsley and pepper for 4-5 minutes. Add chicken and cook 5 minutes. Add broth or water and bring to a boil. Reduce heat, cover and simmer 20 minutes. Add kohlrabies, cover and simmer 20 minutes. Add carrots and simmer 15 minutes more or until all vegetables are tender. Add thin strips of deribbed kohlrabi leaves the last 10 minutes if desired.

KOHLRABIES – FREEZING

HOW TO FREEZE KOHLRABIES[2]

Cut off tops and roots of small to medium kohlrabies. Wash and peel. Leave whole, slice 1/4-inch thick or dice in 1/2- inch cubes. Blanch in water, whole bulbs 3 minutes; diced or sliced bulbs 1 minute. [Cool immediately in cold water. Drain, package and freeze.]

The earth is the Lord's, and the fulness thereof; the world and they that dwell therein.
Psalm 24:1

NOTES

Lettuce
and
Salad Greens

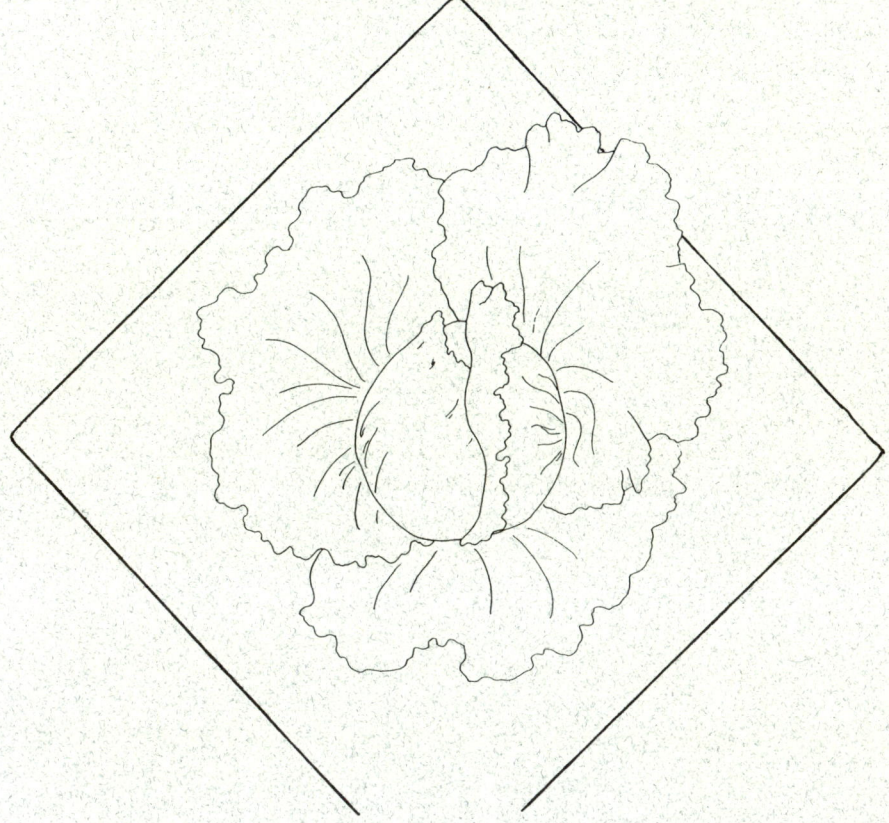

Lettuce is one of the most universally grown of all the garden vegetables. Not only is it very easy to grow, it is adaptable to just about every climate zone in North America.

Lettuce enthusiasts can choose from four main types of lettuce. The first, crisphead or iceberg type, is the large, firm, crisp, head lettuce seen in supermarkets. It is also the hardest to grow in home gardens.

Butterhead lettuce also forms heads, but they are more loosely contained than crisphead varieties.

Leaf lettuce comes in various shapes and flavors. It doesn't form heads and is very easy to grow.

Romaine or *cos* lettuce forms upright, cylindrical heads that have a sharper flavor than other types.

Some of the non-traditional salad greens that are gaining in popularity are arugula, endive, chicory and watercress.

While different varieties have their own unique characteristics, use the four types interchangeably in recipes.

Lettuce grows best under cool spring skies. To take advantage of the best lettuce weather, sow seeds as soon as your ground can be worked in the spring. For leaf lettuce plant ¼- ½ inch deep and thin to 4 to 6-inch final spacing. Midsummer planting for fall crops works well, too.

Head lettuce can be grown from seed or more commonly from transplants. Sow seeds ¼ to ½-inch deep, thinning to 12-14 inches between plants. Start transplants 3-4 weeks before setting out. Lettuce can survive temperatures down to 20 degrees.

Hot weather and warm, dry soil cause lettuce to bolt (form seeds) and get bitter. To extend the lettuce season, provide shade for the plants once the temperature reaches 80 degrees.

The traditional way to use lettuce is, of course, in salads. For variety, try lettuce braised in butter, cream of lettuce soup or stir fried lettuce with mushrooms and onions. Lettuce can also be cooked like spinach and eaten as a vegetable.

Salad greens are low in calories and high in fiber. Some varieties have significant levels of beta carotene, folate, vitamin C, calcium, iron and potassium. Green leafy varieties tend to be higher in nutrients than the iceberg types.

Yield: 1 lb. lettuce = 24 cups chopped

LETTUCE AND SALAD GREENS – SOUPS

LETTUCE SOUP

2 T. chopped onion	1/2 tsp. salt
2 T. butter	1/2 tsp. thyme
2 T. flour	1/8 tsp. pepper
2 c. boiling water	2 c. light cream or whole milk
2 bouillon cubes	2 c. chopped lettuce

Sauté onion in butter. Blend in flour. Add water gradually, stirring constantly. Add bouillon cubes and seasonings. (Replace water and bouillon with 2 c. chicken broth if desired.) Cook 10 minutes. Add cream and lettuce. Heat through.

Variation: Sauté 8 c. chopped lettuce with the onions, about 3 minutes. Omit flour. Add everything but cream and simmer 5 minutes. Cool slightly then puree in a blender. Return soup to the kettle and add cream. Heat through.

WATERCRESS SOUP

2 c. watercress	6 c. water or chicken broth
3 medium potatoes, peeled and	1/2 tsp. salt or to taste
diced	1/8 tsp. pepper
1 c. chopped onion	

Wash and dry watercress. Add potatoes and onions to water. Bring to a boil then simmer 15 minutes or until potatoes are tender. Add watercress and cook 10 minutes longer. Season to taste.
Variation: Substitute arugula for watercress.

LETTUCE AND SALAD GREENS – SALADS

SALAD FOR TWO

1 small head of Bibb or Boston	1/2 small red onion, sliced and
lettuce	separated into rings
1/4 lb. spinach, stems removed or	4 radishes, sliced
watercress	1/4 c. French dressing

Tear lettuce and spinach into bite-size pieces; place in a salad bowl. Top with onions and radishes. Add dressing and toss lightly.

OLD FASHIONED LETTUCE SALAD

2 bunches leaf lettuce, washed and
    chilled
1/2 c. light cream

1/2 T. sugar
1/4 tsp. salt
1/4 c. vinegar

Tear lettuce in bite size pieces (6 cups). Just before serving, mix remaining ingredients. Pour over lettuce and toss.

WILTED LETTUCE SALAD

1 head lettuce
4 slices bacon
2 T. bacon drippings
2 T. vegetable oil

1/4 c. vinegar
1 T. sugar
1/4 tsp. salt

Wash lettuce. Tear into bite-size pieces. Pat dry. Fry bacon then remove from skillet. Save 2 T. drippings. Add remaining ingredients and bacon; bring to a boil, stirring well. Pour over lettuce and toss lightly to coat leaves. Serve at once.

Variation: Use dandelion greens instead of lettuce.

DANDELION SALAD WITH HORSERADISH

6 c. young dandelion leaves
2 hard boiled eggs, chopped
4 slices bacon, cooked, drained
    and crumbled
1 T. minced onion

1 tsp. prepared horseradish or
    mustard
1/2 c. olive or vegetable oil
2 T. lemon juice
1 tsp. sugar
1/4 tsp. salt

Wash dandelion very thoroughly, removing any tough stems. Dry well. Combine dandelion, eggs and bacon in a salad bowl. Whisk together remaining ingredients and pour over salad. Toss to coat and serve at once.

That if thou shalt confess with thy mouth the Lord Jesus, and shalt believe in thine heart that God hath raised him from the dead, thou shalt be saved. For with the heart man believeth unto righteousness; and with the mouth confession is made unto salvation.
Romans 10:9,10

GREENS AND BACON SALAD

8 slices bacon, cut into bite-size
   pieces
2 qt. broken salad greens
3 hard boiled eggs, sliced
8 cherry tomatoes, halved
1/3 c. mayonnaise
2 T. sugar

2 T. vinegar
2 T. salad oil
2 tsp. dry mustard
1 tsp. paprika
1/2 tsp. salt
1/4 tsp. garlic salt

Fry bacon until crisp and drain on paper towels. Put greens in salad bowl; arrange eggs, bacon and tomatoes on top. Combine remaining ingredients and serve with salad.

CAESAR SALAD

1 clove garlic, cut in quarters
1/3 c. cooking oil
1/2 tsp. salt
1/8 tsp. pepper
2 qt. romaine lettuce

1 egg
2 T. lemon juice
1/4 c. grated Parmesan cheese
1 c. seasoned croutons
6 anchovy fillets (optional)

In small container, marinate garlic in oil 30 minutes; add salt and pepper. Place torn romaine lettuce in salad bowl. Discard garlic pieces, saving oil. Pour oil over lettuce; toss lightly. Boil egg 1 minute and break over salad; add lemon juice and toss again. Add cheese and croutons; toss. Garnish with anchovies. Serve immediately.

SUMMER SALAD

leaf lettuce
1/2 head lettuce in bite-size pieces
1 c. diagonally sliced celery
1 c. sliced radishes

2 c. sliced raw cauliflower
1 green pepper, thinly sliced
1/2 tsp. salt
1/3 c. crumbled blue cheese

Line bowl with leaf lettuce. Arrange head lettuce and remaining vegetables in bowl; add salt. Sprinkle blue cheese over. Serve with dressing.

Hint: An ice "jacket" keeps the crunch in summer salads. Fit two bowls of different sizes together and pack crushed ice in between.

GREEK SALAD

1/4 c. olive or vegetable oil	1/2 large head lettuce or salad
1/4 c. vinegar	greens
1/2 tsp. sugar	2 tomatoes, diced or cut in wedges
1/2 tsp. salt	1 cucumber, diced or sliced
1/8 tsp. oregano	1/4 c. diced or sliced red onion
1/8 tsp. dry mustard	1/4 c. pitted black olives
	1/2 c. feta cheese, crumbled

Combine first six ingredients in a jar with a lid; shake well. Tear lettuce into bite-size pieces; put in a salad bowl. Add remaining ingredients, crumbling cheese on top. Just before serving, pour dressing over salad and toss lightly.

LETTUCE AND FRUIT SALAD

1 large head romaine lettuce	1 unpeeled apple, sliced
1 1/2 c. mixed dried fruit	1/2 unpeeled cucumber, thinly
(apricots, prunes, raisins)	sliced
1/3 c. radishes, sliced	1/2 c. toasted wheat germ
1 c. alfalfa sprouts	

Line salad bowl with lettuce. Arrange dried fruit, radishes, sprouts, apple and cucumber on lettuce. Sprinkle with wheat germ. Serve with Creamy Honey Dressing.

VEGETABLE SALAD

8 c. broken romaine, leaf and ice	1 small red onion sliced thin
berg lettuce	1 c. cubed cheddar cheese
1 small yellow squash, sliced thin	1/2 c. olive or vegetable oil
1 small red pepper, seeded and	1/4 c. vinegar
sliced thin	salt and pepper

Toss together salad greens, squash, pepper, onion and cheese cubes. Mix oil and vinegar in a cruet and let everyone add their own dressing, salt and pepper, or serve with dressing of your choice.

LAYERED SALAD

2 qt. chopped iceberg lettuce
1/2 c. chopped celery
1/2 c. chopped green pepper
1/2 c. chopped onion
1 1/2 c. peas, cooked and drained

1 1/2 c. mayonnaise
3 T. sugar
1 1/2 c. shredded Cheddar cheese
8 slices bacon, fried and crumbled

Place the above ingredients in layers in the order given in a 13 x 9 pan. Cover. Chill at least 8 hours. Cut into squares to serve.

LAYERED GARDEN PASTA SALAD

7 or 8 oz. macaroni shells
1/2 c. sliced green onions
1/4 c. imitation bacon bits
1 c. mayonnaise or salad dressing
1/4 c. lemon juice
3 T. grated Parmesan cheese
1 tsp. sugar

1/2 tsp. garlic powder
4 c. bite-size pieces salad greens
1 medium zucchini, sliced
1 c. sliced cauliflower florets
1 c. broccoli florets
2 medium tomatoes, cut into wedges

Cook macaroni and drain. Rinse with cold water; drain. Stir together macaroni, onions and 2 T. of the imitation bacon. Mix mayonnaise, lemon juice, cheese, sugar and garlic powder. In 3 1/2 quart salad bowl, layer salad greens, macaroni mixture, zucchini, cauliflower, broccoli and tomatoes. Pour dressing evenly over top. Cover and refrigerate at least 2 hours. Sprinkle with 2 T. imitation bacon just before serving. Refrigerate any remaining salad.

CHEF SALAD

2 medium heads lettuce
4 green onions, thinly sliced
3 large tomatoes
1 c. cooked ham strips
1 c. cooked beef strips

1 c. cooked chicken strips
2 c. Swiss or Cheddar cheese strips
2 hard boiled eggs, sliced

Wash lettuce. Tear into bite-size pieces and arrange into a shallow salad bowl. Arrange remaining ingredients on the lettuce. Serve with a dressing of your choice.

TACO SALAD

1 lb. ground beef	1 head lettuce, torn
1 onion chopped	2 c. grated Cheddar cheese
2 c. canned kidney beans	4 tomatoes, chopped
1 tsp. chili powder	tortilla chips
1/2 tsp. salt	French dressing

Brown ground beef and onion. Add kidney beans, chili powder and salt. Simmer 5 minutes. Cool. Mix remaining ingredients in a large salad bowl and add meat mixture. Toss. Add or pass French dressing.

HOT CHICKEN SALAD

4 c. thin strips of chicken	1 small onion, chopped
1/4 c. corn starch	1 c. diagonally sliced celery
1/4 c. vegetable oil	1 tsp. salt or to taste
1/8 tsp. garlic powder	1/4 c. soy sauce or to taste
1 large tomato, peeled and chopped	2 c. chopped lettuce
4 oz. can water chestnuts, drained	hot cooked rice
4 oz. can mushrooms, drained	

Coat chicken with cornstarch. Heat oil in skillet and stir fry until it loses its pink color. Sprinkle with garlic powder, add tomato, water chestnuts, mushrooms, onion and celery. Stir and sprinkle with salt. Add soy sauce and stir again. Cover, reduce heat and simmer 5 minutes. Lightly toss chicken mixture with lettuce. Serve on hot rice.

LETTUCE AND SALAD GREENS – DRESSINGS

BASIC VINAIGRETTE

1 c. olive or vegetable oil	1/8 tsp. white pepper or black
1/3 c. vinegar	pepper
1/4 tsp. salt	

Whisk together, or shake together in jar. Serve chilled.

Hint: Brighten your salads with edible flowers such as the following: apple blossoms, begonias, calendula, day lilies, geraniums, honeysuckle, lilac, nasturiums, pansies, roses, squash blossoms and tulips. Use only flowers you know are edible—some flowers are poisonous.

ITALIAN DRESSING

1 1/3 c. vegetable oil
2/3 c. vinegar
1 clove garlic, split
1 tsp. dry mustard

1/2 tsp. celery salt
1/2 tsp. dried basil leaves
1/2 tsp. dried oregano leaves
1/4 tsp. pepper

Combine ingredients in jar. Cover; shake vigorously. Chill to blend flavors. Remove garlic; shake again before serving over tossed green salads. Makes 2 cups.

FRENCH DRESSING

1/2 c. olive or vegetable oil
1/4 c. vinegar or lemon juice
1/2 tsp. salt

1/4 tsp. dry mustard
1/4 tsp. paprika

Put in a jar, close tightly and shake vigorously. Chill and shake well before using.

CELERY SEED DRESSING

1/3 c. sugar
2 T. lemon juice
1 T. vinegar
1 tsp. salt

1/2 tsp. paprika
1/2 tsp. dry mustard
1 tsp. celery seed
2/3 c. salad oil

Combine ingredients in a jar, cover and shake vigorously. Refrigerate until used.

HONEY CELERY SEED DRESSING

3/4 c. honey
3/4 c. salad oil
1/2 c. sugar
1/2 c. lemon juice or vinegar
2 tsp. prepared mustard

1 1/2 tsp. paprika
1 tsp. celery seed
3/4 tsp. salt
1/2 thin slice onion

Stir ingredients 20 seconds or until well mixed. Makes about 2 1/4 cups.

HONEY POPPY SEED DRESSING

1/3 c. vegetable oil	2 tsp. poppy seeds
1/4 c. honey	1/2 tsp. salt
2 T. cider vinegar	

In a small bowl or jar with tight-fitting lid, combine all ingredients; shake well. Serve over a green salad or fresh fruit. Refrigerate. Makes about 2/3 cup.

CREAMY HONEY DRESSING

1/2 c. mayonnaise	1 T. honey
1/2 c. sour cream	1 T. milk
2 T. lemon juice	1/2 tsp. vegetable or sesame oil

Combine mayonnaise, sour cream, lemon juice, honey, milk and oil. Mix well. Refrigerate until ready to serve. Makes 1 cup.

CREAMY CUCUMBER DRESSING

1 c. sour cream	1 T. minced onion
1/2 c. chopped, seeded cucumber	1 T. lemon juice
2 T. chopped fresh dill or 2 tsp.	2 tsp. sugar
dried dill weed	1/8 tsp. garlic salt

Stir all ingredients together until well blended. Cover and refrigerate overnight to blend flavors.

CREAMY ITALIAN DRESSING

1 c. mayonnaise or salad dressing	1 tsp. paprika
2 T. lemon juice	1/2 tsp. salt
1 T. sugar	1/2 tsp. dry mustard
1 T. milk	1/8 tsp. pepper

Whisk together all ingredients. Cover and refrigerate at least 2 hours before serving.

BUTTERMILK DRESSING

1 c. buttermilk	1/2 tsp. basil
1 c. mayonnaise or salad dressing	1/4 tsp. Worcestershire sauce
1 T. fresh dill or 1 tsp. dried dill	1/8 tsp. garlic powder
1 T. chopped fresh parsley	1/8 tsp. onion powder

Whisk all ingredients together in a small bowl. Cover and refrigerate at least 12 hours to blend flavors.

Variation: Whisk together 1 c. buttermilk, 1/2 c. mayonnaise or salad dressing, 1/4-1/2 c. sugar and 1/4 c. vinegar.

LOW FAT BUTTERMILK DRESSING

1 c. buttermilk	1 tsp. sugar
1/3 c. vinegar	1/4 tsp. salt
1 thinly sliced green onion	1/8 tsp. ground red pepper
2 T. chopped fresh dill or 2 tsp. dry dill weed	

Whisk together all ingredients or put in a blender for 15 seconds.

THOUSAND ISLAND DRESSING

1 c. mayonnaise or salad dressing	1/2 tsp. paprika
1/4 c. chili sauce or ketchup	1/8 tsp. pepper
2 T. sweet pickle or relish	2 hard boiled eggs, chopped
1 T. finely chopped onion	(optional)

Stir together all but eggs and mix well. Gently stir in eggs.

GREEN ONION DRESSING

1 1/2 c. mayonnaise or salad dressing	1/4 c. light syrup
1/2 c. chopped parsley or 1 T. dried parsley	2 T. lemon juice
1/3 c. finely chopped green onion	1 T. Worcestershire sauce
	1/4 tsp. pepper

Combine all ingredients. Mix well. Cover and chill. Makes 2 cups.

BACON DRESSING

1 1/2 c. mayonnaise or salad
   dressing
1/4 c. light corn syrup
1/4 c. milk

6 slices bacon, cooked, drained
   and crumbled
1 T. finely chopped onion
1 tsp. parsley
1/4 tsp. pepper

Stir all ingredients until well blended. Cover and chill. Makes 2 1/4 cups.

BLENDER MAYONNAISE

2 eggs
1 tsp. dry mustard
1 tsp. salt
1 tsp. sugar
1/2 tsp. paprika

1/4 tsp. celery salt
dash of pepper or cayenne
1/3 c. lemon juice or vinegar
2 c. salad oil

Chop first 8 ingredients and 1/4 c. oil 5 seconds. Add remaining oil in a fine steady stream through top opening while motor runs, about 60 seconds, or until thick and smooth. If necessary, stop motor and push ingredients into blades. Makes about 2 2/3 cups.

COOKED SALAD DRESSING

1 c. sugar
1/2 c. vinegar
2 eggs, beaten
1 T. butter

1/4 tsp. salt
1 c. mayonnaise
2 tsp. mustard

Cook first 5 ingredients until thickened. Cool. Stir in mayonnaise and mustard.

Out of the same mouth proceedeth blessing and cursing. My brethren, these things ought not so to be. Doth a fountain send forth at the same place sweet water and bitter? Can the fig tree, my brethren, bear olive berries? either a vine, figs? so can no fountain both yield salt water and fresh.

James 3:10-12

LETTUCE AND SALAD GREENS – SANDWICHES

LETTUCE SANDWICH SPREAD

1/2 c. chopped lettuce
3 T. chopped green pepper
3 T. chopped celery
3 T. chopped cucumber

2 T. chopped onion
1 hard boiled egg, chopped
1/4 c. mayonnaise

Combine all ingredients and spread on bread.

LETTUCE AND SALAD GREENS – SIDE AND MAIN DISHES

HOW TO COOK LETTUCE

Bring 1/4-inch of salted water to a boil and add torn lettuce. Return to a boil, reduce heat and simmer. Simmer tender lettuce like iceberg or loose leaf 1-3 minutes. Simmer hardier lettuce like escarole or romaine for 5-10 minutes.

DANDELION SOUFFLÉ

1/2 lb. tender dandelion leaves
2 T. butter
2 T. finely chopped onion
6 egg yolks
4 T. butter
4 T. flour

1 1/2 c. milk
1/2 c. grated Swiss or Cheddar
   cheese
1/2 tsp. salt
1/8 tsp. pepper
6 egg whites

Wash and chop dandelion. Heat 2 T. butter and sauté onion 2-3 minutes. Add dandelion and cover. Reduce heat and cook 4-5 minutes. Uncover and turn heat on high to evaporate moisture for several minutes, but do not brown. Beat egg yolks. Set aside. Heat 4 T. butter, add flour then gradually stir in milk. Bring to a boil, stirring constantly and boil 1 minute. Mix a small amount of hot sauce into yolks then add yolks to hot sauce. Stir in dandelion, cheese, salt and pepper. Cool slightly. Beat egg whites until soft peaks form. Stir 1/2 c. egg whites in soufflé mixture to lighten it. Fold in remaining egg whites. Pour into a buttered soufflé dish. Bake at 350° for 35-40 minutes or until golden brown and puffy.
Variation: Substitute arugula, chicory, escarole or romaine lettuce for dandelion.

127

LETTUCE AND SALAD GREENS – MISCELLANEOUS

TOASTED CROUTONS

4 slices firm bread
2 T. butter
1/4 tsp. salt

1/4 tsp. garlic powder
1/8 tsp. pepper

Cut crusts from bread. Spread both sides with butter. Cut slices into 1/2-inch cubes. Place in a 13 x 9 baking pan. Sprinkle with remaining ingredients. Bake at 400° for 10-15 minutes or until golden brown. Cool completely.

HERB VINEGAR

2 c. fresh herb leaves, minced

1 qt. apple cider or white wine vinegar

Combine in a large jar at room temperature for one week, shaking daily. Strain out herbs; pour vinegar into a bottle and seal.

And God said, Behold, I have given you every herb bearing seed, which is upon the face of the earth, and every tree, in the which is the fruit of a tree yielding seed; to you it shall be for meat. And to every beast of the earth, and to every fowl of the air, and to every thing that creepeth upon the earth, wherein there is life, I have given every green herb for meat: and it was so. And God saw every thing that he had made, and, behold, it was very good. And the evening and the morning were the sixth day.

Genesis 1:29-31

Melons

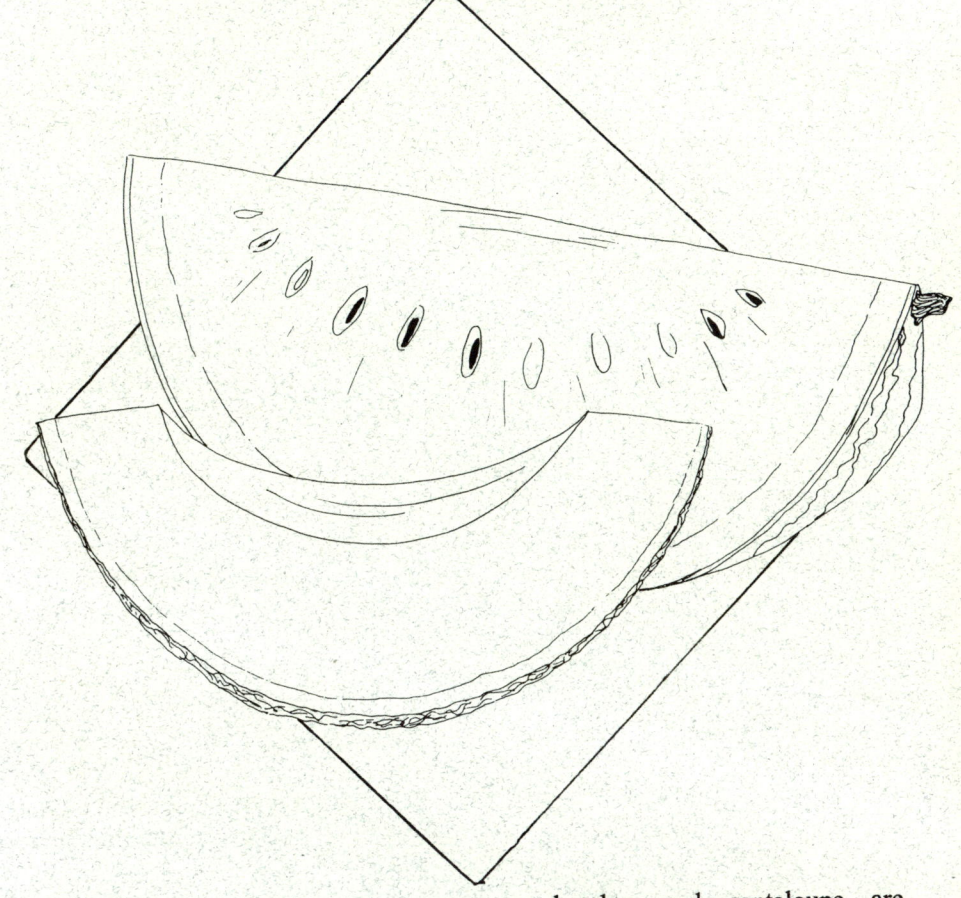

Practically speaking, the terms muskmelon and cantaloupe are interchangeable for the orange-fleshed, musk-flavored melons grown in North America. Technically, though, muskmelon refers to the netted, ribbed rind melons while cantaloupes have a rough, warted rind.

The melons grown in North America are almost exclusively muskmelons. Cantaloupes are more common in Europe. While disagreements stand on nomenclature, few argue that summer would suffer irreparably without the sweet, musky flavor of these tantalizing fruits.

Another type of melon, the honey dew, is smooth skinned, more mildly flavored and light green to white fleshed. Honey dews are categorized with casaba, crenshaw and Persian melons as winter melons—so called because they mature late and require long, hot summers to ripen. Some of the new honey dew varieties are shorter seasoned and do well even in cooler areas.

Watermelons, are in a different genus than the above melons. They generally require more hot weather than muskmelons to mature.

Melons can be direct seeded in areas with long, hot summers. Plant after danger of frost. Sow three seeds ½ inch deep every 18 inches and then thin to one plant. Space rows 6-8 feet apart. In northern areas, or to get an earlier crop, melons can be started with transplants. Start seeds in individual pots 4-6 weeks before setting outside. Smaller plants (ideal transplants have one or two true leaves) will sustain less transplant shock. Water your plants liberally before and after setting out.

In the short, cool summers of central Wisconsin we grow watermelons and muskmelons successfully using a black plastic mulch with row covers. With this method, plants should be started so they are ready to transplant about 2-3 weeks before your expected frost free date. The plastic mulch keeps weeds down in the row, preserves soil moisture and warms the soil. Row covers offer frost protection and greenhouse-like growing conditions during the early, cool part of the summer. Remove row covers when most vines have female flowers. (Female flowers have a fruit bulb immediately behind the flower.) Take row covers off on a cloudy day or at dusk to avoid sun shock.

Melons like light, well drained, fertile soil with plenty of moisture. Soil moisture is less critical after fruit set has occurred.

Knowing when to pick a melon is as much an art as a science. It is extremely difficult to learn other than by doing. Here are a few tips to go by.

Muskmelons are ripe when the rind turns from green to yellowish-tan and the vine slips from the melon with only slight pressure.

Honey dew melons are cut from the vine when the rind turns a pale yellow.

Watermelons are ripe when at least three of the curly tendrils (must include the tendril nearest the melon) on the vine between the melon and the main stalk are brown and dried. Some growers prefer to check the color of the ground spot where the melon touched the ground. When the watermelon is ripe the spot turns from white to yellow.

Melons are most satisfying served cold. Just remove the seeds and enjoy!

You can keep watermelons for 2-3 weeks in the refrigerator. Muskmelons will store for 1-2 weeks, depending on variety.

Yellow melons are high in vitamin A, most varieties are good sources of vitamin C and potassium. Though they are sweet when ripe, they are relatively low in calories. Melons also contain cancer-fighting bioflavonoids.

MELONS WITH PINEAPPLE

1 c. watermelon balls	1/2 c. syrup from canned
1 c. muskmelon balls	pineapple
1 can (2 1/2 c.) pineapple chunks	1/2 c. orange juice
	2 T. lemon juice

Chill fruits. Drain pineapple; combine pineapple syrup with juices. Place fruits in individual serving bowls and pour juice on top.

MELON FRUIT COCKTAIL

1 c. melon balls	1 c. strawberries, whole or sliced
1 c. drained pineapple chunks	1/4 c. lemon juice
1 c. orange sections	2-4 T. sugar
2 bananas, sliced	

Combine fruit. Blend lemon juice and sugar. Spoon over fruit and chill. If desired, garnish with mint leaves.

MUSKMELON MOLDS

3 oz. pkg. strawberry, cherry or	2 muskmelons
orange gelatin	salad dressing
2 c. pineapple juice	

Dissolve gelatin in 1 c. boiling pineapple juice. Add remaining juice; chill until slightly thickened. Cut muskmelons in half; remove seeds. Remove fruit, leaving 1/2-inch shell. Chop fruit; fold in gelatin mixture. Put melon halves in small bowls to steady and pour gelatin mixture into the shells. Chill until firm—at least 4 hours. Cut into wedges; serve with salad dressing.
Variation: Use water for part of the pineapple juice.

And the Lord God took the man, and put him into the garden of Eden to dress it and to keep it. And the Lord God commanded the man, saying, Of every tree of the garden thou mayest freely eat: But of the tree of the knowledge of good and evil, thou shalt not eat of it: for in the day that thou eatest thereof thou shalt surely die.

Genesis 2:15-17

MELON RING WITH HONEY COCONUT DRESSING

3 oz. pkg. orange-flavored gelatin
3 oz. pkg. lemon-flavored gelatin
1 1/2 c. orange juice
1/2 c. lemon juice

1 1/2 c. cold water
3 c. mixed melon balls—
    muskmelon and honeydew
additional melon balls for garnish

Combine gelatin, orange and lemon juice in a saucepan. Heat to boiling over low heat, stirring constantly. Remove from heat. Add cold water and continue stirring until gelatin is dissolved. Chill until slightly thickened, then stir in melon balls. Pour into lightly oiled 6 1/2 c. ring mold. Chill until firm. Unmold and fill center with additional melon balls. Serve with Honey-Coconut Dressing. (Below.)

HONEY COCONUT DRESSING

2 T. honey
1-2 T. lemon juice

1/4 c. flaked coconut
1 c. sour cream

Combine ingredients and blend well. Chill and serve on fruit salads.

HAM SALAD IN MUSKMELON RINGS

2 c. diced, cooked, lean ham
3/4 c. diced celery
1/3 c. mayonnaise

1/2 tsp. dry mustard
1 muskmelon, chilled
salad greens

Mix ham and celery; cover and chill. When ready to serve, mix mayonnaise with mustard and combine with ham mixture. Cut 4 rings from center of a whole melon. Discard seeds and cut rind off rings. Place melon rings on salad greens. Pile salad onto fruit ring.

MELONS – MISCELLANEOUS

MUSKMELON SMOOTHIE

1 1/2 c. diced muskmelon
1 1/2 c. sliced, peeled peaches
1 1/4 c. orange juice or pineapple
    juice

1/4 c. powdered milk
1/2 tsp. vanilla

Combine every thing in a blender. Blend until smooth.

WATERMELON ICE

8 c. 1-inch watermelon pieces   1/4 c. lemon juice
1 c. sugar

Remove seeds from melon. Place 4 c. melon pieces, sugar and lemon juice in a blender. Blend until smooth and sugar is dissolved. Repeat with remaining melon. Mix and pour into 2 ice cube trays. Freeze until firm, about 2 hours.

WATERMELON SLUSH

2 c. water   1 T. lemon juice
1/4 c. sugar   6 c. seeded watermelon cubes
12 oz. can frozen fruit punch   2 liter bottle lemon-lime soda or
    concentrate   ginger ale

Combine water and sugar. Bring to a boil, stirring until sugar is dissolved. Boil gently, uncovered, for 3 minutes. Remove from heat and stir in fruit punch until dissolved. Combine half of the lemon juice and half of the melon cubes in a blender. Blend until smooth. Repeat with the other half. Stir melon mixture into the fruit punch mixture. Mix and pour into a freezer container. Cover and freeze at least 8 hours. To serve scrape with a spoon to form slush. Fill cups at least half full with slush. Slow pour in lemon-lime soda until cups are filled.

WATERMELON POPSICLES

Put chunks of seeded watermelon in the blender and puree. Pour into popsicle molds or paper cups. If using a paper cup insert a stick when the melon is partially frozen.

He hath made every thing beautiful in his time: also he hath set the world in their heart, so that no man can find out the work that God maketh from the beginning to the end.
Ecclesiastes 3:11

131

MELONS – CANNING AND FREEZING

SPICED WATERMELON RIND

rind from 1 large watermelon
(approximately 20 lb.)
16 c. water
1 c. salt
8 c. sugar
2 lemons, thinly sliced

2 T. whole cloves
2 T. whole allspice
8 1-inch pieces stick cinnamon
4 c. cider vinegar
4 c. water

Peel outer green skin from rind. Cut into 1-inch cubes to make about 16 c. of cubes. Combine 8 c. of the water and 1/2 c. salt in a large bowl; add 8 c. of the rind. Repeat with remaining rind water and salt. Refrigerate both bowls overnight. The next morning drain rind; put into a large kettle and cover with fresh water. Bring to a boil then simmer 10 minutes. Drain. While rind drains elsewhere, put remaining ingredients in the same kettle. Bring to a boil; stir in rind. Return to a boil; lower heat and simmer 1 hour, stirring often. Ladle into 8 hot, half-pint jars. Seal and process 15 minutes in boiling water canner.

HOW TO FREEZE MELONS[2]

Select firm-fleshed ripe melons. Cut in half, remove seeds and peel. Cut into uniform cubes or balls. Pack into containers and cover with thin syrup [4 c. water to 2 c. sugar]. Serve while still partially frozen for best texture. Melons tend to develop a rubbery texture when frozen and fully thawed.

MUSKMELONS WITH BLUEBERRIES AND PEACHES

Combine firm but ripe melon balls with blueberries and sliced peaches. Add sugar to taste. Let set a little so sugar dissolves. Stir carefully and put in freezer containers. Serve while still partially frozen.

The sleep of a laboring man is sweet, whether he eat little or much: but the abundance of the rich will not suffer him to sleep.

Ecclesiastes 5:12

Okra

From its stronghold in the south, okra has been making inroads into northern gardens. Though it is steeped with a strong southern reputation, it can be grown without offense in most areas of North America. If you can grow sweet corn, eggplants or cucumbers, then the climate in your area is right for okra.

Okra does best in summer's heat after the ground is completely warmed and danger of frost is past. Sow seeds 1/2 inch deep, 8-10 inches apart in rows 3-4 feet apart. Or start indoors 5 weeks before your frost-free date. Plastic mulch and row covers are helpful to get an earlier crop, especially in northern areas. If space is limited, use dwarf varieties that won't get over three feet tall. Standard strains get up to seven feet tall.

Okra comes from the Hibiscus family. Its gorgeous yellow flowers with dark centers bear a striking resemblance to the Hibiscus flower.

Pods develop quickly after flowers appear and are ready to use when they reach 2-4 inches in length. To keep pods from over maturing okra needs to be picked every other day (move over zucchini, here's your competition). This also helps new pods to set. Over ripe okra is stringy and tough. Discard it. Wear gloves and long sleeves when picking okra to protect from its spiny leaves. Gloves also help prevent the rash some people develop from okra leaves.

One of okra's most valued characteristics is for some cooks its biggest turn off. Cut okra, while cooking, secretes a thick, slimy, mucilaginous substance that is prized as a natural thickener in gumbo soups and stews. For others, the slime forever banishes okra from their kitchen and table.

To prevent the slimy affect, try cooking okra whole or breading and frying sliced okra.

Okra should be used fresh. It keeps for only one or two days in the refrigerator.

Okra is a good source of vitamins A and C, folate and potassium. It is high in fiber and low in fat and calories.

Yield: 1 lb. fresh okra = 8 cups whole = 4 cups sliced

OKRA – SOUPS

OKRA SOUP

4 T. butter
1/4 c. rice
1/4 c. chopped onion
1 diced green pepper
2 ribs celery

3 c. peeled, seeded and chopped
   tomatoes
4 c. water
1 1/2 tsp. salt
2 c. sliced okra pods

Heat butter. Sauté rice, onion, peppers and celery for 5 minutes. Add tomatoes, water and salt. Bring to a boil, reduce heat and simmer, covered, until rice is tender. Add okra and simmer 15 minutes more.

OKRA SOUP WITH CHICKEN

2 T. butter
2 c. sliced okra
1 c. diced onion
1/2 c. diced green pepper
1/4 c. chopped fresh parsley
4 c. peeled, seeded and chopped
   tomatoes

4 c. chicken broth
1/2 c. uncooked rice
1-2 c. diced, cooked chicken
2 c. corn
1 tsp. basil
salt and pepper to taste

Heat butter in a large kettle. Sauté okra, onion, pepper and parsley for 10 minutes. Add tomatoes and broth and bring to a boil. Reduce heat and stir in rice. Simmer 20 minutes. Add chicken and corn; simmer 5 more minutes. Season to taste.
Variation: Substitute turkey or smoked sausage pieces for chicken.

OKRA – SIDE AND MAIN DISHES

HOW TO COOK OKRA

Brush fuzz off of okra with a vegetable brush. Cut off the stems without cutting the pod open. Bring 1/2-inch of water to a boil. Add 1 lb. okra pods and 1/2 tsp. salt. Return to a boil, reduce heat then cook 5-7 minutes. Cook sliced okra 3-5 minutes.

WHOLE FRIED OKRA

1 lb. 1-2 inch okra pods
2 eggs
1/2 c. milk

1 tsp. salt
vegetable oil
1 c. crushed cracker crumbs

Wash and dry okra. Remove stems. Beat eggs and add milk and salt. Heat 1-inch of oil in a skillet with high sides. Dip okra into the egg mixture then coat with crumbs. Fry in hot oil until crisp and lightly browned. Drain on paper towels. sprinkle with salt and pepper.

SLICED FRIED OKRA

1 lb. okra, cut into 1/2-inch slices
1/2 c. cornmeal
1/2 tsp. salt

1/8 tsp. pepper
1/2 c. vegetable oil

Cook okra in 1 c. water and 1/2 tsp. salt, about 10 minutes. Mix cornmeal, salt and pepper. Toss okra cornmeal mixture until okra is completely coated. Heat oil. Cook and stir okra in oil until brown.

OKRA BACON SAUTÉ

okra
flour

4 slices bacon

Cut okra into 1/2-inch slices and coat with flour. Sauté with bacon until deep brown and crisp.

OKRA FRITTERS

1 qt. vegetable oil
1 1/2 c. sliced okra (1/4-inch
    slices)
1/2 c. water
1 1/2 c. flour

2 tsp. baking powder
3/4 tsp. salt
1/2 tsp. chili powder
1 c. milk
1 egg, beaten

Heat oil to 360°. Bring okra and water to a boil. Reduce heat. Cover and cook 2 minutes. Drain well on paper towels. Combine flour, baking powder, salt and chili powder in large bowl. Beat milk and egg the stir into flour mixture just until combined. Stir in okra. Drop 5 T. batter into hot oil. Fry 2-3 minutes or until golden brown. Remove fritters with a slotted spoon and drain on paper towel. Repeat with remaining mixture.

OKRA AND SUMMER SQUASH

2/3 c. water
1 tsp. salt
1 c. slivered carrots
1 1/2 c. sliced summer squash
(1/4-inch thick)

1 1/2 c. sliced okra (1/2-inch thick)
1 c. diagonally sliced green onions
(1-inch pieces)
dash pepper
3 T. butter

Combine water and salt and bring to a boil. Add carrots and cook, covered, about 5 minutes. Add squash, okra and onions and cook about 3 minutes longer or until tender crisp. Drain and season with pepper and butter.

OKRA AND TOMATOES

8 slices bacon, diced
1/4 c. yellow corn meal
1 tsp. chili powder
3/4 tsp. salt
1/8 tsp. pepper

1 medium onion, chopped
2 1/2 c. 1/4-inch slices okra
3 green or red tomatoes, peeled
and coarsely chopped

Brown bacon; drain. Place corn meal, chili powder, salt and pepper in a plastic bag. Shake, then add okra, shaking until well coated. Fry onion in the bacon drippings until tender. Add okra and tomatoes. Bring to a boil; cook approximately 5 minutes, stirring frequently. Garnish with bacon.

OKRA TOMATO RICE SKILLET

3 slices bacon, diced
1 medium onion
1 c. sliced okra (1/4-inch slices)
2 large tomatoes, peeled and cut
into 1 1/2-inch chunks
1 c. uncooked long grain rice

3/4 c. hot water
1 1/4 tsp. salt
1/2 tsp. basil
1/8 tsp. pepper
3 drops hot pepper sauce

Brown bacon; drain on paper towel. Add onion and okra to bacon drippings. Cook, stirring occasionally until okra is tender. Stir in bacon and remaining ingredients; bring to a boil. Reduce heat. Cover and simmer 20 minutes or until rice is tender.

SEAFOOD GUMBO

1/2 c. flour
1/4 c. vegetable oil
2 T. butter
1 1/2 c. chopped onion
1 c. chopped green pepper
1/2 c. chopped celery
3 c. sliced okra
4 c. peeled and chopped tomatoes
5 c. water

1 tsp. salt or to taste
1 tsp. hot pepper sauce
1 tsp. parsley
1/2 tsp. thyme
1 1/2 lb. boned, cubed firm white
    fish
1 lb. peeled raw shrimp
4 c. cooked hot rice

Combine flour and oil in a heavy saucepan making a thick paste. Cook over medium heat, stirring constantly until mixture turns reddish brown, 15-20 minutes. Heat butter in a skillet and sauté onions, pepper, celery and okra for 10 minutes. Add tomatoes, water and seasonings. Mix in the browned paste and simmer 30 minutes. Add the fish and shrimp and cook approximately 10 minutes. Serve on the hot rice.

OKRA – CANNING AND FREEZING

HOW TO CAN OKRA[1]

Hot Pack: Wash pods and trim ends. Leave whole or cut into 1-inch pieces. Cover with hot water and boil 2 minutes. Fill jars with hot okra and cooking liquid, leaving 1-inch headspace. Add 1 tsp. salt for quarts or 1/2 tsp. for pints.

Process in a pressure canner; pints 25 minutes and quarts 40 minutes. Process at 10 lb. of pressure at elevations below 1000 feet above sea level and 15 lb. above 1000 feet above sea level. Dial gauges should be at 11 lb. of pressure up to 2000 feet above sea level.

HOW TO FREEZE OKRA

Select young tender pods. Wash, and separate into two sizes: 4-inches or under and larger than 4-inches. Remove stems. Scald the small pods three minutes, cool, drain and package. Scald the larger pods five minutes. Cool immediately in cold water, cut into 1-inch lengths, package and freeze.

Onions

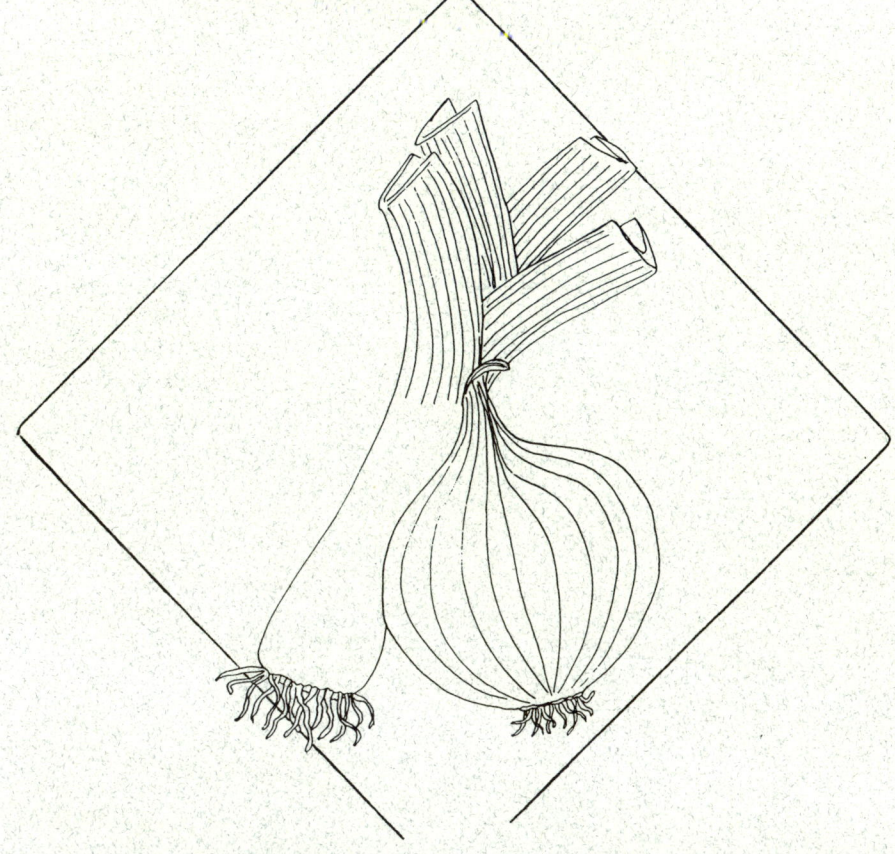

I suppose it's a good thing that my wife Elsie does most of the cooking at our house. If it were up to me, everything would have onions in it. Well at least the hot dishes, salads and sandwiches. The zippy, zesty onion and its relatives—leeks, shallots, garlic and chives—are some of the most ubiquitous of all the vegetables. Onions are probably included as an ingredient in more recipes in this book than any other vegetable.

Not only is the onion widely used in American cuisine, it's easy to grow, too. Onions are either short day (form bulbs with 12 hours of daylight) or long day (form bulbs with 14-16 hours of daylight).

Short day onions are suited for southern areas. Planted in the fall, they form bulbs early the following summer as days lengthen to about 12 hours. Short day onions can be planted in the north for scallions since they don't form bulbs in the longer daylight of the north.

Long day onions are planted in the spring for harvest as bulbs in the fall. In spring and early summer the tops and roots are developing. Then, once daylight stretches to 14 hours, the plants' energy is diverted to bulb production.

Onions do best in fertile, well drained, sandy soil with plenty of humus. They can be grown from seed, onion sets or transplants. Onions are available in red, yellow or white varieties.

Onion sets can be set out as soon as your soil is workable in the spring. Plant 1-2 inches deep every 4 inches for bulb onions. Or plant every 1-2 inches and use as scallions or green onions until you have a spacing of 4-5 inches for bulb onions.

Start onion plants about 12 weeks before setting outside. If your transplants get too leggy, cut them back with a scissors. Plant in the same way as onion sets.

Bunching onions or scallions are a non-bulbing perennial type that develops no or very small bulbs. Bunching onions are easy to start from seed. Sow seeds ½ inch deep every 1-2 inches and thin to 3-4 inches between plants.

You can start using onions as soon as they reach scallion size and continue to use them throughout the summer. If there are any left by late summer, they should be just right for winter storage onions.

Harvest bulb onions when the stems break over and turn brown. Pull and allow the bulbs to dry in the garden for 2-3 days. Trim stems 1 ½ inches above the bulb. Brush the dirt off and cure in an airy place in crates or mesh bags for another 2 weeks. Then store in a cool, dry location. They should last through the winter.

Use onions in soups, sandwiches and salads or stuffed, scalloped, baked, pickled or boiled. The possibilities are limited only by your imagination!

Yield: 1 lb. raw onion = 4 cups chopped

Garlic

Garlic grows in bulbs that break apart into individual cloves. Another type, elephant garlic, is milder and up to six times larger than the bulbed garlic. Garlic is usually started in the fall by planting individual cloves 1 inch deep, 2-4 inches apart in rows 2 feet apart. Your garlic is ready to harvest the following year when the tops turn yellow and fall over. Allow the bulbs to dry in the sun for 2-3 days then braid or tie in bunches. Store in a cool, dry place.

Garlic is used to flavor meats, stews and soups. It can be added to sauces, dips and dressing.

The health benefits of garlic have been widely touted. These benefits include lowering blood pressure and blood cholesterol. Garlic has been reported as an anticancer agent, as well as antibacterial and antiviral.

Shallots

Shallots are similar in appearance to garlic, but smaller and brown skinned instead of white. Shallots are multipliers, meaning one clove divides through the summer into 6-10 clumps of 3 or 4 cloves each. Plant cloves in the spring or fall (preferred), 1-2 inches deep and 6 inches apart.

Harvest the following summer with fall plantings; the same year with spring plantings. Shallots are ready to use when the tops turn brown.

Shallot flavor falls somewhere between an onion and garlic. You can replace 1 medium onion with 3 or 4 shallots in most recipes. Shallots are prized for their delicate, subtle flavor. Quite tender, shallots cook quickly.

Store shallots as you store onions, though they don't keep as long as onions do.

Yield: 1 lb. garlic or shallot cloves = 4 cups sliced

Chives

Also from the onion family, chives are grown for their leaves instead of bulbs. Chives are available either as regular chives or garlic chives. Start chives indoors 6-8 weeks before setting out. Sow 15-20 seeds ½ inch deep in a 6 inch pot. Transplant the whole clump into the garden. Chives are perennials that need to be divided every few years to keep them from getting overgrown.

Harvest chives by cutting leaves with a scissors about 2 inches above the ground. Chives are best if used before they flower.

Properly dried, chopped chives will keep for an extended time in sealed containers.

Leeks

Also called "poor man's asparagus", leeks are valued for their mild, sweet flavor. While onions make a dish oniony, the milder leeks meld with, and enhance, the flavors in the foods they're cooked with.

Leeks are large, non-bulbing, members of the onion family. They require a growing season in the 110-130 day range. Because of the days to maturity, it's best to start with transplants instead of direct seeding.

Start plants in February or March to set out as soon as your soil can be worked in the spring. Plant seedlings 6 inches apart, in holes dibbled about 6 inches deep. Only a few inches of leaf needs to be exposed. Don't firm the soil around the plants.

As the leeks grow, hill up the soil several times during the summer on either side of your row. This will maximize the white edible portion of the leek.

Although larger leeks (1 ½ inches across) are sweeter, you can start using them once they are ¾ inch across. Because of the way they're grown, leeks need to be thoroughly washed to remove any grit. Trim off the root and the dark green leaves. Then slit lengthwise on one side to within 1 ½ inches of the base. Gently separate the leaves and wash by holding under running water.

Use leeks in salads, casseroles and soups. They can also be left whole and eaten as a cooked vegetable—braised, boiled or steamed. Overcooked leeks turn mushy and slippery, so watch cooking times carefully.

Unwashed leeks will keep in the refrigerator for 2-3 weeks. If your winters are mild, mulch unused leeks in the garden and you can enjoy fresh leeks all winter.

Leeks are a good source of vitamin C, with some niacin and calcium.

Yield: 1 lb. fresh leeks = 6 cups sliced

FRENCH ONION SOUP

2 T. butter
2 T. vegetable oil
6 large onions, sliced
2 T. flour
1 tsp. salt

1/4 tsp. pepper
6 c. beef broth (part can be water)
6-8 slices French bread
3 c. grated Swiss cheese

Heat butter and oil in a large skillet or kettle. Add onions and cook 10-15 minutes, stirring several times. Stir in flour, salt and pepper. Add broth and simmer for one hour. Meanwhile cut each slice of French bread into four pieces and toast under broiler. Pour hot soup into 6 or 8 oven proof bowls. Top with French bread croutons and sprinkle with cheese. Broil just long enough to melt cheese and brown slightly.

CREAM OF LEEK SOUP

4 to 6 medium leeks
1/4 c. butter
3 T. flour
2 tsp. chopped chives

1/2 tsp. salt
6 c. milk or light cream
2 chicken bouillon cubes (optional)

Thinly slice leeks, discarding top green portion. Sauté leeks in butter 8-10 minutes or until tender, stirring occasionally. Stir in flour, chives, and salt; add milk and bouillon. Cook over medium heat, stirring occasionally, until soup boils 1 to 2 minutes. Garnish servings with nutmeg if desired.
Variation: Substitute 2 c. chopped onions for the leeks.

LEEK POTATO SOUP

3 T. butter
4 c. sliced leeks
1 lb. potatoes, peeled and diced
4 c. chicken broth

1/8 tsp. pepper
1 bay leaf
1/2 c. sour cream
4 slices fried, crumbled bacon

Melt butter in a 3-qt. saucepan. Add leeks and cook until tender. Stir in potatoes, broth, pepper and bay leaf; bring to a boil. Reduce heat; cover and simmer approx. 20 minutes. Remove bay leaf. Cool slightly. Blend mixture, half at a time, until smooth. Pour blended mixture back into saucepan. Gradually stir in sour cream. Cook over low heat for 3 minutes. Serve hot and garnish bowls with bacon.

TURKEY ONION RICE SOUP

1 lb. ground turkey	1/2 tsp. poultry seasoning
1 c. chopped onion	1/2 tsp. thyme
1/2 c. finely chopped carrots	1/8 tsp. pepper
6 c. chicken broth	1/2 c. flour
1/2 c. uncooked wild rice	2 c. milk

Crumble ground turkey into 6-qt. saucepan; stir in onion and carrots. Cook and stir over medium-high heat for 3 to 5 minutes or until turkey is lightly browned. Stir in chicken broth, rice, poultry seasoning, thyme and pepper. Bring to a boil; reduce heat. Cover; simmer 45 to 55 minutes or until rice is tender. Place flour in small bowl; gradually add milk, blending until smooth. Stir flour mixture into soup. Cook and stir over medium heat until soup bubbles and thickens slightly.

ONION FAMILY – SALADS

TOMATO ONION SALAD

4 large tomatoes, peeled and sliced	1/2 tsp. salt
1 large onion, sliced	1/2 tsp. dry mustard
3/4 c. vegetable oil	1/2 tsp. paprika
1/4 c. vinegar	1/8 tsp. pepper

Layer tomatoes and onions in a large bowl. Combine remaining ingredients in a jar. Cover tightly and shake until well blended. Pour over salad. Cover and refrigerate at least 2 hours, stirring occasionally.

ONION FAMILY – DIPS, SAUCES AND BUTTERS

SOUR CREAM AND ONION DIP

1 c. sour cream	1 tsp. Worcestershire sauce
1/4 c. finely chopped onion	1/4 tsp. salt or seasoned salt
1 T. chopped fresh parsley	1/8 tsp. pepper

Combine ingredients; cover and refrigerate at least 2 hours before serving.

ONION SAUCE

2 T. butter
1 small onion
1 T. flour

1/4 tsp. salt
1/8 tsp. pepper
1 c. milk

Melt butter. Add onion and cook until tender. Stir in flour, salt and pepper until blended. Cook 2 minutes, but do not brown. Gradually sit in milk. Stir constantly until mixture boils and thickens. Serve over asparagus or carrots.

SHALLOT BUTTER

1/2 c. butter   1-2 minced shallots

Heat together over moderate heat until melted. Good with green beans or peas.

ONION FAMILY – SANDWICHES

ONION PEPPER EGG SANDWICH

1/4 c. chopped onion
1/2 green pepper, chopped
3 T. butter
6 eggs

6 T. milk
3/4 tsp. salt
1/8 tsp. pepper

Sauté onion and green pepper in butter. Beat remaining ingredients and pour into skillet; scramble with onion and peppers, just until set. Top with a slice of cheese if desired. Eat with hamburger buns or bread.

HOT HAM AND BEEF SANDWICH WITH ONION

1 loaf French or Italian bread
6 slices Swiss cheese
6 slices cooked ham

6 slices cooked turkey, beef or
meat loaf
1 large onion, thinly sliced

Cut bread in half lengthwise. Arrange slices on the bottom half of the bread and cover with top half. Cut diagonally in 6 or 8 portions. Wrap in foil. Bake at 350° approximately 20 minutes.
Variation: Add tomato or green pepper slices.

ONION FAMILY – SIDE AND MAIN DISHES

HOW TO COOK ONIONS

Bring 1-inch of water to a boil. Add 1 lb. whole onions and 1/2 tsp. salt or to taste. Return to a boil; reduce heat and simmer 10-20 minutes or until tender. Time will vary with the size of the onions.

CREAMED ONIONS

4 c. pearl onions, peeled	1/2 c. chopped fresh parsley
6 T. butter	1/2 tsp. paprika
6 T. flour	salt and pepper to taste
3 c. milk	

Boil onion until just barely tender 10-15 minutes. Melt butter in a large kettle. Blend in flour; gradually add milk, stirring constantly until mixture thickens and boils. Add onions and remaining ingredients and heat through.

ONION RINGS

1 large onion	1/2 c. flour
vegetable oil for deep frying	3/4 tsp. baking powder
2/3 c. milk	1/4 tsp. salt

Cut onion into 1/4-inch slices and separate into rings. Heat oil 1-inch deep to 375°. Beat remaining ingredients until smooth. Dip rings into batter letting excess batter drip back into bowl. Fry a few rings at a time until golden brown—about 2 minutes. Turn one time. Drain and serve hot.

BAKED GLAZED ONIONS

1 lb. small white onions, peeled	1 T. lemon juice
1/4 c. butter	1/2 tsp. salt
1/4 c. brown sugar	1/4 tsp. ground ginger

Cook onions in salted water 15 minutes; drain. Melt butter in a 1 1/2-qt. baking dish in the oven. Stir in remaining ingredients. Add onions and coat with mixture. Arrange in a single layer; cover. Bake at 325° for 30 minutes, turning onions 2-3 times.

LEEKS AU GRATIN

12 medium to large leeks
1 1/4 c. beef or chicken bouillon
1 c. water
1/4 c. butter
1/4 c. flour

1/2 tsp. salt
1/4 tsp. pepper
1 c. grated Swiss or American
    cheese

Trim the leeks, removing roots and all but 2-inches of the green leaves. Wash thoroughly. Combine the bouillon and water and bring to a boil. Lower heat and add leeks. Simmer, covered, for 7-10 minutes, or until leeks are barely tender. Drain and reserve liquid—there should be about 2 cups. Place leeks in a buttered shallow baking dish. Melt the butter in a saucepan and stir in the flour. Gradually stir in the reserved liquid. Cook, stirring constantly, until thickened and smooth. Stir in the salt and pepper and 3/4 c. of the cheese. Cook until the cheese is melted. Pour sauce over leeks. Sprinkle with remaining cheese. Place under broiler or in a hot oven and cook until top is golden brown.
Variation: Use 6 large onions instead of leeks.

ONION AND GREEN BEAN CASSEROLE

3 c. sliced onions
1/3 c. butter
1/4 c. flour
1 1/2 tsp. salt
1/4 tsp. dry mustard

1/4 tsp. pepper
2 c. milk
1 c. shredded Cheddar cheese
3 c. lightly cooked green beans
2 T. bread crumbs

Sauté onion slices in butter until they are limp. Blend in flour, salt, mustard and pepper. Add milk, stirring constantly, until mixture thickens. Add cheese and green beans. Put into shallow 2-qt. casserole and sprinkle with bread crumbs. Bake at 350° for 30 minutes.

And he showed me a pure river of water of life, clear as crystal, proceeding out of the throne of God and of the Lamb. In the midst of the street of it, and on either side of the river, was there the tree of life, which bare twelve manner of fruits, and yielded her fruit every month: and the leaves of the tree were for the healing of the nations.

Revelation 22:1,2

ONION TOMATO CASSEROLE

4 c. thinly sliced onion
4 medium-size ripe tomatoes,
    peeled and sliced
1 tsp. salt
1/4 tsp. pepper

1/2 tsp. basil
6 slices American cheese
1/2 c. seasoned bread crumbs
3 T. melted butter

In 1-inch boiling water, in medium saucepan, cook onions, covered, 10 minutes; drain. In a buttered 1 1/2-qt. casserole, layer in order, half of tomatoes and onions; sprinkle with half of salt, pepper and basil; top with half of cheese. Repeat. Toss bread crumbs with butter; sprinkle over top of casserole. Bake at 350°, uncovered, 30 to 35 minute.

ONION POTATO BASKETS

3 baking potatoes
3 T. olive oil, divided
1/2 tsp. salt
1/4 tsp. pepper
2 c. diced onions

1/2 c. light cream
1/2 c. shredded Swiss cheese
1 egg, lightly beaten
2 T. chopped parsley

Coarsely shred peeled potatoes. Stir in 2 T. oil, salt and pepper, tossing to coat well. Place 1 1/2 T. potato mixture into each of 12 greased muffin pan cups, pressing into tin to create a crust. Bake at 425° for 22 to 25 minutes or until golden brown. Meanwhile, in large skillet, sauté onion in remaining oil until tender, about 5 to 6 minutes. Add cream; cook 2 to 3 minutes more or until slightly thickened. Remove from heat; cool slightly. Stir in cheese, egg and parsley. Spoon about 1 T. onion mixture into each potato cup. Reduce oven to 400°; bake 10 to 12 minutes more or until center is set. Serve warm.

And I looked, and behold a white cloud, and upon the cloud one sat like unto the Son of man, having on his head a golden crown, and in his hand a sharp sickle. And another angel came out of the temple, crying with a loud voice to him that sat on the cloud, Thrust in thy sickle, and reap: for the time is come for thee to reap; for the harvest of the earth is ripe. And he that sat on the cloud thrust in his sickle on the earth; and the earth was reaped.

Revelation 14:14-16

ONION PIE

1 1/2 c. flour
1/2 tsp. salt
1 1/2 tsp. caraway seed (optional)
1/2 c. shortening
2-3 T. cold water
3 c. thinly sliced onion

3 T. butter
2 eggs
1/2 c. milk
1`1/2 c. sour cream, divided
3 T. flour

Make dough by mixing flour, salt and caraway seed. Cut in shortening and add enough water to make dough soft but not sticky. Roll out on a floured surface and put in a 10-inch pie pan. Bake at 450°, 12 to 15 minutes. Meanwhile, sauté onions in butter until light brown. Spoon into baked pie shell. Beat eggs well and add milk, 1 1/4 c. sour cream and salt. Blend flour with remaining 1/4 c. of sour cream. Mix into the egg mixture and pour over onions in pie shell. Bake at 325° for 30 minutes or until firm in center. Garnish with crisp bacon if desired.

EASY ONION AND CHEESE QUICHE

26 soda crackers
1/4 c. melted butter
6 slices bacon
1 c. chopped onion

2 c. shredded Swiss cheese
2 eggs, slightly beaten
3/4 c. sour cream

Combine crackers and butter and press into the bottom and sides of a 9-inch pie plate. Cook bacon until crisp. Drain and crumble. Save 2 T. drippings to cook onion in. Cook onion until tender, about 10 minutes. Combine rest of ingredients with onion and pour into shell. Bake at 375° for 35-40 minutes or until knife inserted in center comes out clean. Let set for 10 minutes before cutting.

ONION CARROT PEPPER SCRAPPLE

3 1/2 c. boiling water
1 1/4 c. yellow corn meal
1 tsp. salt
1/8 tsp. pepper
1/2 c. finely chopped onion

1/3 c. finely chopped carrot
1/4 c. finely chopped pepper
1 c. chopped peanuts
2 T. butter

Place boiling water in the top of a double boiler. Slowly add corn meal, salt and pepper, stirring constantly until thickened. Add the chopped vegetables. Place top of double boiler over simmering water and cook 1 hour. Stir in peanuts and pour into a 9 1/2 x 5 1/2 loaf pan, spreading to the edges. Chill 3 1/2 to 4 hours. Cut into 1-inch slices. Heat butter in a skillet and brown scrapple slices on both sides. Serve warm.

BREAKFAST BURRITOS WITH ONIONS

1 lb. bulk sausage
1 onion, chopped
1/2 green pepper chopped
4 oz. can mushroom pieces,
    drained

8 7-inch flour tortillas
6 eggs, beaten
1 c. shredded Cheddar cheese

Brown sausage. Drain; saving 2 T. drippings. Add onion, pepper and mushrooms; sauté about 5 minutes. Meanwhile, scramble the eggs in another skillet. Divide sausage evenly on the tortillas; cover with evenly divided eggs and cheese. Fold up the bottom of the tortilla and roll up. Serve with salsa if desired.

LIVER AND ONIONS

2 T. butter
1 T. oil
3 large onions, sliced thin
1 1/2 lb. beef liver

flour
1/2 tsp. salt or to taste
1/4 tsp. pepper
2-3 T. butter

Heat oil and butter and cook onions slowly for 20 minutes, stirring occasionally. While onions cook, cut the liver into 12 even slices. Dust liver with flour and sprinkle with salt and pepper. Melt butter in a skillet and brown liver on both sides over medium-high heat, just until liver loses its pink color. Add more butter if needed. To serve, place onions on a platter and top with liver slices.

FRIED CHICKEN AND ONIONS

1 frying chicken, cut up
1 tsp. salt
1/8 tsp. pepper

2 large onions, sliced
1/2 c. water

Put chicken, skin side down, in a single layer in a large skillet. Sprinkle with salt and pepper; place onion slices on top. Cover tightly. Cook over low heat 30 minutes then tilt lid so liquid will evaporate. Cook another 20 minutes then remove chicken. Add water to onions; stir and mix in browned bits from the pan. When liquid evaporates, spoon onions over chicken and serve.

144

BAKED FISH AND ONIONS

2 T. oil
2 T. butter
6 c. sliced onions
1/4 c. flour
2 c. milk
1 c. light cream
1/2 tsp. salt or to taste

1/4 tsp. pepper
1 c. grated Swiss and Parmesan
   cheese
1 1/2-2 lb. cod fillets
2 T. butter
1/2 c. bread crumbs

Heat oil and butter and sauté onions 20 minutes, stirring frequently. Stir in flour; gradually add milk and cream, stirring constantly. Bring to a boil; reduce heat and simmer 15 minutes. Season with salt and pepper. Spread 1/3 of the onion sauce in a casserole, top with 1/3 of the cheese. Cover with cod fillets then sprinkle 1/3 of the cheese on top. Pour on remaining onion sauce and top with remaining cheese. Sauté bread crumbs in butter and sprinkle on the casserole. Bake at 400° for 20 minutes or until casserole is bubbly.

PORK CHOPS AND ONIONS

6 large pork chops
2 T. vegetable oil
2 1/2 c. sliced onions
1 tsp. seasoned salt

1/2 tsp. sage
1/2 c. water
1 bouillon cube, dissolved in 1 c.
   hot water

Cut fat from chops and brown in oil. Remove. Add onions and seasonings to skillet. Stir in 1/2 c. water; cover and steam-fry until water evaporates. Place chops in shallow baking dish. Top with onions. Dissolve bouillon cube in 1 c. water and pour over onions. Cover and bake at 350° for 1-1 1/2 hours.

And another angel came out of the temple which is in heaven, he also having a sharp sickle. And another angel came out from the altar, which had power over fire; and cried with a loud cry to him that had the sharp sickle, saying, Thrust in thy sharp sickle, and gather the clusters of the vine of the earth; for her grapes are fully ripe.

Revelation 14:17,18

145

LEEKS WITH WILD RICE CORN AND SAUSAGE

1 1/4 c. wild rice
2 T. butter
6 oz. smoked sausage, cut into
    1/4-inch cubes
1 1/4 c. chopped leeks, white parts
    only
3/4 c. diced (1/4-inch) carrots

2 c. fresh corn kernels
1 c. long grain white rice
4 tsp. dried thyme
1/8 tsp. cayenne pepper
4 1/2 c. chicken stock, plus more
    if needed

Cover wild rice in lightly salted, boiling water. Cook 8 minutes. Remove from heat. Drain and reserve. Heat butter in large, deep-sided pan over medium heat until hot. Add sausage, leeks, carrots and corn and cook, stirring constantly, 5 minutes. Add wild and white rices, thyme, cayenne and stock and bring mixture to simmer. Reduce heat to low and simmer, covered, until all liquid has been absorbed, 25-30 minutes. Taste rice and if not quite tender enough, add 1/2 c. extra stock and cook, covered, about 5 minutes more until liquid is absorbed. Remove from heat. Stir in salt to taste. (Rice can be prepared 1 day ahead. Reheat, covered, in 350° oven until hot, 15-20 minutes.)

ONION FAMILY – BISCUITS AND MUFFINS

GREEN ONION BISCUITS

1 T. butter
1 c. sliced green onions
2 c. flour
4 tsp. baking powder
2 tsp. sugar

1/2 tsp. onion salt
1/2 tsp. cream of tarter
1/2 c. shortening
2/3 c. milk

Melt butter. Add onions; cook until barely tender. Mix together dry ingredients. Cut in shortening until mixture forms coarse crumbs. Add onions and milk. Mix quickly with a fork, just until dough leaves the side of the bowl. Knead dough 10 strokes on a lightly floured surface. Roll dough 3/4-inch thick and cut with a 2-inch biscuit cutter. Place on an ungreased cookie sheet. Bake at 450° approximately 12 minutes.

ONION MUFFINS

1 1/2 c. flour	1 egg
1 tsp. sugar	1 c. buttermilk
1 1/2 tsp. baking powder	2 T. butter, melted
1/2 tsp. soda	1/4 c. grated onion
1/2 tsp. salt	1 T. melted butter
1/2 tsp. dried dill	1 T. poppy seeds

Mix together flour, sugar, baking powder, soda, salt and dill. Whisk egg with buttermilk, 2 T. butter and grated onion. Blend with dry ingredients, stirring just until moistened. Spoon into greased muffin tins. Brush top with 1 T. melted butter and sprinkle with poppy seeds. Bake until golden at 400° for 15-20 minutes. Makes 10 muffins.

ONION FAMILY – CANNING AND FREEZING

HOW TO CAN ONIONS[1]

Hot Pack: Sort for uniform size, about 1-inch in diameter. Peel; wash. Cover with boiling water and cook gently 5 minutes. Drain, saving cooking water for processing. Fit onions closely in jar, leaving 1-inch headspace. Add 1 tsp. salt for quarts or 1/2 tsp. salt for pints. Fill with boiling water or cooking liquid, leaving 1-inch headspace.

Process in a pressure canner; pints 25 minutes and quarts 30 minutes. Process at 10 lb. of pressure if you live up to 1000 feet above sea level. Process at 15 lb. if you live above 1000 feet above sea level. Dial gauges should be at 11 lb. of pressure up to 2000 feet above sea level.

And the angel thrust in his sickle into the earth, and gathered the vine of the earth, and cast it into the great winepress of the wrath of God. And the winepress was trodden without the city, and blood came out of the winepress, even unto the horse bridles, by the space of a thousand and six hundred furlongs.

Revelation 14:19,20

PICKLED ONIONS

4 qt. tiny pickling onions, peeled
1 c. salt
1 gal. water
8 c. vinegar

2 c. water
1 c. sugar
3-4 cloves garlic, crushed
2 T. mixed pickling spice

To peel onions cover with boiling water; let stand 2 minutes. Drain; cool and peel. Combine 1 gal. cold water and 1 c. salt; pour over onions. Let stand 12-18 hours or overnight. Drain and rinse thoroughly. Drain again. While onions are draining, prepare pickling solution by combining vinegar, water, sugar, crushed garlic and mixed pickling spice. Simmer 15 minutes. Pack onions into pint jars. Pour boiling hot pickling solution over onions in the jars, leaving 1/2-inch headspace. Cover and process in boiling water for 10 minutes. Makes 8 pints.

ONION SALSA

5 c. peeled, cored and chopped
    tomatoes (about 3 lb.)
5 c. chopped onions
    (about 1 1/2 lb.)
1 medium seeded and chopped red
    pepper
1 medium seeded and chopped
    yellow pepper

2 seeded and chopped jalapeno
    peppers
2 T. minced cilantro
2 cloves garlic, minced
1 tsp. salt
3/4 c. vinegar
2 drops hot pepper sauce

Combine all ingredients in a large kettle. Bring mixture to a boil; reduce heat and simmer 10 minutes. Carefully ladle hot salsa in hot jars, leaving 1/2-inch headspace. Wipe rim and threads of jar with a clean damp cloth. Place lid on jar and adjust. Process 15 minutes in a boiling water canner. Makes about 3 pints.

I am the good shepherd, and know my sheep, and am known of mine.

John 10:14

148

CANNED SLOPPY JOE WITH ONION

4 lb. lean ground beef	2 c. water
3 c. onion, chopped	1 T. salt
1 1/2 c. green pepper, chopped	1 T. sugar
1 16 oz. can tomato sauce	1 T. prepared mustard
2 c. tomato ketchup	3/4 tsp. black pepper

Sauté beef and onions. Pour off excess fat. Add remaining ingredients, bring to a boil and simmer 5 minutes. Pack into jars, leaving 1-inch headspace. Adjust lids. Process in a pressure canner 75 minutes for pints; 90 minutes for quarts. Process at 10 lb. of pressure for elevations below 1000 ft. above sea level and 15 lb. for elevations above 1000 ft.

HOW TO FREEZE ONIONS[2]

Peel, wash, chop or slice onions. Wrap in aluminum foil or other wrap in amounts used most, e.g. 1/4 or 1/2 c. Place these small packages in another container. Freeze. No blanching is necessary. After 3 to 6 months in 0 degrees F. storage, they tend to loose their flavor.

So also is the resurrection of the dead. It is sown in corruption; it is raised in incorruption: It is sown in dishonour; it is raised in glory: it is sown in weakness; it is raised in power. It is sown a natural body; it is raised a spiritual body. There is a natural body, and there is a spiritual body.

I Corinthians 15:42-46

NOTES

Parsnips

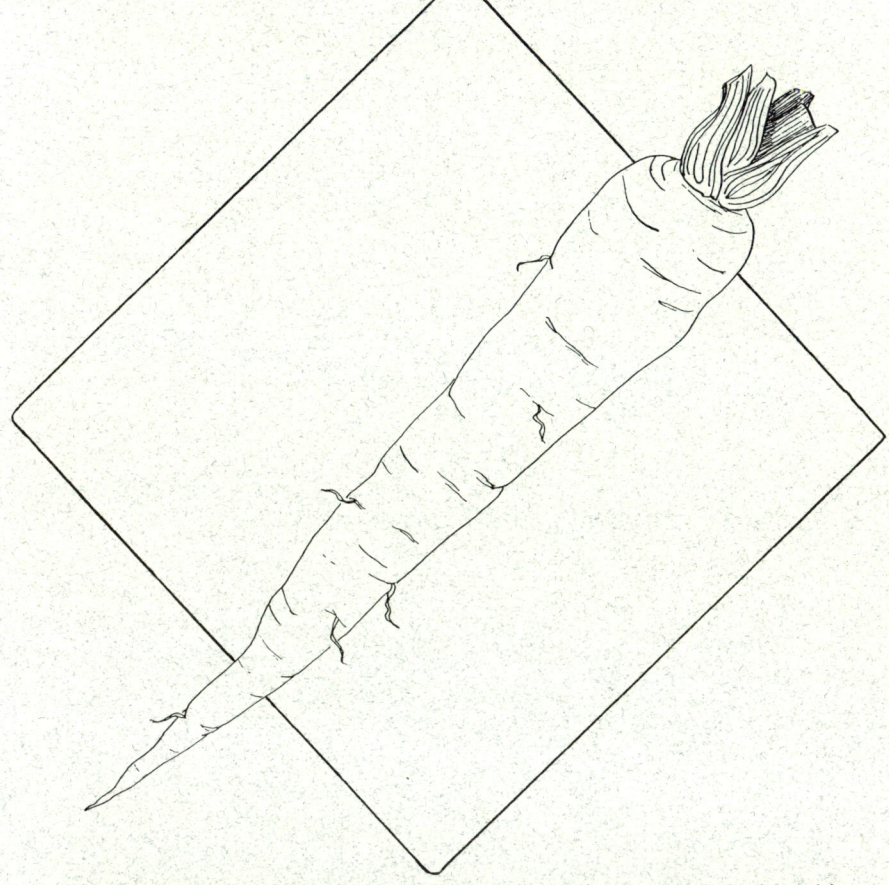

Parsnips, a long season crop, reward the patient gardener with white roots 12-18 inches long, packed with a surprisingly sweet, nutty flavor that is perfected by a hard frost.

Like carrots, parsnips require loose soil that is deeply tilled. Heavy, clayey soils result in malformed, fibrous roots.

If your soil is too tight and poorly drained, try planting your parsnips on a ridge. Make the ridge by piling loose topsoil onto the row until you have a ridge 12-15 inches high. Flatten the top of the ridge with a hoe or shovel and plant your sees on top of the hill. This gives the roots plenty of loose soil to burrow into.

Plant seeds as soon as your soil can be worked in the spring. Sow ¼ to ½-inch deep one inch apart, thinning to a final spacing of 4-5 inches. To keep the soil from drying out before germination, place a board or burlap over the row until the seeds start coming up (may take 3 weeks).

Parsnips are best harvested in the fall after a hard frost. They can be kept for most of the winter by layering in sand and storing in a cool cellar. Or mulch heavily and dig them throughout the winter.

Parsnips substitute well for carrots in recipes. Add parsnips to soups, stews pot roasts and salads. Or enjoy them alone as a cooked vegetable. Peel, slice or chunk parsnips according to recipe directions. Sometimes in larger, or stored parsnips, the center core is tough and needs to be removed.

Parsnips are low in calories and high in fiber and carbohydrates. They contain some vitamin C, folate and potassium.

Yield: 1 lb. fresh parsnip = 3 cups sliced or diced

PARSNIP CHOWDER

4 slices bacon	1 c. milk
1 small onion, chopped	1 c. cream
3 c. diced parsnips	pepper
2 c. diced potatoes	2 T. butter
1 tsp. salt	

Brown bacon. Remove from kettle and cook onion in the drippings about 5 minutes. Add parsnips, potatoes, salt and just enough water to cover. Bring to a boil then reduce heat and simmer 15-20 minutes or until vegetables are tender. Add milk, cream and pepper and heat through. Stir in butter. Garnish with bacon.

PARSNIPS – SIDE AND MAIN DISHES

HOW TO COOK PARSNIPS

Bring 1-inch of water to a boil in a large skillet. Add whole, peeled parsnips and salt to taste. Return water to a boil. Reduce heat and simmer 20-30 minutes. Cook chunked parsnips 15-20 minutes. Cook sliced parsnips 8-15 minutes. Add butter or browned butter.

SAUTÉED PARSNIPS

4 c. thinly sliced parsnips	1/2 tsp. salt or to taste
2 T. butter	pepper

Sauté parsnips in butter until tender crisp, 5-8 minutes. Add salt and pepper to taste.

HERBED PARSNIPS

1/4 c. butter	12 medium, hot, cooked parsnips
1/8 tsp. thyme	salt and pepper to taste
1/8 tsp. marjoram	1/4 c. minced parsley

Melt butter in saucepan; add thyme, marjoram and parsnips and cook until parsnips are lightly browned. Add salt and pepper to taste. Serve sprinkled with parsley.

GLAZED PARSNIPS

6 medium parsnips
1/3 c. brown sugar
1/4 tsp. ground cloves

3 T. orange juice
3 T. butter

Scrape parsnips and cut into chunks. Cook in salt water for 8 minutes. Drain and place in a shallow baking dish. Combine sugar and cloves and sprinkle over parsnips. Drizzle juice over sugar and dot with butter. Bake at 400° for 15 minutes, basting occasionally.

SWEET SOUR PARSNIPS

8 medium parsnips, peeled and
    sliced
3 T. sugar
3 T. vinegar
2 T. butter
1/2 tsp. salt

1/2 tsp. cinnamon
1/4 tsp. nutmeg
1/4 tsp. cloves
1 tsp. cornstarch
1/4 c. water

Cook parsnips 10-15 minutes or until tender crisp. Drain and remove. In same saucepan add all but cornstarch and water. Cook over medium heat, stirring constantly until mixture boils. Combine cornstarch and water. Stir into saucepan until mixture boils and thickens. Reduce heat and stir in parsnips. Heat through.

PARSNIP STIR FRY

2 T. vegetable oil
6 c. grated parsnips
1/2 c. chopped green onions

1/4 tsp. thyme or ground ginger
2 T. soy sauce (optional)

Heat oil in a large skillet. Add parsnips, onions and spice. Stir fry 4-5 minutes.

PARSNIP FRITTERS

3 c. cooked parsnips
2 eggs, beaten
1 c. milk
1 T. flour

1 T. sugar
1/2 tsp. salt
3 T. butter

Mash parsnips. Mix in everything but butter. Heat butter in a skillet and drop parsnip mixture into the skillet by spoonfuls. Brown on both sides.

PARSNIP LOAF

3 c. cooked, mashed parsnips
4 eggs, slightly beaten
1 c. milk
1 c. cream
1 c. dried bread crumbs

1/4 c. chopped onion
1 T. dried celery leaves
1 1/4 tsp. salt
1/4 tsp. pepper

Combine all ingredients, mixing well. Pour into a buttered casserole. Bake at 350° for 45 minutes or until golden brown.

PARSNIPS WITH ACORN SQUASH

1 1/2 lb. parsnips
2 small acorn squash

1 1/4 c. maple syrup
2 T. butter

Peel parsnips. Quarter lengthwise then cut into 3-inch pieces. Cut squash in half. Scoop out center and cut, unpeeled, into 1/2-inch strips. Place parsnips and squash in a large skillet. Cover and cook 10 minutes. Drain. Heat maple syrup in the same skillet. Add butter and stir until melted. Return parsnips and squash to skillet. Cook over medium heat about 15 minutes, basting frequently. Arrange squash around the outside of a serving dish. Spoon parsnips in the center. Drizzle syrup over all.

PARSNIPS IN STEW

2 lb. beef, cubed
1 c. water
2 beef bouillon cubes
1 clove garlic, minced
1 bay leaf
6 medium parsnips

6 medium carrots
12 small white onions
1 1/2 tsp. salt
1/4 tsp. pepper
2 T. flour

Brown beef on all sides in a large kettle. Add water, bouillon, garlic and bay leaf. Cover and simmer 1 1/2 hours. Meanwhile, peel and chunk parsnips and carrots; peel onions. Add to meat, baste with pan liquid, sprinkle with salt and pepper. Cover and simmer 45 minutes or until vegetables are tender. Mix flour with water and stir into stew to thicken. Boil one minute.

PARSNIPS – BAKED GOODS AND DESSERTS

PARSNIP CAKE

4 eggs
1 1/4 c. sugar
1 1/4 c. vegetable oil
2 c. flour
2 tsp. cinnamon

2 tsp. baking powder
1 tsp. baking soda
3 c. peeled, grated parsnips
1 c. chopped nuts

Beat together eggs, sugar and oil. Mix in dry ingredients. Fold in parsnips and nuts. Pour into a 10-inch tube pan or 13 x 9 cake pan. Bake at 350° for 50-60 minutes.

PARSNIP NUT BREAD

1 1/2 c. flour
1 c. whole wheat flour
1/2 c. brown sugar
2 1/2 tsp. baking powder
1 tsp. baking soda
1/2 tsp. salt

2 eggs
1 c. warm water
2 T. vegetable oil
1 c. peeled grated parsnips
1/2 c. chopped pecans

Combine dry ingredients. Beat together eggs, water and oil. Combine with dry ingredients. Fold in parsnips and nuts. Pour batter into a buttered 8 x 4 loaf pan. Bake at 375° for 1 hour.

BLENDER PARSNIP PIE

1 c. light cream
3/4 c. sugar
2 c. peeled, chunked parsnips,
　　　cooked
1 T. flour
1 tsp. vanilla

1/2 tsp. salt
1/2 tsp. cinnamon
1/2 tsp. nutmeg
1/4 tsp. cloves
2 eggs
1 unbaked 9-inch pie shell

Put ingredients into the blender in order given. Beat until smooth then pour into the unbaked pie shell. Bake at 350° for 45 minutes or until done.

HOW TO FREEZE PARSNIPS[2]

Remove tops, wash, peel, slice or dice (1/2-inch pieces). Blanch for 2 minutes. [Cool immediately in cold water; drain and freeze.]

He spake also this parable; A certain man had a fig tree planted in his vineyard; and he came and sought fruit thereon, and found none. Then said he unto the dresser of his vineyard, Behold, these three years I come seeking fruit on this fig tree, and find none: cut it down; why cumbereth it the ground? And he answering said unto him, Lord, let it alone this year also, till I shall dig about it, and dung it: and if it bear fruit, well: and if not, then after that thou shalt cut it down.

Luke 13:6-9

NOTES

Peas

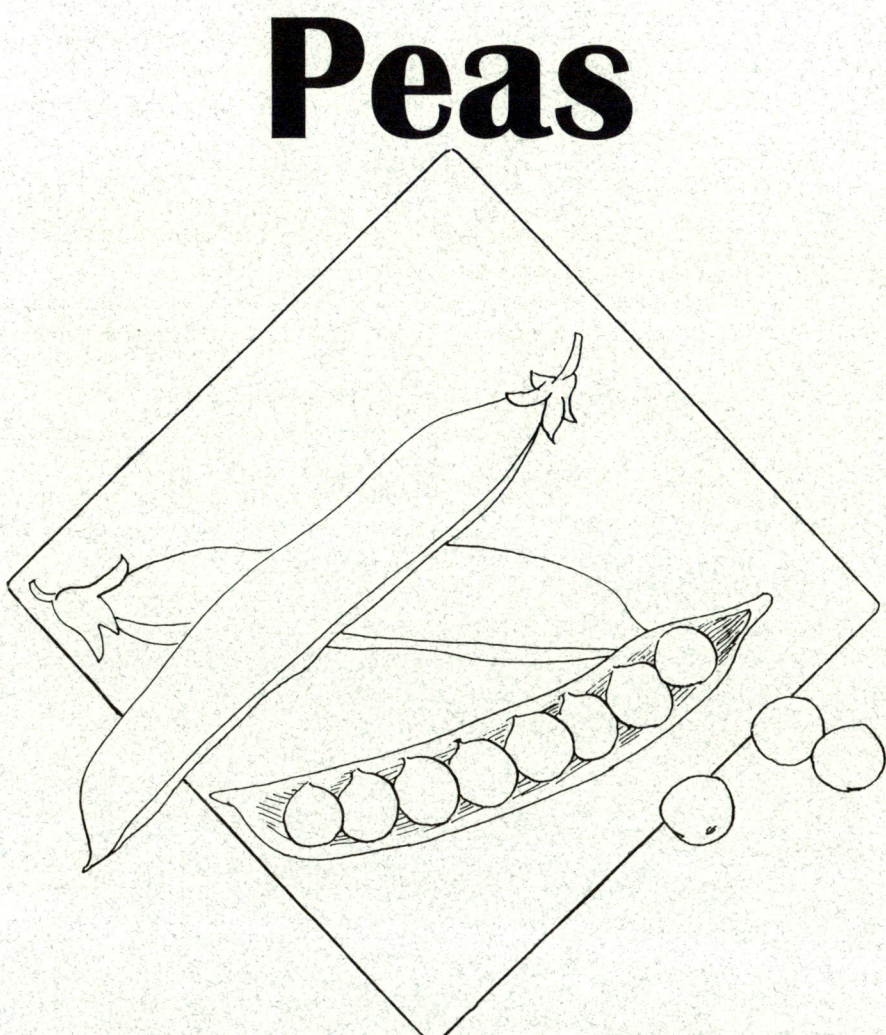

Peas are a cool weather crop that can be grown in most regions of the country.

There are three main types of garden peas—shell peas that need to be shelled before using, snow peas that are picked when pods are thin and peas just starting to develop and sugar snap peas, an edible pod pea that is picked when the pods are well-filled like shell peas.

Don't confuse blackeyed peas, which are actually beans, with garden peas.

Peas do not tolerate hot weather so plant them early in the spring as soon as your soil can be worked. Sow ½ -1 inch deep about 1 inch apart in rows 2-3 feet apart.

Tall varieties do best with a fence or trellis to grow on. Chicken wire stretched between steel posts set 6-8 feet apart works fine. Plants with short growing habits benefit from staking too, but it's not as critical. Peas are easier to pick and they don't rot as fast if given something to climb on.

Peas mature over a 2-3 week period and are best if picked every 3-4 days to keep them from over ripening. Shell peas and sugar snap peas should fill the pod well, but shouldn't be cracked or squarish. Over mature, their sugars convert to starch, making them tougher and less tasty.

Sugar turns to starch in peas that are picked and left at room temperature, too. They're best picked in the early morning and used or frozen as soon as possible.

Pick snow peas when the pods are thin and peas very small.

Shell peas need to be shelled before eating. Use them raw as a snack or boil or steam for a cooked vegetable.

Sugar snap peas can be used in the shell, however, they do need to be destringed. Just pull the stem down one side and the tail down the other side. Eat them raw with dips or as a cooked vegetable.

Snow peas are delicious in stir-fries or as a cooked vegetable. They may or may not have strings that need to be pulled.

Peas are rich in vitamins A and C, thiamine, riboflavin and potassium.

Keep unshelled, unwashed peas for 4-5 days in the refrigerator.

Yield: 1 lb. unshelled peas = 4-5 cups unshelled = 1 ¼ cups shelled
1 bushel = 30 lb. = 12-15 pints

PEAS – SOUPS

RICE AND PEA SOUP

5 c. chicken broth
3/4 c. long grain white rice
1/4 c. butter
1/4 c. finely chopped onion

2 c. peas
1/2 tsp. salt or to taste
1/8 tsp. pepper

Bring broth to a boil. Add rice, cover and simmer approximately 20 minutes. Meanwhile heat butter and sauté onion until light brown. Add peas, salt and pepper; cook 3-5 minutes more. Add pea mixture to cooked rice.

CREAM OF PEA SOUP

2 T. butter
1 onion, minced
1 tsp. chopped celery leaves
2 T. flour

2 c. milk (or use some vegetable
     water)
2 c. cooked peas
1/2 tsp. salt
1/8 tsp. pepper

Melt butter; add onion and celery. Sauté for 10 minutes. Blend in flour and when well mixed add liquid slowly, stirring constantly. Put peas in the blender. Add to white sauce; season, mix well and heat through.

PEAS – APPETIZERS

FILLED SNOW PEAS

48 snow peas
2 1/2 c. finely chopped cooked
     shrimp or chicken
1 c. finely chopped celery
1/2 c. mayonnaise
1/4 c. finely chopped onion

1/4 c. finely chopped parsley
1 T. lemon juice
3/4 tsp. salt
1/2 tsp. sugar
1/8 tsp. pepper

Bring 1 1/2 quarts water to a boil and add peas. Blanch 1 minute. Immediately put into cold water then string and split open peas. Pat dry. Stir together shrimp or chicken and remaining ingredients. Fill each pea with mixture. Cover and refrigerate until ready to serve. Makes 48 appetizers.

NEW POTATO SALAD WITH PEAS

1 lb. tiny new potatoes, quartered
2 c. bias sliced pea pods
1/4 c. sour cream
1/4 c. mayonnaise or salad
    dressing

1 tsp. dried dill weed
1 T. snipped chives
salt
bibb or romaine lettuce

Cook potatoes, covered, in a small amount of boiling water for 8 minutes. Add peas to saucepan with potatoes. Cover and cook 2 to 4 minutes. Drain thoroughly; cool. Stir together sour cream, mayonnaise, dill, chives and salt. Cover; chill. Line salad plates with lettuce. Mound potato mixture in center. Drizzle dressing over each.

CREAMY PEA POTATO SALAD

12-16 tiny new potatoes
2 c. shelled fresh peas
1/2 c. mayonnaise or salad
    dressing
1/2 c. sour cream
1 T. prepared mustard

1/2 tsp. salt
1/2 c. finely chopped onion
1/2 c. sliced radishes
1/2 c. shredded Swiss cheese
    (optional)

Scrub potatoes; cook, covered in boiling salted water for 10 to 15 minutes or until tender; drain. Cool; quarter. Cook peas, covered, in small amount of boiling water 5 to 10 minutes. Drain; cool. Combine mayonnaise, sour cream, mustard and salt. In a bowl, combine potatoes, peas and onion. Add dressing. Toss lightly to coat mixture. Cover; chill thoroughly. Just before serving, add radishes and mix gently. Sprinkle cheese over top, if desired.

Build ye houses, and dwell in them; and plant gardens, and eat the fruit of them.
Jeremiah 29:5

RAW PEA SALAD

2 c. shelled peas
2 c. chopped cauliflower
1 1/2 c. diced celery
1/2 c. chopped green onion
1/2 lb. bacon, fried and crumbled
1 c. mayonnaise or salad dressing

1/2 c. sour cream (optional)
1/4 c. sugar
1 T. vinegar
1/2 tsp. seasoned salt
2 T. cream (optional)

Combine peas, cauliflower, celery, onion and bacon in a salad bowl. Mix remaining ingredients together and toss with salad. Chill before serving.
Variation: Add diced cheddar cheese, salted nuts or sunflower seeds.

PEAS – SIDE AND MAIN DISHES

HOW TO COOK PEAS

Bring 1-inch of water to a boil. Add 4 c. shelled peas and 1 tsp. salt. Return to a boil; reduce heat and simmer for 5 minutes. Serve buttered or plain.

PEAS WITH MUSHROOMS AND ONIONS

4 oz. can mushrooms, drained
1/4 c. chopped onion
2 T. butter

2 c. peas, cooked and drained
1/2 tsp. salt
1/8 tsp. pepper

Sauté mushrooms and onion in butter until tender. Add remaining ingredients and serve immediately.

PEAS ALMONDINE

4 c. peas
2/3 c. chopped bacon
1/4 c. minced onion

1/3 c. slivered almonds
1/2 tsp. salt or to taste
1/2 c. whipping cream

Cook peas in salted water. Cook onion and bacon in skillet until lightly browned. Drain. Add peas, almonds and salt and cook until heated through. Stir in cream and heat.

CREAMED PEAS

4 c. shelled peas
1/4 c. butter
1/4 c. flour
1/2 c. cooking water

1/2 c. light cream or milk
1 tsp. sugar
1/8 tsp. pepper

Cook peas in salted water. Melt butter in a skillet and add flour. Gradually stir in cooking water and cream. Cook until thickened, stirring constantly. Add sugar and pepper. Gently stir in peas.

CREAMED POTATOES WITH PEAS

1 lb. small, early red potatoes
2 T. butter
1/4 c. chopped onion
2 T. flour
1 1/4 tsp. salt

1/2 tsp. dill weed
1/8 tsp. pepper
1 1/2 c. milk
1 1/2 c. peas, cooked

Cook unpeeled potatoes in boiling water until tender, 20 to 25 minutes. Drain and cool enough to handle; peel if desired. Set aside. In same saucepan, combine butter and onion. Cook until onion is tender. Blend in flour, salt, dill and pepper. Stir in milk, mixing well. Cook until mixture boils, stirring constantly. Boil 1 minute. Add potatoes and peas. Heat through.
Variation: When early potatoes are not available, use 4 medium potatoes. Cook and cut into pieces before adding to sauce.

SAUTÉED SUGAR SNAP AND SNOW PEAS

1/4 c. butter

1 lb. sugar snap or snow peas

Heat butter in a large skillet. Add peas and cook 2 to 3 minutes, stirring often.

SNOW PEAS WITH PINEAPPLE

1/2 lb. snow peas
1 c. water
1/2 tsp. salt

8 oz. can pineapple chunks,
    drained
2 T. butter

Remove tips and strings from peas. Bring water and salt to a boil. Add peas and cook 2-3 minutes. Cook pineapple in butter until hot. Add drained pea pods; toss and heat through.

SNAP PEA STIR FRY

3 c. snap peas

2 T. broth or water

2 T. cornstarch

2 tsp. soy sauce

2 T. vegetable oil

1 tsp. sugar

6 T. broth or water

Prepare peas by removing strings. Combine 2 T. broth with cornstarch and soy sauce. Set aside. Heat oil and add peas Stir until peas are all coated with oil then add sugar and remaining water. Cover and cook 3 minutes. Add cornstarch mixture while stirring. Stir until thickened.

Variation: Add 1/4 c. chopped green onion with snap peas

SNOW PEA AND PORK STIR FRY

1/2 lb. boneless pork

2 tsp. cornstarch

2 T. soy sauce, divided

4 T. vegetable oil, divided

3 c. snow peas

1/2 tsp. salt

1/2 tsp. sugar

1/4 c. broth or water

Cut pork into short, 1/4-inch thick strips. Combine cornstarch and 1 T. soy sauce. Stir in pork strips. Marinate 20-30 minutes. Heat 2 T. oil in a large skillet and add peas. Stir fry for 2 minutes then remove from the skillet. Heat remaining oil and stir fry pork until lightly browned. Add broth and cover for 2 minutes. Add peas, remaining soy sauce and sugar. Stir until heated through.

FRIED RICE WITH PEAS

1/4 c. butter

1/3 c. chopped onion

2 c. shelled peas or chopped snow
  peas

2 1/2 c. cooked rice

1 T. soy sauce

1/8 tsp. pepper

2 eggs, well beaten

Heat butter and sauté onions 1 minute. Add peas and stir fry 3 minutes. Add rice, soy sauce and pepper. Stir fry until hot. Add eggs stirring constantly until eggs cook.

Variation: Add diced cooked chicken or mushrooms with the onions.

PEAS WITH NOODLES AND HAM

1 lb. fettucini or egg noodles	1 c. grated Parmesan cheese
2 c. thin ham strips	1/2 c. whipping cream
1 T. butter	salt and pepper to taste
2 c. shelled peas	

Cook noodles in boiling salted water until barely tender. Sauté ham in butter until slightly browned. Meanwhile cook peas 4-5 minutes; drain. Toss together drained noodles, peas and ham. Add the cheese and cream. Season to taste and serve.
Variation: Sauté 2 c. sliced mushrooms along with ham.

CHICKEN CASSEROLE WITH PEAS

3 T. margarine	2 c. chopped, cooked chicken
1/4 c. chopped onion	1 1/2 c. chicken broth
1 T. flour	1 can cream of chicken soup
1 bouillon cube	2 c. peas
1 tsp. salt	2 c. diced potatoes
1/4 tsp. pepper	1 c. diced carrots

Melt margarine and sauté onions several minutes. Add flour, seasoning and chicken. Sauté until chicken is slightly browned. Add broth and soup. Stir until smooth. Add vegetables. Bake in a covered casserole at 350° for 1 hour.

PEAS – CANNING AND FREEZING

HOW TO CAN SHELLED PEAS[1]

Raw Pack: Shell and wash peas. Fill jars loosely to within 1-inch of top. Add 1 tsp. salt for quarts and 1/2 tsp. for pints. Fill with boiling water, leaving 1-inch headspace. (Note: Freeze sugar snap and snow peas for best quality.)

Hot Pack: Shell and wash peas. Cover with boiling water; bring to a boil. Fill jars loosely with hot peas to within 1-inch of top. Add 1 tsp. salt for quarts and 1/2 tsp. salt for pints. Fill jars with boiling cooking liquid, leaving 1-inch headspace.

Process in a pressure canner; pints or quarts for 40 minutes. Process at 10 lb. of pressure at elevations below 1000 feet above sea level. Process at 15 lb. at elevations above 1000 feet above sea level. Dial gauges should be at 11 lb. of pressure up to 2000 feet above sea level.

REFRIGERATOR PICKLED SNOW PEAS

1 lb. snow peas, string removed	1 T. pickling spice
1 1/2 c. vinegar	1/2 tsp. salt
1/2 c. sugar	

Bring 2 quarts of water to a boil. Fill a large bowl with ice water right away, too. Add snow peas to boiling water; blanch 20 seconds. Immediately drain peas and plunge into ice water. Let peas cool about 5 minutes. Drain well. Pack peas into 2 pint jars. Bring vinegar, sugar, pickling spice, salt and 1/3 c. water to a boil. Boil 2 minutes. Pour boiling liquid over peas. Cover jars and refrigerate at least 2 days before using.

HOW TO FREEZE PEAS

Shelled Peas: Shell peas and wash. Blanch 1 1/2 minutes. Cool immediately in cold water, package and freeze.

Snow Peas: Choose tender, young pods. Wash; remove stems and strings. Leave whole. Blanch 1 to 1 1/2 minutes. Cool immediately in cold water, package and freeze.

Sugar Snap Peas: Wash. Remove stems and strings; leave whole. Blanch for 2 minutes. Cool immediately in cold water, package and freeze.

But he answered and said, Every plant, which my heavenly Father hath not planted, shall be rooted up.

Matthew 15:13

NOTES

Peppers

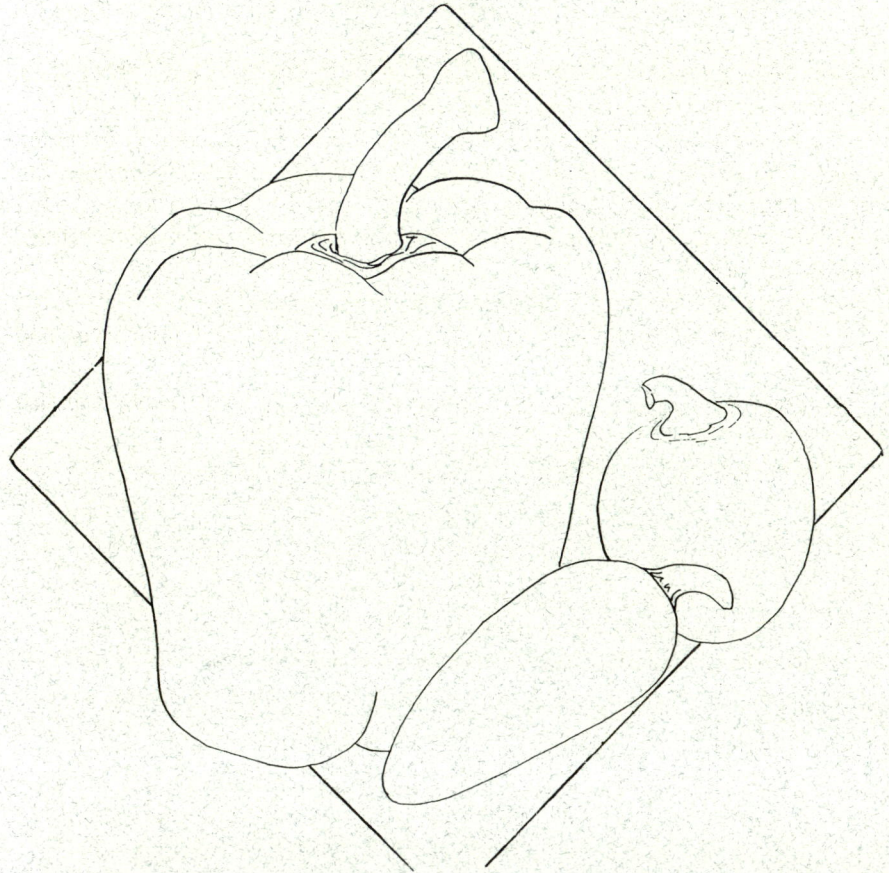

Perhaps more temperamental than most of the garden vegetables in regard to their temperature and nutrient requirements, peppers are still a good choice for the home garden. Their foliage is beautiful, their colors inviting and their flavors appealing.

Peppers come in two classes—sweet and hot. Shapes and sizes vary considerably from round, to bell-shaped, to elongated, to banana shaped. Peppers—sweet and hot—start out some shade of green and ripen to red, yellow, purple or brown. Sweet peppers get sweeter and milder as they ripen, but they're always sweet. I haven't been able to verify this, but my own in-garden tests indicate that hot peppers get hotter as they mature. They are always hot.

Especially in the north, start your peppers with plants instead of direct seeding. Transplants should be started 8-10 weeks before setting out after all danger of frost. Plastic mulch and row covers are helpful in short season areas. Plant 18 inches apart in rows 2-3 feet apart.

Pepper plants may become stunted and refuse to flower if cold stressed. If it's too hot the flowers drop and won't set fruit (nighttime temperatures must be between 60 and 75 degrees for fruit set to occur). If they get too much nitrogen you get beautiful foliage, but no peppers. And sometimes there are no peppers for no apparent reason.

Having said all that, peppers really are not that hard to grow. Most years 4-6 plants will keep a family well supplied.

Pick sweet peppers as soon as they are full size and the skin is thick and firm. For colored peppers just leave them on the plant longer. Hot peppers are harvested at full size—either green or red.

Use peppers raw with dips or in salads; add them to vegetable stir-fries; stuff and bake; chop into relishes, sauces and salsas.

Peppers are low-calorie and high in vitamins A and C.

Be careful when cutting hot peppers. They will burn your eyes and sensitive skin. Wear protective gloves.

Peppers will keep in the refrigerator for at least one week. They can also be dried or frozen.

Yield: 1 lb. fresh peppers = 3 ½ cups diced = 1 ½ pints

PEPPERS – SALADS AND DRESSINGS

COLE SLAW WITH PEPPERS

3 c. shredded cabbage
1 c. chopped green pepper
3/4 c. grated or sliced carrots
1/2 c. chopped onion

2 T. chopped fresh parsley
3/4 c. mayonnaise or salad
    dressing

Mix thoroughly, chill and serve.

GREEN PEPPER DRESSING

1 c. olive or vegetable oil
3 T. vinegar
1 tsp. salt
1 tsp. sugar

1/2 tsp. paprika
1/4 c. chopped green pepper
2 T. chopped onion
1 T. chopped fresh parsley

Thoroughly mix all ingredients. Chill. Shake well just before serving.

PEPPERS – SANDWICHES

PEPPER HAM ONION HOAGIES

1 T. oil
2 green bell peppers, cut into 1/4-
    inch strips
2 medium onions, thinly sliced

2 c. ham, cut into 1/4-inch strips
4 hoagie rolls, split and toasted
8 thin slices mozzarella cheese

Heat oil in a skillet over medium heat. Sauté peppers and onions, stirring often, until softened, 5-7 minutes. Add ham to skillet; stir until ham is hot, 1 minute. Line inside of each hoagie roll with 2 slices cheese; divide ham mixture and spread evenly over cheese. Cut rolls in half and serve.

PEPPERS – SIDE AND MAIN DISHES

ROASTED PEPPERS

Put peppers under the broiler or on a grill and broil 2-3 minutes per side. Rotate until the entire pepper is blistered and slightly charred. Then quickly place in a paper bag for 10-20 minutes. Peel and cut into slices. This recipe can also be used to peel peppers if they have tough skins.

SAUTÉED SWEET PEPPERS

3 large green, red or yellow
    peppers
3 T. butter

1/4 c. chopped onion
salt and pepper to taste

Remove seeds and membranes from peppers. Cut into strips or dice. Heat butter in a large skillet and add peppers and onions. Sauté about 5 minutes—a little longer if the peppers are real thick.
Variations: Add strips of zucchini and serve with rice. Or add chopped mushrooms and add to scrambled eggs or an omelet.

STUFFED PEPPERS

6 medium large sweet peppers

Cut tops off peppers; remove seeds and membranes. Place peppers in enough boiling water to cover. Blanch 3 minutes. If you like crisp peppers, don't blanch at all. Put peppers upright in a baking dish that has 1/4-inch of water in it. Stuff with one of the following stuffings or use leftover casseroles.

STUFFING FOR PEPPERS I

1 lb. ground beef or sausage
1 c. chopped onion
1/2 tsp. salt
1/8 tsp. pepper

1 1/2 c. peeled, seeded and
    chopped tomatoes
1/2 c. water
1/2 c. uncooked rice
1 c. shredded cheese

Brown meat and onions together. Season with salt and pepper. Add tomatoes, water and uncooked rice. Cover and simmer until rice is tender, about 20 minutes. Add more water if needed. Stuff peppers and sprinkle with cheese . Place upright in a baking dish. Bake uncovered at 375° for 20-25 minutes.
Variation: Add 1 or 2 chopped hot peppers and 1 T. chili powder with onions. Delete rice and water and add 2 c. cooked kidney beans.

I am the true vine, and my Father the husbandman. Every branch in me that beareth not fruit he taketh away: and every branch that beareth fruit, he purgeth it, that it may bring forth more fruit.

John 15:1, 2

166

STUFFING FOR PEPPERS II

2 c. diced, cooked ham	1/4 c. minced onion
1 1/2 c. cooked rice	1/2 tsp. salt
1 c. peeled, seeded and chopped	1/4 tsp. pepper
tomatoes	

Combine all ingredients and stuff peppers. Place upright in a baking pan with 1/4-inch of water in it. Sprinkle with cheese if desired. Bake uncovered at 375° for 30 minutes.

STUFFING FOR PEPPERS III

1 c. diced, cooked roast beef	1 c. bread crumbs or cooked rice
(leftovers are fine)	1/4 c. finely chopped onion
1 c. chopped, seeded and peeled	1/2 tsp. salt or to taste
tomatoes	1/8 tsp. pepper

Mix ingredients and stuff peppers. Put in a baking dish with 1/4-inch water. Bake at 375° for 30 minutes.

PEPPERS AND POTATOES

4 medium potatoes, peeled and	1/2 c. chopped onion
cubed	1/4 c. butter
1/2 c. diced green pepper	1/2 tsp. salt
1/2 c. diced red pepper	dash of pepper

Cook potatoes in boiling salt water 15 minutes or until tender. Drain. Sauté peppers and onion in butter until tender crisp. Stir in potatoes; sprinkle with salt and pepper. Cook, stirring carefully, 5 minutes or until potatoes are lightly browned.

PEPPERS AND BROWN RICE

1 c. brown rice	1/2 c. finely chopped red bell
2 1/2 c. water or chicken broth	pepper
1 tsp. butter	1/2 c. finely chopped yellow bell
1 T. soy sauce	pepper
1 T. vegetable oil	1/2 c. finely chopped green onion

Simmer rice, water, butter and soy sauce approximately 35 to 40 minutes or until rice is tender and liquid is absorbed. Sauté peppers and onion in oil until tender. Toss with rice and heat through. Season to taste.
Variation: Use 1 c. long grain white rice and simmer 20 to 30 minutes.

PEPPERS AND ONIONS WITH COD

2 T. olive or vegetable oil	1 tsp. salt
1 green pepper cut into strips	1/2 tsp. oregano
1 red pepper cut into strips	1/8 tsp. pepper
1 onion sliced thin	1 1/2 lb. cod fillets, cut into 6
1 clove garlic, minced	pieces

Heat oil in a large skillet. Sauté peppers, onion and garlic for 4 minutes. Add the seasonings. Push vegetables to the edge of the skillet and add cod fillets. Cover and cook for 3 minutes. Turn the fish, cover and cook 2 to 3 minutes more or until fish is opaque. Spoon the pepper mixture over the fish and serve.

QUICK CHICKEN FAJITAS WITH PEPPERS

1 lb. boneless chicken breast	salt and pepper to taste
1 T. oil	2/3 c. chunky salsa
1 green pepper in 1/4-inch strips	1 1/2 tsp. chili powder
1 medium onion, thinly sliced	8 8-inch flour tortillas

Cut chicken into thin strips. Heat oil in a large skillet. When hot add chicken, pepper and onion. Stir fry 4 minutes or until chicken is lightly browned. Drain. Sprinkle lightly with salt and pepper. Combine salsa and chili powder and add to chicken; cook and stir until thoroughly heated. Warm tortillas. Place about 1/2 c. of the mixture on each tortilla. Fold up bottom; fold in sides and secure with a toothpick, leaving top open. Serve with sour cream if desired.

QUICK PEPPER CHICKEN

1/4 c. vegetable oil	2 large green peppers, sliced in
1 broiler-fryer chicken, cut up	strips
1 tsp. salt, divided	1 large red pepper, sliced in strips
1 tsp. chili powder, divided	2 large onions, sliced in rings

In large heavy kettle over medium-high heat, heat oil. Add chicken and sprinkle with 1/2 tsp. salt and 1/2 tsp. chili powder. Cook until chicken is browned on one side, about 5 minutes. Turn chicken and sprinkle with remaining salt and chili powder; cook about 5 minutes longer or until chicken is browned. Reduce heat to medium-low; cover and continue cooking about 30 minutes longer or until fork can be inserted in chicken with ease. Drain off any accumulated fat and discard. Increase heat to medium-high; add peppers and onions and cook about 5 minutes, stirring often, until onion is tender. To serve, sprinkle chicken lightly with chili powder, if desired.

PEPPER STEAK

2 lb. round or flank steak, 1-inch thick	1 clove garlic, minced
1/4 c. soy sauce	1/2 tsp. ground ginger
1/4 c. water	1/4 tsp. pepper
3 large green peppers	1/2 c. beef bouillon
2 large onions	1 T. cornstarch
1/4 c. vegetable oil	1 tsp. sugar

Freeze steak 1 hour for easier cutting. Cut into 1/8 to 1/4-inch strips. Combine soy sauce and water; stir in meat strips. Set aside. Remove seeds from peppers and slice into thin strips. Slice onions thin. Heat oil. Drain meat, saving liquid. Stir fry meat until lightly brown. (Doing it in two batches works best.) Remove meat from skillet. Stir fry peppers, onions, garlic, ginger and ground pepper for 3 minutes. Return meat to pan. Combine reserved liquid with bouillon, cornstarch and sugar; stir into meat mixture. Bring to a boil, stirring constantly—boil one minute. Serve over hot rice.

BAKED PASTA WITH PEPPERS

1 lb. ground beef	4 T. grated Parmesan cheese, divided
2 c. green, red and yellow bell pepper strips	1 tsp. oregano
1 c. sliced onion	2 c. shredded mozzarella cheese, divided
1 (26 oz.) jar spaghetti sauce (or 3 cups homemade sauce)	3 c. cooked ziti or macaroni

Brown ground beef with peppers and onions until meat is browned and peppers begin to soften; drain. Return pepper mixture to saucepan; stir in spaghetti sauce, 2 T. Parmesan cheese, oregano, 1 cup mozzarella and pasta. Spoon into 13 x 9 baking dish. Sprinkle with remaining mozzarella and Parmesan cheese. Bake uncovered at 375° for 30 minutes or until hot and bubbly.

Herein is my Father glorified, that ye bear much fruit; so shall ye be my disciples.

John 15:8

169

PEPPERS – CANNING AND FREEZING

HOW TO CAN PEPPERS—HOT OR SWEET[1]

Wash and remove stem and seeds of peppers. Wear gloves if working with hot peppers. To peel, heat in 400° F. oven or broiler until skins blister—6 to 8 minutes. Let peppers cool. Cover with a damp cloth. Remove skins with a knife blade. Flatten peppers and pack in layers in jars. Add 1/2 tsp. salt per pint. Add 1 T. vinegar or lemon juice to each pint. Fill jars with boiling water, leaving 1-inch headspace.

Process in a pressure canner for 35 minutes. Use only pint or 1/2 pint jars, quarts are unsafe for peppers. Process at 10 lb. of pressure for elevations up to 1000 feet above sea level; 15 lb. of pressure for elevations over 1000 feet above sea level. Dial gauges should be at 11 lb. of pressure up to 2000 feet above sea level.

PICKLED PEPPERS

4 qt. long red, green or yellow peppers (hot or sweet)	2 1/2 qt. vinegar
1 1/2 c. salt	2 c. water
1 gal. cold water	1/2 c. sugar
	2-3 cloves garlic, crushed

Wash peppers; cut two small slits in each pepper. Wear rubber gloves while handling hot peppers. Dissolve salt in water; pour over peppers and let stand 12 to 18 hours in a cool place. Drain, rinse and drain thoroughly. Pack peppers into hot, pint or half pint jars. Combine remaining ingredients and simmer 15 minutes. Remove garlic and pour boiling hot solution over peppers, leaving 1/2-inch headspace. Cover and process in boiling water canner for 10 minutes. Makes 7 to 8 pt.

SWEET PICKLED PEPPER RINGS

3 lb. ripe peppers	1 3/4 c. cider vinegar
3/4 c. pickling salt	1 3/4 c. sugar
2 T. pickling spice	

Stem and seed peppers; cut into 1/4-inch rings. Put peppers and salt in a large non-aluminum bowl; cover with water. Soak 6 to 8 hours. Tie pickling spices in cheese cloth. Combine vinegar, sugar, spice bag and 3/4 c. plus 2 T. water in a 4 qt. saucepan. Bring to a boil and boil 10 minutes. Drain pepper rings, rinse with cold water and drain again. Add to the syrup and bring to a boil again. Boil steadily 10 to 12 minutes. Put peppers into jars. Discard spice bag and add syrup to jars, leaving 1-inch headspace. Process 10 minutes in a boiling water canner.

170

SWEET PEPPER TOMATO RELISH

4 qt. green tomatoes	2 oz. mixed pickling spices
4 qt. onions	11 1/4 c. (5 lb.) sugar
24 sweet red and green peppers	8 c. vinegar
2 bunches celery	

Cut and seed tomatoes; halve onions and peppers. Let tomatoes, peppers and onions stand overnight in 5 % salt brine (3/4 c. salt in 1 gal. water). Drain. Next day, grind peppers with the celery. Squeeze out as much juice as possible. Tie spices loosely in bag; bring sugar, vinegar and spices to a boil; then add ground, drained vegetables. Cook until onions are tender and mixture is clear. Remove spice bag. Pour hot relish into jars and cover. Process 10 minutes in boiling water. Makes 9 to 10 pints.

JALAPENO PEPPER SALSA

3 c. chopped jalapeno peppers	2 T. minced cilantro
(seed if desired)	2 tsp. oregano
3 c. peeled and chopped tomatoes	1 1/2 tsp. salt
1 c. chopped onion	1/2 tsp. cumin
3 cloves garlic, minced	3/4 c. vinegar

Wear rubber gloves while chopping hot peppers. Combine all ingredients in a large kettle. Bring to a boil; reduce heat and simmer 10 minutes. Put hot salsa into pint or 1/2 pint jars, leaving 1/2-inch headspace. Process 15 minutes in a boiling water canner.

HOW TO FREEZE PEPPERS[2]

Wash thoroughly. Cut out stem end and remove seeds of green or red peppers. Halve slice or dice. Pimiento peppers can be peeled by roasting in a 400° oven until peel is charred. Remove charred skin by rinsing pimientos in cold water. A sharp knife or vegetable peeler can assist in removing skins. Hot peppers can be frozen whole. [Put in containers and freeze.] Do not blanch.

The wicked worketh a deceitful work: but to him that soweth righteousness shall be a sure reward.

Proverbs 11:18

NOTES

172

Potatoes

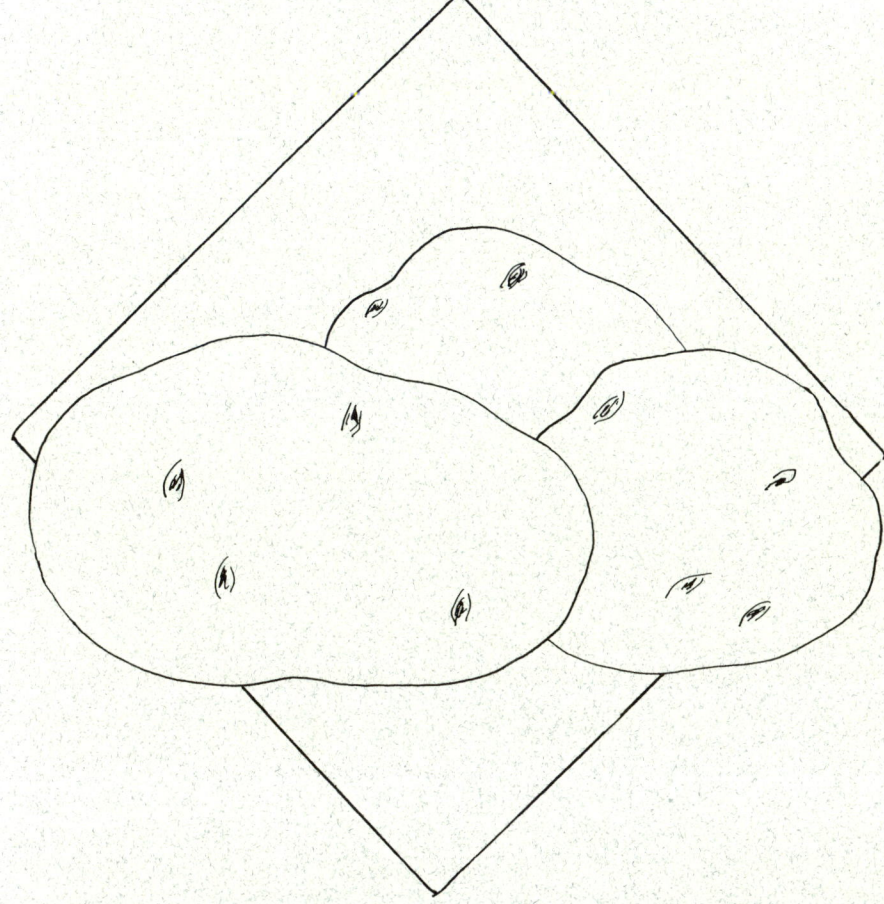

If there is a king in the vegetable world that reigns supreme, I suppose it would be the potato. More potatoes are eaten than any other vegetable in North America. Estimated consumption is around 120 pounds per capita, per year.

Potatoes are versatile, they're nutritious and absolutely delicious. Potatoes store easily too, making them available at a reasonable price year round.

Potatoes adapt to diverse soil types and climates, however, they do best where summers are on the cool side and the soil is rich, loose and well drained. Potatoes prefer slightly acidic (ph 4.8-5.4) soil.

Plant potatoes as soon as your soil can be worked in the spring. Frost damages the foliage, but setback to the plant is minimal.

Use only certified seed potatoes to help prevent disease. Plant small potatoes (1-2 inches) whole, cut larger ones to 2 inch size making sure each piece has at least two eyes. Cut potatoes should be laid out for 1-2 weeks before planting so the cut surface cures. (All of the gardening books recommend this step, but we traditionally cut and plant the same day with excellent results.) If the potatoes have sprouts, leave them on.

Plant potatoes 4 inches deep, 12 inches apart in rows 2-3 feet apart. Hill up the row when plants are 5-6 inches high and again 2 weeks later.

Potatoes grow from side sprouts that develop just below the soil surface so exercise care when hoeing and tilling to prevent damage to the new potatoes.

If you have heavier soil with poor drainage you may want to consider this alternative which we picked up from an old-timer in our neighborhood. We plant potatoes just beneath the soil surface. If the potatoes have long sprouts on, it's all right to leave them exposed. As soon as the potatoes emerge (a week or so earlier than for deeper plantings) I begin hilling loose soil around the shoots. We continue to hill frequently (1 or 2 times a week or whenever my hoe is handy) until blossoms appear. By that time, the potato plants are on top of a hill of loose topsoil 10-12 inches high. The potatoes develop inside the hill, high and dry and well protected from the rotting that might occur with deeper plantings.

Misshapen, knobby, split or hollow potatoes result from erratic growing conditions caused by a dry period that arrests growth followed by rains and a new growth spurt. Watering on a regular basis will prevent the problem.

There are many varieties of potatoes to choose from including: russets, reds and whites. Short season varieties can be dug sooner, but don't have the storage qualities of a long-season potato. The higher starch content of russets makes them more mealy and a good choice for baking or mashing. Norland—an early red potato low in starch is good for boiling and salads. Most of the potatoes are in the medium starch range and are sold as all-purpose potatoes; a good choice for general use.

You can begin harvesting potatoes by robbing the tiny ones from the sides of the stalk soon after flowers develop. These new potatoes (any potato that is dug before it is mature is considered a new potato) should be dug only as you need them, because they don't keep well.

Potatoes for storage should be left in the ground until they're fully mature—when the vines are dead. Allow newly dug potatoes to dry for 2-3 hours in the sun. Brush the dirt off then store in a dark, cold cellar. They should keep for most of the winter.

Of the myriad ways to prepare a potato, these are the more common: baked, boiled, steamed, sautéed, scalloped, fried, mashed and (opinions vary on this one) raw.

Potatoes are high in starch, vitamins C and B6 and potassium.

Yield: 1 lb. unpeeled = 3 cups sliced or chopped

1 bushel = 50 lb.

POTATO SOUP

2 T. butter
3/4 c. chopped onion
4 medium potatoes, peeled and
    diced

1/2 tsp. salt or to taste
1/8 tsp. pepper
2 c. water
3 c. milk

Heat butter in a large saucepan. Sauté onion until soft. Add potatoes, salt, pepper and water. Cover and cook 20 minutes or until potatoes are tender. Add milk and heat through.

Variations: For Swiss potato soup stir in 1-2 c. grated Swiss cheese after potatoes are tender. For chili potato soup add 1 tsp. chili powder and 1/2 tsp. oregano after potatoes are tender. For Hungarian potato soup mix 1/4 c. flour and 1 1/2 tsp. paprika into a cup of sour cream. Stir into tender potatoes. Bring to a boil after adding milk and cook 1 minute.

POTATO RIVEL SOUP

4 medium potatoes, peeled and
    sliced
1 large onion
3 1/2 c. water
1 tsp. salt or to taste

1/8 tsp. pepper
1 egg
1 c. flour
1/2 tsp. salt
4 c. milk

Combine potatoes, onion, water, salt and pepper in a large, heavy saucepan. Cover and simmer 15 minutes. Meanwhile make rivels (tiny dumplings) by beating egg and adding four and 1/2 tsp. salt. Mix well. Rub small amounts of dough between palms over simmering soup, allowing tiny pieces of dough to drop into soup, forming rivels. Simmer 5 minutes or until rivels are tender and soup is thick. Add milk and heat through.

But whosoever drinketh of the water that I shall give him shall never thirst; but the water that I shall give him shall be in him a well of water springing up into everlasting life.

John 4:14

CREAMY POTATO SOUP

2 c. water
2 c. diced potatoes
1/2 c. diced carrots
1/2 c. diced celery
1/4 c. chopped onion
1 tsp. salt

1/4 tsp. pepper
1/4 c. butter
1/4 c. flour
2 c. milk
2 c. cheddar cheese, grated

Combine water, potatoes, carrots, celery, onion, salt and pepper in a large kettle. Boil 10-12 minutes. Meanwhile melt butter. Add flour and stir until smooth. Slowly add milk; cook until thickened. Add cheese and stir until melted. Add cheese sauce to underained vegetables. Heat through.
Variations: Add a cup of diced, cooked chicken, turkey or ham to the cheese sauce.

CHEESEBURGER POTATO SOUP

1 lb. ground beef
3 medium potatoes, peeled and
    cubed
1/2 c. chopped celery
1/2 c. chopped onion
2 T. chopped green pepper
    (optional)

1 T. instant beef bouillon
1/2 tsp. salt
1 1/2 c. water
2 1/2 c. milk
3 T. flour
1 c. shredded Cheddar or
    American cheese

In a 3-quart saucepan, brown beef; drain off excess fat. Stir in potatoes, celery, onion, pepper, bouillon, salt and water. Cover and cook until vegetables are tender, 15 to 20 minutes. Blend 1/2 c. milk with flour. Add to saucepan along with remaining milk. Cook and stir until thickened and bubbly. Add cheese and stir just until cheese melts.

FISHY POTATO CHOWDER

2 T. butter
1/2 c. finely chopped onion
2 T. flour
1 tsp. salt
1/4 tsp. pepper

3 c. water or fish stock
2 c. peeled, diced potatoes
3 c. milk
1 1/2 c. flaked, cooked fish

Heat butter in a large kettle. Sauté onions about 5 minutes. Add flour, salt and pepper to onions; stir. Add water and potatoes. Bring to a boil then reduce heat and simmer 15 to 20 minutes. Stir occasionally. Add milk and fish. Heat over low heat until heated through, stirring occasionally. Sprinkle with parsley if desired.

CLASSIC POTATO SALAD

1 c. mayonnaise or salad dressing	5 c. cooked, cubed potatoes
2 T. vinegar	1 c. chopped celery
1 tsp. prepared mustard	1/2 c. chopped onion
1 tsp. salt	3 hard boiled eggs
1/2 tsp. celery seed (optional)	1/2 c. chopped sweet pickle or
1/8 tsp. pepper	pickle relish (optional)

Stir together mayonnaise, vinegar, mustard, salt, celery seed and pepper. Add remaining ingredients; mix lightly. Chill.
Variation: Add 1/4 c. chopped green pepper or radishes.

CHUNKY POTATO SALAD

2 lb. small red potatoes, quartered	1 c. diced celery
	1/2 c. sliced green onions
3 c. cubed Cheddar cheese	3/4 c. Italian salad dressing
1 c. 1/2-inch sweet red or green pepper pieces	

Cook potatoes in salted water until tender, about 10 minutes. Drain potatoes and cool to room temperature. Meanwhile combine cheese, peppers, celery and onions. Add potatoes and toss with dressing.

HOT GERMAN POTATO SALAD

6 bacon slices, cut into 1/2-inch pieces	2 T. sugar
	1/2 tsp. salt
1 c. chopped onion	1/4 tsp. pepper
3/4 c. vinegar	5 to 6 c. cooked sliced potatoes

Fry bacon until crisp. Pour off all but 1/4 c. bacon drippings. Stir onion, vinegar, sugar, salt and pepper into drippings. Cook and stir over low heat, uncovered, until mixture simmers. Pour over potato slices in bowl and toss lightly to combine. Season to taste with salt. Garnish with crumbled bacon slices.

POTATOES – SIDE AND MAIN DISHES

HOW TO COOK POTATOES

Peel 6 medium potatoes and cut into 1-inch chunks. Bring 1-inch of water to a boil. Add potatoes and 3/4 tsp. salt. Return to a boil; reduce heat and simmer about 15 minutes. Cook whole, peeled potatoes 25-30 minutes. Cook whole, unpeeled new potatoes 15-20 minutes.

CREAMED POTATOES

6 c. sliced, peeled potatoes
1/4 c. butter
1/4 c. flour
1/2 c. reserved liquid or water

1/2 c. light cream or milk
1 tsp. salt or to taste
1/4 tsp. pepper

Cook potatoes 10-15 minutes or until tender. Melt butter on low heat. Add flour, stirring until smooth. Gradually blend in water or reserved cooking liquid and cream; cook until thickened on low heat. Add salt and pepper. Add cooked potatoes to cream sauce. Combine gently.
Variation: Add 1/4 c. finely chopped dill or 1 tsp. dill weed or add chives.

PARSLIED POTATOES

18-20 small new potatoes, cooked
    and drained
1/4 c. butter

2 T. snipped parsley or 1 tsp. dry
    flakes
1/8 tsp. celery salt or seasoned
    salt (optional)

Potatoes can be peeled or unpeeled. In same saucepan used to cook potatoes, melt butter; stir in parsley and celery salt. Add potatoes; toss lightly.
Variation: Add 1/4 tsp. dill weed for dilled potatoes.

MASHED POTATOES

8 medium peeled potatoes, cooked
1 tsp. salt

1/4 c. butter
1/3-1/2 c. milk

Drain cooked potatoes. Mash. Add remaining ingredients except milk; gradually add milk, beating until light and fluffy. If desired, top with additional butter and sprinkle with pepper or paprika.

BAKED MASHED POTATOES WITH CHEESE

2 1/2 c. cooked potatoes, mashed
3 T. milk
2 T. margarine

1 T. chopped chives
1/2 lb. process cheese, cubed
1/4 c. grated Parmesan cheese

Combine potatoes, milk, margarine and chives; beat until fluffy. Stir in half of process cheese. Spoon into 1-quart casserole; sprinkle with Parmesan cheese. Bake at 350°, 20-25 minutes or until thoroughly heated. Sprinkle with remaining cheese; continue baking until cheese begins to melt.

BAKED POTATOES

Wash potatoes; prick 2-3 times with a fork. Bake at 400° for 45-60 minutes until tender. Using paper towels to protect hands from heat, roll potatoes between hands to make inside potato mixture light and mealy. Make a cross slit on top of potato to force potato up through the slit. Top with butter, salt and pepper and/or one of these toppings: sour cream, chives, crumbled cooked bacon, chopped green onions, shredded cheddar cheese or parsley.

TWICE BAKED POTATOES

4 large baking potatoes
8 strips bacon
1/2 c. chopped onion
1/4 c. grated Parmesan cheese

1 c. sour cream
1 tsp. salt or to taste
1/2 tsp. pepper
1/4 c. melted butter

Prick washed potatoes with a fork and bake at 400° for 1 hour. While potatoes cool for easier handling, fry bacon until crisp. Remove bacon and leave 2-3 T. drippings. Sauté onion 5 minutes. Cut potatoes in half lengthwise; scoop out pulp. Add to onions. Add cheese, sour cream, salt, pepper and crumbled bacon. Mix thoroughly. Heat through. Spoon into potato shells; drizzle with melted butter. Sprinkle with paprika if desired. Bake at 350° for 15-20 minutes. Can be made ahead and heated just before serving.

BAKED POTATOES WITH CHIVES

6 medium potatoes, peeled and
    thinly sliced
1 tsp. salt

1/4 tsp. pepper
6 T. butter
3 T. snipped chives

Butter a shallow casserole with lid. Gently toss potatoes with salt and pepper. Layer a third of potato slices in a circle around bottom of prepared casserole. Dot with 2 T. butter; sprinkle with 1 T. chives. Repeat twice. Bake, covered, 30 minutes at 425°. Remove lid; bake 10 minutes longer. To serve, invert on platter.

177

EASY POTATO BAKE

6-8 potatoes, grated   1 c. hot milk
1/2 c. finely chopped onion   6 T. melted butter
3 eggs, well beaten   1 tsp. salt

Mix ingredients and pour into a buttered baking dish. Bake at 350° for 1 hour and 15 minutes.

PARMESAN POTATOES

1/2 c. butter   3/4 c. Parmesan cheese
8 medium potatoes, peeled   1 tsp. salt
3/4 c. flour   1/8 tsp. pepper

Preheat oven to 375°. Melt butter on a cookie sheet with sides. Meanwhile cut each potato into 6-8 wedges. Mix together flour, Parmesan cheese, salt and pepper. Dip wet potatoes in flour mixture and place on pan with melted butter in a single layer. Bake at 375° for 1 hour, turning once. Sprinkle with parsley if desired.
Variation: For a different method to coat potatoes—combine flour, cheese, salt and pepper in a plastic bag and shake well. Add potatoes and shake until well coated.

FRIED POTATOES

1/4 c. butter   1/2 tsp. salt
5-6 medium potatoes, peeled and   1/4 tsp. pepper
     thinly sliced

Melt butter in a large skillet. Add potatoes, salt and pepper. Cover and fry over medium-low heat for 12-15 minutes. Uncover, turn potatoes and brown other side for 10 minutes. Loosen occasionally.
Variation: Add 1/4 c. finely chopped parsley.

FRENCH FRIED POTATOES

large raw potatoes   salt
vegetable oil

Peel potatoes and cut into thick slices then cut lengthwise as wide as they are thick. Let stand in ice water for 1 hour. Drain and pat dry with a cloth. Fry a few at a time in deep vegetable oil at 325°. Drain on crumpled paper towel. Spread generously with salt.

OVEN FRENCH FRIED POTATOES

6 medium potatoes   salt
1/2 c. vegetable oil

Cut potatoes into 3/8-inch sticks. Heat oil in a roasting pan in a 450° oven for 3 minutes. Remove pan and spread potatoes in one layer. Bake 25-30 minutes, stirring occasionally. Drain on crumpled paper towels and sprinkle with salt.
Variation: Dip each potato stick into oil and arrange in a single layer on a cookie sheet.

SCALLOPED POTATOES

6 medium potatoes   1 tsp. salt
1 onion, thinly sliced   dash of pepper
3 T. butter   2 1/4 c. milk
2 T. flour

Peel and slice potatoes. Cook potatoes and onions in salted water for five minutes to keep from curdling. Drain and layer 1/2 of the potatoes in a buttered 2-quart casserole. Melt butter and stir in flour, salt and pepper. Gradually add milk, stirring until it thickens. Pour half of the sauce over the potatoes in the casserole. Add remaining potatoes then remaining sauce. Bake; uncovered, at 400° for 35 minutes or until top is browned and potatoes are tender.
Variations: Stir 1 c. shredded cheese into the white sauce for cheese potatoes. Slice in hot dogs or cooked ham cubes.

SCALLOPED POTATOES WITH CHEESE AND PEPPERS

5 c. sliced potatoes   3/4 c. milk
2 T. flour   1/2 c. chopped green pepper
1 tsp. salt   1/2 c. chopped onion
dash of pepper   2 T. pimiento strips (optional)
1/2 lb. process cheese, cubed

Coat potatoes with combined flour and seasonings. Place in 12 x 8 baking dish. Heat cheese and milk over low heat; add green pepper, onion and pimiento. Pour cheese sauce over potatoes. Bake at 350° for 50 minutes or until potatoes are done.

POTATOES AU GRATIN

1/4 c. butter	1 1/2 c. milk
1 onion, chopped	2 c. grated American cheese
1/4 c. flour	4 c. cooked, cubed potatoes
1 tsp. salt	1/4 c. fine, dry, bread crumbs
1/4 tsp. pepper	1 T. butter

Melt butter in saucepan; cook onion until soft. Add flour, salt and pepper and mix. Add milk gradually and stir and cook until thickened. Add cheese and stir until melted. Arrange potatoes and cheese sauce in layers in 1 1/2-quart casserole and top with buttered crumbs. Bake at 350° about 30 minutes.

POTATO DUMPLINGS

1 qt. water	2 eggs, slightly beaten
1 tsp. salt	1 tsp. baking powder
5 c. mashed potatoes	1 tsp. salt
1 1/2 c. flour	

In saucepan, bring water and 1 tsp. salt to a boil. In bowl, combine remaining ingredients; mix until fluffy. Roll into 1-inch balls; drop into gently boiling water cook about 7 minutes. Drain; serve warm. Serve with roast beef and gravy.

POTATO PANCAKES

4 c. grated raw potatoes	1 tsp. salt
1 onion, grated	1/4 tsp. pepper
3 eggs, beaten	vegetable oil
1/4 c. flour	

Mix all ingredients but the oil. Heat enough oil in a skillet to cover the bottom. Use a 1/4 c. measure to pour the batter into the skillet. Flatten a little if necessary. Fry until golden brown. Turn and fry on the other side. Pancakes may be kept warm in a 300° oven while frying more.

POTATO BACON OMELET

8 slices bacon, diced	12 eggs, beaten
1 1/2 c. diced, peeled potatoes	2 T. water
(1/4-inch pieces)	1/4 tsp. pepper
1/4 c. finely chopped onion	2 T. vegetable oil
1 tsp. salt, divided	cheese (optional)
3 T. chopped fresh parsley	

Fry bacon until browned. Drain on paper towel. Pour off all but 2 T. drippings. Add potatoes and onions to drippings. Cook until potatoes are tender and golden. Stir in bacon and parsley. Set aside. Beat eggs, water, pepper, and salt. Stir into potatoes until well blended. Heat oil in skillet and pour egg and potato mixture into heated skillet. Cook, lifting cooked egg portion around the edge so uncooked portions runs underneath. Cook until mixture is set, but top is creamy. Fold in half and slide onto serving platter. If desired, sprinkle top with cheese before folding.

POTATO EGG CASSEROLE

1/2 lb. bacon	1/2 tsp. salt
1/4 c. fine dry bread crumbs	1/8 tsp. pepper
6 medium potatoes, cooked and	8 oz. sour cream
peeled	1/2 c. milk
6 hard boiled eggs, sliced	1 T. flour
2 T. minced chives	

Fry bacon in skillet. Remove bacon and drain all but 1 T. of drippings. Sauté bread crumbs in drippings until brown. Slice potatoes. Crumble bacon. Arrange half of the potatoes in a buttered, shallow 2-quart baking dish. Spread eggs, bacon and chives on top; sprinkle with salt and pepper and top with remaining potatoes. Combine sour cream, milk and flour. Mix well and pour over potatoes. Sprinkle with crumbs. Bake at 350° for 25 minutes or until crumbs are brown.

For all flesh is as grass, and all the glory of man as the flower of grass. The grass withereth, and the flower thereof falleth away: But the word of the Lord endureth for ever. And this is the word which by the gospel is preached unto you.

I Peter 1:24,25

181

POTATO AND VEGETABLE STUFFING

2 c. sliced celery
1 c. chopped onion
1/2 c. butter
1 1/4 c. water
4 tsp. chicken-flavor instant
    bouillon or 4 chicken
    bouillon cubes

16 c. dry bread cubes (about 28
    slices)
2 medium potatoes, peeled, cooked
    and cubed
1 c. chopped zucchini
1 c. shredded carrot
2 tsp. poultry seasoning
3/4 tsp. rubbed sage

In large skillet, cook celery and onion in butter until tender. Add water and bouillon; cook until bouillon dissolves. In large bowl, combine remaining ingredients; add bouillon mixture. Mix well. Loosely stuff turkey just before roasting if desired. Place remaining stuffing in greased baking dish. Bake at 350° for 30 minutes or until hot. Refrigerate leftovers.

POTATOES O'BRIEN

3 T. vegetable oil
1/2 c. chopped onion
1/2 c. chopped green pepper
1/2 c. chopped sweet red pepper

4 medium red potatoes, diced
1/4 c. beef broth or water
1/2 tsp. Worcestershire sauce
1 tsp. salt

Heat oil and sauté the vegetables for 4 minutes. Combine the remaining ingredients and pour over the vegetables. Cover and cook 10 minutes or until potatoes are tender. Stir occasionally. Uncover and cook 3 minutes longer or until the liquid is absorbed.

PORK CHOPS WITH POTATOES AND PEPPERS

1 lb. new potatoes, sliced 1/4-inch
    thick
1 small onion, cut in thin wedges
1 red or green bell pepper, cut in
    strips

1 tsp. oregano
1 tsp. salt, divided
2 T. olive or vegetable oil
4 pork chops (1/2-inch thick)
1/4 tsp. garlic powder

Season potatoes, onions and peppers with oregano and 1/2 tsp. salt. Heat oil in skillet over medium-high heat. Add vegetables and cook 10-12 minutes or until potatoes are slightly brown and tender. Remove vegetables from skillet. Keep warm. Season pork chops with remaining salt and garlic powder. Add more oil to skillet if needed. Over medium heat, sauté pork chops, covered, 8-10 minutes per side or until done. Drain. Return cooked vegetables to skillet with pork chops. Cover and heat 3-5 minutes. Serve.

CHICKEN AND POTATO SKILLET WITH VEGETABLES

1 lb. chicken or turkey breast
6 new red potatoes, unpeeled,
   quartered
1/2 c. sliced carrots
1 c. chicken broth or water
2 tsp. cornstarch

4 T. butter, divided
1 c. sliced yellow summer squash
   or zucchini
1 c. broccoli florets
2 garlic cloves, minced
1-2 tsp. dried tarragon leaves

Cut chicken breast into thin strips. In large skillet, combine potatoes, carrots and chicken broth; bring to a boil. Reduce heat to low; cover and simmer 10-12 minutes or until tender crisp. Drain, reserving broth in small bowl. Stir cornstarch into broth; mix well. Set aside. Remove potatoes and carrots from skillet; keep warm. Melt 2 T. butter in same skillet over medium-high heat. Add chicken. Cook and stir 3-5 minutes or until lightly browned. Remove from skillet; keep warm. Melt remaining 2 T. butter in same skillet over medium-high heat. Add squash, broccoli, garlic and tarragon; cook and stir 4-6 minutes or until vegetables are tender crisp. Add potato mixture, chicken and broth mixture; cook and stir until thoroughly heated and sauce thickens slightly.

BEEF STEW WITH POTATOES

2-3 lb. beef chuck, cut into 2-inch
   pieces
1 tsp. salt
1/4 tsp. pepper
3 c. beef broth (or 3 beef bouillon
   cubes in 3 c. hot water)

4 potatoes, peeled and quartered
4 carrots, cut into 1-inch chunks
6-8 small onions
1 c. 1-inch celery pieces
1/4 c. flour
1/4 c. cold water

Preheat heavy, 6-quart kettle for 3 minutes over medium heat. Brown beef cubes on all sides, about 10 minutes. Add salt, pepper and broth or bouillon. Cover and bring to a boil; reduce heat and simmer 45 minutes. Add potatoes, carrots, onions and celery. Bring to a boil then reduce heat and simmer for 45 minutes or until vegetables and meat are tender. In small bowl combine flour and cold water. Increase heat to medium. Slowly stir flour mixture into broth to thicken. Bring to a boil and heat thickened, about 3 minutes.

POTATO CHOCOLATE CAKE

2 c. sugar
1 3/4 c. flour
3/4 c. cocoa
1 1/2 tsp. baking powder
1 1/2 tsp. soda
1 tsp. salt

2 eggs
1 c. milk
1/2 c. vegetable oil
2 tsp. vanilla
1 c. mashed potatoes

Combine dry ingredients. Add eggs, milk, oil, vanilla and potatoes; beat on medium speed 2 minutes. Pour batter into a buttered 13 x 9 cake pan. Bake at 350° approximately 40 minutes or until toothpick inserted in the center comes out clean. Cool and frost with chocolate frosting. (See following recipe.)
Variation: Replace potatoes with 1 c. boiling water. Add after beating 2 minutes.

CHOCOLATE FROSTING

6 T. soft butter
2 2/3 c. powdered sugar
1/2 c. cocoa

1/3 c. milk
1 tsp. vanilla

Beat butter. Add sugar and cocoa alternately with milk. Stir in vanilla. Use less cocoa if desired.

BUTTERMILK POTATO PUFFS

1 1/2 c. hot, unsalted mashed
     potatoes
1/3 c. butter, melted
2 c. sugar
3 eggs, slightly beaten
1 c. buttermilk

1 tsp. vanilla
5 1/2 c. flour
4 tsp. baking powder
1 1/2 tsp. soda
1 tsp. salt
1 tsp. nutmeg

Combine potatoes, butter, sugar, eggs, buttermilk and vanilla. Gradually stir in combined dry ingredients. Chill and drop rounded tsp. into 375° oil. Fry until golden brown; drain on paper towel. Roll into sugar.

RAISED POTATO DOUGHNUTS

4 c. milk	1/2 c. warm water
1 c. butter	2 eggs, beaten
2 c. mashed potatoes	1 1/2 tsp. salt
1 1/4 c. sugar	10 c. flour
2 T. yeast	

Scald milk. Melt butter in milk and add potatoes and sugar. Cool. Dissolve yeast in water. Add to lukewarm milk mixture. Add eggs and salt. Gradually stir in flour. Add more flour if needed. Let dough rise in a warm place until double in size (about 1 hour). Punch dough down and roll out 1/2-inch thick on a floured surface. Cut with a doughnut cutter. Let rise until doubled (about 45 minutes). Deep fry at 375° 1 to 1/2 minutes per side. Don't overcrowd fryer or skillet or the temperature of the oil will drop too much. Sugar by shaking a few doughnuts at a time in a plastic bag containing sugar.

Variation: Glaze with a glaze made by mixing 2 c. powdered sugar, 1/4 c. milk and 1 tsp. vanilla.

POTATO CINNAMON ROLLS

2 pkg. (or 2 T.) yeast	2 c. mashed potatoes
2 c. lukewarm water	1 c. sugar
4 c. flour	1 T. salt
1 c. butter, melted	6 c. flour
5 eggs, beaten	

Mix yeast, water and 4 c. flour. Let rise 1 hour. Add butter, eggs, potatoes, sugar, salt and 6 c. flour; knead. Let rise 2 hours. Roll out 1/2-inch thick on a floured surface. Spread soft butter on dough and sprinkle with brown sugar and cinnamon. Roll up and cut into slices. Put in buttered pans 1/2-inch apart. Let rise until double. Bake at 350° for 15 to 20 minutes or until done. Cool slightly then frost or glaze.

And why take ye thought for raiment? Consider the lilies of the field, how they grow; they toil not, neither do they spin: And yet I say unto you, That even Solomon in all his glory was not arrayed like one of these.

Matthew 6:28, 29

POTATOES – CANNING AND FREEZING

HOW TO CAN POTATOES—WHOLE OR CUBED

Hot Pack: Wash. Pare; cut into 1/2-inch cubes. Choose 1 to 2-inch potatoes if they are to be canned whole. Keep in salt water to prevent darkening. Drain. Cook cubed potatoes 2 minutes in boiling water, whole potatoes 10 minutes. Pack hot. Add 1 tsp. salt for quarts, 1/2 tsp. for pints. Cover with fresh boiling water, leaving 1-inch headspace.

Process in a pressure canner; pints 35 minutes and quarts 40 minutes. Process at 10 lb. pressure at elevations below 1000 feet above sea level. Process at 15 lb. of pressure at elevations above 1000 feet above sea level. Dial gauges should be at 11 lb. of pressure up to 2000 feet above sea level.

HOW TO FREEZE POTATOES[2]

Wash, peel and remove deep eyes, bruises and green surface coloring. Cut into 1/3 to 1/2- inch cubes. Blanch 3 to 5 minutes. [Cool immediately in cold water, drain, package and freeze.]

HOW TO FREEZE HASH BROWN POTATOES[2]

Cook potatoes in peel until nearly done. Peel, grate and form into desired shape. Freeze on a tray then package.

HOW TO FREEZE FRENCH FRIED POTATOES[2]

Peel and cut into 3/8-inch strips. Rinse in cold water to remove surface starch and dry thoroughly with towel. Partially fry in deep fat at 360° F. until very light golden brown. Prepare just enough potatoes to cover bottom of fryer. Drain well and chill in refrigerator. Freeze on a tray, then package.

HOW TO FREEZE MASHED POTATOES

Prepare mashed potatoes (pg. 176). Form into mounds or patties. Freeze on a tray, then package, separating layers with 2 pieces of wrap for easier use.

Pumpkins

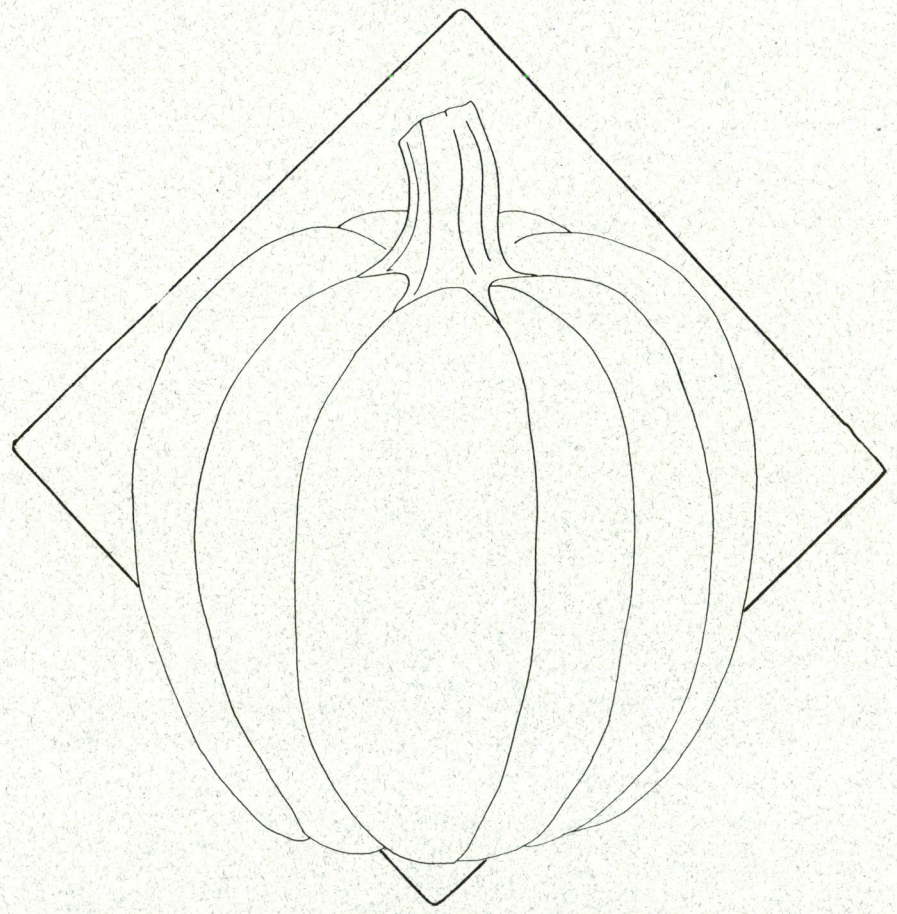

When the frost is on the punkin'
and the fodder's in the shock...*

Pumpkins, with their brilliant orange color have come to symbolize summer's end and fall's harvest. Native to the Americas and cultivated by the Indians, pumpkins have been a part of American gardens from the colonial period.

Pumpkins come in many shapes and sizes. Field pumpkins have coarser, stringier flesh than the more fine grained, sweeter pie pumpkins. Some varieties are sold as dual purpose—decorative or eating.

Pumpkins can be grown in most areas of North America. They should be sowed after soil is warm and danger of frost is past. Plant seeds ½ inch deep 1 foot apart in rows 8-10 feet apart. Thin to a final spacing of 2-3 feet between plants.

In northern areas it's best to start with plants instead of direct seeding. Start them in individual pots 3-4 weeks before your frost free date. Ideal transplants have 1 or 2 true leaves. Black plastic mulches are helpful to speed growth and keep weeds down.

To prevent disease, rotate pumpkins on a three year basis with non-cucurbits. (Cucurbits include pumpkins, squash, melons, cucumbers and gourds.)

Pumpkins are ripe when they take on a deep orange color. Mature pumpkins can tolerate moderate frost without damage to the flesh. At temperatures of 55-60 degrees, in dry conditions, pumpkins will last for 1-2 months.

Use pumpkins as a cooked vegetable, in soups and in vegetable combination dishes. Pumpkin pies, pumpkin cookies and pumpkin breads are always favorites. Pumpkin can be substituted for winter squash in recipes.

Pumpkins are high in fiber and low in calories. In addition, they are an excellent source of beta carotene, vitamin C and potassium. Pumpkin seeds are a good source of B vitamins, vitamin E and fiber.

Yield: 7 lb. whole pumpkin = 3 ½ lb. flesh
1 lb. peeled pumpkin = 4 cups chopped

...Oh, it sets my heart a-clickin' like
the tickin' of a clock,
When the frost is on the punkin' and
the fodder's in the shock.*

*From When the Frost is on the Punkin
by James Whitcomb Riley.

PUMPKIN SOUP

4 c. cubed raw pumpkin, peeled	1 medium onion, quartered
1/4 c. butter	1 T. parsley
1/4 c. water	1/2 bay leaf
2 carrots, peeled, cut into pieces	1/4 tsp. thyme
4 c. chicken broth	1 tsp. salt
2 ribs celery, cut into pieces	pepper

In large saucepan, cook pumpkin in butter a few minutes. Add water and carrots; cover and simmer 30 minutes or until pumpkin is tender. Simmer remaining ingredients in another covered saucepan 30 minutes. Strain to remove celery and onion. Process pumpkin and carrots in blender until smooth. Stir in broth. Heat to serving temperature. Serve in a hollowed out pumpkin if desired.

PUMPKINS – SIDE AND MAIN DISHES

HOW TO COOK PUMPKIN

Bring 1-inch of salted water to a boil in a large kettle. Add unpeeled pumpkin chunks. Return to a boil; reduce heat and simmer, covered, 25 to 30 minutes or until fork tender. Drain. Peel when cool enough to do so. Or peel 1 1/2 to 2-inch chunks and cook about 10 minutes after water returns to a boil.

BAKED PUMPKIN

1 medium pumpkin	1/2 tsp. salt
3/4 c. sugar	2 T. butter
1 tsp. cinnamon	

Peel and cube pumpkin. Place in a shallow baking pan. Combine sugar, cinnamon and salt; sprinkle over pumpkin. Dot with butter. Cover and bake at 350° for 30 minutes.

BAKED PUMPKIN TO USE IN A RECIPE

Cut a small pumpkin in half and clean out cavity. Place flesh side down in a cake pan or cookie sheet with sides. Add a little water. Bake at 350° for 1 1/2 hours or until pumpkin is fork tender. Scrape out and mash or puree in the blender. Use in recipes that call for mashed pumpkin or freeze for later use.

Pumpkin can also be cut into 3-inch unpeeled pieces and baked, covered, at 375° approximately 40 minutes. Cool, peel and mash, or puree in a blender.

BAKED CUSHAW OR PUMPKIN

1 medium cushaw	2 tsp. vanilla
2 T. flour	2 c. sugar
1 c. butter	1/2 tsp. baking powder
2 eggs	1 tsp. cinnamon

Cut cushaw in pieces; scrape out seeds and boil until tender. Peel when cool. Mix cushaw with the rest of the ingredients with a mixer. Place in a large casserole dish. Bake at 350° until brown on top.

DEEP FRIED PUMPKIN OR WINTER SQUASH

pumpkin or winter squash	1 c. flour
vegetable oil to deep fry—2 inches	1/4 tsp. salt
1 egg	1/4 tsp. cinnamon
1 c. ice water	

Slice pumpkin into 1/4-inch pieces. Beat together eggs and ice water. Add flour, salt and cinnamon, mixing with a fork until barely combined. Dip pumpkin into batter and fry in hot (350°) oil. Cook 4-5 minutes; drain. Fry only a few at a time. If pumpkin is not very dry, dip into flour before dipping into batter.

Hint: Pumpkins, winter squash and sweet potatoes can often be used interchangeably in recipes.

WHOLE STUFFED PUMPKIN

1 small pumpkin	1/2 c. sliced mushrooms
1 lb. pork sausage	1 egg, beaten
1 c. chopped onion	1/2 c. sour cream
1 c. chopped celery	1/4 tsp. salt

Cut the top of the pumpkin off and scoop out seeds. Place the pumpkin in a large kettle and cover with boiling water. Simmer 30 minutes or until tender. Meanwhile, sauté sausage, onions, celery and mushrooms until browned. Combine egg, sour cream and salt. Mix with meat. Fill well drained pumpkin. Bake at 350° approximately 30 minutes.

PUMPKIN WAFFLES

2 c. flour	1/2 tsp. salt
2 tsp. baking powder	3 eggs, beaten
1/4 tsp. cinnamon	1 3/4 c. milk
1/4 tsp. ginger	1/2 c. vegetable oil
1/4 tsp. nutmeg	3/4 c. cooked, mashed pumpkin

Mix dry ingredients together. Mix in remaining ingredients. Bake in a hot waffle iron.

ROASTED PUMPKIN SEEDS

2 c. pumpkin or squash seeds	1 1/2 tsp. salt
2 T. vegetable oil	

Spread unwashed seeds on a cookie sheet. Sprinkle with oil and salt. Bake at 250°, stirring frequently, for approximately 1 hour or until seeds are dry and evenly brown. Crack shells to remove seeds before eating, unless you have a hullless variety. Cool and store in a tight container.

Wherefore, if God so clothe the grass of the field, which to day is, and tomorrow is cast into the oven, shall he not much more clothe you, O ye of little faith? Therefore take no thought, saying, What shall we eat? or, What shall we drink? or, Wherewithal shall we be clothed?

Matthew 6:30,31

189

PUMPKINS – BAKED GOODS AND DESSERTS

PUMPKIN MUFFINS

3 c. flour	1 tsp. nutmeg
1 c. sugar	1 c. milk
4 tsp. baking powder	1 c. mashed pumpkin
1 tsp. salt	1/2 c. butter, softened
1 tsp. cinnamon	2 eggs, beaten

Put all ingredients in bowl in order given. Mix just enough to blend. Bake at 400° for about 20 minutes. Makes 20 muffins.

PUMPKIN WALNUT COOKIES

2 1/2 c. flour	1 1/2 c. brown sugar
2 tsp. baking powder	2 eggs
1 tsp. soda	1 c. mashed pumpkin
1 tsp. cinnamon	1 tsp. vanilla
1/2 tsp. nutmeg or ginger	1 1/2 c. chopped walnuts
1/2 c. soft butter	

Combine dry ingredients and set aside. Cream butter and sugar until fluffy. Beat in eggs. Stir in pumpkin and vanilla. Add flour mixture; mix well. Stir in walnuts. Drop by rounded teaspoons 1-inch apart on greased cookie sheets. Bake at 375° for 12-14 minutes.
Variation: Add 1 c. chocolate chips instead of walnuts or delete both and frost with pumpkin frosting. (See following recipe for frosting.)

PUMPKIN FROSTING

1 T. butter	1/4 tsp. cinnamon
1 T. milk	powdered sugar
1/4 c. pumpkin	

Beat together butter, milk, pumpkin and cinnamon. Add enough powdered sugar until frosting is the right consistency.

The sluggard will not plow by reason of the cold; therefore shall he beg in harvest, and have nothing.

Proverbs 20:4

PUMPKIN BARS

4 eggs	2 tsp. baking powder
1 2/3 c. sugar	1 tsp. soda
3/4 c. vegetable oil	1 tsp. cinnamon
2 c. mashed pumpkin	1/2 tsp. nutmeg
2 c. flour	1/2 tsp. salt

Mix eggs, sugar, oil and pumpkin until light and fluffy. Stir in remaining ingredients. Spread out evenly on a greased 15 x 10 pan. Bake at 350° for 20-25 minutes. Frost with cream cheese frosting.

CREAM CHEESE FROSTING

3 oz. soft cream cheese	1 tsp. vanilla
1/2 c. margarine	2 c. powdered sugar

Cream together cream cheese, margarine and vanilla. Add sugar and mix well.

PUMPKIN CHOCOLATE CHIP CAKE

2 c. flour	3/4 c. vegetable oil
1 tsp. salt	2 c. sugar
2 tsp. soda	2 eggs
2 tsp. baking powder	1 tsp. vanilla
1 tsp. cinnamon	1 c. nuts
2 c. mashed pumpkin	1 c. chocolate chips

Sift together flour, salt, soda, baking powder and cinnamon. Mix pumpkin, oil, sugar, eggs, and vanilla. Blend with dry ingredients. Add chopped nuts and chocolate chips. Pour into 13x 9 baking pan. Bake at 350° for 25-30 minutes or until done. Eat plain or frost with cream cheese or chocolate frosting. Cake freezes well.

But this I say, He which soweth sparingly shall reap also sparingly; and he which soweth bountifully shall reap also bountifully.

II Corinthians 9:6

PUMPKIN BREAD

1 1/2 c. sugar
1/2 c. oil
2 eggs
1/3 c. water
1 1/2 c. flour
2 tsp. baking powder

1 tsp. soda
1 tsp. cinnamon
1/2 tsp. nutmeg
1/2 tsp. salt
1 c. mashed pumpkin
1/2 c. chopped nuts (optional)

Beat together sugar, oil, eggs and water. Combine dry ingredients and add to sugar mixture. Mix well. Add pumpkin and nuts; mix well. Pour into a buttered 9 x 5 loaf pan. Bake at 350° approximately 60 minutes.

Variation: To make oatmeal pumpkin bread combine 1 c. quick oatmeal with 1 c. hot milk and let cool. Add to sugar, oil and eggs. Delete water. Add dry ingredients and pumpkin.

PUMPKIN CINNAMON ROLLS

1 1/3 c. milk
1/2 c. butter
2 c. cooked, mashed pumpkin
1/2 c. sugar
1 1/2 tsp. salt
4 eggs

2 pkg. (2 T.) yeast
8 c. flour
1/4 c. melted butter
1 c. brown sugar
4 tsp. cinnamon

Heat milk and 1/2 c. butter just until warm. Combine pumpkin, sugar and salt; add milk. Beat in eggs and yeast Add flour. Mix, cover and let rise until double in size. Turn out on floured surface and knead until smooth. Roll out into two rectangular shaped pieces of equal size. Brush on melted butter. Mix sugar and cinnamon and sprinkle on dough. Roll dough jelly-roll style, starting with the long end. Slice into 1-inch circles. Place on lightly greased cookie sheets or round cake pans with rolls almost touching each other. Let rise in a warm place until double in size. Bake at 350° for 20 minutes. Frost if desired.

PUMPKIN PIE

2 eggs
1 c. brown sugar
1 tsp. cinnamon
1/2 tsp. ginger
1/4 tsp. nutmeg

1/2 tsp. salt
2 c. cooked, mashed pumpkin
12 oz. can evaporated milk (or 1
    c. milk and 1/2 c. cream)
1 unbaked pie shell

Beat eggs until frothy. Add remaining filling ingredients in order; beat just until blended. Pour into pie shell. Bake at 425° for 15 minutes. Reduce to 350° and bake 45 minutes longer or until an inserted toothpick comes out clean.

PIE CRUST

| 1 1/3 c. flour | 1/2 c. shortening |
| 1/2 tsp. salt | 3 T. ice water |

Combine flour and salt. Cut in shortening. Add water, a little at a time while stirring with a fork. Roll out on floured surface.

Variation: WHOLE WHEAT PIE CRUST

1/2 c. whole wheat flour	1/3 c. + 1 T. shortening
1/2 c. flour	2 T. finely chopped pecans
1/2 tsp. salt	2 1/2 T. ice water

Combine flours and salt. Cut in shortening. Mix in nuts. Sprinkle ice water, 1 T. at a time, over pastry mixture, tossing lightly with a fork. Roll out on a floured surface to fit pie plate. Do not stretch. Crimp edges.

PUMPKIN PIE WITH CREAM CHEESE

8 oz. cream cheese	1 tsp. cinnamon
1/4 c. sugar	1/4 tsp. ginger
1/2 tsp. vanilla	1/4 tsp. nutmeg
1 egg	dash of salt
9-inch unbaked pie shell	1 c. evaporated milk
1 1/4 c. pumpkin	2 eggs, slightly beaten
1/2 c. sugar	

Combine softened cream cheese, sugar and vanilla, mixing well. Add egg and blend well. Spread on the bottom of unbaked pie shell. Combine remaining ingredients and mix well. Carefully pour over cream cheese mixture. Bake at 350° for 65 minutes or until knife inserted in center comes out clean.

Therefore they shall come and sing in the height of Zion, and shall flow together to the goodness of the Lord, for wheat, and for wine, and for oil, and for the young of the flock and of the herd: and their soul shall be as a watered garden; and they shall not sorrow any more at all.

Jeremiah 31:12

PUMPKIN PIE SQUARES

1 c. flour
1/2 c. quick oats
1/2 c. packed brown sugar
1/2 c. butter
2 c. mashed pumpkin
2 12 oz. cans evaporated milk
4 eggs
1 1/2 c. sugar

2 tsp. cinnamon
1 tsp. ginger
1/2 tsp. cloves
1 tsp. salt
1/2 c. packed brown sugar
1/2 c. chopped pecans
2 T. butter

Combine the first 4 ingredients until crumbly; press into a greased 13 x 9 baking pan. Bake at 350° for 20 minutes or until golden brown. Meanwhile, beat pumpkin, milk, eggs, sugar, spices and salt until smooth; pour over crust. Bake for 45 minutes. Combine remaining ingredients; sprinkle over top. Bake 15-20 minutes longer or until a knife inserted near the center comes out clean. Keep refrigerated.

PUMPKIN MARSHMALLOW DESSERT

3 1/2 c. miniature marshmallows
1 c. mashed pumpkin
1/2 tsp. cinnamon
1/4 tsp. ginger

1 c. crushed graham crackers
1/4 c. butter, melted
2 c. whipped topping

In large saucepan, melt marshmallows with pumpkin and spices over low heat, stirring until smooth. Cool about 15 minutes. Meanwhile, combine crushed graham crackers with melted butter; reserve 1/4 c. for topping. Pat remaining crumbs firmly into the bottom of an 8-inch square baking dish. Fold whipped topping into cooled marshmallow mixture and spread over crust. Top with reserved crumbs and chill.

FROZEN PUMPKIN DESSERT

3 c. crushed graham crackers
2/3 c. melted butter
1/2 c. sugar
2 qt. soft vanilla ice cream
2 c. pumpkin, cooked and mashed

1 c. brown sugar
1/2 tsp. salt
1/2 tsp. nutmeg
2 tsp. cinnamon

Mix first 3 ingredients; press into 13 x 9 pan. Spread ice cream on the crust. Blend remaining ingredients and pour over ice cream. Freeze. Cut into squares and serve plain or with whipped topping.

PUMPKIN CHEESECAKE

1 c. graham cracker crumbs	5 eggs
1/2 tsp. cinnamon	2 c. mashed pumpkin
1/4 c. melted butter	1 tsp. vanilla
3-8 oz. pkg. cream cheese,	1/4 c. flour
softened	1/2 tsp. cinnamon
1 c. sugar	1/4 tsp. nutmeg

Combine crumbs, cinnamon and butter. Press into the bottom of a 9-inch spring form pan. Refrigerate. Beat cream cheese and sugar until smooth. Beat in eggs and vanilla. Add pumpkin and mix well. Beat in flour, cinnamon and nutmeg until smooth. Bake at 325° approximately 1 hour or until edge is set but center is still soft. Chill at least 2 hours before serving.

PUMPKINS – CANNING AND FREEZING

HOW TO CAN CUBED PUMPKIN[1]

Hot Pack: Wash, remove seeds; peel. Cut into 1-inch cubes. Boil 2 minutes in water. **Do not mash or puree.** [Put hot into jars and] cover with hot cooking liquid or boiling water, leaving 1-inch headspace.

Process in a pressure canner; pints 55 minutes and quarts 90 minutes. Process at 10 lb. of pressure at elevations below 1000 feet above sea level. Process at 15 lb. pressure at elevations over 1000 feet above sea level. Dial gauges should be at 11 lb. of pressure up to 2000 feet above sea level.

SPICED PUMPKIN PECAN BUTTER

3 1/2 c. cooked, mashed pumpkin	4 1/2 c. sugar
1 c. toasted, chopped pecans	1 box fruit pectin
1 T. pumpkin pie spice	1/2 tsp. butter

Measure pumpkin, pecans and pumpkin pie spice into a large kettle. Measure sugar into separate bowl. Stir fruit pectin into pumpkin mixture. Add butter. Bring mixture to full rolling boil on high heat, stirring constantly. Quickly stir in all sugar. Return to full rolling boil and boil exactly 1 minute, stirring constantly. Remove from heat. Skim off any foam with metal spoon. Ladle quickly into five 1 cup jars, filling to within 1/8-inch of tops. Wipe jar rims and threads. Cover with lids. Screw bands tightly. Process in a boiling water bath for 5 minutes.

HOW TO FREEZE PUMPKIN[2]

Wash pumpkin. Cut or break into uniform pieces [or cut in half] and remove seeds. Place cut side down on baking sheet and bake at 350 to 400 degrees F., until tender. Cool. Scoop out pulp; mash or put through ricer; thoroughly chill before packaging, leaving 1-inch headspace in rigid containers.

HOW TO FREEZE PUMPKIN PIE MIX[2]

Prepare pie mix from your favorite recipe by adding milk, egg, sugar and spices (except cloves) before freezing. Leave 1-inch headspace.

But seek ye first the kingdom of God, and his righteousness; and all these things shall be added unto you. Take therefore no thought for the morrow; for the morrow shall take thought for the things of itself. Sufficient unto the day is the evil thereof.
Matthew 6:33,34

Radishes

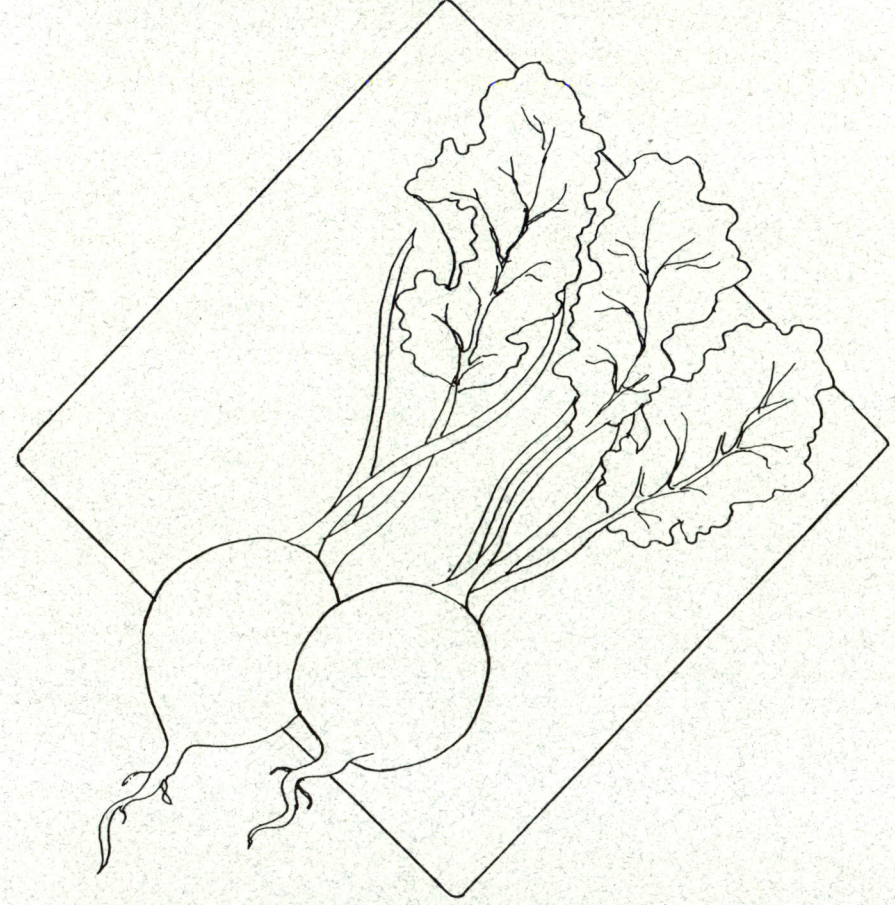

Radishes are one of the first vegetables to reward the early gardener, finally breaking the long winter drought of fresh vegetables.

Sow radishes as soon as your soil can be worked in the spring. Radishes do not tolerate 80 degree weather so plant early and harvest before hot weather arrives. Mid to late summer plantings can be successful for fall crops, too.

Plant seeds ½ inch deep, ½ inch apart in a band 3 to 4 inches wide. Thin to final spacing of 1-2 inches between plants. Radishes will be ready to harvest 30-45 days after planting. Growth that is checked by dry weather, hot weather or poor fertilization yields a disappointing combination of small, bitter radishes.

Harvest radishes as soon as they're ready. They get tough and bitter if left in the ground after they're mature.

To prevent root maggot infestation, spray the soil with insecticides or cover the row with a nylon mesh to keep flies from laying eggs beside the plants.

Choose from red, white, mixed red and white or black colored radishes. The black Spanish radish is especially adapted for fall crops. Shape varies from round to elongated. Sizes range from 1-4 inches.

Radishes are perfect raw, in salads, sandwiches or as a cooked vegetable. They will keep for 1-2 weeks refrigerated. Fall radishes can be layered in moist sand and be kept for up to 2 months in a cool cellar.

Radishes contain vitamin C. They're low calorie and high fiber.

Yield: 1 lb. fresh radishes = 3 cups

RADISHES – SALADS, DIPS AND SANDWICHES

RADISH COLESLAW

4 c. finely shredded cabbage
1/2 c. radishes, sliced thin

1 1/2 T. minced scallions or
    onions
1/2 c. French dressing

Mix all ingredients together.

RADISH DIP

2 c. washed and trimmed radishes
2 T. minced onion
8 oz. cream cheese, softened
1/2 c. sour cream

1 T. chopped chives
1/2 tsp. seasoning salt or to taste
1/8 tsp. pepper

Chop radishes. Mix remaining ingredients and add radishes.

RADISH CREAM

8 oz. sour cream
1 c. finely chopped radishes
1/4 c. finely chopped chives

1/2 tsp. salt
1/4 tsp. pepper

Mix everything together. Chill. Good on baked potato.

RADISH SANDWICHES

Butter French bread or regular bread and top with radish slices. Sprinkle with salt

RADISHES – SIDE AND MAIN DISHES

CREAMED RADISHES

4 c. radishes, trimmed
2 T. butter
2 T. flour

1 1/2 c. milk
3/4 tsp. salt or to taste
1/8 tsp. pepper

Cut radishes in half. Cook 8-10 minutes. Drain. Melt butter and stir in flour. Add milk and stir until thickened. Add radishes and heat through. Season.
Variations: For curried creamed radishes, add 1/2 tsp. curry powder to the butter along with flour.

RADISH STIR FRY

1 T. vegetable oil
1 garlic clove, minced
1/2 c. sliced scallions, including
    green tops

3 c. sliced radishes
2 T. soy sauce

Heat the oil in a wok or large skillet. Stir fry the vegetables for 4-5 minutes or until the radishes are tender crisp. Add the soy sauce and stir to coat. Serve immediately.

DEEP FRIED RADISHES

1 1/2 c. flour
1/2 c. cornstarch
1 tsp. baking powder
cold water as needed
2 T. sugar
2 T. ketchup
2 T. cider vinegar

2 T. pineapple juice
soy sauce to taste
2 tsp. cornstarch mixed with 2
    tsp. water
vegetable oil for deep frying
sliced radishes

Mix together the flour, cornstarch and baking powder with enough cold water to form the consistency of heavy cream. Make sure there are no lumps. Refrigerate until thoroughly chilled. To make the dipping sauce, heat together the sugar, ketchup, vinegar and juice in a small pan. Bring to a boil. Add enough soy sauce to color the mixture lightly. Then add the cornstarch mixed with water. Return to a boil and cook until thickened. Heat the oil to 375° . Dip radishes into the chilled batter and allow excess to drip off before gently placing it—using a slotted spoon—in the hot oil. Remove with slotted spoon and drain on paper towels. Serve immediately with dipping sauce.

Variation: Use zucchini, carrots, mushrooms or eggplant instead of, or with, the radishes.

MASHED RADISHES AND POTATOES

Boil equal amounts of radishes and potatoes together until soft. Mash together and season with butter, salt and pepper.

What fruit had ye then in those things whereof ye are now ashamed? for the end of those things is death. But now being made free from sin, and become servants to God, ye have your fruit unto holiness, and the end everlasting life.

Romans 6:21,22

RADISH POTATO PANCAKES

2 c. white radishes, grated
4 large potatoes, grated
1 onion, grated
3 eggs, beaten

1/2 c. flour
1/2 tsp. salt
1/4 tsp. pepper

Mix well and fry in small amounts of oil or butter over medium heat until browned on both sides.

RADISHES – CANNING

REFRIGERATOR PICKLED RADISHES

1 T. pickling spice
1 c. cider vinegar
1/2 c. sugar

2 tsp. salt
3/4 c. water
5 c. red radishes

Tie pickling spice in a cheese cloth bag. Bring all ingredients but radishes to a boil. Reduce heat and simmer 10 minutes. Meanwhile, trim radishes. Cut any large radish in half. Place radishes in a bowl and pour hot mixture over them. Cover and refrigerate overnight before using.

Again, the kingdom of heaven is like unto treasure hid in a field; the which when a man hath found, he hideth, and for joy thereof goeth and selleth all that he hath, and buyeth that field.

Matthew 13:44

NOTES

Rhubarb

Rhubarb is so famous for its pies that some people call it the pie plant. It is a hardy perennial that grows well in any area that can give it at least two months of below freezing weather each winter.

Rhubarb is started either by dividing an existing plant or by purchasing root crowns from a nursery. Plant crowns 2 inches deep with 3 feet between plants and 5 feet between rows. No stalks should be harvested the first year and for only 1 to 2 weeks the second year. After that you should be able to harvest rhubarb for 6 to 8 weeks. Pick by twisting the stems off near the base. Never use rhubarb leaves. They contain the toxin oxalic acid. Don't take more than ½ of the stalks at any one time. To keep your plants producing to their full potential, remove all seed pods as they form during the harvest season.

Rhubarb can be kept for at least 1 week in the refrigerator.

In addition to the pies already mentioned, rhubarb is good cooked like applesauce, made into jam or used as a complement to strawberries in salads and fruit compotes.

Rhubarb is high in vitamin C and potassium.

Yield: 1 lb. rhubarb stalks = 4 cups chopped

RHUBARB – BEVERAGES

RHUBARB PUNCH

4 c. small pieces of rhubarb	1/2 c. orange juice
4 c. water	1/3 c. lemon juice
2 c. sugar	2 liters ginger ale

Cook rhubarb in water until soft. Strain through a cloth lined strainer. Add sugar to the liquid and bring to a boil, stirring constantly. Add juices. Chill. Add ginger ale just before serving.

RHUBARB – SALADS

RHUBARB STRAWBERRY SALAD

6 c. 1/2-inch rhubarb pieces	2 T. lemon juice
1 c. sugar	1 pint strawberries, stemmed and
3/4 c. water	sliced
3 oz. pkg. strawberry gelatin	lettuce leaves

Bring rhubarb, sugar and water to a boil. Reduce heat and simmer 10-15 minutes, stirring occasionally. Remove from heat. Dissolve gelatin in the rhubarb. Add lemon juice. Cool until slightly thickened. Fold in strawberries. Pour into a 6 c. mold; chill until firm—about 3 hours. Unmold onto a lettuce lined serving plate.

RHUBARB – SAUCES

STEWED RHUBARB

8 c. 1-inch rhubarb pieces	1 c. water
1 1/4 c. sugar	

Bring everything to a boil in a heavy saucepan. Reduce heat and simmer 10-15 minutes or until rhubarb is tender. Add more or less sugar according to taste. Serve with whipped cream, whipped topping or ice cream.
Variation: Cook rhubarb in 2 c. of water then stir in a 3 oz. pkg. of strawberry gelatin after rhubarb is tender.

RHUBARB STRAWBERRY SAUCE

3-4 c. 1-inch rhubarb pieces
3/4 c. sugar
1/2 c. water

1/4 tsp. salt
2 c. halved strawberries
2 T. butter

Bring rhubarb, sugar, water and salt to a boil. Reduce heat and cook 10 minutes, stirring occasionally. Add strawberries and cook 3-5 minutes longer, or until rhubarb is tender. Remove from heat and add butter. Serve sauce warm or cold over ice cream, angel food cake, pudding or baked custard.

RHUBARB PINEAPPLE SAUCE

4 c. diced rhubarb
1 1/2 c. sugar

14 oz. can pineapple chunks
2 T. orange juice (optional)

Bring rhubarb, sugar and juice from the pineapple to a boil. Reduce heat and simmer until rhubarb is soft. Stir in orange juice. Pour over pineapple chunks to serve.

RHUBARB –BAKED GOODS AND DESSERTS

RHUBARB MUFFINS

1 1/4 c. brown sugar
1/2 c. vegetable oil
1 egg
2 tsp. vanilla
1 c. buttermilk
1 1/2 c. finely diced rhubarb
1 c. chopped nuts (optional)

2 1/2 c. flour
1 tsp. soda
1 tsp. baking powder
1/2 tsp. salt
1 tsp. melted butter
1/3 c. sugar
1 tsp. cinnamon

Combine brown sugar, oil, egg, vanilla and buttermilk. Stir in rhubarb and nuts. In another bowl combine flour, soda, baking powder and salt. Add to rhubarb mixture, stirring only until blended. Spoon into lined or buttered muffin tins. Mix remaining ingredients and sprinkle on top of batter. Bake at 375° for approximately 25 minutes.

RHUBARB BREAD

1 1/2 c. packed brown sugar	1 tsp. salt
1 c. buttermilk or sour milk	1 tsp. vanilla
2/3 c. cooking oil	1 1/2 c. chopped rhubarb
1 egg	1/2 c. chopped nuts
2 1/2 c. flour	1/2 c. sugar
1 tsp. soda	1 T. butter

In large bowl, blend first four ingredients until smooth. (To make sour milk, use 1 T. vinegar plus enough milk to equal 1 c.) Add flour, soda, salt and vanilla; blend well. Stir in rhubarb and nuts. Pour batter into 2 buttered 8 x 4 loaf pans. Combine remaining ingredients until crumbly; sprinkle over batter. Bake at 325° for 60-70 minutes until toothpick inserted in center comes out clean. Cool in pans 10 minutes; remove and cool completely.

Variation: For a coffee cake, bake in buttered 9 x 9 pan 40-50 minutes.

RHUBARB CAKE

1 1/2 c. brown sugar	1 tsp. vanilla
1/2 c. butter	2 c. flour
1/2 tsp. salt	2 c. finely diced rhubarb
1 egg	1/2 c. sugar
1 c. buttermilk	1 tsp. cinnamon
1 tsp. soda	1/4 c. sliced almonds (optional)

Cream brown sugar and butter. Add salt and egg. Stir in buttermilk (or make sour milk by adding 1 T. vinegar to enough milk to make 1 c.), soda, vanilla and flour. Add rhubarb. Combine sugar , cinnamon and nuts; sprinkle on cake. Bake in a 13 x 9 pan at 350° approximately 35 minutes.

RHUBARB UPSIDE-DOWN CAKE

2 T. butter	1 egg
1 c. brown sugar	2 c. flour
2 c. diced rhubarb	2 1/2 tsp. baking powder
1/4 c. butter	1/2 tsp. salt
1 c. sugar	1 c. milk

Melt 2 T. butter in a 9 x 9 cake pan. Add brown sugar and rhubarb. Cream together butter and sugar. Add the egg and beat. Combine the dry ingredients and add alternately with the milk. Pour over rhubarb and bake at 375° for 40-45 minutes. Turn upside-down on plate to serve. Serve with milk, cream or ice cream.

203

STREUSEL RHUBARB CAKE

2 c. flour
1/2 c. sugar
2 tsp. baking powder
1 tsp. salt
1/4 c. butter
1 c. milk
1 egg

4 c. sliced rhubarb
3 T. strawberry or raspberry
   gelatin
3/4 c. sugar
1/2 c. flour
1/2 c. rolled oats
1/4 c. butter

Combine first seven ingredients. Blend 1 minute at low speed; beat 2 minutes at medium speed. Spread into a buttered 13 x 9 pan. Top batter with rhubarb; sprinkle with gelatin. In small bowl, combine remaining sugar, flour and oats. Cut in butter until crumbly. Sprinkle over rhubarb mixture. Bake at 350° for 35-40 minutes. Serve warm or cooled, topped with whipped cream, if desired.

RHUBARB AND ORANGE COFFEE CAKE

1 1/3 c. flour
1 1/2 tsp. baking powder
1/4 tsp. salt
1 T. grated orange rind
1/4 c. butter
3/4 c. sugar

1/2 c. orange juice
1 egg, slightly beaten
1 1/3 c. 1-inch rhubarb pieces
2 T. sugar
1/2 tsp. cinnamon

Combine flour, baking powder, salt and orange rind. Beat together butter and sugar until light and creamy. Stir in juice and egg until well mixed. Add dry ingredients and mix only until evenly moistened. Fold in rhubarb. Pour into a 9 x 9 cake pan. Combine sugar and cinnamon and sprinkle over batter. Bake at 350° for 30 minutes.

RHUBARB CINNAMON ROLLS

2 c. flour
2 T. sugar
1 T. baking powder
1 tsp. salt
6 T. vegetable oil
2/3 c. milk

3 c. diced rhubarb
butter
cinnamon
1 c. white sugar
1 c. brown sugar
2 c. water

Combine flour, sugar, baking powder, salt, oil and milk to make dough. Roll dough into a rectangle on a floured surface. Spread rhubarb on dough. Roll up like a log, beginning on the wide side. Slice into rounds and put into a cake pan. Dot with butter and sprinkle with cinnamon. Cook remaining ingredients together for 5 minutes and pour over the rhubarb rounds. Bake at 375° for 30 minutes. Serve with milk, cream or ice cream.

BAKED RHUBARB PUDDING

2 eggs
1 c. sugar
1 tsp. vanilla

1/4 c. flour
3 c. finely chopped rhubarb

Beat together eggs, sugar, vanilla and flour. Stir in rhubarb. Pour into a buttered 1 1/2-quart casserole. Bake at 350° for 40 minutes or until pudding is firm. Serve warm with whipped cream or ice cream.
Variation: Make a crust by mixing 1 c. flour and 1/3 c. powdered sugar with 1/4 c. butter. Press crust into a 9 x 9 baking pan. Pour pudding on top of crust. Bake at 350° for 35-40 minutes.

EASY RHUBARB DESSERT

4 c. diced rhubarb
1 c. sugar
3 oz. pkg. strawberry gelatin

1 box yellow cake mix
2 c. water

Put ingredients in order given into a 9 x 13 pan. DO NOT STIR. Bake at 350° for 50 minutes. Serve warm with milk or ice cream.

RHUBARB CUSTARD DESSERT

2 c. flour
1 T. sugar
1 c. butter
1 1/2 c. sugar
2 T. cornstarch
3 c. diced rhubarb

1/2 c. light cream or milk
1/4 c. orange juice
3 egg yolks, slightly beaten
3 egg whites
3 T. sugar
1 tsp. vanilla

In large bowl, combine flour, 1 T. sugar and butter until crumbly. Press flour mixture into ungreased 13 x 9 pan. Bake at 375° for 15-20 minutes until light golden brown. Meanwhile, combine sugar and cornstarch. Add rhubarb, milk and orange juice. Cook over medium heat until rhubarb is tender and mixture is thickened, stirring constantly. Remove from heat. Stir small amount of hot mixture into egg yolks; add to cooked rhubarb. Return to heat just until filling boils. Set aside to cool. Beat reserved egg whites until frothy. Add 3 T. sugar gradually, beating continuously, until stiff peaks form. Blend in vanilla; set aside. Remove baked crust from oven; reduce heat to 350°. Pour rhubarb mixture over crust. Spoon egg whites on top, spreading to cover and sealing to edges. Bake 12 to 15 minutes until top is golden brown. Cool before serving.

RHUBARB CRISP

6 c. diced rhubarb
1 1/2 c. sugar
6 T. flour
1 c. brown sugar

1 c. oatmeal
3/4 c. flour
1 tsp. cinnamon
1/2 c. butter, melted

Combine rhubarb with sugar and 6 T. flour; place in a 13 x 9 cake pan. Combine the remaining ingredients and sprinkle over rhubarb. Bake at 375° for 40-45 minutes.
Variation: Sprinkle 3/4 c. raisins over rhubarb before adding crumbs. Reduce sugar to 1 1/4 c.

RHUBARB CRUNCH

1 c. flour
3/4 c. uncooked oatmeal
1 c. brown sugar, packed
1/2 c. melted butter
1 tsp. cinnamon

4 c. diced rhubarb
1 c. sugar
1 c. water
2 T. cornstarch
1 tsp. vanilla

Combine first 5 ingredients. Press half of the crumbs into a greased 9 x 9 cake pan. Spread rhubarb on the crumbs. Combine remaining ingredients and bring to a boil while stirring. Pour on top of the rhubarb, then top with remaining crumbs. Bake at 350° for 1 hour.

RHUBARB PIZZA

1/2 c. sugar
1/4 c. butter
2 T. vegetable oil
1 egg
1 1/4 c. flour
1 tsp. baking powder

3 c. diced rhubarb
3 oz. pkg. strawberry or cherry
    gelatin
1/2 c. sugar
1/2 c. flour
1/4 c. butter, melted or soft

Beat together first 4 ingredients. Add flour and baking powder. Press into a well buttered 12-inch pizza pan. Put rhubarb on crust. Sprinkle with gelatin. Combine remaining ingredients and crumble on top. Bake at 350° for 45 minutes.

RHUBARB CUSTARD PIE

1 1/2 c. sugar
3 T. flour
2 eggs, beaten
1/2 tsp. nutmeg

1 T. butter
3 c. diced rhubarb
1 unbaked pie shell

Mix sugar, flour, beaten eggs, nutmeg and butter. Beat well. Add rhubarb. Pour into unbaked pie shell. Bake at 350° for 40-45 minutes.
Variation: Before baking, top with crumbs made by combining 3/4 c. flour, 1/2 c. brown sugar and 1/3 c. butter.

RHUBARB CREAM PIE

1/2 c. brown sugar
1/2 c. sugar
1/2 c. flour
1 unbaked 9-inch shell

2 1/2 c. diced rhubarb
1 c. evaporated milk, cream or
whole milk

Combine sugars and flour. Spread half of the mixture in the bottom of the pie crust. Add rhubarb. Mix the remaining sugar mixture with the milk and pour over rhubarb. Bake at 400° for 15 minutes; reduce heat to 350° for 30 minutes or until done.

RHUBARB STRAWBERRY PIE

1 1/4 c. sugar
1/4 c. quick cooking tapioca or
flour
1/4 tsp. ground nutmeg
3 c. diced rhubarb

2 c. fresh strawberries, sliced
1/8 tsp. almond extract (optional)
pastry for a double crust pie
1 T. butter

Combine sugar, tapioca and nutmeg. Add rhubarb and strawberries. Add extract. Mix gently and let stand 10-15 minutes to blend flavors. Pour mixture into an unbaked 9-inch pie shell. Dot with butter. Cover with top crust. Cut slits into the top crust. Seal and flute edges of pie crust. Bake at 350° for 45-50 minutes until fruit bubbles and pie is golden. (See recipe for a double top crust on page 195.)
Variation: Weave a lattice top out of dough.

RHUBARB RAISIN PIE

3/4 c. sugar
2 T. flour
3 c. diced rhubarb

1 egg, beaten
1/2 c. raisins
pastry for a double pie crust

In medium mixing bowl, combine sugar and flour. Add rhubarb and toss to coat. Stir in egg and raisins. Transfer filling to an unbaked 9-inch pie shell. Cover with top crust. Cut slits in top crust; seal and flute edge. Cover edge with foil. Bake at 375° for 25 minutes. Remove foil and bake for 20-25 minutes more or until top is golden and rhubarb is tender. (See recipe below for a double crust pie below.)

PASTRY FOR A DOUBLE CRUST PIE

2 1/4 c. flour
1/2 tsp. salt

2/3 c. shortening
1/3 c. ice water

Combine flour and salt. Cut in shortening. Add water, a little at a time, while stirring with a fork. Roll out on a floured surface. Ease into a pie plate. Do not stretch dough. Trim edges and flute if desired.

RHUBARB – CANNING AND FREEZING

HOW TO CAN RHUBARB[4]

Hot Pack: Wash, trim and cut into 1/2-inch pieces. Add 1/2 c. sugar to each quart of rhubarb. Let stand at room temperature 3-4 hours to draw out juice, [or add 1/4 c. water for each cup of rhubarb.] Heat slowly to boiling and pack hot, leaving 1/2-inch of headspace.

Process in a boiling water canner, pints and quarts, for 15 minutes.

For every tree is known by his own fruit. For of thorns men do not gather figs, nor of a bramble bush gather they grapes. A good man out of the good treasure of his heart bringeth forth that which is good; and an evil man out of the evil treasure of his heart bringeth forth that which is evil: for of the abundance of the heart his mouth speaketh.
Luke 6:44,45

RHUBARB JAM

2 1/2 lb. rhubarb
1 c. water
6 1/2 c. sugar
1 box fruit pectin

1/2 tsp. butter
2-3 drops red food coloring
(optional)

Finely chop rhubarb. Do not peel. Place in a 4-quart saucepan. Add water and bring to a boil. Reduce heat, cover and simmer 2 minutes or until rhubarb is soft. Measure 4 1/2 c. into a 6 to 8-quart saucepan. Measure sugar into a separate bowl. Stir pectin into rhubarb. Add butter. Bring to a full rolling bowl on high heat, stirring constantly. Quickly stir in all sugar. Return to a full rolling boil. Boil 1 minute stirring constantly. Remove from heat. Skim foam. Add coloring if desired. Ladle quickly into six 1-cup prepared jars, leaving 1/8-inch headspace. Process in a boiling water canner 10 minutes.

HOW TO FREEZE RHUBARB

Wash, trim and cut rhubarb into 1 or 2-inch pieces. Pack raw or blanch for 1 minute and chill in ice water for better flavor and color retention. Pack raw rhubarb without sugar; sweetening is optional for blanched rhubarb. [To sweeten use 1 c. sugar for every 4 c. rhubarb. (Measure rhubarb before blanching.)][2]

To freeze rhubarb sauce prepare your favorite sauce as for table use. Chill and pack into containers, leaving 1-inch headspace.[2]

Rhubarb can be frozen in the summer and made into jam during the winter. Pack correctly measured quantities. Do not add sugar.

Fresh and frozen rhubarb can usually be used interchangeably in recipes

RHUBARB PRESERVES

5 c. finely chopped rhubarb
4 c. sugar

3 oz. pkg. red gelatin

Mix rhubarb and sugar and let stand to form its own juice. Bring to a boil and boil approximately 10 minutes or until rhubarb falls apart. Remove from heat. Add gelatin and stir well. Put in freezer containers and freeze.

NOTES

Salsify

Known as the vegetable oyster, salsify is a root crop with a distinct oysterlike flavor. Salsify is a biennial that is usually grown as an annual. It has long (2-3 feet) grass-like leaves and purple flowers if allowed to grow the second year.

Scorzonera or black salsify has black roots and is in a different genus, but grown similarly and used similarly to the more common white root salsify.

Like all root crops, salsify does best in rich, loose, fertile soil that has been deeply tilled. Plant salsify as soon as your soil can be worked in the spring. Sow 1/2 inch deep and thin to a final spacing of 3 inches after seedlings are 2 inches tall.

Roots attain a length of about 8 inches by harvest time in the fall before the ground freezes. In mild-winter areas, under heavy mulch, salsify can be over wintered and dug in the spring.

Use salsify raw, cooked, in soups or with meats. Place scraped, chopped salsify in cold water with lemon juice or vinegar to prevent discoloration before cooking.

SALSIFY – SOUPS

SALSIFY SOUP
(MOCK OYSTER SOUP)

1 1/2 c. peeled, diced salsify   1 T. butter
1 1/2 c. water   salt and pepper to taste
1 qt. whole milk

Cook salsify in salt water until tender. Add remaining ingredients and heat. Serve with crackers.

SALSIFY – SIDE AND MAIN DISHES

HOW TO COOK SALSIFY

Bring 1-inch of water to a boil. Add one pound of peeled salsify and 1/2 tsp. salt or to taste. Return to a boil; simmer 15-20 minutes or until fork tender.

MOCK OYSTERS

salsify, cooked   butter
egg   salt and pepper to taste
flour or bread crumbs

Roll boiled salsify in egg, dip in flour or bread crumbs; sauté in butter until tender. Season to taste.

BAKED SALSIFY

2 c. cooked salsify   2 eggs
3 c. crushed crackers   3 c. milk
1/2 tsp. salt or to taste   2 T. butter
1/8 tsp. pepper

Layer salsify and crackers in a buttered baking dish. Sprinkle each layer of salsify with salt and pepper. End with crackers on top. Beat eggs and add milk. Pour over crackers. Dot with butter. Bake at 350° for 35 minutes.

NOTES

212

Spinach

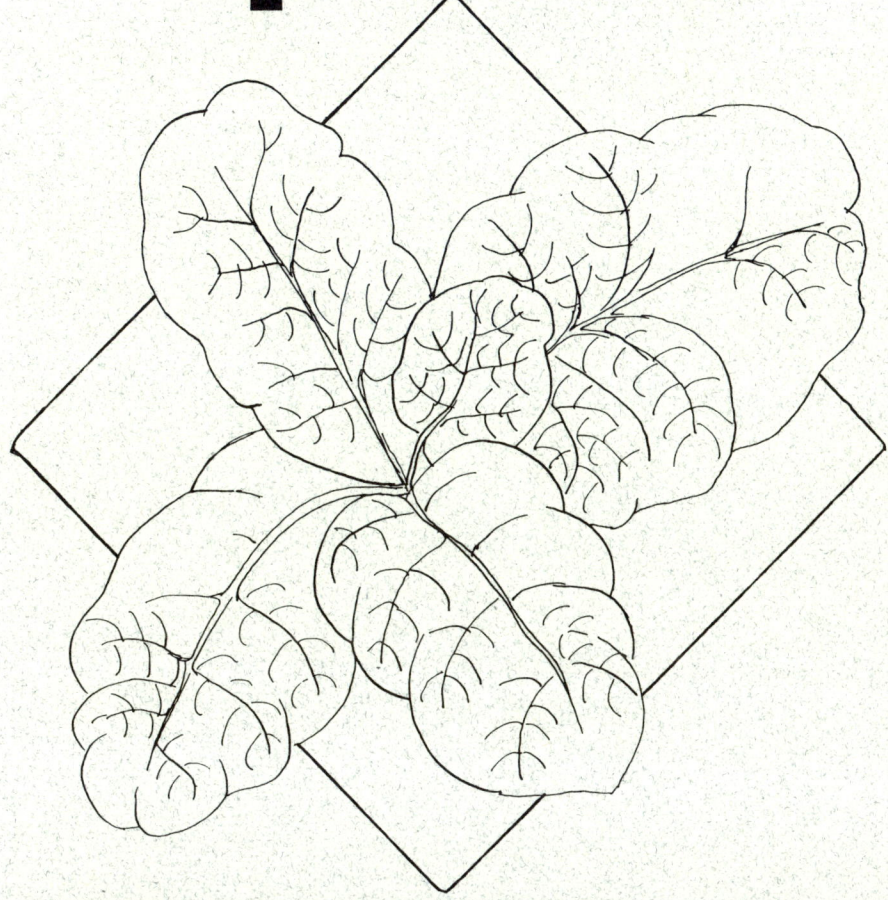

Spinach is an early season green vegetable that can be enjoyed before the beans, corn, peppers and tomatoes begin ripening. Being a cool weather crop, that bolts and gets bitter in hot weather, spinach should be sowed as soon as possible in the spring. Late summer plantings for a fall crop give good results, too. Some varieties are sold as bolt resistant, giving a longer picking season.

Sow seeds ½ inch deep 2 inches apart in a band 6 inches wide. Thin the rows by harvesting entire plants for a final spacing of 4-5 inches. Thinnings are super for salads and soups.

Harvest when leaves are 6-8 inches long before seeds form. In older leaves remove the stems by folding the leaf lengthwise with the underside of the leaf toward you. With your other hand pull the stem out.

Unwashed spinach keeps for 3-4 days in the refrigerator.

Use spinach in salads and soups, or steam, blanche or sauté as a cooked green. Avoid aluminum pans for spinach because it gives it a grayish color. Spinach becomes mushy and water logged if over cooked.

Recipes with Florentine in the name indicate spinach as an ingredient.

Spinach provides high levels of vitamin A, folate, vitamin C and potassium.

Yield: 1 lb. fresh spinach = 3 cups steamed
1 bushel = 12 lb. = 8-12 pints

SPINACH–SOUPS

SPINACH SOUP

8 c. spinach
6 c. milk
3 hard boiled eggs

1/2 tsp. salt or to taste
1/8 tsp. pepper
2 T. butter, browned

Wash spinach and cook 3-5 minutes without adding water. Chop spinach in the kettle with a knife. Add remaining ingredients. Heat through but do not boil.

CREAMY SPINACH SOUP

8 c. chopped spinach
1 1/2 c. water
1/2 tsp. sugar
1/2 tsp. salt or to taste
1/8 tsp. pepper

1 bouillon cube (optional)
4 c. milk
2 T. flour
2 T. butter

Combine spinach, water, sugar and seasonings. Bring to a boil then simmer 3 minutes. Add milk and bring to a boil. Cream together flour and butter. Add to soup and stir until it thickens.

SPINACH–SALADS

SPINACH SALAD

1 lb. young spinach leaves
1 small red onion, sliced or
    chopped
3 hard-boiled eggs, chopped
6 slices bacon, cooked and
    crumbled

1 c. oil
1/3 c. vinegar
1/3 c. sugar
2 tsp. prepared mustard
1 tsp. celery seeds (optional)
1/2 tsp. salt

Remove stems from spinach, wash leaves in lukewarm water and pat dry. Tear into bite-size pieces. Mix spinach, onion, eggs and bacon. Combine remaining ingredients in a jar with a tight lid. Shake well. Pass dressing with salad.
Dressing Variation: Combine 2/3 c. salad dressing, 2 T. vinegar, 2 T. sugar and 1/2 tsp. salt and pour over salad.

SPROUTY SPINACH SALAD

6 c. young spinach leaves, torn
2 c. alfalfa or bean sprouts
2 c. raw mushrooms, sliced
1 cucumber, peeled and sliced
4 green onions, sliced
1 c. shredded Swiss or Cheddar
    cheese

2/3 c. olive or vegetable oil
1/4 c. vinegar
1 tsp. mustard
1 tsp. sugar
1/4 tsp. salt
1/8 tsp. pepper

Toss together spinach, sprouts, mushrooms, cucumber, onions and cheese. Combine remaining ingredients in a pint jar and cover tightly. Shake until thickened. Pour dressing over salad just before serving; toss.
Variation: Delete cheese and add several tomatoes cut into wedges.

WILTED SPINACH SALAD WITH MARINATED MUSHROOMS

1/2 lb. fresh mushrooms
1/4 c. vegetable oil
3 T. lemon juice
1/2 tsp. salt

1/8 tsp. crushed garlic
1 lb. fresh spinach
4 slices bacon
1 small red onion, sliced

Rinse, pat dry and slice mushrooms. Combine oil, lemon juice, salt and garlic; bring to a boil. Pour over mushrooms in bowl; toss. Cover and marinate at room temperature for 15 minutes. Wash and tear spinach into bite-size pieces. In a large skillet fry bacon until crisp. Remove bacon and drain on paper towels; crumble and set aside. Separate onion slices into rings. Sauté rings in bacon fat until limp, about 2 minutes. Add spinach, 1/3 at a time, to skillet; sauté until limp, about 1 minute. Add spinach mixture to mushrooms along with reserved bacon; toss well.

SPINACH AND APPLE SALAD

1 lb. fresh young spinach
1 red or yellow delicious apple,
    thinly sliced
1/2 c. sunflower seeds

4 sliced green onions
3 T. olive or vegetable oil
2 T. lemon juice
1/2 tsp. salt

Wash spinach and tear into salad bowl. Add apple slices, sunflower seeds and onions. Combine remaining ingredients and toss with salad. Sprinkle with fresh ground pepper if desired.

ORIENTAL SPINACH SALAD

1 lb. torn young spinach
1 can water chestnuts or
   1 c. chopped celery
1 c. bean sprouts
2 hard boiled eggs
5 strips bacon, cooked and
   crumbled

1 c. vegetable oil
3/4 c. sugar
1/4 c. vinegar
2 tsp. Worcestershire sauce
3/4 c. ketchup
1/4 tsp. salt
1 medium onion, diced

Mix first 5 ingredients in a large salad bowl. Mix remaining ingredients in a jar with lid; shake well. Pour over spinach just before serving.

SPINACH AND CHICKEN SALAD

4 c. fresh young spinach, torn
2 medium zucchini, sliced
2 medium oranges, peeled,
   sectioned, cut into 1/2-inch
   pieces
1 1/2 tsp. chili powder
1/4 tsp. salt
1/4 tsp. cayenne pepper

1/8 tsp. garlic powder
2 T. oil
1 lb. chicken breast, sliced thin
1/4 c. chopped red onion
1 T. sugar
1/2 c. orange juice
2 T. lemon juice

In large bowl, combine spinach, squash and oranges; set aside. Combine chili powder, salt, cayenne and garlic powder. Add chicken strips; toss to coat. Heat oil in 12-inch skillet over medium-high heat until oil sizzles, about 1 minute. Add chicken. Cook 2 minutes on each side or until lightly browned. In small bowl, combine onion, sugar, orange juice and lemon juice; blend well. Add to chicken in skillet. Cook 2 minutes, stirring occasionally. Spoon chicken mixture over spinach mixture, toss gently to coat. Serve immediately.

SPINACH – DIP AND SANDWICHES

SPINACH DIP

1 c. chopped, cooked spinach
1 c. mayonnaise or salad dressing
1/2 c. sour cream

1/2 c. finely chopped onion
1 1/2 tsp. parsley flakes
1/2 tsp. garlic salt or seasoned salt

Combine and chill. Serve with vegetables or crackers.

ENGLISH MUFFINS WITH EGGS AND SPINACH

6 hard-boiled eggs, chopped
2 c. spinach, finely chopped
1/2 c. sour cream
1/4 c. chopped green pepper
1/4 c. shredded carrots

4 English muffins, split, toasted
8 thick slices American cheese, cut
   in half diagonally
4 crisply cooked bacon slices,
   crumbled

Combine eggs, spinach, sour cream, peppers and carrots; mix lightly. Top muffin halves with egg mixture, cheese and bacon. Broil until cheese begins to melt.

SPINACH – SIDE AND MAIN DISHES

HOW TO COOK SPINACH

Bring 1/4-inch water to a boil. Add 1 lb. spinach and 1/4 to 1/2 tsp. salt or to taste. Return to a boil. Simmer 2-4 minutes depending on the age of the spinach. Drain immediately. Do not overcook. Spinach can also be cooked in the water that clings to washed leaves. Cook 3-5 minutes. Eat plain, buttered or with a white sauce and crumbled bacon.

SAUTÉED SPINACH

2 lb. spinach
2 T. butter

1/2 tsp. salt
1/8 tsp. pepper

Wash and trim spinach. Drain well. Heat butter in a large skillet. Add spinach and sauté 3-5 minutes, stirring often. If the spinach is older, cover pan and let cook several minutes. Add salt and pepper.
Variation: Sauté 1/2 c. chopped onion several minutes before adding spinach. Use 1 T. vegetable oil and 1 T. butter instead of all butter.

CREAMY SPINACH

3 lb. fresh spinach
1/2 c. whipping cream
1 tsp. salt

1/8 tsp. pepper
pinch of ground nutmeg (optional)

Carefully wash spinach. Heat cream. Slowly sauté spinach in cream until wilted, turning often. Sprinkle seasoning on.
Variation: Replace cream with 1/4 c. butter.

216

SPINACH FRIED RICE

3 T. vegetable oil
1/4 lb. mushrooms, finely
    chopped
4 green onions, cut into 1-inch
    pieces
1 c. shredded carrot

1 lb. spinach, washed, trimmed
    and coarsely chopped
3 eggs, beaten
3 c. cooked rice
1/4 c. chopped fresh cilantro
    (optional)
3 T. soy sauce

Heat oil over high heat. Add mushrooms, onions and carrots and stir until tender. Add spinach. Cover and cook 1 minute. Reduce heat to medium. Add eggs and stir until eggs are cooked—approximately 2 minutes. Stir in rice, cilantro and soy sauce. Heat through.

SPINACH PARMESAN

2 lb. fresh spinach
1/4 tsp. sugar
1/2 tsp. salt
2 T. sour cream

1/2 c. grated Parmesan cheese
4 drops Tabasco sauce (optional)
salt and pepper to taste

Wash spinach. Place in kettle with sugar and salt but no water. Cover. Cook 3-5 minutes. Drain off any liquid. Chop spinach. Stir in sour cream and Parmesan cheese until well combined. Add Tabasco sauce, salt and pepper to taste.

SAVORY SPINACH SQUARES

4 eggs
2/3 c. milk
1/4 c. melted butter
1/2 c. minced onion
2 T. dry parsley flakes
1 tsp. Worcestershire sauce
1 1/2 tsp. salt

1/2 tsp. thyme
1/2 tsp. nutmeg
2 c. cooked rice
1 1/2 lb. spinach, cooked and
    drained
2 c. shredded, processed
    American cheese

Beat eggs; add combined milk, butter, onion, parsley flakes, Worcestershire sauce, salt, thyme and nutmeg; mix well. Combine remaining ingredients; add egg mixture and mix well. Pour into a greased shallow 2-quart baking dish. Bake at 350° for 40 to 45 minutes. Cut into squares and serve.

OVEN OMELET WITH SPINACH AND TOMATO

1 T. vegetable oil
1 onion, chopped
1 clove garlic, minced
1/2 lb. spinach, coarsely chopped
1 tomato, chopped

6 eggs
1 c. shredded Cheddar cheese
1/2 tsp. salt
1/2 tsp. basil
1/8 tsp. pepper

Heat oil in a broiler-proof skillet. Add onion and garlic; cook until tender. Drain spinach and tomato on paper towel then add to onion. Cover and cook until spinach wilts. Beat eggs and remaining ingredients until well blended; pour into skillet. Reduce heat. Cover and cook 4-5 minutes or until eggs are set around edge, but still runny in the center. Broil, 6-inches from heat, until the top is lightly browned, about 2 minutes. To serve, cut into wedges.

Variation: Use 1/2 lb. fresh mushrooms instead of tomatoes. Add with onions.

SPINACH QUICHE

4-6 strips bacon
3 eggs
2 c. finely chopped, cooked
      spinach, well-drained
1 1/4 c. light cream
1 c. shredded Swiss cheese

1/2 tsp. salt
1/4 tsp. nutmeg
1/8 tsp. pepper
1 9-inch unbaked pie shell with a
      fluted edge

Fry, drain and crumble bacon. Beat eggs briefly. Squeeze spinach to remove water and add to eggs. Add bacon and remaining ingredients, mix and pour into the pie shell. Bake at 375° approximately 30 minutes. Let stand 10 minutes before cutting.

SPINACH – CANNING AND FREEZING

HOW TO CAN SPINACH[1]

Can only freshly picked, tender spinach that has been thoroughly washed. Cut out tough stems and ribs. Steam in a cheesecloth bag or steamer for 3-5 minutes or until well wilted. Pack hot, loosely. Cover with boiling water leaving 1-inch headspace. Add 1/2 tsp. salt to pints and 1 tsp. to quarts.

Process in a pressure canner, pints for 70 minutes, quarts 90 minutes. Process at 10 lb. of pressure at elevation up to 1000 feet above sea level. Process at 15 lb. of pressure at elevations over 1000 feet above sea level. Dial gauges should be at 11 lb. of pressure up to 2000 feet above sea level.

HOW TO FREEZE SPINACH[2]

Cut off large, tough stems; discard all damaged leaves. Wash thoroughly several times. Blanch 1 lb. spinach in 2 gal. water. Blanch for 1 1/2 to 2 minutes. [Cool immediately in cold water, drain, package and freeze.]

And he spake a parable unto them, saying, The ground of a certain rich man brought forth plentifully: And he thought within himself, saying, What shall I do because I have no room where to bestow my fruits? And he said, this will I do: I will pull down my barns, and build greater; and there will I bestow all my fruits and my goods. And I will say to my soul, Soul, thou hast much goods laid up for many years; take thine ease, eat, drink, and be merry. But God said unto him, Thou fool, this night thy soul shall be required of thee: then whose shall those things be, which thou hast provided? So is he that layeth up treasure for himself, and is not rich toward God.

Luke 12:16-21

NOTES

Straw-berries

      Strawberries are perhaps America's most popular fruit. They are extremely versatile and are easily adaptable to most areas of North America. Strawberries burst on the summer scene with a flare of color and flavor in June in most areas.

      To start your own strawberry patch, buy plants from a reputable nursery to avoid spreading disease. Plant strawberries in the spring, setting the crowns at ground level so no roots are exposed. Allow 24-inches between plants and 4 to 5-feet between rows. Remove any flowers that develop the first summer to help promote growth in the mother plant and the daughter plants that develop from runners.

To get more even spacing, runners can be hand spaced, allowing a minimum of 4-inches between plants. Spacings of less than 4-inches will decrease size and yield of your bed. Too many strawberry plants inhibit production just like weeds do.

Weed control is critical during the first summer. Frequent hoeing around the mother plant before runners set and tilling between rows is advisable.

In the fall, cover the rows with clean straw mulch. Straw with a lot of weeds in it will seed new weeds all over your strawberry patch. The mulch will protect the plants from extreme cold and keep the ground from going through root damaging freeze/thaw cycles. Remove straw in the spring once new growth is beginning and put it between the rows. It will make picking more pleasant and help keep the weeds from growing.

Strawberries are irresistible picked fresh from the garden. The ones that make it to the table, are excellent plain, with sugar and milk, in pies, in sauces or cooked into jam.

Nutritionally, strawberries are a good source of vitamin C, folate and potassium. In addition, they have bioflavonoids that help reduce the risk of cancer.

Yield: 1 qt. = 1 1/2 lb
 1 qt. fresh = approximately 1 pt. frozen mashed or sliced (yield depends on the size of the strawberries.

STRAWBERRIES – SOUPS

FRUIT SOUP WITH STRAWBERRIES

2 qt. milk
1/2 c. sugar
1 tsp. vanilla
2 c. fresh sliced or crushed
    strawberries

1 c. fresh blueberries or crushed
    peaches
2-3 bananas, sliced

Combine all ingredients. Serve cold. Use Chex®, mini-shredded wheat or fresh bread cubes for "crackers".

STRAWBERRIES – SALADS

STRAWBERRY BLUEBERRY BANANA SALAD

1 c. sliced strawberries
1 c. blueberries
1 banana, sliced

1 c. shredded coconut
1 c. miniature marshmallows
1 c. sour cream or vanilla yogurt

Gently fold together strawberries, blueberries, banana, coconut, marshmallows and sour cream until evenly combined. Refrigerate until serving time. Recipe can easily be doubled.
Variation: Delete the banana and add 1 1/2 c. strawberries and blueberries.

FROZEN STRAWBERRY PINEAPPLE SALAD

8 oz. pkg. cream cheese
2 T. mayonnaise
16 oz. can crushed pineapple,
    drained

2 c. sliced strawberries
3 bananas, sliced
8 oz. whipped topping

Mix cheese and mayonnaise together. Add all other ingredients. Put into a 13 x 9 pan and freeze. Can also be frozen in lined muffin tins. Set at room temperature a little before serving. Serve plain or on lettuce.
Variation: Delete pineapple and bananas and add more strawberries.

STRAWBERRY SPINACH SALAD

2 T. sesame seeds
1 1/2 lb. spinach
1/3 c. vegetable oil
1/3 c. vinegar

1 T. sugar
1 T. minced onion
1/2 tsp. paprika
2 c. strawberries, halved

Heat and stir sesame seeds in a skillet until golden; set aside. Wash spinach thoroughly; dry on paper towels and tear into bite size pieces. Chill. Blend oil, vinegar, sugar, onion and paprika. Mix together spinach, strawberries, dressing and seeds.

STRAWBERRIES – SIDE AND MAIN DISHES

STRAWBERRY OMELET

2 c. whole strawberries
1 T. sugar
4 eggs, separated

1/2 tsp. salt
1 T. lemon juice
1 T. butter

Toss strawberries with sugar. Beat egg whites until they stand in firm peaks. Beat yolks and salt in another bowl, until thick. Beat in lemon juice. Fold in egg whites until no streaks of yellow show. Melt butter in a skillet. Pour in eggs. Cook, lifting cooked portion around the edge so uncooked eggs flow underneath. Cook until mixture is set. Remove to a serving plate. Spoon 1/2 of the strawberries onto 1/2 of the omelet. Fold omelet over the berries. Spoon remaining berries on top.

STRAWBERRIES – BAKED GOODS AND DESSERTS

STRAWBERRY MUFFINS

1/2 c. butter, softened
1 c. sugar
2 eggs
2 c. flour
2 tsp. baking powder

1/4 tsp. salt
2/3 c. milk
1 tsp. grated lemon rind
1 c. strawberries, chopped
1 T. cinnamon sugar

Cream butter in large bowl; gradually add sugar and eggs, creaming until light and fluffy. Mix dry ingredients and add to creamed mixture alternately with milk. Stir in lemon rind and fold in berries. Spoon batter into lined or buttered muffin pans, filling each 2/3 full. Sprinkle sugar lightly over top of batter. Bake at 375° for 15-18 minutes. Makes 12 muffins.

STRAWBERRY BREAD

3 c. flour
2 c. sugar
1 tsp. salt
1 tsp. soda
1 tsp. cinnamon

3 eggs, well beaten
3/4 c. vegetable oil
2 1/2 c. sliced strawberries,
  drained
1 c. chopped pecans (optional)

Combine dry ingredients. Add eggs and oil, stirring briefly. Fold in berries and nuts. Spoon batter into two 8 x 4 buttered loaf pans. Bake at 350° about 1 hour. Freezes well.

STRAWBERRY PIE

1 1/4 c. sugar
2 c. water
3 T. cornstarch
1/8 tsp. salt

3 oz. pkg. strawberry gelatin
1 qt. strawberries, whole or
  halved
1 baked 9-inch pie shell

Cook sugar, water, cornstarch and salt until it thickens. Add gelatin and stir to dissolve. Cool. Put strawberries into cooled, baked pie shell. Spoon gelatin mixture over strawberries. Top with whipped topping or sweetened whipped cream.

FLUFFY STRAWBERRY PIE

2/3 c. boiling water
3 oz. pkg. strawberry gelatin
1/2 c. cold water
ice cubes

8 oz. frozen whipped topping,
  thawed
1 c. chopped strawberries
1 graham cracker crumb crust

In large bowl stir boiling water into gelatin until dissolved. In a separate bowl mix cold water and ice to make 1 1/4 cups. Stir into gelatin until slightly thickened. Remove any remaining ice. Stir in whipped topping until smooth. Mix in strawberries. Refrigerate 30 minutes or until mixture will mound. Spoon into crust. Refrigerate 4 hours or until firm. Before serving, garnish with additional whipped topping and strawberries, if desired.

Ye shall know them by their fruits. Do men gather grapes of thorns, or figs of thistles? Even so every good tree bringeth forth good fruit; but a corrupt tree bringeth forth evil fruit. A good tree cannot bring forth evil fruit, neither can a corrupt tree bring forth good fruit.

Matthew 7:16-18

STRAWBERRY PUDDING PIE

4 oz. cream cheese, softened
1 T. milk
1 T. sugar
1 T. lemon juice
8 oz. frozen whipped topping,
    thawed, divided

1 graham cracker pie crust
2 c. strawberries, halved
2 c. cold milk
2 pkg. (4-serving size) vanilla or
    lemon pudding

Beat cream cheese, 1 T. milk and sugar in medium bowl with wire whisk until smooth. Stir in juice. Stir in 1 1/2 c. of whipped topping. Spread evenly on bottom of crust. Press strawberries into cream cheese layer. Pour 2 c. milk in large bowl. Add pudding mixes. Beat with wire whisk 1 minute. Let stand 1 minute or until thickened. Gently stir in remaining topping. Spoon over strawberries in crust. Refrigerate 4 hours or until set.

STRAWBERRY SHORTCAKE

2 eggs
1 c. sugar
1 c. milk
1 tsp. vanilla
2 1/2 c. flour
2 tsp. baking powder

1/2 tsp. salt
2 T. melted butter
1 qt. strawberries, sliced
1 c. cream, whipped or 2 c.
    whipped topping

Beat eggs. Add sugar, milk and vanilla. Stir in dry ingredients and add melted butter. Pour into two 8-inch cake pans. Bake at 375° for 25-30 minutes. Spread 1/2 of the whipped cream on one cake. Add 1/2 of the berries. Top with the other cake and layer cream and berries on it.
Variation: Eat shortcake with milk and strawberries and delete cream.

QUICK STRAWBERRY SHORTCAKE

1 pt. vanilla ice cream, softened
2 c. prepared biscuit mix

4 c. sweetened strawberries
2 c. heavy cream, whipped

Add ice cream to biscuit mix and mix only until dry ingredients are dampened. Fill greased muffin pans about 2/3 full. Bake at 425° about 15 minutes. Remove from pan and cool; split in half. Allow one cake for each serving. Top halves with fruit and whipped cream or ice cream. Makes 12 "muffins".
Variation: Delete cream and eat with milk.

STRAWBERRY CHEESECAKE

2 c. graham cracker crumbs
1/2 c. butter, melted
1/4 c. sugar
6 oz. pkg. strawberry gelatin
2 c. boiling water

8 oz. cream cheese
8 oz. carton frozen whipped
topping
1 1/2 c. sliced strawberries

Combine crumbs, butter and sugar. Press into a 13 x 9 pan. Dissolve gelatin in boiling water. Cool until slightly thickened. Beat cream cheese, then add whipped topping. Beat 2 minutes and stir into gelatin. Add strawberries. Pour into crust and chill.

STRAWBERRY PIZZA

3/4 c. butter, softened
1/2 c. powdered sugar
1 1/2 c. flour
8 oz. pkg. cream cheese
1/2 c. powdered sugar
1/4 c. whipping cream

4 c. strawberries, sliced
1/2 c. pineapple or orange juice
1/4 c. powdered sugar
1 T. cornstarch
1 tsp. lemon juice

Cream butter and sugar. Mix in flour, then press into a greased 12-inch pizza pan. Bake at 300° for 25-28 minutes or until lightly browned. Cool. Mix cream cheese and powdered sugar. Whip cream and fold into cream cheese. Spread on the cooled crust. Arrange berries over the filling. Bring remaining ingredients to a boil and boil 1 minute, stirring constantly. Cool slightly, then drizzle over berries. Chill at least 1 hour before serving.

STRAWBERRY GELATIN PIZZA

12 oz. strawberry gelatin
2 1/2 c. boiling water

1 c. whipped topping
2 c. sliced strawberries

Combine gelatin and boiling water. Stir until gelatin is completely dissolved. Spray a pizza pan with cooking spray. Pour gelatin into the pan. Refrigerate for 3 hours or until firm. Spread topping over gelatin, leaving 1/2-inch of space around the edge. Top pizza with strawberries. Cut into wedges. Lift from pan with spatula.
Variation: Use any flavor gelatin or different fresh fruit.

STRAWBERRY CREAM PUFFS

1 c. water
1/2 c. butter
1 tsp. sugar
1/4 tsp. salt
1 c. flour
4 eggs

2 c. strawberries, washed and
    hulled
4 T. sugar, divided
1 c. heavy cream
1/2 tsp. almond extract

Bring water, butter, sugar and salt to a full rolling boil in a large saucepan. Add flour all at once. Stir vigorously with a wooden spoon until mixture forms a thick smooth ball. Remove from heat; cool slightly. Add eggs one at a time, beating well after each one until paste is shiny and smooth. Drop by rounded T. into 6 even mounds, 2-inches apart on a cookie sheet. Bake at 400° for 40 minutes or until puffed and golden brown. Cool completely. To make filling slice berries and add 3 T. sugar. Chill at least 30 minutes. Beat cream with remaining sugar and the extract until stiff. Cut a slice from the top of the puffs and remove any soft dough. Fold berries into cream and put about 1/3 c. into each one. Replace tops and sprinkle with powdered sugar if desired.

STRAWBERRY TAPIOCA PUDDING

4 c. water
1/2 c. plus 1 T. baby pearl tapioca
3 oz. pkg. strawberry gelatin
2/3 c. sugar

1 1/2 c. whipping cream
3-4 bananas
2 c. strawberries

Bring water to a boil. Add tapioca. Turn off heat and let stand until tapioca is clear, about 15 minutes. Reheat and add dry gelatin and sugar. Cool. When completely cool, whip cream and add. Add bananas and strawberries.

STRAWBERRY PINEAPPLE DESSERT

1 angel food cake
22 oz. can lemon pie filling
22 oz. frozen whipped topping,
    thawed

20 oz. can pineapple chunks,
    drained
4 c. strawberries, sliced

Cut angel food cake in half. Tear half the cake into bite-size pieces. Place cake pieces in bottom of 3-quart glass bowl. In large bowl combine pie filling and whipped topping. Spread half of filling mixture over cake pieces. Layer half of the pineapples and strawberries over filling mixture. Tear remaining half of cake into bite-size pieces; place cake pieces over filling. Repeat layers with remaining ingredients. Cover with plastic wrap; refrigerate at least 4 hours before serving.

FROZEN STRAWBERRY DESSERT

2 1/4 c. graham cracker crumbs
1/2 c. sugar
3/4 c. butter, melted
1/2 gal. vanilla ice cream

1/2 c. pineapple juice
1/4 c. cornstarch
1 c. sugar
2 c. crushed frozen strawberries

Combine cracker crumbs, sugar and melted butter. Mix well and press firmly into 13 x 9 pan. Bake at 350° for 15 minutes. Soften ice cream and spread over cool crust. Place in freezer until glaze is ready. Cook pineapple juice, cornstarch and sugar until thick, stirring constantly. Add strawberries and cool. Spread over ice cream and freeze until ready to use. Remove from freezer about 15 minutes before serving.
Variation: Replace pineapple juice with water. Add 1 T. lemon juice to water.

STRAWBERRY ICE

4 c. strawberry halves
7 oz. marshmallow creme

1 T. lemon juice
1 T. grated lemon peel

Process strawberries in a blender until smooth. Gradually add strawberries to marshmallow creme and beat with an electric mixer, mixing until well blended. Mix in juice and peel. Pour into 9-inch square pan; freeze until almost firm. Coarsely chop mixture; spoon into chilled bowl. Beat with electric mixer until smooth; freeze.

STRAWBERRY ICE CREAM

6 c. milk
3 pkg. (3 T.) unflavored gelatin
1/2 c. water
3 c. sugar

1/2 tsp. salt
4 c. whipping cream
3 T. vanilla
4 c. crushed strawberries

Heat milk almost to a boil. Soften gelatin in water and add to hot milk. Add sugar and salt. Cool, but do not let it congeal before adding cream, vanilla and strawberries. Freeze in a 6-quart ice cream freezer.

EASY STRAWBERRY ICE CREAM

4 c. crushed strawberries
1 1/2 c. sugar
1 pt. whipping cream

1 qt. milk
1 T. vanilla
1/2 tsp. salt

Mix strawberries and sugar and let stand 30 minutes. Add remaining ingredients and freeze in a 4 or 6-quart ice cream freezer.

227

STRAWBERRY PUNCH

4 c. strawberries	1/4 c. lemon juice
2 c. sugar	2 liters ginger ale
4 c. water	

Blend strawberries in the blender. Boil sugar and water 3 minutes, stirring to dissolve sugar. Cool. Add lemon juice. Add strawberries and ginger ale just before serving.

STRAWBERRY PINEAPPLE PUNCH

1 1/4 c. sugar	46 oz. can pineapple juice
4 c. water	1 1/2 c. crushed strawberries
12 oz. can pink lemonade, thawed	1 liter ginger ale

Boil the sugar and water 5 minutes, stirring to dissolve the sugar; cool. Add undiluted lemonade and pineapple juice. When ready to serve add strawberries and ginger ale.

STRAWBERRY BANANA SMOOTHIE

2 c. strawberries	1 c. sliced bananas
2 c. orange juice	1/2 c. powdered milk

Combine everything in a blender and process until smooth.

CREAMY STRAWBERRY SMOOTHIE

1 1/2 c. strawberries	1 pt. strawberry or vanilla ice
1 qt. milk	cream

Combine all ingredients in a blender at high speed about 1 minute.

But the wisdom that is from above is first pure, then peaceable, gentle, and easy to be intreated, full of mercy and good fruits, without partiality, and without hyprocisy.

James 3:17

STRAWBERRIES – MISCELLANEOUS

STRAWBERRY SAUCE I

2 c. fresh strawberries   1/4 c. water
1/2 c. sugar

Crush 1/2 c. of berries. Dissolve sugar in water and bring to a boil; stir in crushed berries. Reduce heat and simmer, uncovered 5 minutes. Remove from heat and pour over the sliced strawberries. Chill thoroughly.
Variation: Stir together 2 c. crushed strawberries and 1 c. sugar until sugar dissolves. Do not cook. Chill.

STRAWBERRY SAUCE II

2 c. crushed strawberries   2 T. cornstarch
1 1/2 c. sugar   1 tsp. butter
1/2 c. water   red food coloring (optional)

Cook berries, sugar, water and cornstarch until mixture thickens. Cook 2 minutes more. Stir in butter and food coloring if desired. Cover surface with a clear plastic wrap. Cool and serve over cheesecake, pound cake or ice cream.
Variation: Add some sliced strawberries.

FRESH STRAWBERRY FROSTING

3 T. butter, softened   1/4 c. crushed strawberries
2 1/2 c. powdered sugar   1 tsp. vanilla

Combine all ingredients, mixing well. Use on angel food and other cakes.
Variation: Use 3 c. powdered sugar and delete butter.

FRUITY STRAWBERRY POPSICLES

1 1/3 c. strawberries   15 oz. unsweetened crushed
2/3 c. evaporated milk   pineapple
                                 2 small ripe bananas

Combine all ingredients in blender. Blend until smooth. Freeze in popsicle forms or paper cups with sticks or plastic spoons.

STRAWBERRIES – JAMS AND PRESERVES

STRAWBERRY JAM

5 c. crushed strawberries   1 box fruit pectin
7 c. sugar   1/2 tsp. butter

Put strawberries into a 6 to 8-quart kettle. Accurately measure sugar into separate bowl. Add fruit pectin and butter to strawberries. Bring to full rolling boil over high heat, stirring constantly. Quickly add sugar. Return to a full rolling boil and boil 1 minute, stirring constantly. Remove from heat. Skim off any foam. Fill prepared jars quickly to 1/4-inch of the top. Process in a boiling water canner for 5 minutes. Begin timing as soon as jars are in boiling water.

NO-COOK STRAWBERRY FREEZER JAM

2 c. crushed strawberries   3/4 c. water
4 c. sugar   1 box fruit pectin (1/3 c.)

Thoroughly mix fruit and sugar in large bowl; let stand 10 minutes. Mix water and fruit pectin in small saucepan. Boil 1 minute, stirring constantly. Remove from heat and stir into fruit. Continue stirring 3 minutes. Ladle quickly into six 1-cup containers. Cover at once with tight lids. Let stand overnight, then store in freezer.

STRAWBERRY RHUBARB JAM

4 c. prepared fruit, (about 1 qt.   6 c. sugar
    fully ripe strawberries and   1 box fruit pectin
    1 1/2 lb. fully ripe rhubarb   1/2 tsp. butter
    and 1/2 c. water)

Stem and crush strawberries, 1 c. at a time. Measure 2 1/4 c. into a 6 to 8-qt. saucepan. Finely chop rhubarb. Do not peel. Place in 2-quart saucepan. Add 1/2 c. water. Bring to a boil. Reduce heat; cover and simmer 2 minutes or until rhubarb is soft. Measure 1 3/4 c. and add to strawberries. Measure sugar into a separate bowl. Stir fruit pectin into fruit. Add butter. Bring mixture to full rolling boil on high heat, stirring constantly. Quickly stir in all sugar. Return to full rolling boil and boil exactly 1 minute, stirring constantly. Remove from heat. Skim off any foam with metal spoon. Ladle into jars, leaving 1/8-inch headspace. Cover with lids. Process in a boiling water canner for 10 minutes, timing as soon as jars are in the water.

STRAWBERRY RASPBERRY BLACKBERRY JAM

2 1/2 c. crushed strawberries
1 1/2 c. crushed raspberries
1 c. crushed blackberries

7 c. sugar
1 box fruit pectin (1/3 c.)
1/2 tsp. butter

Crush fruit thoroughly, one cup at a time. Put in a large kettle. Measure sugar into separate bowl. Stir fruit pectin into fruit in kettle. Add butter. Bring mixture to full rolling boil on high heat, stirring constantly. Quickly stir in all sugar. Return to full rolling boil and boil exactly 1 minute, stirring constantly. Remove from heat. Skim off any foam with metal spoon. Ladle quickly into prepared jars, filling to within 1/4-inch of tops. Process in boiling water for 5 minutes. Makes about 8 (1 c.) jars.

STRAWBERRY PRESERVES

1 1/2 qt. strawberries
5 c. sugar

1/3 c. lemon juice

Slice berries; combine with sugar then let stand 3-4 hours. Bring slowly to boil, stirring occasionally until sugar dissolves. Add lemon juice. Cook rapidly until berries are clear and syrup is thick, about 10-12 minutes. Pour into a shallow pan and let stand uncovered, 12-24 hours in a cool place. Heat mixture, pour hot preserves into hot jars. Process 5 minutes in a boiling water canner.

STRAWBERRIES – CANNING AND FREEZING

HOW TO CAN STRAWBERRIES[4]

Canning is not as desirable as freezing to preserve strawberries. They tend to fade and lose flavor. The following method will yield the best results for canned strawberries.

Hull and wash firm, ripe berries. Use 1/2 to 3/4 c. sugar for each quart of hulled berries and sprinkle over a thin layer of berries in a shallow pan. Continue to layer and sprinkle berries until you have enough for a batch. Allow to stand in a cool place 5 to 6 hours to draw out juice. Carefully heat to simmering. Do not boil. Pack hot in pint jars, leaving 1/2-inch headspace.

Process in boiling water for 15 minutes.

STRAWBERRY RHUBARB SAUCE

8 c. strawberries
3 lb. rhubarb
2 1/2 c. sugar

1/2 c. water
1 T. lemon juice

Wash and hull strawberries. Halve large berries. Cut rhubarb into 1-inch pieces. Combine all ingredients in a large kettle. Bring to a boil and boil 1/2 minute. Pack into pint jars, leaving 1/2-inch headspace. Process 15 minutes in a boiling water canner.

HOW TO FREEZE STRAWBERRIES

Sugar Pack: Wash and drain berries. Slice or crush berries then sprinkle with sugar to taste; mix until sugar is dissolved. Pack and freeze.

Unsweetened Loose Pack: Place on tray in a single layer; freeze for 1-2 hours; or until completely frozen. Repack into freezer bags and return to freezer.

And he said also to the people, When ye see a cloud rise out of the west, straightway ye say, There cometh a shower; and so it is. And when ye see the south wind blow, ye say, There will be heat; and it cometh to pass. Ye hypocrites, ye can discern the face of the sky and of the earth; but how is it that ye do not discern this time? Yea, and why even of yourselves judge ye not what is right?

Luke 12:54-57

Summer Squash

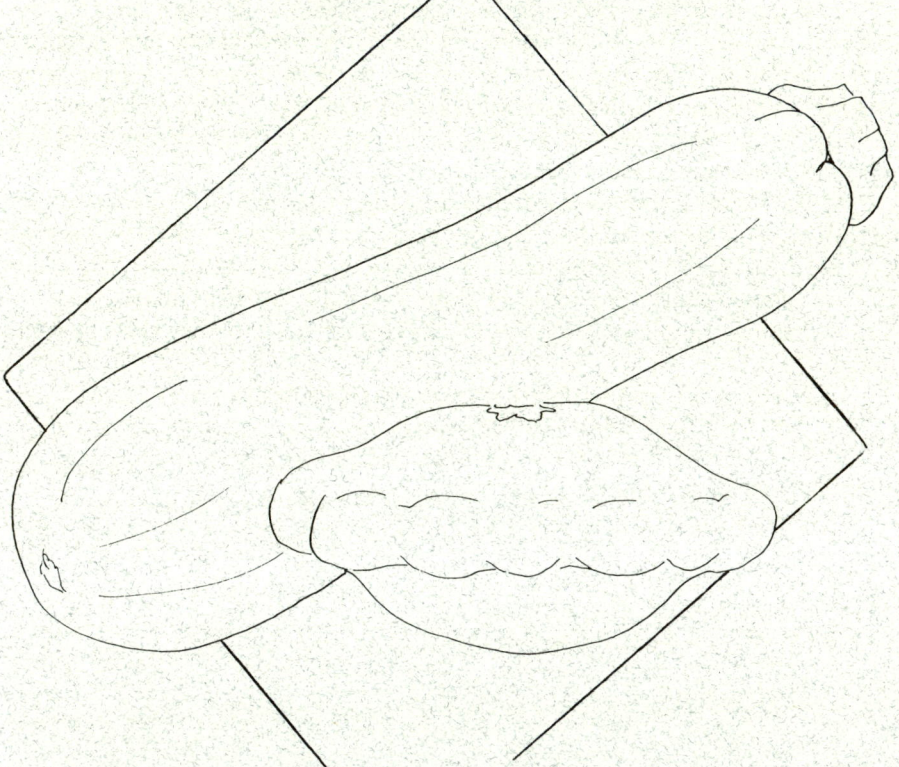

    Summer squash is a general term for more than 70 different varieties of fast-growing, tender-skinned, soft-fleshed, bland-tasting squash. Zucchini is by far the most famous (or is it infamous?) of all the summer squash. Some other common types are yellow squash—either straight or crookneck—and scallops (also called patty pans).

    Summer squash are easy to grow by direct seeding after the soil is warm and danger of frost is past. Plant seeds ½ inch deep every 6-12 inches, thinning to a final spacing of 18 inches for bush plants and 2-3 feet for vining plants. Squash seeds are susceptible to rotting in cool wet soils; minimum germination temperatures are 60 degrees; the ideal is 70 degrees.

For an earlier crop start seeds indoors in individual pots, 3-4 weeks before setting out. Black plastic mulch and row covers are well suited for growing summer squash.

Pick summer squash while the seeds are small and tender. Seeds and skin can both be eaten at this stage. Under ideal growing conditions, summer squash need to be picked every 2-3 days to keep them from getting too big. Discard overgrown, misshapen or soft tipped squash—there will be more good ones tomorrow.

All summer squash can be used interchangeably in recipes. Preferences are due to size, color and shape rather than to flavor.

Because of their bland flavor, summer squash lend themselves to many different cooking applications, taking on the flavor of whatever they're cooked with. Try using them as a substitute for rice, pasta or potatoes. Young, tender summer squash are excellent raw with dips or in salads. They're also delicious steamed, fried, sautéed, stuffed or baked in breads. Squash flowers are edible too, with some new varieties developed especially for their flowers.

As a testament to their extreme versatility, I suspect there have been more recipes inspired by the zucchini than by any other vegetable. Whole cookbooks have been devoted to zucchini squash.

Summer squash provide some vitamin A and C as well as folate.

Summer squash keep for about 7-10 days refrigerated; they can't be winter stored.

Yield: 1 lb. summer squash = 4 cups sliced or diced
1 bushel = 40 lb. = 32-40 pints

SUMMER SQUASH–SOUPS

ZUCCHINI BROCCOLI POTATO SOUP

1/4 c. butter
1 onion, chopped
3 medium zucchini, chopped
1 bunch broccoli, chopped
6 c. chicken broth
2 medium potatoes, peeled and
    shredded

1 tsp. salt or to taste
1 tsp. celery seed (optional)
1 tsp. cumin (optional)
1/4 tsp. pepper
1 c. light cream or whole milk

Heat butter and sauté onion several minutes. Add the zucchini and broccoli, sautéing lightly for 5 minutes or until tender crisp. Stir in broth. Add potatoes and seasonings. Bring to a boil then cook 10 minutes or until the vegetables are tender. Stir in cream and heat through.

SUMMER SQUASH–SALADS

SUMMER SQUASH SALAD

2 small zucchini
2 small yellow squash
2 tomatoes
1 small onion, chopped
1/2 c. olive or vegetable oil

2 T. vinegar or lemon juice
1/4 tsp. salt
1/4 tsp. basil
1/8 tsp. pepper

Cut squash into thin slices. Blanch one minute (if desired). Cool quickly and pat dry. Slice or chop tomatoes. Mix squash, tomatoes and onions in a bowl. Whisk remaining ingredients. Pour over salad just before serving.
Variation: Combine vegetables and serve with a favorite dressing.

Hint: Cut young summer squash into strips to eat with dip.

SUMMER SQUASH—SANDWICHES

ZUCCHINI PITA SANDWICHES

1/2 c. plain yogurt
1/2 c. shredded zucchini
1/4 tsp. dill weed
8 boiled ham slices
2 pita bread rounds, cut in half

1/2 c. alfalfa sprouts
tomato slices
4 slices process American cheese
cut in half

Combine yogurt, zucchini and dill weed; mix well. Spread one ham slice with one T. yogurt mixture; cover with second ham slice; roll up. Fill bread with sprouts, ham roll, tomatoes and cheese. Top with remaining yogurt mixture.

SUMMER SQUASH – SIDE AND MAIN DISHES

HOW TO COOK SUMMER SQUASH

Bring 1-inch of water to a boil. Add 3-4 c. sliced zucchini and 1/2-1 tsp. salt or to taste. Return to a boil, reduce heat, cover and simmer for 2 to 3 minutes or until tender crisp. Drain.

ZUCCHINI PARMESAN

4-5 small zucchini
2-3 T. butter
1/2 tsp. salt

1/8 tsp. pepper
2 T. grated Parmesan cheese

Halve squash lengthwise and across; cut into 3-inch long sticks. Sprinkle with salt and let drain 30 minutes. Squeeze lightly to remove water. Heat butter and sauté zucchini 3-5 minutes. Season to taste. Sprinkle with cheese and serve.
Variations: Sprinkle with 1/3 c. cheddar cheese instead of Parmesan cheese. For dilled zucchini delete cheese and toss with 1 tsp. dill weed instead.

The husbandman that laboureth must be first partaker of the fruits.

II Timothy 2:6

234

SAUTÉED SQUASH

2 small zucchini	1 green pepper, chopped
2 small yellow squash	(optional)
3 T. butter	1/2 tsp. salt or to taste
1 small onion, chopped	1/8 tsp. pepper

Cube, slice or cut squash into strips. (Sprinkle with salt and let drain 30 minutes if desired.) Heat the butter in a large skillet and add the squash and onion. Sauté, stirring frequently, about 5 minutes. Sliced squash will take less time. Large cubes may take a little longer. Season to taste.
Variation: Leave 3 1/2 to 4-inch squash whole for sautéed baby squash.

PAN FRIED SQUASH

zucchini, yellow, crookneck or	butter
patty pan squash	salt and pepper
flour	

Cut squash into 1/4-inch rounds. Dip in flour and fry in hot butter until golden-brown, turning once. Sprinkle with salt and pepper.

STIR FRIED ZUCCHINI

3 T. vegetable oil	1 T. sesame seeds (optional)
4-5 small zucchini, cut into strips	1 T. soy sauce
1/2 c. chopped onion	1/2 tsp. salt

Heat oil in a large skillet. Add zucchini and onion and stir fry 3-5 minutes, or until tender crisp. Add remaining ingredients and mix.

BROILED ZUCCHINI

Cut 8 small zucchini in half lengthwise. Brush with melted butter. Sprinkle with salt and pepper. Broil 5 to 6 inches from heat until tender, 10-12 minutes.

BAKED ZUCCHINI SLICES

2 6-inch zucchini	1 c. bread crumbs
1/4 tsp. salt	grated Parmesan cheese
1 egg, beaten	1/4 c. butter

Peel and cut zucchini into 1/2-inch slices. Add salt to beaten egg. Dip zucchini slices in egg, then in bread crumbs. Arrange the slices on a cookie sheet. Sprinkle each slice with Parmesan cheese and dot with butter. Bake at 375° for 35 minutes.

DEEP FRIED SUMMER SQUASH

thinly sliced squash rounds
vegetable oil for deep frying,
    2-inches deep
2 eggs

2 c. ice water
2 c. flour
1/2 tsp. salt

Beat eggs and ice water. Add flour and salt and mix just to combine. Dip squash into batter, dipping into flour first if wet. Cook 4-5 minutes. Remove with a slotted spoon. Drain on crumpled paper towel. Fry only a few at a time so oil stays hot.
Variation: Deep fry squash blossoms. Pick only male blossoms (those without tiny squash at the base of the flower) or the plants will quit bearing. Keep in ice water until ready to fry, then pat dry, dip in batter and fry.

GRILLED ZUCCHINI AND OTHER VEGETABLES

2 small zucchini
2 small summer squash
2 small eggplant
1 red onion

1 red pepper
olive or vegetable oil, as needed
vinegar, as needed

Cut zucchini, summer squash and eggplant lengthwise twice to obtain 4 wedges from each. Cut onion into 8 wedges. Cut red pepper lengthwise into 8 strips. Marinate in olive oil and vinegar for at least 30 minutes. Grill over medium-high heat, first one side and then the other, being careful not to burn. When both sides are charred and somewhat soft to the touch, the vegetables are done.

BAKED ZUCCHINI AND TOMATOES

2 medium zucchini, sliced
2 tomatoes, peeled and chopped
2 onions, sliced
1/2-1 tsp. salt

pepper
butter
1 c. dry bread crumbs

Layer zucchini, tomatoes and onions in a buttered casserole. Sprinkle each zucchini layer with salt and pepper and dot with butter. Sprinkle crumbs on top. Bake, uncovered, until vegetables are done, about 25 minutes.
Variation: Layer 2 c. shredded mozzarella cheese with other ingredients.

BAKED ZUCCHINI AND TOMATOES WITH CHEESE SAUCE

8 c. sliced zucchini
1/2 c. chopped onion
6 T. butter, divided
2 T. flour
1/2 c. milk
1/2 tsp. salt

1/2 lb. process American cheese,
cubed
2 tomatoes, peeled and chopped
1 1/2 c. fresh bread crumbs
2 T. butter, melted

Sauté zucchini and onion in 4 T. butter for 5 minutes. Melt 2 T. butter in a small saucepan. Add flour, then stir in milk. Stir until milk thickens and boils. Add cheese cubes; stir until melted. Layer 1/2 of zucchini mixture, tomatoes and cheese sauce in a 13 x 9 pan. Repeat layers. Top with crumbs tossed with melted butter. Bake at 350° for 35 minutes.

SCALLOPED SUMMER SQUASH

4 c. diced squash, cooked
1 tsp. salt
1/8 tsp. pepper
2 T. butter
30 soda crackers

1 1/2 c. scalded milk
2 eggs, beaten
1 medium onion, chopped
American cheese slices

Drain excess water from squash. Add salt, pepper, butter and crackers to milk. Add squash, eggs and onion. Bake in a covered casserole at 350° for 1 hour. Uncover and put cheese slices on top; bake until melted.

ZUCCHINI QUICHE

3 c. grated zucchini
1 c. finely chopped onion
1 c. Swiss or mozzarella cheese
1 unbaked, 9-inch pie shell
1/2 c. light cream or whole milk

3 eggs
1/2 tsp. salt
1/2 tsp. basil or oregano
1/4 tsp. thyme

Wrap zucchini in a dish towel and squeeze to remove excess water. Combine zucchini, onion and cheese. Spread into the unbaked pie shell. Briefly beat together remaining ingredients and pour over zucchini mixture. Bake at 400° for 20 minutes. Reduce heat to 350° and bake 20 more minutes or until knife inserted in the center comes out clean.

STUFFED SCALLOP SQUASH

4 squash
4 slices bacon, cooked crisp
1/2 c. onion, chopped

3/4 c. bread crumbs
1/4 c. milk

Cook squash in boiling salted water for 10 minutes. Drain and cool. From the stem end cut a small slice; scoop out center, leaving 1/2-inch rim. Chop the squash which has been removed very finely. Sprinkle the squash cups lightly with salt. Saute onion in bacon drippings; add crumbs, milk and reserved squash. Fill cups; sprinkle crisp bacon on top. Place in a shallow baking pan. Bake at 350° for 25-30 minutes.

STUFFED ZUCCHINI

6 medium zucchini
1/2 c. chopped onion
2 T. butter
1 c. chopped tomato
1 tsp. salt

1/4 tsp. poultry seasoning
1/8 tsp. pepper
1 1/2 c. shredded Cheddar cheese
4 slices crisply cooked bacon,
    crumbled

Trim ends of zucchini. Cook, covered, in boiling salted water 5-8 minutes; drain. Cut in half lengthwise. Scoop out centers; chop. Sauté onion in butter until tender; combine with chopped zucchini, tomato, seasonings, cheese and bacon. Fill zucchini. Arrange in a 13 x 9 pan. Bake at 350° for 30 minutes.

STUFFED ZUCCHINI BOATS

2 10-inch zucchini
12 oz. pork sausage
1/2 c. chopped onion
1/2 c. chopped green pepper
1/2 c. chopped red sweet pepper
1 c. corn

4.5 oz. jar mushrooms, drained
1 c. tomatoes, peeled, seeded and
    chopped
1/4 c. grated Parmesan cheese
1 T. parsley flakes
1 c. shredded mozzarella cheese

Trim ends from zucchini and cook in boiling water for 10 minutes. Slice each in half lengthwise. Cut thin slices from the bottom so each half will sit upright. Remove seeds, leaving 1/2-inch pulp on all sides. Place on ungreased jelly roll pan. Set aside. In large skillet, brown sausage, onion and peppers; drain well. Stir in corn, mushrooms, tomato, Parmesan cheese and parsley flakes. Spoon sausage mixture evenly into zucchini halves. Cover with foil. Bake at 350° for 25-35 minutes or until thoroughly heated. Remove foil. Sprinkle mozzarella cheese on each filled zucchini. Broil 6-8 inches from heat for 2-3 minutes or until cheese melts. (See variation Page 223.)

238

Variations (for stuffed zucchini boats): Brown 1 lb. hamburger, 1 c. chopped onion and 1 c. chopped sweet peppers. Add 2 c. cooked rice and 1-2 c. spaghetti sauce, white sauce or cheese sauce. Sprinkle with cheese if desired.
Stuff squash with your favorite casserole ingredients or casserole leftovers.

SQUASH FRITTERS

4 c. shredded squash	1/8 tsp. pepper
1/3 c. finely chopped onion	2 eggs, beaten
(optional)	1/2 c. flour
1/2 tsp. salt	vegetable oil

Wrap shredded squash in dish towel and squeeze out as much liquid as possible. Combine squash with onion, salt, pepper and eggs. Mix well. Stir in flour. Heat 1 T. oil in a skillet over medium-high heat. Drop in 4 rounded T. zucchini mixture and press down to form 3-inch pancakes. Cook 4-5 minutes or until golden brown, turn once. Repeat with remaining batter, adding oil as needed.

ZUCCHINI POTATO PATTIES

1 1/2 c. shredded zucchini	1 tsp. parsley
1 1/2 c. peeled, shredded potato	1 tsp. salt
1/4 c. chopped onion	1 tsp. pepper
1/4 c. flour	3 eggs, slightly beaten

Squeeze excess liquid out of zucchini. In a large bowl, toss zucchini, potato and onion with flour. Stir in remaining ingredients. Heat a small amount of oil in a large skillet over medium heat. Drop zucchini mixture (about 1/4 c.) into skillet to form patties. Fry until golden brown, turn and brown second side. If desired, top with a slice of cheese after turning.

ZUCCHINI OMELET

2 c. thinly sliced zucchini	1 tsp. salt or to taste
1 onion	1/8 tsp. pepper
2-3 T. butter	1/2 c. shredded cheese (optional)
6 eggs	

Quarter zucchini lengthwise then slice thin. Chop onion fine. Sauté zucchini and onion in butter for 4 minutes, stirring occasionally. Meanwhile, beat eggs and add salt and pepper. Pour over zucchini and stir quickly to mix. Cook, lifting cooked egg around the edge of the pan so the uncooked portion runs underneath. Slide pan back and forth to prevent sticking. Cook until mixture is set, but top is creamy. Sprinkle half with cheese and fold in half. Slide onto a serving dish.

SUMMER SQUASH TOMATO SKILLET

1 large onion	2 tomatoes, peeled and chopped
1 clove garlic	1 tsp. salt
3 T. olive or vegetable oil	1 tsp. thyme
1 yellow squash	1 tsp. basil
1 zucchini	1/4 tsp. pepper

In a large skillet, sauté onion and garlic in oil until soft. Trim, halve and slice yellow squash and zucchini. Add to skillet and sauté 3 minutes. Stir in tomatoes and seasonings. Cover and cook until vegetables are tender crisp and liquid is absorbed.

ZUCCHINI AND YELLOW SQUASH WITH CREAM

1 medium zucchini, sliced thin	1/4 tsp. salt or to taste
1 medium yellow squash,	1/8 tsp. pepper
sliced thin	1 c. cream
2 T. butter	1/2 tsp. dill weed

Sauté squash in butter. Season with salt and pepper. Add cream and simmer for 10-15 minutes. Mix well with dill. Serve hot.

YELLOW SQUASH WITH HERBED RICE

1/2 c. chopped onion	1 tsp. oregano or Italian
1 c. chopped celery	seasoning
4 T. butter, divided	1/2 tsp. parsley
1 c. uncooked rice	3 c. sliced crookneck or yellow
2 1/2 c. chicken broth	squash
1 tsp. salt or to taste	

Sauté onion and celery in 2 T. butter. Do not brown. Add rice and stir. Add broth, salt and herbs. Bring to a boil. Reduce heat and cook, covered, until rice is tender. Meanwhile, sauté squash in remaining butter. Add squash to rice.

Hint: Blanch zucchini pieces to be used in salads 1 minute or use them raw.

ZUCCHINI WITH PASTA

8 oz. tubular or spiral pasta
1/2 c. olive or vegetable oil
1 clove garlic
1/2 lb. sliced mushrooms
2-3 small zucchini, sliced thin
2 small carrots, sliced

1 red pepper, seeded and sliced
    thin
1 T. chopped fresh parsley
salt and pepper to taste
Parmesan cheese

Cook pasta according to directions. Heat oil and sauté garlic until slightly browned. Add vegetables and stir. Sauté 3-5 minutes or until tender crisp, stirring frequently. Toss with parsley and drained pasta. Season to taste. Sprinkle with grated cheese before serving.

ZUCCHINI STEW

2 T. vegetable oil
3 lb. boneless beef chuck roast,
    cut into 1-inch pieces
1/2 tsp. salt
1 c. thick and chunky salsa
2 medium zucchini, cut into 3/4-
    inch pieces

15 oz. can black beans, rinsed
    and drained or 1 pt. kidney
    beans
1 c. corn
2 T. corn starch dissolved in 3 T.
    water

Heat oil in a large kettle. Add beef (1/2 at a time) and brown evenly. Pour off drippings. Season with salt. Stir in salsa and broth. Bring to a boil; reduce heat to low. Cover tightly and simmer 1 1/4 hours or until tender. Stir in zucchini, beans and corn. Bring to a boil; reduce heat to low. Cover tightly and simmer 15 minutes longer or until vegetables are tender. Add cornstarch mixture; cook and stir 1 minute or until thickened and bubbly. Serve with chopped tomatoes, chopped cilantro and sour cream if desired.

ZUCCHINI MEAT LOAF

2 lb. ground beef
2 c. coarsely grated zucchini
1 c. milk
1 c. bread or cracker crumbs
1 onion, finely chopped
1 egg, beaten

1 tsp. salt
1 tsp. Italian seasoning
1 tsp. parsley
1/4 tsp. pepper
1/2 c. grated Parmesan cheese
    (optional)

Combine all ingredients. Mix thoroughly. Pack into a loaf pan. Bake at 350° for 1 1/4 hours.

ZUCCHINI LASAGNA

1/2 lb. ground beef
1 garlic clove, minced
1 c. tomatoes, peeled, seeded and
    chopped
1 tsp. Italian seasoning

1 tsp. salt
2 8-inch zucchini, sliced
    lengthwise
1 c. cottage cheese
1 c. grated mozzarella cheese

Cook ground beef and garlic in a skillet until lightly browned. Stir in tomatoes and seasonings; bring to a boil. Arrange slices of zucchini in the bottom of an 8-inch baking dish. Spoon on half of beef mixture and half of cottage cheese. Sprinkle with half of mozzarella cheese. Repeat layering. Bake at 350° for 40 minutes.

TURKEY ZUCCHINI SKILLET

1 T. butter
2 T. lemon juice
2 garlic cloves, minced
1/2 tsp. basil
1 lb. turkey breast, cut into thin
    strips

2 c. fresh mushrooms, sliced
2 small zucchini, thinly sliced
1/4 c. thinly sliced green onions
1/2 tsp. oregano

Melt butter in a large skillet over medium-high heat. Stir in lemon juice, garlic, basil and oregano. Add turkey. Cook until lightly browned. Remove from skillet; keep warm. Add mushrooms, zucchini and onions to same skillet; cook and stir over medium-high heat until zucchini is tender crisp. Arrange vegetables and turkey on a large serving platter.

SAUSAGE ZUCCHINI STIR FRY

2 medium zucchini, cut in half
    lengthwise
1 lb. bulk sausage
1 can cream of mushroom soup

1/2 c. thinly sliced onion
1 clove garlic, minced
1 tomato cut in wedges

Cut zucchini into 1-inch pieces. Shape sausage into 16 meatballs. Brown in skillet. Pour off fat. Add remaining ingredients except tomato. Cover; simmer 15 minutes or until done, stirring often. Add tomatoes; heat.

Hint: Recipes for zucchini, yellow squash, crookneck squash and scalloped squash are interchangeable in most recipes.

242

BEEF STIR FRY WITH ZUCCHINI

2 cloves garlic, crushed
1 T. olive or vegetable oil
1 lb. beef round steak, cut into 1/8
    to 1/4-inch thick strips
salt and pepper to taste
2 small zucchini, thinly sliced

1 c. cherry tomato halves or
    peeled and seeded tomato
    wedges,
1/4 c. Italian salad dressing
2 c. hot cooked spaghetti
1 T. grated Parmesan cheese

Sauté garlic in hot oil 1 minute. Add beef strips, half at a time; stir fry about 2 minutes. Season with salt and pepper, if desired. Remove with slotted spoon; keep warm. Add zucchini to same skillet; adding more oil if needed. Stir fry 2 to 3 minutes or until tender crisp. Return beef to skillet with tomatoes and dressing; heat through. Pour beef mixture over hot pasta; sprinkle with Parmesan cheese.

PORK ZUCCHINI PINEAPPLE STIR FRY

1/3 c. soy sauce
1/3 c. vinegar
2 T. vegetable oil, divided
4 cloves garlic, finely chopped
1/2 tsp. pepper
1 lb. pork tenderloin, cut into 1-
    inch pieces
1 1/2 c. sliced zucchini

1 c. sliced mushrooms
1 c. chopped red or green bell
    pepper
20 oz. can pineapple chunks,
    drained
1/4 c. sliced green onion
hot cooked rice

Combine soy sauce, vinegar, 1 T. oil, garlic and pepper in a small bowl; set aside. Combine pork with 1/2 c. reserved soy sauce mixture in shallow non-metallic dish. Cover; marinate 15 minutes in refrigerator. Heat 1 T. oil over medium-high heat in large skillet. Drain pork, discard marinade; add to skillet. Cook 3 minutes or until pork is cooked; remove from pan. Add zucchini, mushrooms and bell pepper to skillet. Cook 3 minutes or until vegetables are tender crisp. Add soy sauce mixture to skillet with pineapple, green onion and pork; heat through. Serve over rice.

And he said, So is the kingdom of God, as if a man should cast seed into the ground; And should sleep, and rise night and day, and the seed should spring up, he knoweth not how. For the earth bringeth forth fruit of herself; first the blade, then the ear, after that the full corn in the ear. But when the fruit is brought forth, immediately he putteth in the sickle, because the harvest is come.

Mark 4:26-29

SAUSAGE AND ZUCCHINI WITH SPAGHETTI

1 1/2 lb. bulk sausage
2 green peppers, seeded and
   chopped
1 c. minced onions
1 clove garlic, minced
3 medium zucchini, shredded

2 c. peeled and chopped tomatoes
1 tsp. basil
1/2 tsp. salt
1/2 c. grated Parmesan cheese
cooked spaghetti

Cook sausage, green peppers, onions and garlic in a large skillet. Drain, when meat is lightly browned. Add the next 5 ingredients. Simmer for 15 minutes. Remove from heat, add cheese; mix well. Serve over spaghetti.
Variation: Add 1/4 c. chopped jalapeno peppers with zucchini and tomatoes.

ZUCCHINI HAM CASSEROLE

3 c. thinly sliced zucchini
2 T. butter
2 T. flour
1 c. milk
1 c. shredded Cheddar cheese
1 1/2 c. cooked, chopped ham

1 onion, sliced
1/2 tsp. salt or to taste
1/8 tsp. pepper
1 c. bread crumbs
2 T. melted butter

Cook zucchini in boiling, salted water about 5 minutes. Drain well. Melt butter in a large skillet and mix in flour. Add milk and stir until thickened and boiling. Stir in cheese and add ham. Place zucchini in bottom of shallow 1 1/2-quart buttered baking dish. Arrange onion slices over zucchini. Sprinkle on salt and pepper. Spoon cheese sauce over vegetables. Top with crumbs and drizzle with butter. Bake at 350° for 20-25 minutes.

ZUCCHINI TUNA CASSEROLE

2 c. shredded zucchini
1/4 c. butter
1 c. sliced celery
1/2 c. chopped onions
1/4 c. flour
2 c. milk

2 cans tuna, drained
1 c. grated Cheddar cheese
1 tsp. salt
1 tsp. parsley
1 tsp. dried dill weed
12 oz. noodles, cooked

Squeeze zucchini lightly to remove excess moisture. Heat butter in a large skillet. Add zucchini, celery and onions. Sauté 5 minutes. Blend in flour. Add milk, stirring until thick. Add remaining ingredients. Put in a casserole and bake at 350° for 20-30 minutes.

ZUCCHINI CHICKEN RICE CASSEROLE

3 T. vegetable oil
1 c. chopped onion
3 c. diced zucchini
2 c. chopped, peeled tomatoes
1 c. sliced mushrooms
3 c. diced, cooked chicken

2 1/2 c. chicken broth or water
1 c. uncooked brown rice
1/2 c. grated Parmesan cheese
1 tsp. salt
1/2 tsp. thyme
1/8 tsp. pepper

Heat oil and sauté onion for 2 minutes. Add zucchini, tomatoes and mushrooms and sauté 3 minutes longer. Combine the vegetables with the remaining ingredients. Stir well and pour into a 13 x 9 pan. Bake at 350° for 1 hour.

ZUCCHINI GROUND BEEF CASSEROLE

1 c. chopped onions
2 green peppers, chopped
2 T. vegetable oil
1 lb. ground beef
2 c. sliced zucchini

2 c. tomatoes, peeled, seeded and
   chopped
1 tsp. dried oregano
1 tsp. dried basil
1 tsp. salt or to taste
pepper

Sauté onions and green peppers for two minutes in hot oil. Add ground beef and brown. Stir in remaining ingredients. Put in a casserole and bake at 350° for 35 minutes.

ZUCCHINI PIZZA CASSEROLE

2-3 6-inch zucchini, unpeeled,
   sliced
2 c. water
1/2 tsp. salt
1 1/2 lb. ground beef
1 onion, chopped
1 c. mushrooms

1 tsp. oregano
1/4 tsp. pepper
1/2 tsp. salt
2-15 oz. cans spaghetti sauce (or 2
   pints homemade sauce)
1 lb. mozzarella cheese, shredded
4 oz. pepperoni (optional)

Prepare zucchini. Bring water to a boil. Add zucchini and salt. Return to a boil; reduce heat and cook 2-3 minutes. Drain well. Brown ground beef and onion. Add mushrooms, seasonings and zucchini. Pour half of the mixture into a casserole. Add 1 can spaghetti sauce, 1/2 of the cheese and 1/2 of the pepperoni. Repeat layers. Bake at 350° for 30 minutes.
Variation: Mix all ingredients, saving some of the cheese to sprinkle on top; bake.

SUMMER SQUASH – BAKED GOODS AND DESSERTS

ZUCCHINI MUFFINS

2 c. flour	2 eggs
1/2 c. brown sugar, packed	3/4 c. milk
3 tsp. baking powder	1/3 c. vegetable oil
1 tsp. cinnamon	1 c. grated zucchini
1/2 tsp. salt	2/3 c. raisins

Combine dry ingredients. Beat eggs, milk and oil. Fold in zucchini and raisins. Add dry ingredients, stirring only until combined. Spoon into muffin tins. Bake at 375° approximately 20 minutes. Makes 12 muffins.
Variation: Use 2 c. whole wheat flour.

ZUCCHINI BREAD

3 eggs	1 1/2 c. raisins
1 1/2 c. sugar	3 c. flour
2 tsp. vanilla	1 tsp. baking powder
1 c. olive or vegetable oil	1 tsp. soda
1 tsp. cinnamon	
3 c. grated, unpeeled zucchini	

Beat the eggs then add the sugar, vanilla, oil and cinnamon. Mix in squash and raisins. Combine and add remaining ingredients. Mix well. Bake in 2-9 x 5 loaf pans at 350° for 1 to 1 1/4 hours, or until done.
Variation: For healthier zucchini bread, use only 1 c. sugar and 1/2 c. oil. Substitute 2 c. whole wheat flour and 1 c. oatmeal for the flour. Add another tsp. baking powder, if desired.

Hint: Sliced, cubed or grated summer squash, like eggplant, is less watery if sprinkled with salt and drained 30 minutes. Squeeze slightly to remove water. Use about 1 tsp. salt to 6 c. squash. Adjust salt in the recipe or rinse and pat dry. For saltless removal of moisture, blanch squash whole for 2-10 minutes, depending on size. Drain, then chop, slice or grate.

ZUCCHINI COOKIES WITH LEMON GLAZE

2 c. flour
1 tsp. baking powder
1/2 tsp. salt
3/4 c. butter
3/4 c. sugar
1 egg, beaten

grated rind of one lemon
1 c. shredded zucchini
1 c. chopped walnuts or pecans
1 c. powdered sugar
1 1/2 T. lemon juice

Combine flour, baking powder and salt; set aside. In a large bowl, cream butter and sugar. Beat in egg and lemon rind. Stir in flour mixture until smooth. Stir in zucchini and nuts. Drop by rounded teaspoons on greased cookie sheets. Bake at 375° for 15-20 minutes or until lightly browned. Drizzle with lemon glaze while still warm. To make glaze, mix powdered sugar and lemon juice until smooth.

ZUCCHINI BROWNIES

3 eggs
1 c. sugar
1/2 c. vegetable oil
1 c. grated zucchini
1 tsp. vanilla

1 1/2 c. flour
1/4 c. cocoa
1 tsp. soda
1/4 tsp. salt
1/2 tsp. cinnamon

Beat eggs, sugar and oil. Add zucchini and vanilla. Combine and add remaining ingredients. Bake in a buttered 13 x 9 pan at 350° for 20-30 minutes.

ZUCCHINI CHOCOLATE CAKE

1 1/2 c. sugar
1/2 c. butter
1/4 c. vegetable oil
3 eggs
1/2 c. milk
1 tsp. vanilla
2 1/2 c. flour

1/2 c. cocoa
1 tsp. baking powder
1 tsp. soda
1 tsp. salt
1/2 tsp. cinnamon (optional)
2 c. shredded, peeled zucchini

Cream sugar, butter and oil. Beat in eggs, milk and vanilla. Combine dry ingredients and add. Stir in zucchini. Pour into a buttered 13 x 9 pan. Bake at 350° approximately 40 minutes.
Variation: Add 1 tsp. grated orange to the batter. Make glaze with 3/4 c. powdered sugar, 1/2 tsp. grated orange peel and 1 T. orange juice. Drizzle over the cake.

247

ZUCCHINI CARROT CAKE

4 eggs
2 c. sugar
1 1/4 c. vegetable oil
2 1/2 c. flour
2 tsp. baking powder
2 tsp. soda
2 tsp. cinnamon
1 tsp. salt

1/2 tsp. ginger
1/2 tsp. allspice
1/2 tsp. nutmeg
2 c. grated zucchini
2 c. grated carrots
1 c. coarsely chopped nuts
    (optional)

Beat eggs and sugar until light. Add oil. Combine dry ingredients and add. Beat several minutes, then stir in remaining ingredients. Pour into a buttered 13 x 9 cake pan or 3 round cake pans. Bake at 350° approximately 40 minutes. Round cake pans will not take as long. Cool 5 minutes before removing from the pan. Eat plain or frost with cream cheese frosting.

ZUCCHINI DESSERT

8 c. peeled, seeded and sliced
    zucchini
1/2 c. lemon juice
1 c. sugar
1 1/2 tsp. cinnamon, divided

1/2 tsp. nutmeg
4 c. flour
2 c. sugar
1 1/2 c. butter, softened

Cook zucchini and lemon juice 5-10 minutes, stirring frequently. Stir in 1 c. sugar, 1 tsp. cinnamon and nutmeg. Remove from heat. Combine remaining ingredients to make a crust. Mix until crumbly. Stir 1/2 c. of the crumbs into the zucchini mixture. Press half of the crumbs into a buttered 15 x 10 x 1-inch pan. Spread zucchini over the crust then crumble the remaining crumbs on the zucchini. Bake at 375° for 35-40 minutes.

YELLOW SQUASH PIE

1 9-inch pie shell, unbaked
3 eggs
1 1/4 c. sugar
1 T. flour
2 T. butter, melted

1 tsp. vanilla
1 tsp. coconut extract
1/4 tsp. salt
2 c. peeled and grated yellow
    squash

Beat eggs briefly then add remaining ingredients. Mix well. Pour into the unbaked pie shell. Bake at 400° for 15 minutes. Reduce heat and bake at 350° about 45 minutes longer or until golden brown.

SUMMER SQUASH – CANNING AND FREEZING

HOW TO CAN SUMMER SQUASH[1]

Raw Pack: Wash but do not peel squash. Trim ends. Cut into 1/2-inch slices; halve or quarter to make uniformly sized pieces. Pack tightly, leaving 1-inch headspace. Add 1/2 tsp. salt to pints and 1 tsp. to quarts. Cover with boiling water, leaving 1/2-inch headspace.

Hot Pack: Prepare squash as for raw pack. Cover with boiling water and boil 2-3 minutes. Pack hot, loosely. Cover with boiling cooking liquid, leaving 1-inch headspace. Add salt as for raw pack.

Process in a pressure canner, pints 25 minutes for raw pack and 30 minutes for hot pack. Process raw pack quarts for 30 minutes and hot pack for 40 minutes. Process at 10 lb. of pressure at elevations up to 1000 feet above sea level. Process at 15 lb. of pressure at elevations over 1000 feet above sea level. Dial gauges should be at 11 lb. of pressure up to 2000 ft. above sea level.

ZUCCHINI PINEAPPLE TO CAN

(Unlike some other zucchini-pineapple recipes, this is a tested recipe and will ensure a safe product if followed precisely.)

4 quarts zucchini, grated or diced	**1 46-oz. can unsweetened**
1 1/2 c. bottled lemon juice	**pineapple juice**
	3 c. sugar

Simmer all ingredients together for 20 minutes. Pack hot into half-pint or pint jars (do not use quarts). Evenly distribute solids and liquid in the jars. Leave 1/2-inch headspace. Process 15 minutes in a boiling water canner. Can be used instead of crushed pineapple.
Variation: Replace pineapple juice with 1 tsp. pineapple extract and 1 12-oz. can frozen pineapple juice concentrate.

For they have sown the wind, and they shall reap the whirlwind: it hath no stalk; the bud shall yield no meal: if so be it yield, the strangers shall swallow it up.

Hosea 8:7

249

ZUCCHINI BREAD AND BUTTER PICKLE

2 gal. thinly sliced zucchini	2 qt. vinegar
1 qt. thinly sliced onions	1 qt. sugar
1/2 c. salt	1 tsp. turmeric
2 qt. water	1/4 c. whole mustard seed

Cover zucchini and onions with salt and water. Let stand 3 hours; drain. Put zucchini and onions in a large kettle. Mix the remaining ingredients and pour over the zucchini and onions. Heat just to a boil. Pack into prepared jars, leaving 1/2-inch headspace. Cover. Process in a boiling water canner for 10 minutes. Makes 8 pints.

ZUCCHINI VEGETABLE MIX

4 qt. cubed, unpeeled zucchini	1/2 c. salt
6 onions, chopped	8 c. vinegar
2 c. carrots, sliced	5 c. sugar
2 c. celery, coarsely chopped	1 T. celery seed
2 heads of cauliflower florets	2 tsp. garlic salt
4 red sweet peppers, chopped	1 tsp. turmeric

Mix vegetables and salt together; let stand for 3 hours. Drain. Combine remaining ingredients in a very large kettle to make syrup. Bring to a boil; add vegetables and cook for 5 minutes. Put vegetables in prepared pint jars. Add hot syrup, leaving 1/2-inch headspace. Adjust lids and process 10 minutes in a boiling water canner.

ZUCCHINI RELISH

10 c. chopped, unpeeled zucchini	2 1/2 c. vinegar
4 c. chopped onion	3 c. sugar
3 green peppers, chopped	1 tsp. turmeric
3 red peppers, chopped	1 tsp. celery seed
1/4 c. salt	

Mix chopped vegetables with salt and let set overnight or 12 hours. Drain well. Combine remaining ingredients and bring to a boil. Add vegetables. Bring to a boil and cook 3 minutes. Put into prepared pint jars leaving 1/2-inch headspace. Put lids on. Process in a boiling water canner for 10 minutes.

HOW TO FREEZE SUMMER SQUASH

Sliced: Choose young squash with tender skin. Wash, slice (or cube); blanch three minutes. Cool immediately in cold water, drain and put into freezer containers. Freeze.

Mashed: Wash, slice and cook in a very small amount of water until just tender. Mash. Pour into a bowl, set in ice water to cool quickly. Package and freeze.

Frozen summer squash works best in baked goods recipes.

Who can find a virtuous woman? for her price is far above rubies. The heart of her husband doth safely trust in her, so that he shall have no need of spoil. She will do him good and not evil all the days of her life. She seeketh wool, and flax, and worketh willingly with her hands. She is like the merchants' ships; she bringeth her food from afar. She riseth also while it is yet night, and giveth meat to her household, and a portion to her maidens. She considereth a field, and buyeth it: with the fruit of her hands she planteth a vineyard.

Provervs 31:10-16

NOTES

Sweet Potatoes

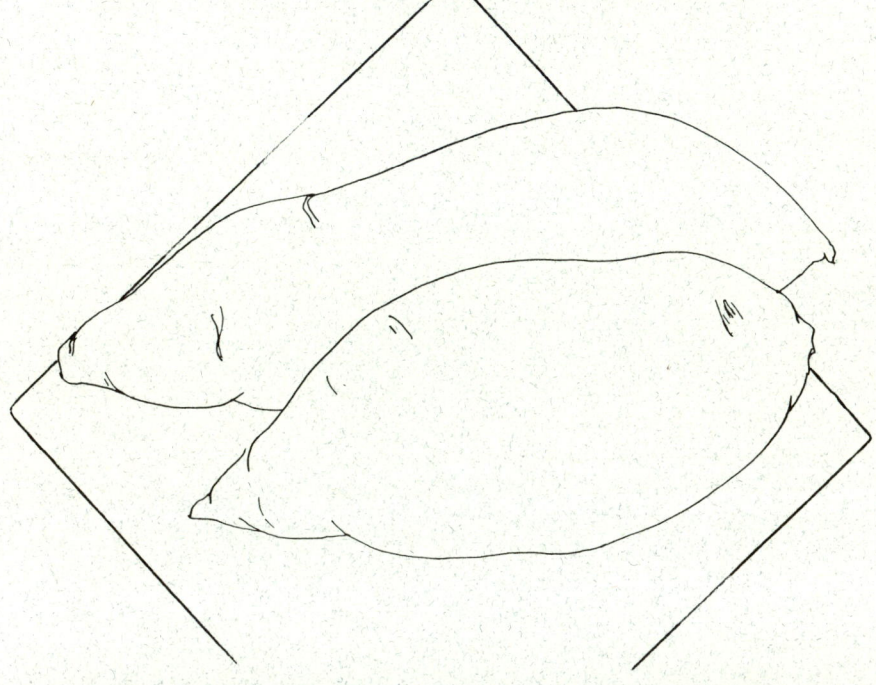

To the purist, sweet potatoes are not yams. To the practicalist, the two terms are interchangeable. Yams are a tropical crop that require 8-11 months to mature. All of the yams grown commercially in the United States and sold in supermarkets are technically sweet potatoes—regardless of what the label says. Enough said. Sweet potatoes are too delicious to get hung up on their name.

Sweet potatoes do best in long, hot summer regions. There are, however, some varieties like Georgia jet, that extend the range of sweet potato production even into the cool summers of central Wisconsin and other northern regions. Days to maturity range from 90 to 140 days.

Sweet potatoes are grown from vine slips that can be purchased from a garden center. Or you can grow your own slips by suspending the small end of a whole sweet potato in water. The top 2/3 of the potato should be out of the water. Start about 10 weeks before your frost free date. Once shoots are 8-10 inches long, break them off at the potato and place the shoots in water to allow them to root. Roots develop in 10-14 days. Keep in water until planting time.

Plant outside after frost danger is past and soil is thoroughly warm. Plant in well-drained, loose soil 12-18 inches apart. Longer spacings yield larger tubers, but quality tends to decrease with bigger potatoes.

If your soil is heavy and poorly drained, plant slips on top of a 12-15 inch ridge. Northern gardeners can benefit immensely from black plastic mulch laid over the ridge. This warms the soil faster and speeds plant growth. If you fertilize, stick to low nitrogen formulations. High nitrogen levels result in long vines and thin, undersized tubers.

Harvest sweet potatoes in the fall when frost danger is imminent. If the leaves are damaged by frost, dig immediately.

To store, allow the sweet potatoes to dry for 2-3 hours. (Avoid direct sunlight.) Then move to a dry, warm (85 degrees) spot for 2 weeks. Store at 55 degrees for 8-24 weeks.

Handle sweet potatoes carefully; they bruise easily; decreasing their storageability.

Sweet potatoes are excellent baked, boiled or glazed with brown sugar.

Sweet potatoes are a good sources of beta carotene, vitamin C and B6, folate and potassium.

Yield: 1 lb. fresh sweet potatoes = 3 cups cubed

SWEET POTATO SALAD

2 c. diced, cold, cooked sweet
potatoes
1 c. chopped celery
1/4 c. chopped green pepper

1/4 c. chopped onion
1/2 c. mayonnaise or salad
dressing

Combine all ingredients. Chill.

SWEET POTATO FRUIT SALAD

2/3 c. mayonnaise
1 T. lemon juice
1 T. honey
2 apples, diced

1 lb. sweet potatoes, cooked,
peeled and cubed
1 lb. seedless grapes
2 bananas, sliced

In a large bowl, combine mayonnaise, lemon juice and honey. Add apples, sweet potatoes and grapes. Toss gently to coat. Cover and refrigerate 2 hours to blend flavors, stirring occasionally. Add bananas and toss gently.

SWEET POTATOES – SIDE AND MAIN DISHES

HOW TO COOK SWEET POTATOES

Bring 1-inch of water to a boil in a large kettle. Add 4 medium sweet potatoes and 1/2 tsp. salt or to taste. Return to a boil. Cover and simmer 20-25 minutes or until fork tender. Drain and peel.

BAKED SWEET POTATOES

Wash medium sweet potatoes. Prick with a fork. Bake at 400° approximately 50 minutes. Cut open and eat with butter and salt.

Be patient therefore, brethren, unto the coming of the Lord. Behold, the husbandman waitheth for the precious fruit of the earth, and hath long patience for it, until he receive the early and latter rain. Be ye also patient; stablish your hearts: for the coming of the Lord draweth nigh.

James 5:7,8

SWEET POTATO CHIPS

4 medium sweet potatoes   **vegetable oil**
2 qt. ice water

Peel sweet potatoes and slice 1/16-inch thick. Soak in ice water 1 hour. Drain and pat dry. Heat enough vegetable oil so it is 2 to 3-inches deep. Fry sweet potatoes at 360° until light brown around the edges, 1-2 minutes. Drain on crumpled paper towels. Sprinkle with salt.

SWEET POTATOES WITH MAPLE SYRUP

1/2 c. maple syrup   **4 c. cooked sweet potatoes, sliced**
1/4 c. butter

Bring syrup and butter to a boil. Boil rapidly for 5 minutes or until thickened. Pour over hot sweet potatoes. Serve warm.

SWEET POTATOES WITH ORANGE JUICE

2 1/2 c. sliced, cooked sweet   **3 T. brown sugar**
**   potatoes**   **1 T. grated orange rind**
3 T. butter   **2 T. orange juice**

Sauté potatoes in butter until browned on one side. Turn and sprinkle with sugar, rind and juice. Cover and brown slowly on the other side.

SKILLET CANDIED SWEET POTATOES

6 medium sweet potatoes   **1/2 c. brown sugar**
1/4 c. butter   **1/4 tsp. salt**

Cook sweet potatoes just until tender. Peel. Melt butter in a skillet. Add sugar and salt. Add sweet potatoes when sugar bubbles. Cook over medium heat, about 20 minutes, turning sweet potatoes occasionally.

The wicked worketh a deceitful work: but to him that soweth righteousness shall be a sure reward.
Proverbs 11:18

BAKED CANDIED SWEET POTATOES

6 medium sweet potatoes
1 c. sugar
3 T. flour
1/2 tsp. salt
2 T. butter

miniature marshmallows
1/2 c. chopped nuts (optional)
1 c. thin cream or evaporated
    milk

Cook sweet potatoes until tender. Drain and peel. Slice 1/2 to 3/4-inch thick and arrange in a buttered casserole or 13 x 9 pan. Combine sugar, flour and salt. Sprinkle over sweet potatoes. Dot with butter, marshmallows and nuts. Pour cream over all. Bake at 350° for 45-50 minutes.

SWEET POTATO CASSEROLE

3 c. mashed, cooked sweet
    potatoes
3/4 c. sugar
1/2 c. melted butter
2 eggs, beaten
1 tsp. cinnamon

1/4 tsp. nutmeg
1/3 c. whole or evaporated milk
1/3 c. melted butter
3/4 c. brown sugar
1/2 c. flour
1 c. chopped pecans

Combine first seven ingredients. Place in a casserole. Make topping by combining the last four ingredients. Sprinkle on the sweet potatoes. Bake at 350° approximately 35 minutes.
Variation: Top with marshmallows instead of topping.

RAW SWEET POTATO CASSEROLE

4 c. grated raw sweet potatoes
3/4 c. milk
1/2 c. sugar
1/2 c. corn syrup
1/2 c. butter, melted
1/2 tsp. salt

1 tsp. cinnamon
1/4 tsp. nutmeg
1/8 tsp. cloves
1/2 c. chopped nuts (optional)
2 eggs, well beaten

Mix together everything but eggs. Add eggs and stir until well blended. Pour into a buttered 1 1/2-quart casserole. Bake at 375° for 50-60 minutes.
Variation: Replace sugar and syrup with 1 c. molasses or honey.

MAPLE SYRUP SWEET POTATO CASSEROLE

4 medium sweet potatoes	1/4 tsp. cinnamon
1/2 c. maple syrup	1/8 tsp. nutmeg
1/2 c. packed brown sugar	1/3 c. chopped pecans (optional)
1/4 c. melted butter	

Slice sweet potatoes crosswise into 1/2-inch slices; cook in boiling water 20 minutes or until fork tender. Let cool to touch, peel and mash. Combine maple syrup, brown sugar, butter, cinnamon and nutmeg; mix well. Add syrup mixture to sweet potatoes; mix well. Pour into an 8 x 8 buttered baking dish; sprinkle with pecans if desired. Bake at 350° for 15-20 minutes.

APPLE SWEET POTATO CASSEROLE

2 sweet potatoes	2 T. cornstarch
1/2 c. water	3 T. water
2 large apples	1/2 c. honey
1 c. apple juice	1/3 c. wheat germ

Cook sweet potatoes in 1/2 c. water until tender about 20 minutes. Peel and slice lengthwise into 1/2-inch thick slices. Lay them in a casserole dish. Peel and core apples, slicing 1/2-inch thick. Lay apple slices on top of sweet potatoes. Bring apple juice to a boil. Combine cornstarch and water. Add to juice, cooking until sauce is clear and thickened. Add honey. Spoon over apples, then top with wheat germ. Bake at 350° for 30-45 minutes or until apples are tender.

ORANGE SWEET POTATO CASSEROLE

6 medium sweet potatoes	3 T. orange juice
3/4 c. brown sugar	1 T. grated orange peel
1/4 c. butter	1/4 tsp. salt

Cook sweet potatoes until tender. Meanwhile, combine remaining ingredients and cook 5 minutes. Drain, peel and mash sweet potatoes. Add sugar mixture, mixing well. Put in a casserole and bake at 350° for 30 minutes.
Variation: Slice sweet potatoes 1/2 to 3/4-inch thick and arrange in a 13 x 9 pan. Pour sugar mixture over sweet potatoes.

PINEAPPLE SWEET POTATO CASSEROLE

6 medium sweet potatoes
1 tsp. salt
6 pineapple slices

1/2 c. brown sugar
1/4 c. butter
3/4 c. pineapple juice

Cook the sweet potatoes in salt water until almost soft. Peel, slice and arrange sweet potatoes in alternate layers with pineapple. Mix sugar and butter together then add pineapple juice. Cook for 3 minutes and pour over sweet potatoes. Bake at 375° for 30 minutes.

CREAMED SWEET POTATOES

3 T. butter
1/3 c. chopped onion
3 T. flour
4 c. milk

2 chicken bouillon cubes
3 c. cooked, mashed sweet
    potatoes

Heat butter. Sauté onion 5 minutes. Stir in flour. Slowly add milk while stirring. Cook until mixture thickens and boils. Add bouillon cubes and stir until dissolved. Add mashed sweet potatoes and heat through.
Variation: Use winter squash instead of sweet potatoes.

SWEET POTATOES AND SAUSAGE

2 lb. sweet potatoes
1/4 c. butter
1 1/2 c. fresh French or Italian
    bread crumbs
1/2 lb. pork sausage

1/2 c. chopped onion
1/2 c. chopped celery
1/2 tsp. poultry seasoning
1/4 tsp. salt
1/8 tsp. pepper

Cook and peel sweet potatoes; mash. Heat butter in a skillet and brown bread crumbs until crisp and brown. Remove crumbs. Add remaining ingredients. Cook until sausage is brown. Drain drippings. Add sweet potatoes and crumbs to sausage and mix well. Put in a well buttered 1 1/2-quart casserole. Bake at 375° for 25 minutes.

SWEET POTATOES WITH PORK CHOPS AND PEARS

1 pt. pear halves
4 medium sweet potatoes, cooked
4 pork chops
salt and pepper

1/2 c. brown sugar
2 T. butter
1/4 tsp. cinnamon

Drain pears, reserving syrup. Peel sweet potatoes and cut crosswise into thick slices. Place in the bottom of a shallow baking dish. Trim excess fat off the chops. Brown slightly. Sprinkle with salt and pepper and place on sweet potatoes. Combine pear juice with remaining ingredients. Heat until sugar dissolves. Spoon half of the syrup over the chops. Bake at 350° for 30 minutes. Remove from the oven and place pear halves around the chops. Spoon remaining syrup over the pears and chops. Bake 30 minutes more or until chops are tender.

SWEET POTATOES IN BEEF STEW

2 lb. cubed stew meat
1 tsp. salt
1/4 tsp. pepper
1 clove garlic, chopped
1/2 c. chopped onion
1/2 c. chopped celery
1 tsp. parsley
4 c. boiling water

4 sweet potatoes, peeled and
  quartered
3 carrots, peeled and cut into
  2-inch pieces
2 white potatoes, peeled and
  quartered
2 c. corn kernels
2 T. flour
1/4 c. water

Heat a large kettle and brown meat on all sides, a few pieces at a time. Remove pieces as they brown. Add salt, pepper, garlic, onion, and celery. Sauté briefly. Add beef, parsley and water. Return to a boil then reduce heat and simmer 1 1/2 hours. Add sweet potatoes, carrots and potatoes. Cook 35 minutes. Add corn and cook another 10 minutes. Combine flour and water. Add to stew while stirring. Stir until stew thickens.

For as the earth bringeth forth her bud, and as the garden causeth the things that are sown in it to spring forth; so the Lord GOD will cause righteousness and praise to spring forth before all the nations.

Isaiah 61:11

SWEET POTATOES – BAKED GOODS AND DESSERTS

SWEET POTATO BISCUITS

1 c. mashed sweet potatoes
1/4 c. vegetable shortening
1 T. sugar
1/2 tsp. soda

3/4 c. buttermilk
2 c. flour
1 T. baking powder
1 tsp. salt

Beat potatoes, shortening and sugar together until well mixed. Dissolve soda in buttermilk and add potato mixture. Combine remaining ingredients and add. Mix well and roll out 1/2-inch thick on a floured surface. Cut with a cutter or in squares. Put on a greased cookie sheet and bake at 400° about 15 minutes.
Variation: Use regular milk and delete soda.

SWEET POTATO MUFFINS WITH WALNUT STREUSEL

1 c. mashed sweet potatoes
1 c. milk
1 egg, beaten
1/4 c. butter, melted
2 c. flour
1/2 c. sugar
2 tsp. baking powder
1 tsp. cinnamon

1/2 tsp. nutmeg
1/2 tsp. salt
3 T. sugar
2 T. chopped walnuts
1 T. flour
1 T. butter
1/4 tsp. cinnamon

Beat sweet potatoes, milk and eggs until smooth; add butter. Combine flour, sugar, baking powder, spices and salt. Stir into sweet potato mixture just until blended. Divide batter evenly among 12 paper-lined muffin cups. Combine remaining ingredients and sprinkle on top, pressing tightly. Bake at 400° for 20-25 minutes.

SWEET POTATO CAKE

2 c. flour
2 c. sugar
2 tsp. baking powder
2 tsp. soda
1/2 tsp. salt

4 eggs
1 1/4 c. vegetable oil
3 c. raw sweet potatoes, grated
1 c. pecans (optional)

Combine dry ingredients. Set aside. Beat eggs. Add oil and sweet potatoes. Add dry ingredients and beat well. Fold in pecans. Pour into a floured tube pan or a 13 x 9 pan. Bake at 350° 50 minutes. Frost with cream cheese frosting if desired.

SWEET POTATO FRITTERS

2 c. mashed sweet potatoes
1 T. butter
1 T. sugar
1 c. milk
2 eggs, separated

1/2 c. flour
1 tsp. baking powder
1/2 tsp. salt
oil for deep frying

Combine sweet potatoes, butter, sugar, milk and egg yolks. Beat until smooth. Combine dry ingredients and add. Fold in stiffly beaten egg whites. Drop by tsp. into 365° oil. Fry until brown. Drain on crumpled paper towels. Sprinkle with powdered sugar.

BLENDER SWEET POTATO PIE

1 1/2 c. mashed sweet potatoes
1 c. sugar
1/4 c. butter, melted
1/2 c. evaporated or whole milk

2 eggs
1 tsp. nutmeg
1 tsp. vanilla
1 9-inch unbaked pie shell

Combine all ingredients except pie shell in the blender. Process until well-blended. Pour into unbaked pie shell. Bake at 350° for 50 to 55 minutes, or until knife inserted in center comes out clean and pie is golden-brown.

COCONUT CUSTARD SWEET POTATO PIE

3 eggs
1/2 c. sugar
1/4 c. brown sugar
1/2 tsp. salt
1 tsp. cinnamon
1/2 tsp. nutmeg

1/4 tsp. ginger
2 c. mashed sweet potatoes
1 c. light cream or evaporated
   milk
1 c. coconut
1 unbaked pie shell

Beat eggs with sugars, salt and spices. Add sweet potatoes and cream; mix well. Fold in coconut. Pour into an unbaked pie shell. Bake at 350° for 50 minutes or until a knife inserted into the center comes out clean. Serve warm or cold.

For God so loved the world, that he gave his only begotten Son, that whosoever believeth in him should not perish, but have everlasting life. For God sent not his Son into the world to condemn the world; but that the world through him might be saved.

John 3:16,17

PECAN SWEET POTATO PIE

1/4 c. butter	1/3 c. milk
1/2 c. brown sugar	1/2 tsp. salt
1 c. mashed sweet potatoes	1 tsp. vanilla
3 eggs, slightly beaten	½ c. chopped pecans
1/3 c. corn syrup	1 unbaked pie shell

Cream butter and sugar. Add potatoes and eggs. Mix well. Add remaining ingredients and pour into the unbaked pie shell. Bake at 425° for 10 minutes. Then reduce heat to 350° and bake another 35-40 minutes.

SWEET POTATOES – CANNING

HOW TO CAN SWEET POTATOES[1]

Boil or steam sweet potatoes 15 to 20 minutes to facilitate removal of skins. Cut into uniform pieces. Pack hot sweet potatoes to within 1-inch of top of jar. Add 1/2 tsp. salt for pints and 1 tsp. for quarts. Cover with either boiling water or medium syrup (3 c. sugar for 4 c. water), leaving 1-inch headspace.

Process in a pressure canner—pints for 65 minutes, quarts 90 minutes. Process at 10 lb. of pressure at elevations up to 1000 feet above sea level. Process at 15 lb. of pressure at elevations over 1000 feet above sea level. Dial gauges should be at 11 lb. of pressure up to 2000 feet above sea level.

And God said, Let the earth bring forth grass, the herb yielding seed, and the fruit tree yielding fruit after his kind, whose seed is in itself, upon the earth: and it was so. And the earth brought forth grass, and herb yielding seed after his kind, and the tree yielding fruit, whose seed was in itself, after his kind: and God saw that it was good. And the evening and the morning were the third day.

Genesis 1:11-13

NOTES

262

Tomatoes

After being shunned by the European colonists early in our country's history, tomatoes have come a long way to stand alone as our most popular garden vegetable. In my mind, a perfectly formed, sun-ripened, flavor packed tomato has come to define excellence from the garden. Much as I enjoy the early onions, radishes, peas, lettuce and spinach it's still that first ripe tomato I really look forward to.

Tomatoes have been adapted to most soil types with good drainage. In addition, with the early varieties available, even northern zones can enjoy ripe tomatoes from the garden.

Because they are a warm weather plant, it's best to start with young, stocky transplants rather than from direct seeding. Garden centers generally have the more popular varieties in stock, but if you have favorites that are less well known you may want to start your own. Plant your seeds indoors 5-6 weeks before setting out side. When the first true leaf develops, transplant to individual pots, burying the stem up to the leaves.

Plants that are over mature—flowers or fruit on the plant—or diseased should be avoided. Plant outside after danger of frost is past or two weeks earlier with plastic mulch and row covers. Bury the stem up to the lower leaves when transplanting. Staked tomatoes can be planted every 18 inches; unstaked allow 3 feet between plants.

Determinate tomatoes set fruit for a limited time and then quit. Indeterminate tomatoes continue to put out vines and set fruit until the vines freeze in the fall. All tomatoes benefit from staking—indeterminates more so than determinates. Staking is any system that keeps foliage and fruit off the ground. This decreases damage from slugs, rot, sun scald and cracking. Tomatoes ripen a bit faster, too, when staked.

Pick the staking method that's easiest for you. Cages, trellises and 4-6 foot stakes work equally well. My favorite method of staking is the basket weave system. I use 5 foot bamboo stakes with two plants between stakes. When the plants are about 18" tall, weave twine on both sides of the stakes and plants parallel to the ground. As the plants grow continue adding 'sets' 4 or 5" apart on the stake. No pruning is necessary when staking determinate tomatoes using this method.

Another method uses steel stakes every 8 feet in your row. Stretch a 9 gauge wire between the tops of the posts. Drop a baler twine from the wire to the base of the main stem of each plant. Prune and spiral the vines up the twine every week.

Tomatoes are ripe when they turn red, yellow, pink or white—whatever color you planted. Keep ripe tomatoes at room temperature out of sunlight; don't refrigerate.

Choose varieties according to use—cherry tomatoes for salads, plum tomatoes for sauces and the standard globe shaped for fresh slicing. Yellow tomatoes are generally lower in acid.

Green tomatoes are also gaining in popularity. Use them for frying, pickling, making mince meat or preserves.

Before heavy frost strikes your tomatoes, choose some green ones or half green for ripening inside. Take only defect-free tomatoes—no cracks, spots or rot—wrap them individually in newspaper or lay them out on newspaper with another one as a cover. Keep them in a warm, dry, dark location. We have enjoyed our own tomatoes up until Christmas using this method. Granted, they're not August vine-ripened tomatoes, but they're every bit as good as supermarket tomatoes and far more satisfying because they come from your own garden.

Nutritionally, tomatoes are rich in vitamins A and C, folate and potassium. They also contain the proven anticancer agent, lycopene.

Yield: 1 lb. whole tomatoes = 2 cups cubed
1 bushel = 50-55 lb. = 38-40 pints

CHUNKY TOMATO SOUP

1 1/2 c. peeled, seeded and finely chopped tomatoes	1/4 c. chopped onion
	1/4 c. flour
2 tsp. sugar	3/4 tsp. salt
1/4 c. butter	3 c. milk

Bring tomatoes and sugar to a boil; simmer 10-15 minutes. Meanwhile, heat butter and sauté onions for 5 minutes. Blend in flour, then slowly add milk while stirring. Cook and stir until thickened. Add hot tomatoes, stirring constantly.
Variation: Process tomatoes in a blender before heating or use tomato juice. Delete flour for a thinner tomato soup.

TURKEY VEGETABLE SOUP WITH TOMATOES

1 lb. ground turkey	1/3 c. uncooked rice, rinsed
1 c. chopped onion	1/4 c. ketchup
1 c. sliced carrots	1 chicken bouillon cube
1 c. sliced celery	1 tsp. basil
6 c. water	1/8 tsp. pepper
2 c. peeled and chopped tomatoes	1 bay leaf

Crumble ground turkey into a large kettle. Stir in onion, carrots and celery. Cook and stir about 5 minutes or until turkey is lightly browned. Stir in water, tomatoes, rice, ketchup, bouillon, basil, pepper and bay leaf. Bring to a boil; reduce heat. Cover; simmer 25-35 minutes or until vegetables and rice are tender.

...that which thou sowest is not quickened, except it die: And that which thou sowest, thou sowest not that body that shall be, but bare grain, it may chance of wheat, or of some other grain: but God giveth it a body as it hath pleased him, and to every seed his own body.
I Corinthians 15:36-38

TOMATOES VINAIGRETTE

10 thick slices tomato
1 c. olive or vegetable oil
1/3 c. vinegar
2 tsp. oregano or basil
1 tsp. salt
1/2 tsp. pepper

1/2 tsp. dry mustard
2 cloves garlic, crushed
crisp lettuce leaves
minced green onion
parsley

Arrange tomatoes in an 8 x 8 x 2 baking dish. Shake next 7 ingredients in a tightly covered jar. Pour over tomatoes. Cover and chill at least 2 hours, spooning dressing on tomatoes from time to time. Just before serving, arrange tomatoes on lettuce leaves. Sprinkle onion and parsley on top. Drizzle with some of the dressing in the pan.

OLD-TIME TOMATO ASPIC

4 c. tomato juice
1/3 c. chopped onion
1/4 c. chopped celery leaves
2 T. sugar
1 tsp. salt
2 small bay leaves

4 whole cloves
2 envelopes (2 T.) unflavored
   gelatin
1/4 c. cold water
3 T. lemon juice
1 c. finely diced celery

Combine tomato juice, onion, celery leaves, sugar, salt, bay leaves and cloves. Simmer 5 minutes. Strain. Soften gelatin in cold water; dissolve in the hot tomato mixture. Add lemon juice. Chill until partially set. Add celery. Pour into 5 or 6 c. ring mold. Chill until set. Serve with chicken salad, if desired.

EGG STUFFED TOMATOES

6 large tomatoes
salt
pepper
6 hard boiled eggs, chopped

1/3 c. mayonnaise
3/4 c. diced celery
2 T. chopped parsley

With a sharp pointed knife, make zig zag cuts about one third way down from the top of tomato all around circumference of tomato; remove top and reserve. Carefully scoop out pulp (save pulp for other uses). Sprinkle tomato shells lightly with salt and pepper; set aside. Combine remaining ingredients and fill tomato shells, piling egg mixture high. Serve on a lettuce lined platter.

TUNA STUFFED TOMATOES

6 large tomatoes
2 cans (6 to 7 oz. each) tuna,
    drained and flaked
1/4 c. minced onion
1/4 c. diced celery

1/4 c. chopped parsley
6 T. mayonnaise
1/2 tsp. salt
1/4 tsp. pepper

Cut a very thin slice from bottom of each tomato so they stand upright; remove stem ends. Cut each tomato into 3 crosswise slices; set aside. Combine remaining ingredients. Using about 1/3 c. tuna mixture for each tomato, spread mixture on two lower slices. Reassemble each tomato; cover with top slice.

CREAM CHEESE AND BACON STUFFED CHERRY TOMATOES

1 qt. cherry tomatoes
8 oz. cream cheese, softened
6 bacon strips, cooked, crumbled

1/4 c. minced green onions
1/4 c. minced fresh parsley
1/2 tsp. Worcestershire sauce

Cut a thin slice off the top of each tomato. Scoop out and discard pulp. Invert the tomatoes on a paper towel to drain. Meanwhile, combine remaining ingredients in a small bowl; mix well. Spoon into tomatoes. Refrigerate until serving.

TACO SALAD WITH TOMATOES

1 lb. ground beef
15 oz. can kidney beans, drained
1 tsp. chili powder
1/2 tsp. salt
1 head lettuce

1 onion, chopped
4 tomatoes, chopped
1 c. shredded cheddar cheese
2-4 c. taco chips
1 c. French dressing

Brown ground beef. Drain excess grease. Add kidney beans, chili powder and salt. Simmer 10 minutes. Tear lettuce into bite size pieces and put in a large bowl. Add tomatoes, onion and cheese. Mix in meat mixture and slightly crushed taco chips. Stir in 1 c. dressing or pass with salad.

ZESTY TOMATO SAUCE

1 1/2 c. finely chopped tomatoes
1/2 c. chopped onion
2 jalapeno peppers, chopped

1 tsp. salt
1/4 tsp. cumin
1/8 clove garlic, crushed

Mix all ingredients. Serve with enchiladas, tacos, burritos or refried beans. Can be refrigerated.

TOMATO AND CHICKEN SANDWICHES

8 slices buttered toast
8 slices cooked chicken
8 slices tomato

salt
1 c. grated American cheese
2 tsp. Worcestershire sauce

Place slices of buttered toast in shallow baking pan. Place chicken on toast and tomato on chicken. Sprinkle with salt. Spread with grated cheese mixed with Worcestershire sauce. Melt cheese under broiler. Serve at once.

HOT TOMATO AND HAM SANDWICHES

8 slices fully cooked ham
8 hamburger buns

8 slices American cheese
8 tomato slices

Brown ham slices on each side. Toast or warm hamburger buns; top with cheese slices; tomato slices and ham. Heat until cheese melts. Serve hot.

SLOPPY JOES WITH FRESH TOMATOES

2 T. butter
1/2 c. diced onion
1/2 c. diced green pepper
2 1/2 c. minced fresh jalapeno
    pepper (optional)
1 tsp. minced garlic
1/2 lb. ground beef

1 c. cooked pinto or kidney beans
1/4 tsp. salt
1/2 tsp. pepper
1 tsp. chili powder
1 c. ketchup
1 c. peeled, diced tomatoes

Heat butter. Sauté onions, green pepper, jalapeno pepper and garlic until onions are translucent. Add the beef and cook, stirring until meat is lightly browned. Drain off all fat. Add the beans, salt, pepper and chili powder. Cook for 1 minute, stirring continually to season evenly. Add the ketchup and tomatoes. Cook uncovered until sauce thickens. Serve on bread or hamburger buns.

Casting all your care upon him; for he careth for you.
I Peter 5:7

TOMATOES – SIDE AND MAIN DISHES

STEWED TOMATOES

6 large ripe tomatoes

2 T. butter

1 T. sugar

1/2 tsp. salt

1/8 tsp. pepper

1/2 tsp. basil

Peel tomatoes and cut into chunks. Melt butter and add tomatoes and remaining ingredients. Simmer 10 minutes or until tomatoes are soft.

Variations: Combine 2 tsp. cornstarch and 2 tsp. water. Stir into tender tomatoes. Cook until thick.

Or add a green pepper, an onion and a clove of garlic to melted butter before adding tomatoes. Cook 5 minutes then add tomatoes.

SAUTÉED TOMATOES

Heat butter in a skillet. Add sliced, unpeeled (unless skins are thick) tomatoes and cook about 2 minutes on each side. Sprinkle with salt, pepper and basil if desired.

BROILED TOMATOES

1 tomato per person

1 tsp. vegetable oil or melted
   butter per tomato

salt and pepper

grated cheese

Cut tomatoes in half horizontally. Brush with oil and sprinkle with salt and pepper. Top with cheese. Broil on a low rack until the tops are browned but not burned, and the tomatoes are heated through.

Variation: Top with bread crumbs instead of cheese.

SCALLOPED TOMATOES

6 c. tomatoes, peeled and cut up

1/4 c. butter

1/4 c. chopped onions

1/4 c. chopped green pepper

salt and pepper to taste

1 T. sugar

1 1/2 c. toasted bread cubes

Cook onions and green peppers in butter until tender. In a 2-quart casserole, mix all ingredients together, except 1/2 c. bread cubes. Sprinkle remaining bread cubes on top and bake at 350° for 30 minutes.

Variation: Top with grated cheese and put under broiler until bubbly brown.

TOMATOES AND SCRAMBLED EGGS

2 tomatoes
1/2 tsp. salt

1 1/2 T. butter
4 eggs

Peel tomatoes. Cut into eighths. Bring tomatoes and salt to a boil and boil 1 minute. Drain juice. Dot with half of the butter. Melt remaining butter in a skillet. Add eggs. When partially cooked, add tomatoes. Stir to mix well.

FRIED GREEN TOMATOES

6 medium green tomatoes
2 eggs
1/4 c. milk
1 c. corn meal, bread crumbs or
     flour

1/2 tsp. salt
1/2 tsp. oregano
1/8 tsp. pepper
2 T. butter
1 T. vegetable oil

Slice tomatoes into 1/4 to 1/2-inch slices. Beat together eggs and milk. Combine corn meal, salt, oregano and pepper. Heat butter and oil in a skillet. Dip tomato slices in egg mixture then in corn meal mixture. Fry tomato slices, turning once, until golden brown on both sides.

SPAGHETTI WITH FRESH TOMATOES

8 medium tomatoes
1/4 c. olive or vegetable oil
1 clove garlic, crushed
1 T. chopped fresh parsley

1 tsp. basil
1 tsp. salt
16 black olives, sliced
8 oz. spaghetti

Peel tomatoes. Chop and seed. Let drain. Combine oil, garlic, parsley, basil, salt and black olives. Add tomatoes and mix well. Cover and set aside at room temperature. Cook spaghetti according to directions. Drain then return to kettle. Add tomato mixture; toss well. Serve with grated Parmesan cheese if desired.

TOMATO CORN CASSEROLE

3 c. fresh corn
6 tomatoes, sliced thick
1 onion, chopped fine
1 green pepper, chopped fine

2 T. butter
salt and pepper
1 c. coarse bread crumbs
4 slices bacon, diced

Spread half the corn in a casserole, cover it with slices of tomato packed closely, sprinkle with half the onion and green pepper; dot with butter. Sprinkle with salt and pepper. Add another layer in the same order. Top the casserole with bread crumbs and diced bacon. Bake at 375° for 40-45 minutes.

TOMATO ZUCCHINI CASSEROLE

2 c. bread crumbs
6 T. melted butter
1 tsp. oregano
2 eggs, beaten
1/2 tsp. salt
2 T. butter
2 c. chopped zucchini

1 green pepper, seeded and
    chopped
1 onion, chopped
1 clove garlic, minced
6 tomatoes, chopped
1 T. chili powder
salt and pepper
2-3 c. grated Cheddar cheese

Combine crumbs, butter, oregano, eggs and salt. Press half of the mixture into a 13 x 9 pan. Heat 2 T. butter in a skillet. Sauté zucchini, pepper, onion and garlic until tender crisp. Add tomatoes; cook 5 minutes. Drain off liquid. Add chili powder, salt and pepper. Spread the mixture on the crust. Cover with cheese and sprinkle with remaining crumbs. Bake at 350° for 45 minutes.

BAKED STUFFED TOMATOES

4 ripe tomatoes
1 small clove garlic, minced
1/4 c. chopped onion
1/4 c. chopped celery
1/4 c. butter

1/2 tsp. salt
1/4 tsp. pepper
1 1/2 c. fresh bread crumbs
1/2 tsp. parsley

Hollow out tomatoes, being careful not to break through the skin. Chop the tomato pulp and set aside. Cook garlic, onion and celery in butter over low heat until onion is transparent. Add chopped tomato, sprinkle with salt and pepper and cook, stirring occasionally, until vegetables are tender. Stir in bread crumbs and parsley and fill tomatoes. Place stuffed tomatoes on a buttered baking sheet. Bake at 350° for 10-12 minutes.
Variation: Halved cucumbers or summer squash may be used instead of tomatoes.

And Jesus said unto them, I am the bread of life: he that cometh to me shall never hunger; and he that believeth on me shall never thirst.

John 6:35

STUFFED TOMATOES WITH MEAT

6 firm, red tomatoes
1/2 lb. sausage or ground beef
olive or vegetable oil
3/4 c. uncooked rice
1 onion, finely chopped

1 clove garlic, minced
1/2 tsp. basil
1/4 c. grated Parmesan cheese
1 tsp. parsley
salt and pepper to taste

Cut tops off unpeeled tomatoes. Remove seeds and reserve the juice. Sprinkle insides with salt and invert to drain. Brown meat, drain fat and set aside. Sauté onion and rice in olive oil in heavy skillet over medium heat until rice is translucent and just turning golden. Combine meat, rice, herbs, cheese and reserved tomato juice. Stuff shells with mixture. Because the rice swells in cooking, fill the shells only half full. Place tomatoes on oiled, shallow baking pan and bake at 350° for 50 minutes or until tomatoes are soft but still firm.

TOMATO STUFFED FISH FILLETS

1 medium tomato, peeled and
    chopped
1/4 c. finely chopped onion
1/4 tsp. basil leaves

1 1/2 lb. fresh flounder or
    haddock fillets
vegetable oil
salt and pepper

Combine tomato, onion and basil; set aside. Brush both sides of fillets with oil; sprinkle with salt and pepper. Place small amount of tomato mixture in center of each fillet. Overlap both ends of fillet over tomato; fasten with wooden picks. Arrange on broiler rack. Broil 3 inches from source of heat, turning once and brushing with vegetable oil. Broil 5 minutes on each side or until fish flakes easily with a fork but is still moist

Jesus said unto her, I am the resurrection, and the life: he that believeth in me, though he were dead, yet shall he live: and whosoever liveth and believeth in me shall never die, Believest thou this?

John 11:25,26

TOMATO CHEESE PIE WITH SALMON

1 1/3 c. flour
1/2 tsp. salt
1/2 c. vegetable shortening
3 T. water
2 c. Cheddar or mozzarella cheese
1 c. cottage cheese
1/4 lb. mushrooms, sliced and
    sautéed
2 T. chopped onions

1/4 c. canned salmon, drained and
    flaked
3-4 ripe tomatoes, cut into thin
    wedges
1 tsp. basil
1 tsp. oregano
1/4 c. chopped green onion
salt and pepper

Combine flour and salt. Cut in shortening with a pastry blender or two knives. Sprinkle with water, tossing lightly. Make a firm ball then roll dough out 1/8-inch thick to fit a 9-inch pie plate. Bake at 425° for 10-15 minutes or until lightly browned. Reduce heat to 325°. Combine cheeses, mushrooms, onions and salmon. Spoon into the baked shell. Arrange tomato wedges in a tightly overlapping circle on mixture. Sprinkle with herbs, green onions, salt and pepper. Bake at 325° for 20 minutes. Cool 15 minutes before cutting.

Variation: Delete salmon.

EASY TOMATO MEAT PIE

2 onions, sliced thin
2 c. sliced cold roast beef or pork
2 T. flour
1 tsp. salt

1/4 tsp. pepper
2 c. peeled, sliced tomatoes
2 c. buttered bread crumbs

Alternate layers of onions and meat in a buttered baking dish. Sprinkle each layer with flour, salt and pepper. Place tomato slices on top. Put bread crumbs on tomatoes. Bake at 350° until brown.

TOMATOES WITH HOT DOGS AND ONIONS

5 tomatoes, sliced thin
2 onions, sliced thin
10 hot dogs, cut into 1-inch pieces

1/2 tsp. basil
1 c. shredded cheese

Layer tomatoes, onions and hot dogs in a large skillet. Sprinkle with basil. Cover; cook over low heat for 30 minutes. Sprinkle cheese on top just before serving.

271

TOMATOES WITH CHICKEN

3 T. butter
3 T. olive or vegetable oil
1 frying chicken cut up
1 qt. tomatoes, peeled and
    chopped

2 cloves garlic, minced
salt and pepper to taste
1/2 tsp. basil
1/2 tsp. oregano

In a large kettle, sauté onions and garlic in butter and oil. Add chicken to brown. Add remaining ingredients and simmer, covered 30-40 minutes or until chicken is done.

CHICKEN STIR FRY WITH TOMATOES

1/4 c. soy sauce
1/2 c. water
2 T. cornstarch
1 chicken breast, cut into 1-inch
    pieces
6 T. vegetable oil
1 medium onion, sliced into rings

2 cloves garlic, minced
1 green pepper, cut into strips
1/2 c. sliced water chestnuts
    (optional)
2 medium tomatoes, cut into
    wedges
cooked rice enough for 4-5 people

Mix soy sauce, water and cornstarch. Marinate the chicken in the mixture for 15 minutes. Heat 3 T. oil in a large skillet and stir fry onion for 1 minute. Add garlic, pepper and water chestnuts and stir fry until vegetables are tender crisp. Remove vegetables. Heat remaining oil in skillet and add chicken mixture. Stir fry 5 minutes or until chicken is cooked. Add vegetables and tomatoes. Cook 2 minutes or until tomatoes are warm. Serve with rice.

BAKED SPAGHETTI WITH TOMATOES

8 oz. spaghetti
2 T. butter
1/4 c. chopped onion
1/4 c. chopped green pepper
2 c. peeled, seeded and chopped
    tomatoes

1/2 tsp. salt or to taste
1/4 tsp. pepper
1/8 tsp. paprika
1 T. sugar
1 c. grated cheese

Cook spaghetti and drain well. Melt butter and sauté onion and green pepper for 5 minutes. Add all but cheese and spaghetti. Simmer 10 minutes. Add cooked spaghetti and mix well. Add 1/2 c. cheese. Put into a buttered baking dish and top with remaining cheese. Bake at 400° for 20-25 minutes.
Variation: Add browned ground beef or sausage.

BEEFY SPAGHETTI WITH TOMATO JUICE

1 lb. ground beef	1 T. vegetable oil
1 c. chopped onion	1 tsp. salt
3 c. broken spaghetti	1 tsp. garlic salt
4 c. tomato juice or peeled,	1 tsp. oregano
chopped tomatoes	1/8 tsp. pepper

Brown ground beef and onion in a large skillet or kettle. Spread broken spaghetti over meat. Combine remaining ingredients and pour over spaghetti; mix. Cook over low heat until spaghetti is tender, about 30 minutes.

STACK SUPPER WITH TOMATOES

2 c. long grain white rice	2 c. chopped onion
1 head lettuce, chopped	1 qt. milk
3 lb. ground beef, browned	1/2 lb. process cheese
2 qt. chopped tomatoes	taco sauce or salsa

Cook rice according to package instructions. Prepare other ingredients. Heat milk and stir in cheese to make cheese sauce. Pass the ingredients in the order given, stacking one on top of the other with the cheese sauce going on last. Top with taco sauce or salsa.

Variation: Delete rice and replace with slightly crushed corn or taco chips.

SWISS STEAK WITH TOMATOES

1/4 c. flour	1-4 oz. can mushroom pieces
1 tsp. salt	1/2 c. finely chopped onion
1/4 tsp. pepper	1/2 c. finely chopped green
2 lb. round steak, cut 1-inch thick	pepper
2 T. vegetable oil	2 c. tomatoes, peeled and chopped

Combine flour with salt and pepper; pound into meat. Heat oil. Brown steak for 5 minutes per side. Add mushrooms, onion, green pepper and tomatoes. Simmer over low heat, covered, for 1 1/2 hours or until tender.

And he said unto me, My grace is sufficient for thee: for my strength is made perfect in weakness. Most gladly therefore will I rather glory in my infirmities, that the power of Christ may rest upon me.

II Corinthinians 12:9

TOMATO GRAVY

6 ripe tomatoes, peeled and
    chopped
2 T. vegetable oil
1 onion, chopped
1 T. sugar

1/2 tsp. salt
1/8 tsp. pepper
1/2 c. water
3 T. flour

Prepare tomatoes. Heat oil and sauté onions 5-10 minutes, stirring occasionally. Add sugar, salt and pepper. Combine water and flour. Stir into tomatoes. Cook and stir until thickened.
Variation: Substitute 1/2 c. cream for the 1/2 c. water.

TOMATO SAUCE

Quarter red ripe tomatoes and cook in a stainless steel kettle on medium heat for 2-3 hours. Strain through a sieve or strainer. One pound of tomatoes makes approximately 1 c. sauce. This can be used immediately or be canned or frozen.

TOMATOES – BAKED GOODS AND DESSERTS

GREEN TOMATO MUFFINS

2 c. flour
1 T. baking powder
1/2 tsp. salt
2 tsp. cinnamon
1 egg

1/4 c. vegetable oil
1/3 c. honey or sugar
1 c. milk
2 c. chopped green tomatoes
1/2 c. raisins

Combine dry ingredients. Beat egg in another bowl then add remaining ingredients. Combine with dry ingredients. Stir just enough to moisten batter. Bake at 425° approximately 25 minutes. Makes 12 muffins.

And Jesus answered them, saying, The hour is come, that the Son of man should be glorified. Verily, verily, I say unto you, Except a corn of wheat fall into the ground and die, it abideth alone: but if it die, it bringeth forth much fruit. He that loveth his life shall lose it; and he that hateth his life in this world shall keep it unto life eternal.
John 12:23-25

TOMATO BREAD

2 c. tomato juice	1/4 c. ketchup
2 T. butter	1/4 c. grated cheese
3 T. sugar	1 pkg. yeast (1 T.)
1 tsp. salt	1/4 c. warm water (110 to 115°)
1/2 tsp. basil	7 c. flour
1/2 tsp. oregano	

Heat tomato juice and butter together until the butter is melted. Add sugar, salt, herbs, ketchup and cheese; allow to cool to lukewarm. Sprinkle yeast on warm water and stir to dissolve. Add tomato mixture and 3 c. flour to yeast. Beat with electric mixer 2 minutes or beat by hand until smooth. Gradually mix in enough remaining flour to make soft dough that leaves the side of the bowl. Turn onto lightly floured board and knead for 8 to 10 minutes, when dough will be elastic and smooth. Place in lightly greased bowl; turn dough over so top is greased. Cover and let rise in warm place until double in size—1 to 1 1/2 hours. Punch down and divide in half. Cover and let rest 10 minutes. Shape into loaves and place in greased, loaf pans. Cover and let rise until almost doubled—about 1 hour. Bake at 375° for 25 minutes or until done.

GREEN TOMATO BREAD

8-10 medium green tomatoes, coarsely chopped	3 1/2 c. flour
	2 tsp. baking soda
2/3 c. raisins	1 1/2 tsp. salt
2/3 c. boiling water	1/2 tsp. baking powder
2/3 c. vegetable shortening	1 tsp. cinnamon
2 1/2 c. sugar	1 tsp. cloves
3 eggs	

Put tomatoes in blender and blend until smooth. Use enough tomatoes to make 2 c. pulp. Soak raisins in boiling water and set aside to cool. Cream shortening and sugar until fluffy. Add eggs, tomato pulp, raisins and soaking water. Beat well. Combine remaining ingredients. Add to tomato mixture, stirring well. Divide batter into two oiled loaf pans. Bake at 350° approximately 60-70 minutes.

And he said, Whereunto shall we liken the kingdom of God? or with what comparison shall we compare it? It is like a grain of mustard seed, which, when it is sown in the earth, is less than all the seeds that be in the earth: But when it is sown, it groweth up, and becometh greater than all herbs, and shooteth out great branches; so that the fowls of the air may lodge under the shadow of it.

Mark 4:30-32

GREEN TOMATO OATMEAL BARS

4 c. finely chopped green tomatoes	1 1/2 c. flour
	1/2 tsp. soda
2 c. brown sugar, packed	1/2 tsp. salt
2 T. lemon juice	2 c. rolled oats
1 tsp. lemon extract	1/2 c. chopped walnuts
3/4 c. butter	

Combine tomatoes, 1 c. sugar and lemon juice. Simmer 15-20 minutes or until mixture is very thick. Remove from heat and stir in lemon extract. Set aside. Cream together butter and the other cup of sugar. Add remaining ingredients. Mix well. Press 2/3 of the crumbs into a buttered 13 x 9 pan. Top with tomato mixture. Sprinkle remaining crumbs on top. Bake at 375° for 30-35 minutes. Cool and cut into bars.

GREEN TOMATO CHOCOLATE CAKE

3/4 c. butter, softened	1/2 c. milk
2 c. sugar	2 1/2 c. flour
3 eggs	1/2 c. cocoa
1 tsp. mint extract (optional)	2 1/2 tsp. baking powder
2 c. coarsely grated green tomatoes	1/2 tsp. soda
	1 tsp. salt
1 tsp. vanilla	1 tsp. cinnamon

Cream butter and sugar. Beat in eggs. Add mint extract, tomatoes, vanilla and milk. Combine dry ingredients and stir into batter. Pour into a buttered and floured 10-inch tube pan. Bake at 350° for 50-60 minutes.

GREEN TOMATO PIE

4 c. green tomato slices	1 tsp. cinnamon
pastry for two 9-inch pie shells	1/4 tsp. nutmeg
1 1/2 c. sugar	1 T. lemon juice (optional)
2 T. flour	2 T. butter

Cover unpeeled tomato slices with boiling water. Let stand 10 minutes; drain. Carefully ease one pie shell into a 9-inch pie plate. Trim edges. Combine sugar, flour and spices. Spread 1/2 c. of the mixture in the pie shell. Arrange well drained tomato slices on top. Sprinkle with lemon juice. Top with remaining sugar mixture. Dot with butter. Cover with the top crust. Make a few slits in it and flute the edges. Bake at 425° for 15 minutes then at 375° for 30 minutes.

TOMATOES – CANNING AND FREEZING

ACIDIFYING CANNED TOMATO PRODUCTS[5]

Since there are so many factors that affect the acidity of canned tomatoes and juice products and because it is impractical if not impossible for the home canner to measure the pH of each container canned, the U.S.D.A. recommends that additional acid be added to most home-canned tomato products. The only exceptions are recipes that contain substantial amounts of vinegar (such as catsup, chili sauce, salsa) or that contain large amounts of low-acid vegetables and must be canned in the pressure canner for times sufficient to destroy botulinum spores (such as tomato-vegetable soup mixtures.)

Citric acid is very effective in increasing the acidity of tomatoes and tomato products without causing noticeable changes in flavor. Bottled lemon juice is the most convenient source of citric acid but other products can be used, if you prefer. A small amount of sugar—one tsp. per quart—can be added to offset the acid taste if desired.

Add 1 T. lemon juice per pint or 2 T. per quart. Measure this amount into the clean jar before filling with tomatoes.

Vinegar is not as effective as citric acid in increasing acidity in tomatoes when used in small amounts. Amounts large enough to significantly change the acidity of canned tomatoes produce a noticeable flavor change. For this reason, vinegar is not recommended as an acidifier in plain canned tomatoes or juice. However, the amount added to ketchup, chili sauce or similar products is adequate for safety, provided the vinegar is added at the very end of the cooking process, as recipes direct.

HOW TO CAN TOMATO JUICE[5]

Select fully red, ripe tomatoes. Wash, remove stems and cut out cores. (Do not use overripe tomatoes or those with damage spots or decay). Cut the unpeeled tomatoes into pieces and put them in a large kettle with a lid. Heat rapidly to simmering. Stir frequently to keep them from scorching. About 23 lb. of raw tomatoes will be needed for 7 qt. of juice; 14 lb. for 9 pt. of juice. Strain the tomatoes through a fine sieve, strainer or a food mill to separate the juice from skins, seeds and fibers. If you have a blender, blend the hot tomatoes for a few seconds before straining to obtain more pulp. After straining, reheat the juice to boiling. Pour into clean hot jars. Add 2 T. lemon juice per quart 1 T. per pint. Add salt, if desired—1/2 tsp. per pint, 1 tsp. per quart. (cont. next page)

Process in a boiling water canner 35 minutes for pints and 40 minutes per quart. Or process in a pressure canner for 20 minutes at 10 lb. of pressure; 15 minutes at 15 lb. of pressure.

TOMATO VEGETABLE JUICE

**8 qt. tomatoes, cored and
    quartered (about 20-25 lb.)
3 medium onions
2 medium carrots, peeled**

**3 stalks celery
2 medium beets, peeled
2 green peppers, cored (optional)
3 T. salt**

Wash, remove stems and core fully red, ripe tomatoes. Quarter and place in a large kettle. Chop or blend onion, celery, beets, carrots and green peppers and add to tomatoes. Heat rapidly to simmering temperature and simmer long enough to cook vegetables thoroughly. Strain through a fine sieve or food mill to separate juice from skin and seeds. Reheat the juice to boiling. Pour into clean hot jars. Add 2 T. lemon juice per qt, 1 T. per pt. Add salt, if desired: 1/2 tsp. per pint, 1 tsp. per quart. Wipe rim of jar and put lids on.

Process in a boiling water canner 35 minutes for pints and 40 minutes for quarts. Or use a pressure canner at 10 lb. of pressure for 20 minutes, or 15 lb. of pressure for 15 minutes.

TOMATO SAUCE, PUREE OR PASTE[5]

Wash, remove stems and cut out cores of fully ripe tomatoes. Cut in pieces and put in a large kettle with a lid. Salt, sugar, bay leaf or garlic may be added for seasoning. Heat rapidly, stirring frequently. Strain, then simmer juice. For a thin sauce reduce the volume by one third; for puree, reduce volume by 1/2 and for paste cook until the mixture rounds up on a spoon. Pour into jars, leaving 1/2-inch headspace. The USDA recommends adding 2 T. lemon juice per quart, 1 T. per pint. Very thick sauce should not be canned in quarts. Add 1/2 tsp. salt per pint, 1 tsp. per quart if none was added earlier. Adjust lids.

Process in a boiling water canner, 35 minutes for pints and 40 minutes for quarts. Or process in a pressure canner for 20 minutes at 10 lb. pressure or 15 minutes at 15 lb. of pressure.

278

TOMATO SAUCE OR PUREE WITH VEGETABLES

8 qt. fully ripe tomatoes, cored
and quartered (about 20-25
lb.)
3 large red and/or green tomatoes,
seeded and chopped
(2 1/4 c.)

3 medium onions, chopped
(1 1/2 c.)
3 medium carrots, chopped
3 stalks celery, chopped
3 T. salt
2 or 3 cloves garlic crushed (opt.)

Place all vegetables in a large kettle and heat quickly to simmering. Simmer until all vegetables are soft. For maximum solids in the sauce, blend and then press through a fine sieve, strainer or food mill to remove skins and seeds. Simmer the strained sauce until thick. For a thin sauce, reduce the volume by one third; for puree, reduce the volume by one half. Stir frequently to avoid sticking. Pour hot into jars, leaving 1/2-inch headspace. Adjust lids.
Process in a <u>pressure canner,</u> pints or quarts for 40 minutes at 10 lb. of pressure or 20 minutes at 15 lb. of pressure.

HOW TO CAN WHOLE TOMATOES[5]

Wash and sort tomatoes. Dip in boiling water for 30 to 60 seconds or until skin splits. Then dip in cold water, slip off skin, and remove cores. Add 2 T. lemon juice to each quart, 1 T. to each pint. Add 1 tsp. salt per quart if desired. Pack raw tomatoes into jars, leaving them whole or cutting them in halves. Press the tomatoes down to produce sufficient juice to cover, or add hot tomato juice to cover the tomatoes. Remove excess air from the jar by running a spatula or knife between the tomatoes and the side of the jar in several places. Adjust lids and process pints and quarts in a boiling water bath for 85 minutes. Or process in a pressure canner, pints or quarts for 40 minutes at 10 lb. of pressure, 25 minutes at 15 lb. of pressure

TOMATO VEGETABLE SOUP[5]

To make soup, combine tomato pulp or juice with a mixture of vegetables such as corn, lima beans, carrots, celery and onion. Such vegetable mixtures must be processed in a pressure canner because of their low acid content. Base the processing time on the vegetable requiring the longest processing. For example, if corn is included, the processing time for quarts would be 85 minutes at 10 pounds pressure.

But the fruit of the Spirit is love, joy, peace, longsuffering, gentleness, goodness, faith, meekness, temperance: against such there is no law.

Galations 5:22,23

279

TOMATO KETCHUP

4 qt. red ripe tomatoes, chopped
1 c. chopped onion
3/4 c. sweet peppers, chopped
1 tsp. mustard seed
1 1/2 tsp. celery seed
1/2 tsp. whole allspice

2 tsp. whole cloves
3-inch cinnamon stick
1 c. sugar
1 T. salt
1 T. paprika
1 1/2 c. cider vinegar

Cook unpeeled, chopped tomatoes, onions and peppers vigorously about 45 minutes. Blend and put through a wire strainer or put through a large crank strainer. Cook strained tomatoes gently, uncovered, until volume is reduced by half. Stir often. Tie spices in a cheesecloth bag and add. Add brown sugar, salt and paprika to puree. Continue cooking over medium heat until very thick (about 1 1/2-2 hours), stirring often. Add vinegar during the last 10-15 minutes of cooking. Remove spice bag and pour hot ketchup into pint or 1/2 pint jars, leaving 1/2-inch headspace. Process 20 minutes in a boiling water canner or freeze.

MILD SALSA

8 c. peeled, seeded and chopped
    tomatoes (about 5 lb.)
2 c. seeded and chopped green,
    red or yellow bell peppers
1 c. chopped onion

2 cloves garlic, minced
2 T. minced cilantro
1 tsp. salt
1/2 c. vinegar
2 drops hot pepper sauce

Combine all ingredients in a large kettle. Bring mixture to a boil; reduce heat and simmer 10 minutes. Carefully ladle hot salsa into hot jars, leaving 1/4-inch headspace. Adjust lids. Process in a boiling water canner for 15 minutes. Makes about 7 half pints.

SALSA WITH JALAPENO PEPPERS

8 c. peeled, seeded and chopped
    tomatoes
3 c. chopped jalapeno peppers
2 c. chopped onion
3 cloves garlic, minced

2 T. minced cilantro (optional)
2 tsp. oregano
1 1/2 tsp. salt
1/2 tsp. cumin
1 1/2 c. vinegar or lemon juice

When seeding or cutting hot peppers, wear rubber gloves to prevent hands from being burned. Combine all ingredients in a large kettle. Bring to a boil; reduce heat and simmer 10 minutes. Carefully ladle hot salsa into hot jars, leaving 1/2-inch headspace. Adjust lids. Process in a boiling water canner for 15 minutes.
Variation: Use part sweet peppers.

280

SALSA WITH HUNGARIAN WAX PEPPERS

10 c. peeled, cored, seeded and
   chopped tomatoes (6 lb.)
5 c. chopped onions
2 c. chopped yellow Hungarian
   wax peppers

1 chopped habanero pepper
4 cloves garlic, minced
2 tsp. salt
3/4 c. vinegar

When seeding or cutting hot peppers, wear rubber gloves to prevent hands from being burned. Combine all ingredients in a large kettle. Bring mixture to a boil; reduce heat and simmer 10 minutes. Carefully ladle hot salsa into hot jars, leaving 1/2-inch headspace. Process 15 minutes in a boiling water canner.

CHILI SAUCE

7 qt. fully ripe tomatoes, peeled,
   seeded and chopped
3 green sweet peppers, seeded and
   chopped
2 red sweet peppers, seeded and
   chopped
2 c. chopped onion

1 c. chopped celery
1 3-inch cinnamon stick
1 tsp. whole cloves
1 tsp. whole allspice
3 T. salt
2 c. sugar
2 c. vinegar

Loosen tomato skins by scalding; core and peel. Chop vegetables coarsely, using a knife, food grinder or food processor. Put them in a large kettle and heat rapidly to simmering. Tie spices in spice bag. Add to chopped vegetables. Simmer 30 to 45 minutes. Remove bag. Add sugar, salt and vinegar to tomato mixture. Boil rapidly for 5 minutes. Pour hot into pint jars, leaving 1/2-inch headspace. Adjust lids. Process for 20 minutes in a boiling water canner.

PIZZA SAUCE

3 lb. onions
2 green peppers
10 qt. tomato juice
2 tsp. crushed red pepper
4-5 12 oz. cans tomato paste
1 pt. olive or vegetable oil
1 c. sugar

1/3 c. salt
1/4 c. parsley flakes
1/4 c. oregano
1/4 c. basil
6 bay leaves
2 garlic cloves

Blend onions and peppers in the blender or chop fine. Cook onions, peppers, tomato juice and crushed red pepper for one hour. Add remaining ingredients and cook another hour, stirring frequently. Pour into jars, leaving 1-inch headspace. Process in a pressure canner, pints for 20 minutes and quarts for 25 minutes. Process at 15 lb. of pressure.

SPAGHETTI SAUCE

10 qt. tomatoes, peeled and
    chopped (about 30 lb.)
1 c. onions (chopped)
1 c. green sweet peppers, chopped
2-4 cloves garlic, minced

4 T. salt
1/4 c. sugar
1 T. basil, crushed
1 T. oregano

Combine all ingredients in a large kettle. Heat rapidly to simmering and simmer until thickened, about 1 1/2 hours. Stir frequently to prevent sticking. Pour boiling sauce into canning jars, leaving 1-inch headspace. Adjust lids. Process in a pressure canner at 15 lb. of pressure, 25 minutes for quarts, 20 minutes for pints. Add browned ground beef, if desired, when the canned spaghetti sauce is reheated for serving.

SPAGHETTI SAUCE WITH BEEF

5 lb. lean ground beef
1 onion, chopped
6 qt. tomatoes, peeled and
    chopped
2 c. green sweet peppers, chopped

1/4 c. parsley chopped (optional)
2 cloves garlic, minced
1 1/2 T. salt
1 T. sugar
1 T. sweet basil

Brown beef and onions; pour off excess fat. Add remaining ingredients, heat rapidly to simmering and simmer until thickened, about 1 hour. Stir frequently. Bring to boil and fill jars, leaving 1-inch headspace. Process in a pressure canner at 15 lb. of pressure, 75 minutes for pints; 90 minutes for quarts. Makes 6-7 pints.

CHILI WITH BEEF AND TOMATOES

3 c. dried pinto or kidney beans
9 c. water
5 tsp. salt
3 lb. ground beef
1 1/2 c. chopped onions

1 c. chopped sweet or hot peppers
1 tsp. black pepper
1/4 c. chili powder
4 c. crushed tomatoes

Wash beans, add water and 2 tsp. salt. Boil 2 minutes, soak 1 hour and drain. Brown ground beef, onions and peppers. Drain off excess fat. Add all other ingredients and simmer 5 minutes. Do not thicken. Fill pint jars, leaving 1-inch headspace. Process in a pressure canner for 75 minutes at 15 lb. of pressure. Do not use quarts. For elevations greater than 2000 feet above sea level check with local extension for process time and pressure. Makes 9 pints.

GREEN TOMATO HOT DOG RELISH

2 qt. green tomatoes, chopped or
    ground
2 qt. cucumbers, chopped or
    ground
1 qt. onions, chopped
3 red sweet peppers, chopped

3 carrots, peeled and ground
1/2 c. salt
2 T. mixed pickling spice
1/2 tsp. cayenne (red) pepper
1 1/2 c. vinegar
3 c. sugar

Chop or grind vegetables; place in a large bowl. Sprinkle with salt and allow to stand overnight in refrigerator or for 6 to 8 hours. Drain thoroughly. Tie spices in a spice bag. Place vinegar and sugar in a large kettle and add the spice bag. Bring to a boil and then add vegetables. Simmer 15-20 minutes, or until vegetables are partially cooked. Pack hot mixture into clean, hot pint canning jars. Cover vegetables with vinegar solution, leaving 1/2-inch headspace. Process in boiling water bath for 10 minutes.

DILLED GREEN TOMATO PICKLES

1 gal. small firm green tomatoes
5-6 ribs celery
5-6 green sweet peppers
garlic

dill
1 qt. vinegar
2 qt. water
1 c. pickling or canning salt

Pack green tomatoes into clean, hot jars. To each quart add a rib of celery and 1 green pepper, seeded and cut in quarters. Add 1 head of dill and 1 or 2 cloves garlic. Combine vinegar, water and salt. Bring to a boil and pour over the vegetables, leaving 1/2-inch headspace. Adjust lids. Process in a boiling water canner for 15 minutes. Allow to stand 4-6 weeks before using in order to develop flavor. Note: this amount of liquid will fill approximately 6 quarts.

MOCK BERRY JAM WITH RIPE TOMATOES

4 c. ripe tomatoes
3 c. sugar

1 T. lemon juice
6 oz. strawberry gelatin

Put tomatoes in the blender then in a saucepan with sugar and lemon juice. Boil 15 minutes. Add gelatin. Boil 5 minutes. Pour into hot jars. Process in a boiling water canner for 10 minutes.

MOCK BERRY JAM WITH GREEN TOMATOES

3 c. ground green tomatoes
2 c. sugar

6 oz. raspberry or blueberry
gelatin

Boil ingredients for 20 minutes. Put in jars. Process in a boiling water canner for 10 minutes.

GREEN TOMATO PIE FILLING

4 qt. chopped green tomatoes
3 qt. peeled and chopped
    tart apples
1 lb. dark raisins
1 lb. white raisins
1/4 c. minced citron, lemon or
    orange peel
2 c. water

2 1/2 c. brown sugar
2 1/2 c. sugar
1/2 c. vinegar
1 c. lemon juice
2 T. cinnamon
1 tsp. nutmeg
1 tsp. cloves

Combine all ingredients in a large saucepan. Cook slowly, stirring often, until tender and slightly thickened—35 to 40 minutes. Fill pint or quart jars with hot mixture, leaving 1/2-inch headspace. Process in boiling water canner for 15 minutes. Makes about 7 quarts.

HOW TO FREEZE TOMATOES

Canning is the method of choice for preserving tomatoes, if that is not an option, then use the following methods to freeze.

Whole tomatoes: Lay whole washed tomatoes in a single layer on a pan in the freezer. When tomatoes are solid, package in large bag, removing single tomatoes as needed. Core and peel while thawing. Whole tomatoes will last about 3 months in the freezer.

Stewed tomatoes: Wash, scald 2 minutes to loosen skins, peel and core. Simmer 10-20 minutes until tomatoes are tender. Cool and package in rigid containers, leaving 1-inch headspace.[2]

Tomato Juice: Wash, core and cut into pieces. Heat to boiling and strain. Cool and package, leaving 1-inch headspace.[2]

But whosoever drinketh of the water that I shall give him shall never thirst; but the water that I shall give him shall be in him a well of water springing up into everlasting life.

John 4:14

Turnips
and
Rutabagas

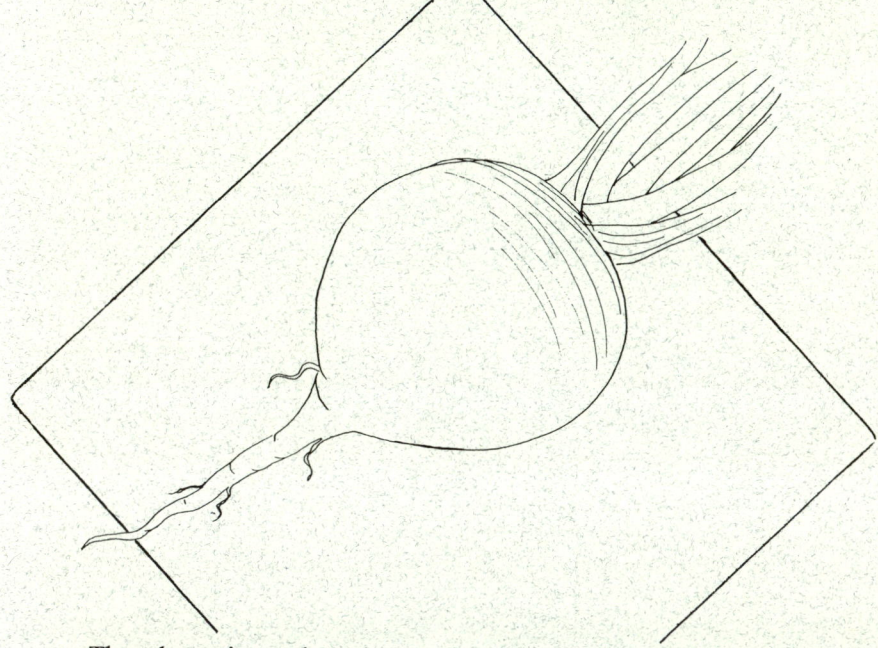

Though turnips and rutabagas are closely related, there are nonetheless, significant differences between the two.

Turnips grow faster, have fuzzy leaves and don't store very long because of their high water content. Rutabagas are a long season (90 day) crop, have smooth leaves and can be stored for extended periods. Most turnips have white flesh; most rutabagas have yellow flesh—with exceptions to both. Turnips have been around much longer—since ancient times—than their rutabaga cousins. Rutabagas were developed in the 1700s by crossing a turnip with a cabbage.

Turnips are grown for spring or fall harvest. Rutabagas are planted in midsummer for harvest in fall after a couple of frosts.

For spring turnips, plant seeds as soon as ground can be worked in sweet, fertile soil ¼- ½ inch deep. Thin plants to a final spacing of 3-5 inches. Rutabagas are planted 90 days before a mid-fall harvest. Thin to a spacing of 6-8 inches.

Both plants can be used for their tops, although turnips are especially prized as greens. Some turnip varieties are grown exclusively as greens, never developing bulbs. You can also harvest greens from your root crop by cutting the tops 1 inch above ground level. The tops regrow and roots continue to develop.

Turnips are fast growing and need a steady supply of water. If growth is checked by hot, dry weather turnips get woody and bitter. Because rutabagas are slower growing, watering is less critical.

Root maggots can be a problem with turnips and rutabagas. Prevent with insecticide sprays or use a row cover to keep flies from laying their eggs around the plants.

Harvest turnip greens early in the season and roots when they are 2-3 inches across. Over ripe turnips get woody fast if left in the ground after they're ready. Rutabagas are ready for harvest in the fall at 3-4 inches across.

Baby turnips can be sliced and eaten raw or boiled without peeling. Larger turnips, and rutabagas, need to be peeled.

Rutabagas are good baked, French fried, glazed, boiled and mashed. Boil, steam, bake or stir-fry turnips.

Keep turnips in the refrigerator for up to 1 week. Rutabagas last about 2 months if stored unwashed in moist sand in a cool cellar.

Turnips contain good levels of vitamin C, calcium and potassium.

Yield: 1 lb. fresh turnips or rutabaga = 3 ½ cups cubed

TURNIPS AND RUTABAGAS—SOUPS

TURNIP SOUP

2 c. grated turnips
2 T. butter
1 onion, finely chopped
2 T. flour

1 tsp. salt
1 qt. milk
chopped parsley

Cook turnips in water until tender. Meanwhile, heat butter and sauté onions 5 minutes. Blend in flour and salt then slowly add milk, stirring constantly until mixture boils. Add cooked turnips.

TURNIP VEGETABLE SOUP

4 white turnips, peeled and grated
1 medium rutabaga, peeled and
    grated
2 carrots, scraped and diced
2 onions, finely chopped
4 large cloves garlic, minced
1/2 c. fresh parsley, chopped
1/2 c. uncooked barley

2 tsp. basil
chicken broth or water to cover
    vegetables (about 4 c.)
2-3 dashes hot sauce
salt to taste
1/2 tsp. pepper
1 tsp. dill weed

Place turnips, rutabaga, carrots and onions in a large soup kettle. Add garlic, parsley, barley and basil. Just barely cover with broth or water. Bring to a boil. Lower heat and simmer, covered, for about 1 hour. Stir in hot sauce, salt, pepper and dill just before serving.

RUTABAGA SOUP

2 T. butter
1 c. chopped onion
4 c. finely diced rutabagas

4 c. chicken broth or bouillon
salt and pepper to taste
1 c. cream

Heat butter in a large kettle. Sauté onion 5 minutes. Add rutabagas, broth, salt and pepper. Simmer until rutabagas are tender, about 15 minutes. Add cream and heat through.

TURNIPS AND RUTABAGAS—SALADS

TURNIP SLAW

6 medium turnips   2 T. sugar
2/3 c. sour cream   1 tsp. salt
2 T. vinegar

Peel and grate turnips. Combine remaining ingredients to make a dressing. Pour over turnips and mix well.

TURNIP CARROT CABBAGE SALAD

1 c. shredded turnips   salt and pepper to taste
1 c. shredded cabbage   French dressing
1 c. shredded carrots

Combine vegetables; season to taste. Serve with French dressing.
Variation: Use shredded beets instead of cabbage.

APPLE RUTABAGA SALAD

1/4 c. mayonnaise   1/4 c. chopped peanuts
1 T. lemon juice   1/2 c. pared, coarsely grated, raw
1 tsp. sugar   rutabaga
1/8 tsp. salt   1 c. shredded cabbage
1/4 c. raisins   1 c. diced, peeled red apples

In a large bowl, combine and mix mayonnaise, lemon juice, sugar and salt. Add remaining ingredients and mix well.

TURNIPS AND RUTABAGAS—SIDE AND MAIN DISHES

HOW TO COOK TURNIPS

Bring 1-inch of water to a boil. Add 3-4 c. cubed turnips and 1/2-1 tsp. salt or to taste. Return to a boil, reduce heat and simmer 10-15 minutes. Cook small whole turnips approximately 20 minutes. Serve plain, buttered or with white or cheese sauce.

CURRIED TURNIPS

3 T. butter
1 medium onion, thinly sliced
1 tsp. thyme
1 tsp. marjoram
1/2 tsp. ginger
1 tsp. salt

1/2 tsp. pepper
3 T. yogurt
2 lb. white turnips, peeled and cut
   into 1-inch cubes
1 tsp. curry powder

Heat the butter in a large deep skillet. Add onion, thyme and marjoram. Cook, stirring constantly, until onion is soft and golden. Add ginger, salt and pepper. Cook over medium heat, stirring constantly, for 3 minutes. Stir in yogurt and cook 3 minutes more. Add the turnips and cook, uncovered, for 5 minutes. Lower heat. Simmer, covered, for about 10 minutes, stirring occasionally. Check for moisture; if necessary, add a little hot water to prevent scorching, a T. at a time—the curry should be dry. When turnips are almost tender, stir in the curry powder. Cook for 10 minutes more. Serve with roast pork or ham.

TURNIPS WITH ONIONS

5 medium turnips, peeled and cut
   into 1/2-inch cubes
2 T. butter
1 medium onion, chopped

3/4 tsp. marjoram
1/2 tsp. salt
1/8 tsp. pepper

Cook turnips 15-20 minutes or until fork tender. Drain. In same saucepan, melt butter. Add onion and cook until tender. Stir in remaining ingredients. Cook approximately 5 minutes, stirring often. Turnips should be golden brown.

CHEESY TURNIPS AND CARROTS

3 c. diced, peeled turnips
2 c. sliced carrots
1/4 tsp. ginger
3/4 c. water
1 tsp. salt, divided
1/2 c. chopped onion

1/2 c. diced celery
3 T. butter
3 T. flour
1/4 tsp. pepper
1 1/2 c. milk
1 c. shredded cheddar cheese

In a saucepan, combine turnips, carrots, ginger, water and 1/2 tsp. salt. Cover and cook for 10-15 minutes or until vegetables are tender; drain and reserve liquid. Set vegetables aside. In a skillet, sauté onion and celery in butter until tender; stir in flour, pepper and remaining salt. Add milk and vegetable liquid; bring to a boil. Cook and stir until thickened and bubbly. Stir in cheese until melted; stir in the vegetables and heat through.

BAKED STUFFED TURNIPS

4 medium tomatoes
2 T. uncooked rice
2 c. water
1 T. butter

1 tsp. salt
1/4 tsp. pepper
4 medium turnips

Chop the tomatoes and add rice, water, butter, salt and pepper. Cook until the rice is soft. Scoop out the centers of the turnips, leaving a shell 1/2-inch thick. Chop turnip centers and add to tomato mixture. Fill centers of turnips. Sprinkle with bread crumbs if desired. Place in a buttered baking dish and add 1/2 c. water. Bake at 350° for 1 hour.

TURNIP SOUFFLÉ

6 medium turnips
2 T. butter
1/2 c. milk
1/2 c. grated cheese

2 egg yolks, well beaten
1/2 tsp. salt
1/8 tsp. pepper
2 egg whites, well beaten

Cook turnips until tender. Drain and mash. Add butter, milk, cheese, egg yolks, salt and pepper. Fold in stiffly beaten egg whites. Pile lightly into a well oiled baking dish. Set in a pan of warm water. Bake at 375° until a knife inserted into the center comes out clean.

IRISH STEW WITH TURNIPS

3 lb. lamb cut into small pieces
water to cover meat
4 allspice berries
2 T. minced parsley
1 c. sliced carrots

3/4 c. diced turnips
3 c. cubed potatoes
1/2 c. sliced onion
salt and pepper

Place meat in a large kettle. Add water to cover, allspice and parsley. Cover; simmer 2 hours. Add vegetables, salt and pepper. Cover; cook 35-40 minutes longer. Thicken gravy if desired. Drop dumplings may be added 15 minutes before cooking is completed.

HOW TO COOK RUTABAGAS

Bring 1-inch of water to a boil. Add 4 c. sliced rutabagas and 1/2-1 tsp. salt. Return to a boil; reduce heat and simmer, covered, 10-20 minutes or until fork tender.

RUTABAGAS WITH BASIL LEMON BUTTER

2 T. butter
1 T. lemon juice
1 tsp. salt
1/4 tsp. basil

1/8 tsp. pepper
3 c. diced, cooked rutabagas, hot
2 T. minced fresh parsley

Melt butter; add lemon juice, salt, basil and pepper. Mix well and pour over hot rutabagas. Sprinkle with parsley. Cover and let stand 5 minutes before serving.

RUTABAGAS AU GRATIN

3 T. butter, divided
2 T. flour
1/4 tsp. salt
1/8 tsp. pepper

1 c. milk
1/2 c. grated Cheddar cheese
2 c. mashed, cooked rutabagas
1/4 c. soft bread crumbs

Melt 2 T. butter in a small saucepan. Add flour and seasonings and blend well; add milk gradually and stir and cook until thickened. Add cheese and stir until melted. Pour sauce over rutabagas in a greased 1-quart casserole. Combine crumbs with remaining butter, and sprinkle on top. Bake, uncovered, at 400° for 15 minutes.

RUTABAGA PUFF

3 c. 1-inch cubes peeled rutabaga
1 1/2 c. boiling water
1/2 tsp. salt
1/2 tsp. sugar
1 c. soft bread cubes
1 T. sugar

1/8 tsp. ginger
1/4 tsp. salt
1/8 tsp. pepper
1/2 c. milk
1 egg
2 T. butter

Combine rutabagas, water, salt and sugar in a saucepan and cook, covered, until tender. Mash. Combine mashed rutabaga, bread cubes, 1 T. sugar, ginger, salt and pepper. Combine milk and egg; stir into rutabaga mixture. Pour into a greased 1-quart casserole and dot with butter. Bake at 350° until top is lightly browned—about 45 minutes.

RUTABAGA POTATO WHIP

3 medium potatoes, peeled
1 large rutabaga, peeled
1 tsp. sugar

3 T. butter
1 tsp. salt
1/8 tsp. pepper

Cut potatoes and rutabaga into chunks. Cook in separate saucepans until tender. Add sugar to rutabaga cooking water. Mash potatoes and rutabaga together. Beat in butter, salt and pepper until smooth and fluffy. Add hot milk if needed.

TURNIPS—DESERTS

TURNIP PIE

2 c. mashed turnips
1 c. milk
3 egg yolks, beaten
3/4 c. brown sugar
1 1/4 tsp. cinnamon
1/4 tsp. cloves

1/4 tsp. ginger
1/4 tsp. nutmeg
1 tsp. salt
3 egg yolks, stiffly beaten
1 unbaked pie shell

Mix turnips and milk. Add the egg yolks, sugar, spices and salt. Mix well. Fold in egg whites. Pour into the pie shell. Bake at 450° for 10 minutes; reduce heat to 375° and bake 20 minutes longer, or until filling is firm.

TURNIPS—GREENS

HOW TO COOK TURNIP GREENS

Bring 1/4-inch of water to a boil. Add one pound of greens and 1/2 tsp. salt, or to taste. Return to a boil and simmer 5-10 minutes, depending on size.

TURNIP GREENS

4 slices bacon
1 onion, chopped

6-8 c. chopped young turnip
          greens
salt and pepper to taste

Fry bacon and remove from the skillet. Sauté onions in the bacon drippings. Add the greens to the skillet. Cover and cook 5-7 minutes. Add crumbled bacon, salt and pepper. Serve immediately.

TURNIPS AND RUTABAGAS—FREEZING

HOW TO FREEZE TURNIPS[2]

Remove tops, wash, peel, slice or dice (1/2-inch). Blanch for 2 minutes. [Cool immediately in cold water; drain, package and freeze.]

HOW TO FREEZE TURNIP GREENS[2]

Cut off large, tough stems; discard all damaged leaves. Wash thoroughly several times. Blanch 1 pound greens in 2 gallons water for 2 minutes. [Cool immediately in cold water; drain, package and freeze.]

HOW TO FREEZE RUTABAGAS[2]

Choose tender, young rutabagas. Wash, remove tops. Peel and slice or dice into 1/4-inch cubes. To mash, press through sieve or ricer after blanching 2 minutes. [Cool immediately, package and freeze.]

Hints: Turnips are good eaten raw, with or without dip or in salad.

Turnips and rutabagas can be used interchangeably in recipes.

NOTES

Winter Squash

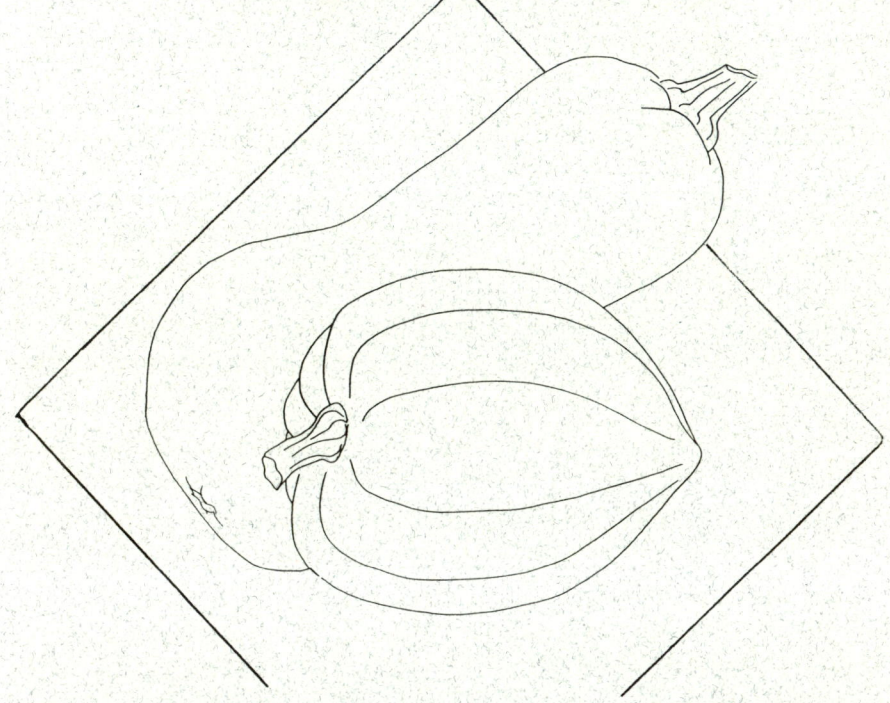

Winter squash are called winter squash because they can be stored over winter for an extended period after harvest in the fall. Size, shape, color, flavor and texture vary widely from one variety to the next. Some of the more common types are—acorn, butternut, buttercup, hubbard and spaghetti. Spaghetti squash are a unique variety with stringy flesh that looks like, and can be substituted for spaghetti.

Most winter squash need from 75 up to 120 days to mature. Northern gardeners can extend their season with plastic mulch and row covers. Using transplants instead of direct seeding will gain time as well. Transplants should be started in individual pots, be 3-4 weeks old and have one or two true leaves.

If you are direct seeding, wait until after danger of frost is past and soil temperatures are in the 60-70 degree range. Like all cucurbits, squash seeds are susceptible to rot in cool wet soil. For bush plants figure a spacing of 18 inches between plants and 5 feet between rows. Vining squash—which most winter squash are—require 10 feet between rows and 3 feet between plants.

Rotate winter squash on a three year basis with non-cucurbits to prevent build up of disease in the soil.

Squash grows best in fertile, well-drained soil. It needs plenty of water, at least until fruit has set. After that water is not as critical.

Winter squash should be fully mature before, harvesting. A good test is to push your thumbnail into the skin. If you can penetrate the skin, the squash is immature and will have a poor, watery flavor. For green varieties, look for a bright orange ground spot (place where the squash touched the ground). The color of the flesh depends on the particular type, but ranges from pale yellow to orange.

A well-ripened squash will withstand light frost, although the thin skinned butternuts are more sensitive and should be harvested before frost.

Harvest winter squash before heavy frost by cutting them from the vine leaving 2-3 inches of stem on the squash. Cure the squash in a sunny, warm location for 1-2 weeks and then move to cool (50-55 degrees), dry storage. They should keep for 3-4 months. Winter squash gets sweeter in storage as the starch converts to sugar.

Winter squash can be used in any recipe that calls for pumpkin. In addition, squash can be served steamed, baked or boiled. Squash soup served in a squash bowl makes an interesting and delicious alternative for your table. Acorn squash are the right size and shape for stuffing and baking.

Winter squash have high levels of vitamin A and some vitamin C, folate and potassium.

Yield: 2 lb. whole squash = 1 lb. peeled = 4 cups diced

WINTER SQUASH SOUP

2 T. butter	1 tsp. salt
1/2 c. flour	1/4 tsp. pepper
1 qt. milk	2 T. minced parsley
2 c. cooked, mashed squash	1/2 tsp. nutmeg
(hubbard, butternut or acorn)	

Melt butter then add flour. Slowly stir in milk. Cook and stir until thickened. Gradually stir in the cooked squash, salt, pepper and parsley. Cook, stirring constantly, until the soup thickens and is hot. Sprinkle nutmeg on top before serving.

SPICY BUTTERNUT SQUASH SOUP

7-8 c. chunks of peeled butternut	1 T. minced fresh ginger or 1/2
squash	tsp. ground ginger
4 c. chicken broth	1/2 tsp. coriander
1 large onion, peeled and chopped	salt and pepper to taste
1 T. curry powder	

Combine squash, broth, onion, curry powder, ginger and coriander in a large kettle. Bring to a boil on high heat; reduce heat to simmer and cover. Simmer 40 minutes. Add more broth if needed. Puree in a food processor or blender in small batches until smooth. Taste and add salt and pepper as needed.

WINTER SQUASH—SALADS

SPAGHETTI SQUASH SALAD

3 c. cooked spaghetti squash	1 tsp. dill weed, optional
2 c. cauliflower, cut in bite size	1 c. sugar
pieces, parboiled	1 T. salt
1 c. celery, sliced thin	1/2 c. vegetable oil
1 medium onion, diced	1 c. vinegar
1 green or red pepper, diced	1 tsp. paprika

Combine squash, cauliflower, celery, onion, pepper and dill weed. Shake rest of the ingredients well in a jar with a tight lid. Pour over vegetables. Chill before serving.

HOW TO COOK WINTER SQUASH

Bring 1-inch of water a boil. Add 3-4 inch pieces of squash and return to a boil. Reduce heat and simmer 10-15 minutes or until tender. Drain, cool and peel then mash or puree. Salt to taste.

HOW TO BAKE WINTER SQUASH

Cut the squash in half and place it upside down on a cookie sheet with sides or a cake pan. Add 1/4-inch of water to the pan. Bake at 350°-375° for 45 minutes to 1 1/2 hours depending on the size of the squash. The squash should be fork tender.

SAUTÉED SQUASH

2-2 1/2 lb. winter squash, coarsely grated	3 T. butter
	salt and pepper to taste

Coarsely grate squash. Heat butter in a large skillet. Add squash and stir until well coated. Cover and cook on low heat approximately 8 minutes or until softened, but not mushy. Season to taste.
Variation: After squash is cooked add 1 T. butter and 1/2 c. cream.

BAKED ACORN SQUASH

Wash, cut in half lengthwise and scrape out seeds and pulp. Dust with salt and pepper; dot with butter. Put cut side up in a pan with 1/2-inch of water. Bake at 375° for 45-50 minutes. Allow 1/2 squash per person.

SWEET BAKED ACORN SQUASH

1 medium acorn squash, cut in half lengthwise	1/4 c. applesauce
1 T. melted butter	1/4 c. maple syrup or brown sugar

Scrape out seed cavity and place cut side down on a baking sheet in 1/4-inch of water. Bake at 375° for 35 minutes. Turn squash over. Fill with remaining ingredients and bake another 15 minutes.

APPLE STUFFED ACORN SQUASH

1 medium acorn squash	2 T. sugar
3 T. melted butter, divided	1/4 tsp. cinnamon
salt	1 tsp. lemon juice
1 baking apple, peeled, cored and chopped	

Cut squash in half lengthwise and remove seeds. Place squash, cut side down, in a baking pan. Add 1/4 to 1/2-inch water and bake at 375° for 35 minutes. Turn cut side up and brush cut surfaces and cavities with butter. Sprinkle lightly with salt. Divide chopped apple evenly into squash cavities. Combine sugar and cinnamon and sprinkle over apples. Sprinkle lemon juice and remaining butter over the apples. Reduce heat to 350° and bake 30 minutes. This recipe can easily be doubled or tripled.

SAUSAGE STUFFED ACORN SQUASH

2 acorn squash	1 c. finely chopped celery
1 lb. bulk sausage	3/4 c. stale bread crumbs
1 c. finely chopped onion	1 c. grated cheese

Cut squash in half lengthwise and remove seeds. Place squash cut side down in a baking pan. Add 1/4 to 1/2-inch water and bake at 375° for 35 minutes. Meanwhile brown sausage and remove from pan. Drain off all but 2 T. drippings. Sauté onion and celery in the drippings about 5 minutes. Remove from heat. Stir in bread cubes. Quickly stir in sausage and cheese. Put into lightly salted squash cavities and bake at 350° for 20-30 minutes.

WHIPPED BUTTERNUT SQUASH

1 butternut squash (about 2 1/2 lb.), peeled, seeded and cubed	3/4 tsp. salt
	2 T. butter
	1 T. brown sugar
3 c. water	1/8 tsp. nutmeg

In a saucepan over medium heat, bring squash, water and 1/2 tsp. salt, if desired, to a boil. Reduce heat; cover and simmer for 20 minutes or until the squash is tender. Drain; transfer to a mixing bowl. Add butter, brown sugar, nutmeg and remaining salt if desired; beat until smooth.

SQUASH PANCAKES

2 eggs
1 c. mashed, dark yellow squash
1 1/2 c. milk
2 T. vegetable oil

1 tsp. vanilla
2 1/2 c. biscuit mix
2 T. brown sugar
1 tsp. cinnamon

Beat together eggs and squash. Add milk, oil and vanilla. Combine dry ingredients and stir in. Fry on a hot, lightly oiled skillet.

WINTER SQUASH FRITTERS

1 c. mashed winter squash
1 egg, beaten
1 T. minced onion
2 T. milk

1/2 c. flour
salt and pepper to taste
1 tsp. baking powder
vegetable oil

Mix squash, egg, onion, milk, flour, salt, pepper and baking powder until well blended. Drop batter by the spoonful into hot oil and fry 3-5 minutes or until golden brown. Turn each fritter once. Drain on paper towels.

WINTER SQUASH BALLS

2 c. mashed winter squash
3/4 c. flour
1/4 c. finely chopped onion
1/2 tsp. baking powder
1/2 tsp. salt

1/8 tsp. pepper
1 egg slightly beaten
3 c. corn flakes, coarsely crushed
oil for deep frying

Combine all but corn flakes and oil. Mix well and shape into 1-inch balls. Roll into crushed corn flakes; coat well. Heat oil to 375°. Fry 4 balls at a time in hot oil about 2 minutes. Drain on paper towels. Serve warm.

SLICED BUTTERNUT SQUASH CASSEROLE

1 medium butternut squash
1/4 c. minced onion
1 c. cracker crumbs
1/2 c. shredded cheddar cheese

salt and pepper to taste
1/4 c. butter
1/4 c. cream or milk

Peel and slice squash. Place alternate layers of squash, onion, crumbs, cheese, salt, pepper and butter in a buttered casserole. Add cream. Cover and bake at 375° for 20 minutes. Uncover and bake 10 minutes more.

BUTTERNUT SQUASH BAKE

1/3 c. butter	3 c. mashed butternut squash
3/4 c. sugar	1/2 c. sugar
2 eggs	1/2 c. chopped pecans
2/3 c. evaporated milk or cream	1/4 c. flour
1 tsp. vanilla	3 T. melted butter
1 tsp. pumpkin pie spice	

Cream butter and sugar. Beat in eggs, milk, vanilla and spice. Stir in squash. Pour into a buttered casserole. Combine remaining ingredients and sprinkle over casserole. Bake at 350° for 45 minutes.

DELICATA SQUASH BAKE

2 c. cooked, peeled and mashed delicata squash (sweet potato squash)	1/8 tsp. pepper
	1/4 tsp. nutmeg
	1 egg, beaten
3 T. melted margarine	1/2 c. chopped nuts
2 T. brown sugar	1 c. drained crushed pineapple
1/2 tsp. salt	

In a medium mixing bowl, combine mashed squash with remaining ingredients. Pour into a well-greased baking dish. Bake at 350° for 30 minutes.

HUBBARD SQUASH BAKE

6 c. peeled and cubed hubbard squash	1/2 c. finely chopped onion
	1 tsp. salt
2 T. butter	1/4 tsp. pepper
1 c. sour cream	

Cook squash until tender, 15 to 20 minutes; drain. Mash squash and stir in remaining ingredients. Mound mixture in an ungreased 1-quart casserole. Bake, uncovered, at 400° for 15 to 20 minutes.

SPAGHETTI SQUASH

| 1 spaghetti squash | garlic salt to taste |
| melted butter | grated Parmesan cheese |

Bake spaghetti squash whole. Pierce the squash several places with a carving fork or knife. Bake at 350° for 45 minute to 1 1/2 hours, depending on size. Cool slightly then cut in half and scoop out seeds. Use fork to remove spaghetti strands. Toss strands with melted butter, garlic salt and Parmesan cheese as desired.

Variation: Boil the squash whole. Pierce the skin and boil 30-60 minutes depending on size. A fork will easily go into the squash if it is done.

SPAGHETTI SQUASH CASSEROLE

2 1/2 lb. spaghetti squash	2 tomatoes, chopped
3 T. vegetable oil	1 c. cottage cheese
1 large onion, chopped	1 c. mozzarella cheese, shredded
1/2 lb. mushrooms, thinly sliced	1 tsp. parsley
2 cloves garlic, minced	1 tsp. dried basil
1 tsp. dried oregano	1 c. bread crumbs
salt and pepper to taste	1/4 c. grated Parmesan cheese

Carefully cut squash in half lengthwise, and scoop out seeds. Arrange halves, cut side down, on greased cookie sheet and bake 45 minutes, or until soft. Using a fork, scoop out spaghetti strands. Heat vegetable oil in large skillet and add onion, mushrooms, garlic, oregano, salt and pepper. Sauté 4 minutes. Add tomatoes and cook, uncovered, on high heat until most liquid has evaporated. Remove from heat. Stir in spaghetti strands, cottage cheese, mozzarella, parsley, basil and bread crumbs. Put in a greased 2-quart casserole. Sprinkle Parmesan on top. Bake at 375° for 40 minutes.

Ye shall know them by their fruits. Do men gather grapes of thorns, or figs of thistles? Even so every good tree bringeth forth good fruit: but a corrupt tree bringeth forth evil fruit. A good tree cannot bring forth evil fruit, neither can a corrupt tree bring forth good fruit. Every tree that bringeth not forth good fruit is hewn down, and cast into the fire. Wherefore by their fruits ye shall know them.

Matthew 7:15-20

SPAGHETTI SQUASH LASAGNA

3 1/2 lb. spaghetti squash
1 lb. ground beef
1 onion, chopped
15 1/2 oz. jar spaghetti squash (or
    1 pt. homemade sauce)
1 tsp. basil

1/2 tsp. oregano
1 tsp. salt
1/8 tsp. pepper
1 c. cottage cheese
1 c. mozzarella cheese

Pierce squash several places with a knife or carving fork. Boil in 4 qt. of water in a large kettle approximately 25-30 minutes or until fork tender. Drain and cool until easy to handle. Fry ground beef and onion until beef is browned. Stir in sauce, basil, oregano, salt and pepper. Reduce heat and simmer 15 minutes. Combine cottage cheese and cheese. Cut squash in half starting by stem. Scoop out seeds. Layer 1/3 of the spaghetti strands in a 13 x 9 baking dish. Top with a third of meat mixture and a third of cheese. Repeat twice. Bake covered at 400° for 15 minutes, then uncovered 5 more minutes. Let stand 10 minutes for easier cutting.

WINTER SQUASH CASSEROLE

2 c. mashed winter squash
4 slices bacon
1/2 c. chopped onion
2/3 c. grated cheddar cheese

1/4 tsp. salt
dash Tabasco or black pepper
1/4 c. buttered bread crumbs

Put squash into medium bowl. Fry bacon until crisp; crumble into squash. Leave about 1 T. drippings in skillet. Fry onion in drippings until transparent; add squash. Add cheese. Add salt and Tabasco sauce or pepper; mix well. Put in a buttered baking dish; top with bread crumbs. Bake at 350° until heated through and crumbs begin to brown—about 25 minutes.

WINTER SQUASH—BAKED GOODS AND DESSERT

Hint: Winter squash can be substituted for pumpkin desserts and baked goods as well as hot dishes.

WINTER SQUASH DOUGHNUTS

1 1/4 c. sugar
2 T. butter
2 eggs, well beaten
1 c. cooked, mashed squash
1 tsp. vanilla
3 c. flour

1 T. baking powder
1/2 tsp. salt
1/2 cinnamon
1/2 tsp. nutmeg
1 c. milk

Cream sugar and butter. Add eggs, squash and vanilla. Combine dry ingredients. Add alternately with milk to the first mixture. Chill dough. Turn onto a lightly floured board. Roll out about 1/3-inch thick. Cut with a floured cutter. Deep fry in hot (365°) vegetable oil until brown. Drain on crumpled paper towels.

EASY BUTTERNUT SQUASH DESSERT

1 tsp. cinnamon
1/2 tsp. ginger
1/4 tsp. cloves
1/4 tsp. nutmeg
2 c. mashed butternut squash

1 1/2 c. sugar
4 eggs
1 can evaporated milk
1 yellow cake mix
1/2 c. butter, melted

Mix together the first 8 ingredients; pour into a 13 x 9 cake pan. Sprinkle dry cake mix onto squash mixture. Drizzle butter on top. Bake at 350° for 30 to 40 minutes. Top with whipped cream or serve with ice cream.

SPAGHETTI SQUASH PIE

1 unbaked pie shell
3 eggs
1 c. sugar
1 T. flour

1 1/2 c. milk
1 tsp. coconut extract
1/4 tsp. salt
1 1/2 c. cooked spaghetti squash

Prepare pastry. Beat eggs slightly. Beat in remaining ingredients except for squash. Stir in squash. Pour into pastry lined pie plate. Bake at 450° for 20 minutes; reduce temperature to 350° and bake until knife inserted in center comes out clean.

I am crucified with Christ: nevertheless I live; yet not I, but Christ liveth in me: and the life which I now live in the flesh I live by the faith of the Son of God, who loved me, and gave himself for me.

Galations 2:20

300

WINTER SQUASH—CANNING AND FREEZING

HOW TO CAN WINTER SQUASH[1]

Wash; remove seeds; pare. Cut into 1-inch cubes. Boil 2 minutes in water. Do not mash or puree. Cover with hot cooking liquid or boiling water, leaving 1-inch headspace.

Process in a pressure canner, pints for 55 minutes, quarts for 90 minutes. Process at 10 lb. of pressure at elevations up to 1000 feet above sea level. Process at 15 lb. of pressure at elevations above 1000 feet above sea level. Dial gauges should be at 11 lb. of pressure up to 2000 feet above sea level.

HOW TO FREEZE WINTER SQUASH

Harvest fully mature squash with a hard rind. Wash, cut in halves and scoop our seeds and membrane. Place cut side down on baking sheet and bake at 375° until tender. Scoop out pulp; mash or put through a food mill, cool, package and freeze. Leave 1-inch headspace in rigid containers.

He which testifieth these things saith, Surely I come quickly. Amen. Even so come Lord Jesus.

Revelation 22:20

NOTES

Vegetable Canning and Freezing Guide

VEGETABLE CANNING—GENERAL INFORMATION

(This section contains general canning information only. For information about a specific vegetable, see the section in the book for that vegetable. Each one will have its own canning and freezing guide. To find how to can corn, see **CORN— CANNING AND FREEZING.**)

To destroy microorganisms that can cause spoilage, low acid vegetables need to be processed in a pressure canner at 240°-250° for a specified time. At sea level, these temperatures are reached at 10 lb. of pressure (240°) and 15 lb. of pressure (250°). Because water boils at lower temperatures at higher elevations, weighted gauge pressure canners should be at 10 lb. for elevations up to 1000 feet above sea level and at 15 lb. for elevations above 1000 feet above sea level. Call your local extension agency for recommendations for your area if unsure about your elevation. (See chart below for dial gauges.)

ALTITUDE	DIAL GAUGE
0-2000 ft.	11 lb.
2001-4000 ft.	12 lb.
4001-6000 ft.	13 lb.
6001-8000 ft.	14 lb.
8001-10000 ft.	15 lb.

Put 2-3 inches of boiling water in the bottom of the pressure canner or follow manufacturers instructions. Set the jars on a rack and fasten lids. Let steam escape through the vent for 10 minutes before placing the pressure regulator on the vent. Start counting time when the correct pressure is reached. Keep the pressure steady by regulating heat.

Let the pressure drop on its own at the end of processing time. It takes approximately 25 minutes for depressurizing, although time may vary.

While most vegetables can be canned with good results, broccoli, Brussels sprouts, cabbage, cauliflower, kohlrabies, rutabagas and turnips are not recommended for home canning.

VEGETABLE FREEZING—GENERAL INFORMATION

(This section contains general information only. For specific instructions about a vegetable, see the **CANNING AND FREEZING** section for that vegetable.)

Freezing vegetables retains more nutrients than other preservation processes. Freeze as soon as possible after harvesting, for the best flavor and vitamin retention.

Most vegetables need to be blanched before freezing. Blanching stops or slows enzyme activity in the vegetables.

To blanch, use at least 1 gallon of water for each pound of vegetables. Use a blancher or a wire basket in a large kettle. Place the basket of vegetables into boiling water. Cover and start timing immediately. (See individual vegetable categories for blanching times.) Keep the heat turned high. Change water occasionally if blanching large amounts of vegetables. Immediately after blanching time is finished, plunge drained vegetables into cold water or ice water. Cooling time should be about as long as blanching time. Drain cooled vegetables well then package and freeze immediately.

Go to the ant, thou sluggard; consider her ways, and be wise: Which having no guide, overseer, or ruler, provideth her meet in the summer, and gathereth her food in the harvest.

Proverbs 6:6-8

Fruit Canning and Freezing Guide

FRUIT CANNING—GENERAL INFORMATION

Canned peaches, plums, pears and apricots are usually superior in quality to frozen. Soft berries on the other hand are better if frozen.

To prevent light colored fruit from darkening when exposed to air, use the antioxidants ascorbic acid, citric acid or lemon juice in water. Mix 1/2 tsp. of a mixture of half ascorbic acid and half citric acid in 1 quart of water. Commercial mixtures are available as well. For lemon juice use 2 T. per quart of water. To prevent darkening, submerge the fruit in the antioxidant solution for 1 minute; drain before packing in jars.

Syrup or other liquid should completely cover the food and fill in around the solid pieces in the jar. Food at the top of the jar darkens if not submerged in liquid.

Sugar helps canned fruit hold its shape, color and flavor. The amount used depends on individual preference and the fruits natural sugar content. The amount of sugar used does not change processing time nor is it a factor in spoilage.

PROPORTIONS FOR SYRUPS[4]

Type of Syrup	Water or Juice	Cups of Sugar	Yield
very light	1 quart	1/2 c.	4 c.
light	1 quart	1 c.	4 1/2 c.
medium	1 quart	2 c.	5 c.
heavy	1 quart	3 c.	5 1/2 c.
very heavy	1 quart	4 c.	6 1/2 c.

It takes about 1 1/2 c. of syrup per quart to cover the fruit.

Fill jars, leaving the recommended headspace between the top of the liquid and the top of the jar. Wipe rims. Tighten lids firmly but not too tightly.

All fruit should be processed in a boiling water canner, carefully observing time for individual fruit. Cover the jars and lids in the canner with at least 1-inch of water. Put the lid on the canner. Begin timing after the water is in a full rolling boil with the jars in the canner. Remove the jars after the processing time is complete. Do not retighten bands even if they seem loose. Remove bands after 24 to 36 hours.

Fruit[4]	Type of Pack and Preparation	Time
Apples	**Hot pack.** Peel, core and cut into pieces. Boil 5 minutes in a thin syrup or water. Pack hot into jars and cover with boiling syrup or water, leaving 1/2-inch headspace.	Pints or Quarts: 20 min.
Applesauce	**Hot pack.** Prepare applesauce, sweetened or unsweetened. Heat to simmering (185-210° F.) and pack hot, leaving 1/4-inch headspace for sieved applesauce or 1/2-inch headspace for chunky applesauce.	Pints: 20 min. Quarts: 25 min.
Apricots	**Raw pack.** Wash, cut in half and remove pits. Pack tightly in jars. Cover with boiling syrup, leaving 1/2-inch head space	Pints: 25 min. Quarts: 30 min.
	Hot pack. Wash, cut in half and remove pits. Heat in syrup and pack hot. Cover with boiling syrup, leaving 1/2-inch headspace.	Pints: 20 min. Quarts: 25 min.
Berries or Grapes *raspberries* *blackberries* *boysenberries* *blueberries* *currants* *elderberries* *gooseberries* *huckleberries*	**Raw pack.** Fill jars with washed berries, shaking gently to get a full pack. Cover with boiling syrup or water, leaving 1/2-inch headspace. Note: freezing produces a more flavorful and attractive product.	Pints: 15 min. Quarts: 20 min.
	Hot pack. Place 1/2 to 3/4 c. water in pan and add berries. Heat for 1 minute. Pack hot, adding boiling water or syrup to cover berries. Leave 1/2-inch headspace.	Pints or Quarts: 15 min.
Cherries, Sweet or Tart	**Raw pack.** Wash. Remove pits if desired. Pack fruit, shaking jar to get a full pack. Cover with boiling syrup or water, leaving 1/2-inch headspace.	Pints or Quarts: 25 min.
	Hot pack. Add 1/2 c. sugar to each quart of pitted or unpitted cherries. Add 1/2 c. water to keep them from sticking. Cover pan and bring to a boil. Pack hot. Cover with boiling syrup or water, leaving 1/2-inch headspace.	Pints: 15 min. Quarts: 20 min.

306

Fruit cocktail	**Hot pack.** Select firm but ripe pineapples, pears and peaches; cut into chunks. Add firm whole seedless grapes. Simmer in light or medium syrup until just heated through. Pack hot into pint or half pint jars to within 1/2-inch of top. Add 2 or 3 halved maraschino cherries to each jar, if desired. Cover with boiling syrup; leave 1/2-inch headspace.	**Half pints or Pints: 20 min.**
Fruit Juices	**Hot Pack.** Wash and crush fruit. To extract juice, heat to simmering and strain through cloth bag or press through sieve or food mill. Add sugar if desired. Reheat to simmering and pack hot, leaving 1/2-inch headspace.	**Pints or Quarts: 5 min.**
Grapefruit or Orange	**Raw pack.** Pare fruit with a sharp or serrated knife, removing white membrane. Remove sections by slipping a sharp, thin-bladed knife between the pulp and membrane of each section. Discard seeds. Pack into pint jars and cover with a boiling syrup, leaving 1/2-inch headspace.	**Pints or Quarts: 10 min.**
Peaches or Nectarines	Wash; dip in boiling water [30 to 60 seconds], then quickly into cold water; peel. Cut in half and remove pits. [Peaches can be pared with a sharp knife instead of blanching. To prevent darkening use one of the solutions described on pg. 283] Slice if desired. Drain before packing or heating. **Raw pack.** Pack raw peaches tightly to within 1/2-inch of top of jar. Cover with boiling syrup or water. Leave 1/2-inch of headspace. **Hot pack.** Heat prepared peaches in hot syrup. Very juicy peaches may be heated with sugar and no added liquid. Pack hot fruit to 1/2-inch of top of jars. Cover with boiling syrup, leaving 1/2-inch headspace.	**Pints: 25 min. Quarts: 30 min.** **Pints: 20 min. Quarts: 25 min.**
Pears	Wash, peel, cut in halves and core. Pack raw or hot, following instructions for peaches.	**See peaches above.**

307

Plums	**Raw pack.** Wash. To can whole, prick skins to keep fruits from bursting. Freestone varieties can be halved and pitted. Pack raw fruit tightly to within 1/2-inch of top of jar. Cover with boiling syrup, leaving 1/2-inch headspace.	Pints: 20 min. Quarts: 25 min.
	Hot pack. Heat to boiling in syrup or juice. If plums are very juicy, they can be heated with sugar and no added liquid. Pack hot and cover with boiling syrup, leaving 1/2-inch headspace.	Pints: 20 min. Quarts: 25 min.

APPLE PIE FILLING

6 qt. blanched, sliced fresh apples
5 1/2 c. sugar
1 1/2 Clearjel or Perma Flo
1 T. cinnamon

2 1/2 c. cold water
5 c. apple juice
1 tsp. nutmeg
3/4 c. lemon juice

Use firm, crisp, tart apples. Wash, peel and core. Prepare slices 1/2-inch wide and place in water containing ascorbic acid to prevent darkening. Blanch 2 quarts at a time for 1 minute in boiling water, then drain. While blanching other batches of apples, keep blanched apples in a covered pot so they will stay warm. Combine sugar, Clearjel and cinnamon in a large kettle with water and apple juice. Add nutmeg. Stir and cook on medium high heat until mixture thickens and begins to bubble. Add lemon juice and boil 1 minute, stirring constantly. Fold in apple slices immediately and fill jars, leaving 1/2-inch headspace. Adjust lids and process in boiling water canner for 25 minutes. Yields 7 quarts.

BLUEBERRY PIE FILLING

6 qt. blueberries
6 c. sugar
2 1/4 c. Clearjel or Perma Flo

7 c. cold water
blue food coloring (optional)
1/2 c. lemon juice

Use fresh, ripe and firm blueberries, or unsweetened frozen blueberries. Wash and drain if using fresh blueberries. Combine sugar and Clearjel in a large kettle. Add water and food coloring. Cook on medium high heat until mixture thickens and begins to bubble. Add lemon juice and boil 1 minute, stirring constantly. Fold in berries immediately and fill jars, leaving 1/2-inch headspace. Adjust lids and process immediately in boiling water canner for 30 minutes. Yields 7 quarts.

CHERRY PIE FILLING

6 qt. tart cherries
7 c. sugar
1 3/4 c. Clearjel or Perma Flo
9 1/3 c. cold water

1/2 c. lemon juice
1 tsp. cinnamon
2 tsp. almond extract (otpional)

Use fresh, very ripe and firm cherries, or unsweetened frozen cherries. Thaw fruit, then collect and measure the juice and use it to replace all or part of the water. Rinse and pit fresh cherries, and hold in cold water. Combine sugar and Clearjel in a large kettle and add water. Add cinnamon and almond extract. Stir mixture and cook over medium high heat until mixture thickens and begins to bubble. Add lemon juice and boil 1 minute, stirring constantly. Fold in cherries immediately and fill jars, leaving 1/2-inch headspace. Adjust lids and process in a boiling water canner for 30 minutes. Yields 7 quarts.

HOW TO FREEZE FRUITS[2]

Most fruits can be preserved by freezing. With the exception of rhubarb, blueberries, cranberries, gooseberries, currants and elderberries, most fruit will have a better color, texture and flavor if they are frozen with sugar.

Many fruits will darken rapidly after peeling due to oxidation, but there are several ways to prevent this color change.

Ascorbic acid (Vitamin C) is effective in preventing oxidation of most fruits. Ascorbic acid, in crystalline or tablet form, is available at drugstores. One teaspoon weighs about 3 grams (3000 mg). Use 1/2 tsp. per quart of water as a dip to hold sliced peaches, apples, pears or similar fruits while you get them ready for packing either with dry sugar or unsweetened. Dip for one minute, then drain and pack. Ascorbic acid may also be added to the syrup for syrup packs (1/2 tsp. per quart of cold syrup), or added directly to fruit purees and juices.

Lemon juice or citric acid can help prevent darkening of some fruits, but are not as effective as ascorbic acid. One T. of lemon juice per quart of water can be used as a dip. There may be a slight but usually unobjectionable flavor change.

Dry sugar pack: The dry sugar pack can be used for many juicy fruits, left whole, sliced or crushed. Cut about 1 quart of fruit into a bowl or shallow pan. If the fruit is one that darkens readily, dip in one of the antioxidants or sprinkle the fruit with dissolved ascorbic acid or other antioxidant. The quantity of sugar depends upon your personal tastes. Sprinkle sugar over the fruit and mix very gently. Sugar will draw juice out of the fruit to form a syrup, even though you do not add water. Some fruits can be sliced or crushed before sugar is added. Using the dry sugar pack instead of syrup has the advantage of not diluting flavor with added water and gives you flexibility in the amount of sugar used.

Dry pack: For a dry pack, pack firmly into containers or crush slightly before packing. No sugar is added. Fruits that darken can be treated with ascorbic acid to preserve color.

Loose pack: For a loose pack, small whole fruits such as raspberries, blueberries and sweet cherries can be spread in a single layer on shallow trays and frozen; then remove them from the tray and package in a freezer container. Label and return to the freezer quickly.

Syrup pack: A 40 per cent syrup is recommended for whole fruits and those that tend to darken. For some mild flavored fruits, a thin syrup (30 %) prevents masking of flavor. Heavier syrups may be needed for very sour fruits. To prepare syrup, dissolve sugar in cold or hot water. If you use hot water, chill the syrup before using. Replacing 1/4 of the sugar with light-colored corn syrup or honey, cup for cup, may improve the texture, flavor and color of fruits. It takes 1/2 to 2/3 cup of syrup for each pint container of fruit.

PROPORTIONS FOR SYRUPS

Type of Syrup		Amount of Water	Amount of Sugar	Yield
Thin	30%	1 quart	2 cups	5 cups
Medium	40%	1 quart	3 cups	5 1/2 cups
Heavy	50%	1 quart	4 cups	6 1/2 cups

Rigid containers work best for fruit packed in syrup or sugar pack. Leave at least 1/2-inch headspace to allow for expansion. Plastic freezer bags work fine for most applications.

Apples

Wash, peel, quarter and core. Slice as desired. Dip in antioxidant; drain well. Dry pack with or without sugar; add antioxidant to syrup if using syrup pack.

Applesauce

Prepare applesauce with or without sugar; chill and pack in rigid containers, leaving 1-inch headspace.

Apricots

Wash. If you intend to peel, dip fruit in boiling water until skins peel easily. May be frozen unpeeled. Halve and remove pits. Dip in antioxidant. Syrup pack, with antioxidant added, is recommended for fruit to be served uncooked. For cooked products, use dry sugar pack. For crushed or pureed, add antioxidant and sugar.

Soft Berries
blackberries
boysenberries
strawberries
raspberries

Sort berries and wash gently. Drain well. For an unsweetened loose pack, place on a tray in a single layer; freeze for 1 or 2 hours, then package. For sugar pack, sprinkle sugar on berries and gently mix until sugar is dissolved; slice strawberries or crush other berries and mix with sugar. Pack. Syrup pack is optional.

Firm Berries
blueberries
cranberries
currants
elderberries
gooseberries
huckleberries

Wash and sort berries. Drain. These berries all freeze well without sweetening. Package after draining or place on a tray in a single layer; freeze for 1 to 2 hours, then package. Syrup pack can be used for berries to be served uncooked. Berries can be crushed and packed with sugar. Antioxidant is not necessary.

Cherries, Sour or Sweet

Stem, sort and wash. Drain and pit. Sweet cherries lose color quickly, so it is advisable to add antioxidant to sugar or syrup in which they are packed. A sugar pack is recommended for all cherries to help in maintaining desirable color and flavor. Syrup pack can also be used.

Fruit Mixtures	Peaches, melon balls, orange or grapefruit sections, whole seedless grapes, sweet cherries and pineapple wedges can be mixed together and frozen in a thin or medium syrup pack. Unsweetened pack or dry sugar pack is not recommended.
Grapes	Wash, sort and pack whole or cut in halves. Remove seeds from seeded varieties. For loose pack, freeze in a single layer on a tray and freeze for 1 to 2 hours, then package. For best quality, freeze in thin or medium syrup.
Juices	Prepare juice from fruit by squeezing (citrus) or by heating crushed fruit, straining or allowing to drip through a jelly bag. Add antioxidant to juices of fruit that darken easily. Sweetening is optional. Package in rigid containers, leaving 1-inch headspace.
Peaches and Nectarines	Wash. Dip in boiling water for 1 to 2 minutes to loosen skins. Cool in cold water and rub off skins. Pit and halve or slice. Drop immediately into antioxidant dip to prevent darkening (or directly into syrup which contains antioxidant). For dry sugar pack, drain and sprinkle with sugar; pack. May be packed without sugar, but quality may not be as good as in a sweetened pack.
Pears	(Some varieties do not freeze satisfactorily and develop a gritty texture. Experiment with one or two containers.) Peel, cut in halves or quarters and remove cores. Heat in boiling thin or medium syrup for 1 or 2 minutes. Remove from syrup and cool. Pack and cover with cold thin or medium syrup which contains antioxidant, leaving 1-inch headspace.
Plums and Prunes	Wash. Leave whole or cut in halves or quarters and remove pits. For unsweetened pack, pack whole fruit into containers. Before serving, dip frozen fruit in cold water for 5 to 10 seconds, remove skins and cover with syrup to thaw. Syrup pack is recommended for cut fruit, using a thin or medium syrup for sweet varieties, heavy syrup for tart. Add antioxidant to syrup. Dry sugar pack is less satisfactory for plums.

ENDNOTES

1 Mennes, Mary E.: Canning Vegetables Safely. Madison: Cooperative
   Extension Publications, University of Wisconsin-Extension, 1995.
   Taken from the chart on pages 8-12. Used with permission.

Note: Process times and canner pressure settings listed under this footnote are
currently accepted standards and not exclusively from the listed source.

All recommendations for adding salt under this footnote should read as
follows: Add ½ teaspoon salt to pints and 1 teaspoon to quarts. Iodized or plain
table salt may be used. If desired, salt may be reduced or eliminated from
canned vegetables.

2 Mennes, Mary E.: Freezing Fruits and Vegetables. Madison: Cooperative
   Extension Publications, University of Wisconsin-Extension. 1991.
   Information taken from pages 5-15. Used with permission.

3 Mennes, Mary E.: How to Make Your Own Sauerkraut. Madison:
   Cooperative Extension Publications, University of Wisconsin-
   Madison. 1994. Steps 1-6 pages 2-4; canning and freezing
   information pages 5 & 6. Used with permission.

4 Mennes, Mary E.: Canning Fruits Safely. Madison: Cooperative Extension
   Publications, University of Wisconsin-Extension, 1996. Chart page 4,
   Proportions for Syrups and chart pages 6-8. Used with permission.

5 Mennes, Mary E.: Tomatoes Tart and Tasty. Madison: Cooperative
   Extension Publications, University of Wisconsin-Extension, 1993.
   From page 3, 7 & 8. Used with permission.

Bibliography

Ballantyne, Janet: *Garden Way's Joy of Gardening Cookbook.* Troy, New York: Garden Way, 1984.

Burrows, Lois M.: *Too Many Tomatoes ... Squash, Beans and Other Good Things: a Cookbook for When Your Garden Explodes.* 1st ed. New York: Harper and Row, 1976.

Doty, Walter L.: *All About Vegetables.* Ramon, CA: Chevron Chemical Company, 1990.

Farm Journal: *Farm Journal's Best-Ever Vegetable Recipes.* Garden City, New York: Farm Journal, Inc., 1984.

Johnny's Selected Seeds: *Johnny's Selected Seeds, Commercial Catalog.* Albion, Me: Johnny's Selected Seeds, 1997.

King James Version: All scripture references are from the King James Bible.

Lane Books: *Vegetable Gardening.* Menlo Park, CA: Lane Books, 1973.

Mennes, Mary E.: *Canning Fruits Safely.* Madison: Cooperative Extension Publications, University of Wisconsin-Extension, 1991.

Mennes, Mary E.: *Canning Vegetables Safely.* Madison: Cooperative Extension Publications, University of Wisconsin-Extension, 1989.

Mennes, Mary E.: *Freezing Fruits and Vegetables.* Madison: Cooperative Extension Publications, University of Wisconsin-Extension, 1984.

Mennes, Mary E.: *How to Make Your Own Sauerkraut.* Madison: Cooperative Extension Publications, University of Wisconsin-Extension, 1984.

Mennes, Mary E.: *Tomatoes Tart and Tasty.* Madison: Cooperative Extension Publications, University of Wisconsin-Extension, 1993.

Morash, Marian: *The Victory Garden Cookbook.* New York: Knopf, 1982.

Reader's Digest: *Foods that Harm Foods that Heal.* Pleasantville: Reader's Digest Association, Inc., 1997.

Town, Marian Kleinsasser: *A Midwest Gardener's Cookbook.* Bloomington: Indiana University Press, 1996.

Index

Acorn Squash, Apple Stuffed 295
Acorn Squash, Baked 294
Acorn Squash, Parsnips with 153
Acorn Squash, Sausage Stuffed 295
Acorn Squash, Sweet Baked 294
Apple Rutabaga Salad 286
Apple Stuffed Acorn Squash 295
Apple Sweet Potato Casserole 256
Asparagus and Cheddar Cheese Soup 1
Asparagus Au Gratin 6
Asparagus, Baked with Eggs 7
Asparagus Brunch Casserole 7
Asparagus Chicken Chowder 2
Asparagus, Chicken Stir Fry with Spaghetti .. 5
Asparagus, Fancy 3
Asparagus, Fried 3
Asparagus, How to Can 8
Asparagus, How to Cook 3
Asparagus, How to Freeze 8
Asparagus Loaf 7
Asparagus Parmesan 5
Asparagus Quiche 6
Asparagus Radish Cucumber Salad 2
Asparagus Soufflé 6
Asparagus Soup 1
Asparagus Soup, Cream of 1
Asparagus Stir Fry 4
Asparagus Stir Fry, Quick 4
Asparagus Vinaigrette 2
Baby Beets in Sour Cream 25
Bacon Dressing 126
Baked Acorn Squash 294
Baked Asparagus with Eggs 7
Baked Beans Using Dry Beans, How to Can 22
Baked Beans, Boston 18
Baked Beans, Horticultural 17
Baked Brussels Sprouts with Cream 38
Baked Cabbage Rolls 49
Baked Candied Sweet Potatoes 255
Baked Carrot Ring with Cheese 57
Baked Cushaw or Pumpkin 188
Baked Eggplant Slices 97
Baked Fish and Onions 145
Baked Glazed Onion 140
Baked Mashed Potatoes with Cheese 177
Baked Pasta with Peppers 169
Baked Pork Chops with Cabbage 50
Baked Potatoes 177

Baked Potatoes with Chives 177
Baked Pumpkin 187
Baked Pumpkin to use in a Recipe 188
Baked Rhubarb Pudding 205
Baked Salsify 211
Baked Spaghetti With Tomatoes 272
Baked Stuffed Tomatoes 269
Baked Stuffed Turnips 288
Baked Sweet Potatoes 253
Baked Whole Fish with Celery Stuffing 73
Baked Zucchini and Tomatoes 236
Baked Zucchini and Tomatoes with Cheese 237
Baked Zucchini Slices 235
Barbecued Lima Beans 17

Bars
   Carrot Bars with Orange Glaze 60
   Green Tomato Oatmeal Bars 276
   Pumpkin Bars 191
   Zucchini Brownies 247
Basic Vinaigrette 122
Bean and Bacon Salad 12
Beef and Celery Stir Fry 71
Beef Stew with Carrots 58
Beef Stew with Kale 108
Beef Stew with Potatoes 183
Beef Stir Fry with Zucchini 243
Beefy Spaghetti with Tomato Juice 273
Beefy Sprout Surprises 39
Beet and Apple Salad 23
Beet and Egg Salad 24
Beet Macaroni Salad 24

Beverages
   Creamy Strawberry Smoothie 228
   Muskmelon Smoothie 130
   Rhubarb Punch 201
   Strawberry Banana Smoothie 228
   Strawberry Pineapple Punch 228
   Strawberry Punch 228
   Watermelon Smoothie 131

Biscuits
   Green Onion Biscuits 146
   Sweet Potato Biscuits 259
Blender Mayonnaise 126
Blender Parsnips Pie 154
Blender Sweet Potato Pie 260
Borscht 23
Boston Baked Beans 18
Braised Chicken with Celery Carrots Onions .. 72

315

Index

Bread

Carrot Bread with Lemon Glaze 61
Corny Cornbread 83
Green Tomato Bread 275
Parsnips Nut Bread 154
Tomato Bread 275
Pumpkin Bread 192
Rhubarb Bread 203
Strawberry Bread 223
Zucchini Bread 246
Bread and Butter Pickles 91
Breakfast Burritos with Onions 144
Broccoli, How to Cook 31
Broccoli and Cauliflower, Marinated 30
Broccoli and Ham Soup 29
Broccoli Carrot Stir Fry 32
Broccoli Cauliflower Salad 30
Broccoli Celery Stir Fry 31
Broccoli Chicken Casserole 34
Broccoli Chicken Noodle Dinner, Quick 33
Broccoli Chicken Stir Fry 32
Broccoli Florets, Oven Fried 31
Broccoli Ham Bake 34
Broccoli Pasta Salad 30
Broccoli Pasta Stir Fry with Cheese 32
Broccoli Potato Soup, Zucchini 233
Broccoli Quiche 33
Broccoli Salad 29
Broccoli Soufflé 33
Broccoli Tuna Casserole 34
Broccoli, How to Freeze 35
Broiled Tomatoes 267
Broiled Zucchini 235
Brussels Chef Salad 37
Brussels Sprouts and Chicken Stir Fry 39
Brussels Sprouts with Bacon 38
Brussels Sprouts with Sour Cream 39
Brussels Sprouts, Baked with Cream 38
Brussels Sprouts, Beefy Surprises 39
Brussels Sprouts, Creamed 38
Brussels Sprouts, Dilled 40
Brussels Sprouts, How to Cook 37
Brussels Sprouts, How to Freeze 41
Brussels Sprouts, Sweet Pickled 40

Butters

Lemon Butter 64
Parmesan Butter 64
Shallot Butter 139
Buttermilk Dressing 125
Buttermilk Potato Puffs 184

Butternut Squash Bake 297
Butternut Squash Casserole, Sliced 296
Butternut Squash Dessert, Easy 300
Butternut Squash Soup, Spicy 293
Cabbage and Corned Beef 51
Cabbage and Ground Beef Casserole 50
Cabbage and Noodles 47
Cabbage Apple Salad 45
Cabbage Au Gratin 47
Cabbage Gelatin Salad 46
Cabbage Refrigerator Sweet Sour Vegetables ... 52
Cabbage Rolls with Corn Syrup 49
Cabbage Rolls, Baked 49
Cabbage Rolls, Stove Top 48
Cabbage Salad, Celeriac and 75
Cabbage Salad, Hot 46
Cabbage Salad, Turnip Carrot 286
Cabbage Sandwich Spread 44
Cabbage Slaw 44
Cabbage Slaw, Creamy 45
Cabbage Slaw, Vegetable 45
Cabbage Soup, Cream of 43
Cabbage Vegetable Stuffing, Turkey Breast 51
Cabbage Wedges, How to Cook 47
Cabbage, Baked with Pork Chops 50
Cabbage, Cauliflower with 65
Cabbage, How to Cook 46
Cabbage, How to Freeze 54
Cabbage, Stir Fried 48
Cabbage, Sweet Sour Red 47
Cabbage, Turkey Minestrone with 44
Caesar Salad 119

Cakes

Carrot Cake 61
Green Tomato Chocolate Cake 276
Parsnip Cake 154
Potato Chocolate Cake 184
Pumpkin Chocolate Chip Cake 191
Rhubarb and Orange Coffee Cake 204
Rhubarb Cake 203
Rhubarb Upside Down Cake 203
Streusel Rhubarb Cake 204
Sweet Potato Cake 259
Zucchini Carrot Cake 247
Zucchini Chocolate Cake 247
Canned Sloppy Joe with Onion 149
Carrot and Celery Stir Fry 57
Carrot and Zucchini Salad 56
Carrot Bars with Orange Glaze 60
Carrot Bran Muffins 59

316

Carrot Bread with Lemon Glaze.................61
Carrot Cabbage Salad, Turnip...........286
Carrot Cake................61
Carrot Cake, Zucchini................248
Carrot Cookies................60
Carrot Ginger Cookies................60
Carrot Marmalade................62
Carrot Pea Soup, Turkey................55
Carrot Pepper Scrapple, Onion................143
Carrot Ring, Baked with Cheese................57
Carrot Salad, Grated................55
Carrot Salad, Pineapple................56
Carrot Sandwich Spread................56
Carrot Soup, Cheesy................55
Carrot Soup, Cream of Celeriac and................74
Carrots Baked in Cheese Sauce................58
Carrots, Cheesy Turnips and................287
Carrots, Chicken and Dumplings with................59
Carrots, Chicken Noodle with Celery and................69
Carrots, Dilled................57
Carrots, Glazed................57
Carrots, How to Can................62
Carrots, How to Cook................56
Carrots, How to Freeze................62
Carrots, Seven Layer Casserole with................58
Carrots, with Beef Stew................58
Cauliflower Au Gratin................66
Cauliflower Beef Stir Fry................66
Cauliflower Pea Casserole................65
Cauliflower Salad................63
Cauliflower Soup with Smoked Sausage................63
Cauliflower Soup, Creamy................63
Cauliflower Vegetable Salad................64
Cauliflower with Cabbage................65
Cauliflower, Fried................65
Cauliflower, How to Cook................64
Cauliflower, How to Freeze................67
Cauliflower, Marinated Broccoli and................30
Cauliflower, Sweet Pickled................67
Cauliflower, Vegetable Pizza with................66
Celeriac and Cabbage Salad................75
Celeriac Grape Pineapple Salad................75
Celeriac Salad................74
Celeriac with Cheese Sauce................76
Celeriac, and Carrot Soup, Cream of................74
Celeriac, How to Cook................75
Celery Dressing................123
Celery Potato Soup................69
Celery Seed Dressing................123
Celery Soup................69

Celery Stir Fry, and Beef................71
Celery Stir Fry, Carrot and................57
Celery Stuffing, Sausage and................74
Celery, Cheesy................71
Celery, Chicken Mix with carrots and Onions....76
Celery, Chicken Noodle Soup with Carrots................69
Celery, Chicken Salad With................70
Celery, Creamed................71
Celery, Curried Turkey and................72
Celery, How to Can................76
Celery, How to Cook................70
Celery, How to Freeze................76
Celery, Sautéed................70
Celery, Stuffed................70
Celery, Turkey Patties with................73
Celery with Braised Chicken Carrots Onions....72
Chard Casserole................108
Chard Salad................104
Chard Soup................103
Chard with Rice................108
Chard, Sautéed................105
Cheese Sauce................64
Cheeseburger Potato Soup................174
Cheesy Carrot Soup................55
Cheesy Celery................71
Cheesy Turnips and Carrots................287
Chef Salad................121
Chicken and Dumplings with Carrots................59
Chicken Asparagus Stir Fry with Spaghetti................5
Chicken Casserole with Peas................162
Chicken Corn Chowder................77
Chicken Corn Noodle Soup................78
Chicken Mix with Celery Carrots Onions................76
Chicken Noodle Soup with Celery Carrots................69
Chicken Salad with Celery................70
Chicken Stew with Kohlrabies................115
Chicken Stir Fry with Tomatoes................272
Chili Sauce................281
Chili With Beef and Tomatoes................282
Chinese Cabbage Salad, Hot................46
Chinese Cabbage with Chicken................43
Chinese Cabbage with Chicken, Stir Fried................48
Chocolate Frosting................184
Chowders
    Chicken Corn Chowder................77
    Fishy Potato Chowder................174
    Lima Bean Chowder................10
    Parsnips Chowder................151
Chow Chow................93
Chunky Potato Salad................175

Index

Chunky Tomato Soup 263
Classic potato Salad 175
Coconut Custard Sweet Potato Pie 260
Cole Slaw to Freeze 54
Cole Slaw with Peppers 165
Collards with Canadian Bacon 106
Cooked Salad Dressing 126

Cookies
    Carrot Cookies 60
    Carrot Ginger Cookies 60
    Pumpkin Walnut Cookies 190
    Zucchini Cookies with Lemon Glaze 247

Corn and Ham Soup 77
Corn and Radish Salad 78
Corn and Sausage, Leeks with Wild Rice 146
Corn Casserole 81
Corn Casserole, Tomato 268
Corn Chowder, Chicken 77
Corn Curry 79
Corn Fritters 80
Corn How to Cook 79
Corn How to Freeze 85
Corn Muffins, Raised 83
Corn Pancakes 80
Corn Pudding 81
Corn Pudding, Easy 80
Corn Quiche 82
Corn Relish 84
Corn Salad 78
Corn Soup, Creamy 77
Corn Tomato Ground Beef Pie 82
Corn, Chicken Noodle Soup 78
Corn, Cream Style, How to Can 84
Corn, Creamed 79
Corn, Lima Beans and 16
Corn, Sautéed 79
Corn, Scalloped 80
Corn, Whole Kernel, How to Can 84
Corny Brunswick Stew 82
Corny Cornbread 83
Cream Cheese Bacon Stuffed Cherry Tomatoes 265
Cream Cheese Frosting 191
Cream of Asparagus Soup 1
Cream of Broccoli Soup 29
Cream of Cabbage Soup 43
Cream of Celeriac and Carrot Soup 74
Cream of Greens Soup 103
Cream of Leek Soup 137
Cream of Pea Soup 157
Creamed Brussels Sprouts 38

Creamed Celery 71
Creamed Corn 79
Creamed Kohlrabies 114
Creamed Onions 140
Creamed Peas 160
Creamed Peas with Potatoes 160
Creamed Potatoes 176
Creamed Radishes 197
Creamed Sweet Potatoes 257
Creamy Cabbage Slaw 45
Creamy Cauliflower Soup 63
Creamy Corn Soup 77
Creamy Cucumber Dressing 124
Creamy Honey Dressing 124
Creamy Italian Dressing 124
Creamy Mayonnaise Sauce 107
Creamy Pea Potato Salad 158
Creamy Potato Soup 174
Creamy Spinach 216
Creamy Spinach Soup 213
Creamy Strawberry Smoothie 228
Croutons, Toasted 128
Cucumber and Tomato Salad 88
Cucumber Dressing, Creamy 124
Cucumber Salad 87
Cucumber Salad, Molded 89
Cucumber Sandwich Spread 89
Cucumber Soup 87
Cucumber Soup, Creamy 87
Cucumbers in Sour Cream 88
Cucumbers in Vinegar and Oil 88
Cucumbers, Dilled 88
Cucumbers, Sautéed 89
Cucumbers, Stir Fried 90
Curried Turkey and Celery 72
Curried Turnips 287
Cushaw, Baked or Pumpkin 188
Dandelion Potato Salad 104
Dandelion Salad 104
Dandelion Salad with Horseradish 118
Dandelion Soufflé 127
Deep Fried Eggplant 97
Deep Fried Pumpkin or Winter Squash 188
Deep Fried Radishes 198
Deep Fried Summer Squash 236
Delicata Squash Bake 297

Desserts
    Baked Rhubarb Pudding 205
    Easy Butternut Squash Dessert 300
    Easy Rhubarb Dessert 205

318

Desserts (cont.)

Easy Strawberry Ice Cream.........................227
Frozen Pumpkin Dessert............................194
Frozen Strawberry Dessert........................227
Pumpkin Cheesecake................................195
Pumpkin Marshmallow Dessert...................194
Pumpkin Pie Squares...............................194
Quick Strawberry Shortcake......................224
Rhubarb Crisp.......................................206
Rhubarb Crunch.....................................206
Rhubarb Custard Dessert..........................205
Rhubarb Pizza.......................................206
Strawberry Cheesecake.............................225
Strawberry Cream Puffs............................226
Strawberry Gelatin Pizza..........................225
Strawberry Ice......................................227
Strawberry Ice Cream...............................227
Strawberry Pineapple Dessert.....................226
Strawberry Pizza....................................225
Strawberry Shortcake...............................224
Strawberry Tapioca Pudding.......................226
Zucchini Dessert....................................248
Dilled Brussels Sprouts..............................40
Dilled Carrots...57
Dilled Cucumbers.....................................88
Dilled Green Tomato Pickles........................283
Dills, Refrigerator...................................90

Dips

Radish Dip...197
Sour Cream and Onion Dip.........................139
Spinach Dip..215
Dilly Beans..20
Dipping Sauce...97

Doughnuts and Rolls

Buttermilk Potato Puff.............................184
Potato Cinnamon Rolls.............................185
Pumpkin Cinnamon Rolls...........................192
Raised Potato Doughnuts...........................185
Rhubarb Cinnamon Rolls...........................204
Sweet Potato Fritters..............................260
Winter Squash Doughnuts..........................300

Dressing

Bacon Dressing......................................126
Basic Vinaigrette...................................122
Blender Mayonnaise.................................126
Buttermilk Dressing................................125
Celery Seed Dressing...............................123
Cooked Salad Dressing..............................126
Creamy Cucumber Dressing.........................124
Creamy Honey Dressing.............................124

Creamy Italian Dressing............................124
French Dressing.....................................123
Green Onion Dressing...............................125
Green Pepper Dressing..............................165
Honey Celery Seed Dressing........................123
Honey Coconut Dressing............................130
Honey Poppy Seed Dressing.........................124
Italian Dressing....................................123
Low Fat Buttermilk Dressing.......................125
Thousand Island Dressing..........................125
Dry Beans, How to Can................................21
Dry Beans, How to Cook..............................18
Easy Butternut Squash Dessert.....................300
Easy Corn Pudding....................................80
Easy Onion and Cheese Quiche......................143
Easy Potato Bake....................................178
Easy Rhubarb Dessert...............................205
Easy Strawberry Ice Cream.........................227
Easy Tomato Meat Pie...............................271
Egg Stuffed Tomatoes...............................264
Eggplant and Beef Pie..............................102
Eggplant Beef Skillet...............................101
Eggplant Casserole...................................98
Eggplant Casserole, Hot Dog and...................101
Eggplant Cheese Sandwiches..........................95
Eggplant Onion and Tomatoes.........................99
Eggplant Parmesan....................................99
Eggplant Patties, Mashed.............................98
Eggplant Pizzas......................................98
Eggplant Salad.......................................95
Eggplant Salad, Roasted..............................95
Eggplant Slices, Baked...............................97
Eggplant, Deep Fried.................................97
Eggplant, Grilled....................................96
Eggplant, How to Cook................................96
Eggplant, How to Freeze.............................102
Eggplant, Sautéed....................................96
Eggplant, Vegetarian Stuffed........................100
Eggplants, Stuffed..................................100
English Muffins with Eggs and Spinach.............216
Fancy Asparagus.......................................3
Fava Beans, Herbed...................................16
Filled Snow Peas....................................157
Fish, Baked and Onions..............................145
Fish, Baked Whole with Celery Stuffing..............73
Fishy Potato Chowder................................174
Fluffy Strawberry Pie...............................223
Four-Day Sweet Gherkins or Chunk Pickles............92
Freezer Cucumber Pickles.............................93
Freezer Sweet Dill Pickles...........................93

Index

French Dressing 123
French Fried Potatoes 178
French Onion Soup 137
Fresh Pack Dill Pickles 91
Fresh Strawberry Frosting 229
Fried Asparagus 3
Fried Cauliflower 65
Fried Chicken and Onions 144
Fried Green Tomatoes 268
Fried Potatoes 178
Fried Rice with Peas 161

Frosting
    Chocolate Frosting 184
    Cream Cheese Frosting 191
    Fresh Strawberry Frosting 229
    Pumpkin Frosting 190
Frozen Pumpkin Dessert 194
Frozen Strawberry Dessert 227
Frozen Strawberry Pineapple Salad 221
Fruit Soup with Strawberries 221
Fruity Strawberry Popsicles 229
Glazed Carrots 57
Glazed Parsnips 152
Grated Carrot Salad 55
Greek Salad 120
Green Bean and Tomato Salad 11
Green Bean Bake 15
Green Bean Casserole, Onion and 141
Green Bean Ham Potato Casserole 15
Green Bean Potato Pancakes 14
Green Bean Salad 11
Green Bean Salad with Limas 12
Green Bean Salad, Raw 11
Green Bean Soup 9
Green Beans with Hard Boiled Eggs 14
Green Beans with Potatoes and Hot Dogs 15
Green Beans with Sour Cream and Bacon 14
Green Beans, How to Cook 13
Green Beans, How to Freeze 22
Green Beans, Stir Fry 13
Green Beans—Unblanched, How to Freeze 22
Green Onion Biscuits 146
Green Onion Dressing 125
Green Pepper Dressing 165
Green Tomato Bread 275
Green Tomato Chocolate Cake 276
Green Tomato Hot Dog Relish 283
Green Tomato Muffins 274
Green Tomato Oatmeal Bars 276
Green Tomato Pie 276

Green Tomato Pie Filling 284
Green, Wax and Italian Beans, How to Can 19
Greens and Bacon Salad 119
Greens and potatoes, mixed 107
Greens Soup, Cream of 103
Greens with Red Pepper 107
Greens, How to Cook 105
Greens, How to Freeze 109
Greens, Turnip 290
Grilled Eggplant 96
Grilled Zucchini and other Vegetables 236
Ground Cherries, How to Can 111
Ground Cherries, How to Freeze 112
Ground Cherry Jam 112
Ground Cherry Pie 111
Ground Cherry Pie with Meringue 111
Ham Salad in Muskmelon Rings 130
Harvard Beets 25
Herb Vinegar 128
Herbed Fava Beans 16
Herbed Parsnips 151
Honey Celery Seed Dressing 123
Honey Coconut Dressing 130
Honey Poppy Seed Dressing 124
Horticultural Baked Beans 17
Hot Cabbage Salad 46
Hot Chicken Salad 122
Hot Chinese Cabbage Salad 46
Hot Dog and Eggplant Casserole 101
Hot German Potato Salad 175
Hot Ham and Beef Sandwich with Onions 139
Hot Mixed Pickle 67
Hot Tomato and Ham Sandwiches 266
How to Bake Winter Squash 294
How to Can Asparagus 8
How to Can Baked Beans Using Dry Beans 22
How to Can Beets 26
How to Can Carrots 62
How to Can Celery 76
How to Can Cream-Style Corn 84
How to Can Cubed Pumpkin 195
How to Can Dry Beans 21
How to Can Beans with Molasses Tomato Sauc 22
How to Can Fresh Lima Beans 21
How to Can Green Soy Beans 21
How to Can Green, Wax, and Italian Beans 19
How to Can Ground Cherries 111
How to Can Okra 136
How to Can Onions 147
How to Can Peppers 170

320

Index

How to Can Potatoes 186
How to Can Rhubarb 208
How to Can Sauerkraut 53
How to Can Shelled Peas 162
How to Can Spinach 218
How to Can Strawberries 231
How to Can Summer Squash 249
How to Can Sweet Potatoes 261
How to Can Tomato Juice 277
How to Can Whole Kernel Corn 84
How to Can Whole Tomatoes 279
How to Can Winter Squash 301
How to Cook Asparagus 3
How to Cook Beet Greens 24
How to Cook Beets 24
How to Cook Broccoli 31
How to Cook Brussels Sprouts 37
How to Cook Cabbage 46
How to Cook Cabbage Wedges 47
How to Cook Carrots 56
How to Cook Cauliflower 64
How to Cook Celeriac 75
How to Cook Celery 70
How to Cook Corn 79
How to Cook Dry Beans 18
How to Cook Eggplant 96
How to Cook Green Beans 13
How to Cook Greens 105
How to Cook Kohlrabies 113
How to Cook Lettuce 127
How to Cook Okra 133
How to Cook Onions 140
How to Cook Parsnips 151
How to Cook Peas 159
How to Cook Potatoes 176
How to Cook Pumpkin 187
How to Cook Rutabagas 288
How to Cook Salsify 211
How to Cook Shell Beans 15
How to Cook Spinach 216
How to Cook Summer Squash 234
How to Cook Sweet Potatoes 253
How to Cook Turnip Greens 290
How to Cook Turnips 286
How to Cook Winter Squash 294
How to Freeze Asparagus 8
How to Freeze Beet Greens 27
How to Freeze Beets 27
How to Freeze Broccoli 35
How to Freeze Brussels Sprouts 41

How to Freeze Cabbage 54
How to Freeze Carrots 62
How to Freeze Cauliflower 67
How to Freeze Celery 76
How to Freeze Corn 85
How to Freeze Eggplant 102
How to Freeze French Fried Potatoes 186
How to Freeze Green Beans 22
How to Freeze Green Beans—Unblanched 22
How to Freeze Greens 109
How to Freeze Ground Cherries 112
How to Freeze Hash Brown Potatoes 186
How to Freeze Kohlrabies 115
How to Freeze Lima Beans 22
How to Freeze Mashed Potatoes 186
How to Freeze Melons 132
How to Freeze Okra 136
How to Freeze Onions 149
How to Freeze Parsnips 155
How to Freeze Peas 163
How to Freeze Peppers 171
How to Freeze Potatoes 186
How to Freeze Pumpkin 196
How to Freeze Pumpkin Pie Mix 196
How to Freeze Rhubarb 209
How to Freeze Rutabagas 291
How to Freeze Sauerkraut 54
How to Freeze Spinach 219
How to Freeze Strawberries 232
How to Freeze Summer Squash 251
How to Freeze Tomatoes 284
How to Freeze Turnip Greens 291
How to Freeze Turnips 291
How to Freeze Winter Squash 301
How to Make Sauerkraut 53
Hubbard Squash Bake 297
Hungarian Wax Peppers, Salsa with 281
Irish Stew with Turnips 288
Italian Dressing 123
Jalapeno Pepper Salsa 171
Jalapeno Peppers, Salsa with 280
Kale and Chicken Soup 103
Kale and Onions 106
Kale or Mustard Greens with Garlic 105
Kale with Sour Cream 106
Kale, Beef Stew with 108
Kidney Bean Casserole 16
Kidney Beans and Sausage over Rice 19
Kohlrabi Radish Salad 113
Kohlrabi Vegetable Salad 113

Index

Kohlrabies with Tomatoes and Peppers........... 114
Kohlrabies, Chicken Stew with........................ 115
Kohlrabies, Creamed... 114
Kohlrabies, How to Cook................................. 113
Kohlrabies, How to Freeze............................... 115
Kohlrabies, Mustard... 114
Kohlrabies, Sautéed.. 114
Lasagna, Zucchini... 242
Layered Garden Pasta Salad............................ 121
Layered Salad... 121
Leek Potato Soup.. 137
Leek Soup, Cream of.. 137
Leeks Au Gratin... 141
Leeks with Wild Rice Corn and Sausage........ 146
Lemon Butter.. 64
Lemon Butter Sauce... 37
Lettuce and Fruit Salad.................................... 120
Lettuce Salad, Wilted....................................... 118
Lettuce Sandwich Spread................................. 127
Lettuce Soup... 117
Lettuce, How to Cook....................................... 127
Lima Bean Chowder... 10
Lima Bean Soup.. 9
Lima Beans and Corn... 16
Lima Beans, Barbecued...................................... 17
Lima Beans, How to Can Fresh.......................... 21
Lima Beans, How to Freeze................................ 22
Lima Beans, Pot Roast with............................... 17
Limas, Green Bean Salad with........................... 12
Liver and Onions.. 144
Low Fat Buttermilk Dressing........................... 125
Maple Syrup Sweet Potato Casserole.............. 256
Marinated Broccoli and Cauliflower................. 30
Mashed Eggplant Patties................................... 98
Mashed Potatoes... 176
Mashed Radishes and Potatoes........................ 198
Meat Loaf, Zucchini... 241
Melon Fruit Cocktail.. 129
Melon Ring with Honey Coconut Dressing..... 130
Melons with Pineapple..................................... 129
Melons, How to Freeze..................................... 132
Mild Salsa... 280
Mixed Greens and Potatoes.............................. 107
Mock Berry Jam with Green Tomatoes........... 284
Mock Berry Jam with Ripe Tomatoes............. 283
Mock Hollandaise.. 3
Mock Oysters.. 211
Molded Cucumber Salad.................................... 89
Muffins
   Carrot Bran Muffins.................................... 59

Green Tomato Muffins..................................... 274
Onion Muffins... 147
Pumpkin Muffins.. 190
Raised Corn Muffins.. 83
Rhubarb Muffins... 202
Strawberry Muffins.. 222
Sweet Potato Muffins, Walnut Streusel..... 259
Zucchini Muffins.. 246
Muskmelon Molds.. 129
Muskmelon Rings, Ham Salad in.................... 130
Muskmelon Smoothie...................................... 130
Muskmelons with Blueberries and Peaches.... 132
Mustard Greens with Garlic, Kale or.............. 105
Mustard Kohlrabies.. 114
Navy Bean Soup... 10
Navy Bean Soup, Old-Fashioned..................... 10
New Potato Salad with Peas............................ 158
No-Cook Strawberry Freezer Jam................... 230
Okra and Summer Squash................................. 135
Okra and Tomatoes... 135
Okra Bacon Sauté... 134
Okra Fritters... 134
Okra Soup... 133
Okra Soup with Chicken.................................. 133
Okra Tomato Rice Skillet................................. 135
Okra, How to Can... 136
Okra, How to Cook... 133
Okra, How to Freeze... 136
Okra, Sliced Fried.. 134
Okra, Whol Fried.. 134
Old-Fashioned Vinaigrette............................... 118
Old-Fashioned Navy Bean Soup...................... 10
Old-Time Tomato Aspic................................... 264
Onion Pie.. 143
Onion and Cheese Quiche, Easy...................... 143
Onion and Green Bean Casserole.................... 141
Onion and Tomatoes, Eggplant......................... 99
Onion Biscuits, Green...................................... 146
Onion Carrot Pepper Scrapple......................... 143
Onion Dip, Sour Cream and............................ 138
Onion Dressing, Green..................................... 125
Onion Hoagies, Pepper Ham........................... 165
Onion Muffins... 147
Onion Pepper Egg Sandwich........................... 139
Onion Potato Baskets....................................... 142
Onion Rice Soup, Turkey................................. 138
Onion Rings.. 140
Onion Salad, Tomato.. 138
Onion Salsa... 148
Onion Sauce.. 139

322

Onion Soup, French 137
Onion Tomato Casserole 142
Onion, Baked Glazed 140
Onion, Canned Sloppy Joe with 149
Onions with Cod, Peppers and 168
Onions, Creamed 140
Onions, Fried Chicken and 144
Onions, Hot Ham Beef Sandwich with 139
Onions, How to Can 147
Onions, How to Cook 140
Onions, How to Freeze 149
Onions, Kale and 106
Onions, Liver and 144
Onions, Pickled 148
Onions, Pork Chops and 145
Onions, Tomatoes with Hot Dogs and 271
Onions, Turnips with 287
Orange Glazed Beets 25
Orange Sweet Potato Casserole 256
Oriental Spinach Salad 215
Oven French Fried Potatoes 179
Oven Fried Broccoli Florets 31
Oven Omelet with Spinach and Tomato 218
Pan Fried Squash 235
Pancakes, Squash (Winter) 296
Parmesan Butter 64
Parmesan Potatoes 178
Parslied Potatoes 176
Parsnip Loaf 153
Parsnip Cake 154
Parsnip Chowder 151
Parsnip Fritters 152
Parsnips in Stew 153
Parsnip Nut Bread 154
Parsnip Stir Fry 152
Parsnips with Acorn Squash 153
Parsnips, How to Cook 151
Parsnips, Glazed 152
Parsnips, Herbed 151
Parsnips, How to Freeze 155
Parsnips, Sautéed 151
Parsnips, Sweet Sour 152
Pastry for Double Crust Pie 208
Pea and Pork Stir Fry, Snow 161
Pea Potato Salad, Creamy 158
Pea Salad, Raw 159
Pea Soup, Cream of 157
Pea Soup, Rice and 157
Pea Soup, Turkey Carrot 55
Pea Stir Fry, Snap 161

Pea, Cauliflower Casserole 65
Peas Almondine 159
Peas with Mushrooms and Onions 159
Peas with Noodles and Ham 162
Peas with Pineapple, Snow 160
Peas with Potatoes, Creamed 160
Peas, Chicken Casserole with 162
Peas, Creamed 160
Peas, Filled Snow 157
Peas, Fried Rice with 161
Peas, How to Can Shelled 162
Peas, How to Cook 159
Peas, How to Freeze 163
Peas, New Potato Salad with 158
Peas, Refrigerator Pickled Snow 163
Peas, Sautéed Sugar Snap and Snow 160
Pecan Sweet Potato Pie 261
Pepper Chicken, Quick 168
Pepper Dressing, Green 165
Pepper Egg Sandwich, Onion 139
Pepper Ham Onion Hoagies 165
Pepper Rings, Sweet Pickled 170
Pepper Scrapple, Carrot Onion 143
Pepper Steak 169
Pepper Tomato Relish, Sweet 171
Peppers and Brown Rice 167
Peppers and Onions with Cod 168
Peppers and Potatoes 167
Peppers, Baked Pasta with 169
Peppers, Cole Slaw with 165
Peppers, How to Can 170
Peppers, Hungarian Wax, Salsa with 281
Peppers, Pickled 170
Peppers, Pork Chops with Potato 182
Peppers, Quick Chicken Fajitas with 168
Peppers, Roasted 165
Peppers, Salsa with Jalapeno 280
Peppers, Stuffed 166
Peppers, Stuffing for, I 166
Peppers, Stuffing for, II 167
Peppers, Stuffing for, III 167
Pickle Relish 92
Pickle, Hot Mixed 67
Pickle, Zucchini Bread and Butter 250
Pickled Beets 26
Pickled Onions 148
Pickled Pepper Rings, Sweet 170
Pickled Peppers 170
Pickled Radishes, Refrigerator 199
Pickled Red Beet Eggs 25

323

Index

Pickles, Bread and Butter 91
Pickles, Four-Day Sweet Gherkins or Chunk 92
Pickles, Freezer Cucumber 93
Pickles, Freezer Sweet Dill 93
Pickles, Fresh Pack Dill 91
Pickles, Refrigerator 90

Pies

Blender Parsnip Pie 154
Blender Sweet Potato Pie 260
Coconut Custard Sweet Potato Pie 260
Fluffy Strawberry Pie 223
Green Tomato Pie 276
Ground Cherry Pie 111
Ground Cherry Pie with Meringue 111
Pecan Sweet Potato Pie 261
Pumpkin Pie 192
Pumpkin Pie with Cream Cheese 193
Rhubarb Cream Pie 207
Rhubarb Custard Pie 207
Rhubarb Raisin Pie 208
Rhubarb Strawberry Pie 207
Spaghetti Squash Pie 300
Strawberry Pie 223
Strawberry Pudding Pie 224
Turnip Pie 290
Yellow Squash Pie 248

Pie Crust 193

Pastry for a Double Crust 208
Pie Crust, Whole Wheat 193
Pineapple Carrot Salad 56
Pineapple Sweet Potato Casserole 257
Pizza Sauce 281
Pork Chops and Onions 145
Pork Chops with Potatoes and Peppers 182
Pork Zucchini Pineapple Stir Fry 243
Pot Roast with Lima Beans 17
Potato and Vegetable Stuffing 182
Potato Bacon Omelet 181
Potato Bake, Easy 178
Potato Baskets, Onion 142
Potato Casserole, Green Bean Ham 15
Potato Chocolate Cake 184
Potato Chowder, Fishy 174
Potato Cinnamon Rolls 185
Potato Doughnuts, Raised 185
Potato Dumplings 180
Potato Egg Casserole 181
Potato Pancakes 180
Potato Pancakes, Green Bean 14
Potato Pancakes, Radish 199

Potato Patties, Zucchini 239
Potato Rivel Soup 173
Potato Salad with Peas, New 158
Potato Salad, Chunky 175
Potato Salad, Classic 175
Potato Salad, Dandelion 104
Potato Salad, Hot German 175
Potato Soup 173
Potato Soup, Cheeseburger 174
Potato Soup, Creamy 174
Potato Soup, Leek 137
Potato Soup, Zucchini Broccoli 233
Potato Whip, Rutabaga 290
Potato, Celery Soup 69
Potatoes and Hot Dogs, Green Beans with 15
Potatoes and Peppers, Pork Cops with 182
Potatoes Au Gratin 180
Potatoes O'brien 182
Potatoes with Cheese and Peppers, Scalloped . 179
Potatoes, Baked 177
Potatoes, Baked with Chives 177
Potatoes, Creamed 176
Potatoes, Creamed Peas with 160
Potatoes, French Fried 178
Potatoes, French Fried, How to Freeze 186
Potatoes, French Fried, Oven 179
Potatoes, Fried 178
Potatoes, Hash Brown, How to Freeze 186
Potatoes, How to Can 186
Potatoes, How to Cook 176
Potatoes, How to Freeze 186
Potatoes, Mashed 176
Potatoes, Mashed Radishes and 198
Potatoes, Mashed with Cheese, Baked 177
Potatoes, Mashed, How to Freeze 186
Potatoes, Mixed Greens and 107
Potatoes, Parmesan 178
Potatoes, Parslied 176
Potatoes, Peppers and 167
Potatoes, Scalloped 179
Potatoes, Twice Baked 177
Potatoes, with Beef Stew 183
Pumpkin Bars 191
Pumpkin Bread 192
Pumpkin Cheesecake 195
Pumpkin Chocolate Chip Cake 191
Pumpkin Cinnamon Rolls 192
Pumpkin Dessert, Frozen 194
Pumpkin Frosting 190
Pumpkin Marshmallow Dessert 194

Pumpkin Muffins 190
Pumpkin or Winter Squash, Deep Fried 188
Pumpkin Pecan Butter, Spiced 195
Pumpkin Pie 192
Pumpkin Pie Mix, How to Freeze 196
Pumpkin Pie Squares 194
Pumpkin Pie with Cream Cheese 193
Pumpkin Seeds, Roasted 189
Pumpkin Soup 187
Pumpkin Waffles 189
Pumpkin Walnut Cookies 190
Pumpkin, Baked 187
Pumpkin, Baked, to use in a Recipe 188
Pumpkin, How to Can Cubed 195
Pumpkin, How to Cook 187
Pumpkin, How to Freeze 196
Pumpkin, Whole Stuffed 189
Quiche
   Asparagus Quiche 6
   Broccoli Quiche 34
   Corn Quiche 82
   Easy Onion and Cheese Quiche 143
   Spinach Quiche 218
   Zucchini Quiche 237
Quick Asparagus Stir Fry 4
Quick Broccoli Chicken Noodle Dinner 33
Quick Chicken Fahitas with Peppers 168
Quick Pepper Chicken 168
Quick Strawberry Shortcake 224
Radish Cole Slaw 197
Radish Cream 197
Radish Dip 197
Radish Potato Pancakes 199
Radish Salad, Corn and 78
Radish Salad, Kohlrabi 113
Radish Sandwiches 197
Radish Stir Fry 198
Radishes and Potatoes, Mashed 198
Radishes, Creamed 197
Radishes, Deep Fried 198
Radishes, Refrigerator Pickled 199
Raised Corn Muffins 83
Raised Potato Doughnuts 185
Raw Beet Salad 23
Raw Green Bean Salad 11
Raw Pea Salad 159
Raw Sweet Potato Casserole 255
Red Beet Salad to Can 26
Refried Beans 18
Refrigerator Dills 90

Refrigerator Pickled Radishes 199
Refrigerator Pickled Snow Peas 163
Refrigerator Pickles 90
Refrigerator Sweet Sour Vegetables Cabbage 52
Rhubarb and Orange Coffee Cake 204
Rhubarb Bread 203
Rhubarb Cake 203
Rhubarb Cake, Streusel 204
Rhubarb Cinnamon Rolls 204
Rhubarb Cream Pie 207
Rhubarb Crisp 206
Rhubarb Crunch 206
Rhubarb Custard Dessert 205
Rhubarb Custard Pie 207
Rhubarb Dessert, Easy 205
Rhubarb Jam 209
Rhubarb Jam, Strawberry 230
Rhubarb Muffins 202
Rhubarb Pineapple Sauce 202
Rhubarb Pizza 206
Rhubarb Preserves 209
Rhubarb Pudding, Baked 205
Rhubarb Punch 201
Rhubarb Raisin Pie 208
Rhubarb Sauce, Strawberry 232
Rhubarb Strawberry Pie 207
Rhubarb Strawberry Salad 201
Rhubarb Strawberry Sauce 202
Rhubarb Upside-Down Cake 203
Rhubarb, How to Can 208
Rhubarb, How to Freeze 209
Rhubarb, Stewed 201
Rice and Pea Soup 157
Roasted Beets 24
Roasted Eggplant Salad 95
Roasted Peppers 165
Roasted Pumpkin Seeds 189
Rutabaga Apple Salad 286
Rutabaga Potato Whip 290
Rutabaga Puff 289
Rutabaga Soup 285
Rutabagas Au Gratin 289
Rutabagas with Basil Lemon Butter 289
Rutabagas, How to Cook 288
Rutabagas, How to Freeze 291
Salads
   Apple Rutabaga Salad 286
   Asparagus Radish Cucumber Salad 2
   Asparagus Vinaigrette 2
   Bean and Bacon Salad 12

325

Index

Beet and Apple Salad...................................... 23
Beet and Egg Salad 24
Beet Macaroni Salad 24
Broccoli Cauliflower Salad........................... 30
Broccoli Pasta Salad 30
Broccoli Salad 29
Brussels Chef Salad 37
Cabbage Apple Salad.................................... 45
Cabbage Gelatin Salad.................................. 46
Cabbage Slaw.. 44
Caesar Salad 119
Carrot and Zucchini Salad 56
Cauliflower Salad.. 63
Cauliflower Vegetable Salad 64
Celeriac and Cabbage Salad 75
Celeriac Grape Pineapple Salad 75
Celeriac Salad 74
Chard Salad 104
Chef Salad 121
Chicken Salad with Celery 70
Chunky Potato Salad 175
Classic Potato Salad.................................... 175
Cole Slaw with Peppers 165
Corn and Radish Salad................................. 78
Corn Salad.. 78
CreamCheeseBaconStuffedCherryTomato 265
Creamy Cabbage Slaw 45
Creamy Pea Potato Salad 158
Cucumber and Tomato Salad........................ 88
Cucumber Salad 87
Cucumbers in Sour Cream............................ 88
Cucumbers in Vinegar and Oil 88
Dandelion Potato Salad............................... 104
Dandelion Salad 104
Dandelion Salad with Horseradish 118
Dilled Cucumbers 88
Egg Stuffed Tomatoes................................. 264
Eggplant Salad 95
Frozen Strawberry Pineapple Salad............ 221
Gjreens and Bacon Salad 119
Grated Carrot Salad 55
Greek Salad 120
Green Bean and Tomato Salad 11
Green Bean Salad.. 11
Green Bean Salad with Limas 12
Ham Salad in Muskmelon Rings 130
Hot Cabbage Salad.. 46
Hot Chicken Salad 122
Hot Chinese Cabbage Salad.......................... 46
Hot German Potato Salad 175

Kohlrabi Radish Salad 113
Kohlrabi Vegetable Salad............................ 113
Layered Garden Pasta Salad 121
Layered Salad... 121
Lettuce and Fruit Salad............................... 120
Marinated Broccoli and Cauliflower 30
Melon Fruit Cocktail................................... 129
MelonRing withHoney Coconut Dressing . 130
Melons with Pineapple 129
Molded Cucumber Salad 89
Muskmelon Molds 129
New Potato Salad with Peas 158
Old-Fashioned Lettuce Salad...................... 118
Old-Time Tomato Aspic 264
Oriental Spinach Salad 215
Pineapple Carrot Salad 56
Radish Coleslaw.. 197
Raw Beet Salad 23
Raw Green Bean Salad 11
Raw Pea Salad... 159
Rhubarb Strawberry Salad 201
Roasted Eggplant Salad 95
Salad for Two 117
Spaghetti Squash Salad 293
Spinach and Apple Salad............................. 214
Spinach and Chicken Salad 215
Spinach Salad 213
Sprouty Salad 214
Strawberry Blueberry Banana Salad........... 221
Strawberry Spinach Salad........................... 222
Stuffed Celery 70
Summer Salad 119
Summer Squash Salad 233
Sweet Potato Fruit Salad............................. 253
Sweet Potato Salad..................................... 253
Taco Salad.. 122
Taco Salad with Tomatoes.......................... 265
Three Bean Salad 12
Tomato Onion Salad 138
Tomatoes Vinaigrette.................................. 264
Tuna Stuffed Tomatoes............................... 265
Turnip Carrot Cabbage Salad 286
Turnip Slaw... 286
Vegetable Cabbage Slaw 45
Vegetable Salad 120
Wilted Lettuce Salad................................... 118
Wilted Spinach Salad with Mushrooms 214
Salad for Two 117
Salsa with Hungarian Wax Peppers 281
Salsa with Jalapeno Peppers 280

Salsa, Jalapeno Pepper 171
Salsa, Mild 280
Salsa, Onion 148
Salsify Soup 211
Salsify, Baked 211
Salsify, How to Cook 211
Sandwiches
    Cabbage Sandwich Spread 44
    Carrot Sandwich Spread 56
    Cucumber Sandwich Spread 89
    Eggplant Cheese Sandwiches 95
    English Muffins with Eggs and Spinach 216
    Hot Ham and Beef Sandwich with Onion .. 139
    Hot Tomato and Ham Sandwiches 266
    Lettuce Sandwich Spread 127
    Onion Pepper Egg Sandwiches 139
    Pepper Ham Onion Hoagies 165
    Radish Sandwiches 197
    Sloppy Joe with Fresh Tomatoes 266
    Tomato and Chicken Sandwiches 266
    Zucchini Pita Sandwiches 234
Sauces
    Cheese Sauce 64
    Dipping Sauce 97
    Lemon Butter Sauce 37
    Mock Hollandaise 3
    Onion Sauce 139
    Rhubarb Pineapple Sauce 202
    Rhubarb Strawberry Sauce 202
    Sour Cream Sauce 31
    Strawberry Sauce I 229
    Strawberry Sauce II 229
    Tomato Sauce 274
    Zesty Tomato Sauce 265
Sauerkraut, How to Can 53
Sauerkraut, How to Freeze 54
Sauerkraut, How to Make 53
Sausage and Celery Stuffing 74
Sausage and Zucchini with Spaghetti 244
Sausage Stuffed Acorn Squash 295
Sausage Zucchini Stir Fry 242
Sautéed Celery 70
Sautéed Chard 105
Sautéed Corn 79
Sautéed Cucumbers 89
Sautéed Eggplant 96
Sautéed Kohlrabies 114
Sautéed Parsnips 151
Sautéed Spinach 216
Sautéed Squash (Summer) 235

Sautéed Squash (Winter) 293
Sautéed Sugar Snap and Snow peas 160
Sautéed Sweet Peppers 166
Sautéed Tomatoes 267
Savory Spinach Squares 217
Scallop Squash, Stuffed 238
Scalloped Corn 80
Scalloped Potatoes 179
Scalloped Potatoes with Cheese and Peppers .. 179
Scalloped Summer Squash 237
Scalloped Tomatoes 267
Seafood Gumbo 136
Seven Layer Casserole with Carrots 58
Shallot Butter 139
Shell Bean Casserole 16
Shell Bean Soup 9
Shell Beans, How to Cook 15
Skillet Candied Sweet Potatoes 254
Sliced Butternut Squash Casserole 296
Sliced Fried Okra 134
Sloppy Joes with Fresh Tomatoes 266
Snap Pea Stir Fry 161
Snow Pea and Pork Stir Fry 161
Snow Peas with Pineapple 160
Soufflés
    Asparagus Soufflé 6
    Broccoli Soufflé 33
    Dandelion Soufflé 127
    Turnip Soufflé 288
Soup
    Asparagus and Cheddar Cheese Soup 1
    Asparagus Soup 1
    Borscht 23
    Broccoli and Ham Soup 29
    Cauliflower Soup with Smoked Sausage 63
    Celery Potato Soup 69
    Celery Soup 69
    Chard Soup 103
    Cheeseburger Potato Soup 174
    Cheesy Carrot Soup 55
    Chicken Corn Noodle Soup 78
    Chicken Noodle Soup with Celery Carrot 69
    Chinese Cabbage with Chicken 43
    Chunky Tomato Soup 263
    Corn and Ham Soup 77
    Cream of Asparagus Soup 1
    Cream of Broccoli Soup 29
    Cream of Cabbage Soup 43
    Cream of Celeriac and Carrot Soup 74
    Cream of Greens Soup 103

Index

Soup (cont.)

Cream of Leek Soup 137
Cream of Pea Soup...................................... 157
Creamy Cauliflower Soup........................... 63
Creamy Corn Soup...................................... 77
Creamy Cucumber Soup............................. 87
Creamy Potato Soup................................. 174
Creamy Spinach Soup.............................. 213
Cucumber Soup.. 87
French Onion Soup.................................... 137
Fruit Soup with Strawberries.................... 221
Green Bean Soup... 9
Kale and Chicken Soup............................ 103
Leek Potato Soup...................................... 137
Lettuce Soup 117
Lima Bean Soup... 9
Nary Bean Soup.. 10
Okra Soup... 133
Okra Soup with Chicken.......................... 133
Old-Fashioned Navy Bean Soup................ 10
Potato Rivel Soup...................................... 173
Potato Soup 173
Pumpkin Soup.. 187
Rice and Pea Soup 157
Rutabaga Soup 285
Salsify Soup... 211
Shell Bean Soup... 9
Spicy Butternut Squash Soup 293
Spinach Soup.. 213
Turkey Carrot Pea Soup.............................. 55
Turkey Minestrone with Cabbage 44
Turkey Onion Rice Soup.......................... 138
Turkey Vegetable Soup with Tomatoes 263
Turnip Soup... 285
Turnip Vegetable Soup 285
Watercress Soup... 117
Winter Squash Soup.................................. 293
Zucchini Broccoli Potato Soup 233
Soup, Shell Bean 9
Sour Cream and Onion Dip....................... 138
Sour Cream Sauce 31
Soy Beans, How to Can Green 21
Spaghetti Sauce 282
Spaghetti Sauce with Beef........................ 282
Spaghetti Squash 298
Spaghetti Squash Casserole 298
Spaghetti Squash Lasagna 299
Spaghetti Squash Pie 300
Spaghetti Squash Salad 293
Spaghetti with Fresh Tomatoes 268

Spaghetti, Baked with Tomatoes 272
Spaghetti, Beefy with Tomato Juice 273
Spiced Pumpkin Pecan Butter........................ 195
Spiced Watermelon Rind 132
Spicy Butternut Squash Soup......................... 293
Spinach and Apple Salad 214
Spinach and Chicken Salad............................ 215
Spinach and Tomato, Oven Omelet with......... 218
Spinach Dip 215
Spinach Fried Rice 217
Spinach Parmesan 217
Spinach Quiche 218
Spinach Salad 213
Spinach Salad with Marinated Mushrooms 214
Spinach Salad, Oriental 215
Spinach Salad, Sprouty 214
Spinach Salad, Strawberry 222
Spinach Sautéed 216
Spinach Soup 213
Spinach Soup, Creamy 213
Spinach Squares, Savory 217
Spinach, Creamy 216
Spinach, English Muffins with Eggs and......... 216
Spinach, How to Can...................................... 218
Spinach, How to Cook.................................... 216
Spinach, How to Freeze 219
Sprouty Spinach Salad 214
Squash (Winter) Pancakes 296
Squash Bake, Butternut.................................. 297
Squash Bake, Delicata.................................... 297
Squash Bake, Hubbard 297
Squash Balls, Winter...................................... 296
Squash Casserole, Sliced Butternut 296
Squash Casserole, Spaghetti 298
Squash Casserole, Winter 299
Squash Doughnuts, Winter 300
Squash Fritters 239
Squash Fritters, Winter 296
Squash Lasagna, Spaghetti 299
Squash Pie, Spaghetti 300
Squash Pie, Yellow.. 248
Squash Salad, Spaghetti 293
Squash Salad, Summer.................................... 233
Squash Sautéed (Winter)................................ 293
Squash Soup, Spicy Butternut......................... 293
Squash Soup, Winter 293
Squash Tomato Skillet, Summer...................... 240
Squash with Cream, Zucchini and Yellow 240
Squash with Herbed Rice, Yellow................... 240
Squash, Baked Acorn 294

Squash, Deep Fried Pumpkin or Winter 188
Squash, Deep Fried Summer 236
Squash, How to Bake Winter 294
Squash, How to Can Summer 249
Squash, How to Can Winter 301
Squash, How to Cook Summer 234
Squash, How to Cook Winter 294
Squash, How to Freeze Summer 251
Squash, How to Freeze Winter 301
Squash, Pan Fried 235
Squash, Sausage Stuffed Acorn 295
Squash, Sautéed 235
Squash, Scalloped Summer 237
Squash, Spaghetti 298
Squash, Stuffed Scallop 238
Squash, Sweet Baked Acorn 294
Squash, Whipped Butternut 295
Stack Supper with Tomatoes 273
Stewed Rhubarb 201
Stewed Tomatoes 267
Stir Fried Cabbage 48
Stir Fried Chinese Cabbage with Chicken 48
Stir Fried Cucumbers 90
Stir Fried Green Beans 13
Stir Fried Zucchini 235

Stir Frys
    Asparagus Stir Fry 4
    Beef and Celery Stir Fry 71
    Beef Stir Fry with Zucchini 243
    Broccoli Carrot Stir Fry 32
    Broccoli Celery Stir Fry 31
    Broccoli Chicken Stir Fry 32
    Broccoli Pasta Stir Fry with Cheese 32
    Brussels Sprouts and Chicken Stir Fry 39
    Carrot and Celery Stir Fry 57
    Cauliflower Beef Stir Fry 66
    Chicken Asparagus Stir Fry, Spaghetti 5
    Chicken Stir Fry with Tomatoes 272
    Parsnips Stir Fry 152
    Pork Zucchini Pineapple Stir Fry 243
    Quick Asparagus Stir Fry 4
    Radish Stir Fry 198
    Sausage Zucchini Stir Fry 242
    Snap Pea Stir Fry 161
    Snow Pea and Pork Stir Fry 161
    Stir Fried Cabbage 48
    Stir Fried Chinese Cabbage with Chicken 48
    Stir Fried Cucumbers 90
    Stir Fried Green Beans 13
    Stir Fried Zucchini 235

Stove Top Cabbage Rolls 48
Strawberries, Fruit Soup with 221
Strawberries, How to Can 231
Strawberries, How to Freeze 232
Strawberry Banana Smoothie 228
Strawberry Blueberry Banana Salad 221
Strawberry Bread 223
Strawberry Cheesecake 225
Strawberry Cream Puffs 226
Strawberry Dessert, Frozen 227
Strawberry Freezer Jam, No-Cook 230
Strawberry Frosting, Fresh 229
Strawberry Gelatin Pizza 225
Strawberry Ice 227
Strawberry Ice Cream 227
Strawberry Ice Cream, Easy 227
Strawberry Jam 230
Strawberry Muffins 222
Strawberry Omelet 222
Strawberry Pie 223
Strawberry Pie, Fluffy 223
Strawberry Pineapple Dessert 226
Strawberry Pineapple Punch 228
Strawberry Pineapple Salad, Frozen 221
Strawberry pizza 225
Strawberry Popsicles, Fruity 229
Strawberry preserves 231
Strawberry Pudding Pie 224
Strawberry Punch 228
Strawberry Raspberry Blackberry Jam 231
Strawberry Rhubarb Jam 230
Strawberry Rhubarb Sauce 232
Strawberry Sauce I 229
Strawberry Sauce II 229
Strawberry Sauce, Rhubarb 202
Strawberry Shortcake 224
Strawberry Shortcake, Quick 224
Strawberry Smoothie, Creamy 228
Strawberry Spinach Salad 222
Strawberry Tapioca Pudding 226
Strawberry, Rhubarb Pie 207
Strawberry, Rhubarb Salad 201
Streusel Rhubarb Cake 204
Stuffed Celery 70
Stuffed Eggplants 100
Stuffed Peppers 166
Stuffed Scallop Squash 238
Stuffed Tomatoes with Meat 270
Stuffed Zucchini 238
Stuffed Zucchini Boats 238

Index

Stuffing for Peppers I 166
Stuffing for Peppers II 167
Stuffing for Peppers III 167
Succotash 16
Summer Salad 119
Summer Squash Salad 233
Summer Squash Tomato Skillet 240
Summer Squash, Deep Fried 236
Summer Squash, How to Can 249
Summer Squash, How to Cook 234
Summer Squash, How to Freeze 251
Summer Squash, Okra and 135
Summer Squash, Scalloped 237
Sweet Baked Acorn Squash 294
Sweet Pepper Tomato Relish 171
Sweet Peppers, Sautéed 166
Sweet Pickled Brussels Sprouts 40
Sweet Pickled Cauliflower 67
Sweet Pickled Pepper Rings 170
Sweet Potato Apple Casserole 256
Sweet Potato Biscuits 259
Sweet Potato Cake 259
Sweet Potato Casserole 255
Sweet Potato casserole, Maple Syrup 256
Sweet Potato Casserole, Orange 256
Sweet Potato Casserole, Raw 255
Sweet Potato Chips 254
Sweet Potato Fritters 260
Sweet Potato Fruit Salad 253
Sweet Potato Muffins with Walnut Streusel 259
Sweet Potato Pie, Coconut Custard 260
Sweet Potato Pie, Pecan 261
Sweet Potato Salad 253
Sweet Potato, Blender Pie 260
Sweet Potatoes and Sausage 257
Sweet Potatoes in Beef Stew 258
Sweet Potatoes with Maple Syrup 254
Sweet Potatoes with Orange Juice 254
Sweet Potatoes with Pork Chops and Pears 258
Sweet Potatoes, Baked 253
Sweet Potatoes, Baked Candied 255
Sweet Potatoes, Creamed 257
Sweet Potatoes, How To Can 261
Sweet Potatoes, How to Cook 253
Sweet Potatoes, Skillet Candied 254
Sweet Sour Parsnips 152
Sweet Sour Red Cabbage 47
Swiss Steak with Tomatoes 273
Taco Salad 122
Taco Salad with Tomatoes 265

Thousand Island Dressing 125
Three Bean Salad 12
Three Bean Salad to Can 12
Toasted Croutons 128
Tomato and Chicken Sandwiches 266
Tomato and Ham Sandwiches, Hot 266
Tomato Aspic, Old-Time 264
Tomato Bread 275
Tomato Bread, Green 275
Tomato Casserole, Onion 142
Tomato Cheese Pie with Salmon 270
Tomato Chocolate Cake, Green 276
Tomato Corn Casserole 268
Tomato Gravy 274
Tomato Ground Beef Pie, Corn 82
Tomato Hot Dog Relish, Green 283
Tomato Juice, How to Can 277
Tomato Ketchup 280
Tomato Meat Pie, Easy 271
Tomato Muffins, Green 274
Tomato Oatmeal Bars, Green 276
Tomato Onion Salad 138
Tomato Pie, Green 276
Tomato Relish, Sweet Pepper 171
Tomato Rice Skillet, Okra 135
Tomato Salad, Cucumber and 88
Tomato Salad, Green Bean and 11
Tomato Sauce 274
Tomato Sauce or Puree with Vegetables 279
Tomato Sauce, Puree or Paste 278
Tomato Sauce, Zesty 265
Tomato Skillet, Summer Squash 240
Tomato Soup, Chunky 263
Tomato Stuffed Fish Fillets 270
Tomato Vegetable Juice 278
Tomato Vegetable Soup 279
Tomato Zucchini Casserole 269
Tomato, Green, Dilled Pickles 283
Tomato, Oven Omelet with Spinach and 218
Tomatoes and Scrambled Eggs 268
Tomatoes Vinaigrette 264
Tomatoes with Chicken 272
Tomatoes with Hot Dogs and Onions 271
Tomatoes with Meat, Stuffed 270
Tomatoes, Broiled 267
Tomatoes, Cherry, Cream Cheese and Bacon 265
Tomatoes, Chicken Stir Fry with 272
Tomatoes, Chili With Beef and 282
Tomatoes, Egg Stuffed 264
Tomatoes, Eggplant Onion and 99

Tomatoes, Fried Green 268
Tomatoes, How to Can Whole 279
Tomatoes, How to Freeze 284
Tomatoes, Mock Berry Jam with Green 284
Tomatoes, Mock Berry Jam with Ripe 283
Tomatoes, Okra and 135
Tomatoes, Sautéed 267
Tomatoes, Scalloped 267
Tomatoes, Sloppy Joes with Fresh 266
Tomatoes, Spaghetti with Fresh 268
Tomatoes, Stack Supper with 273
Tomatoes, Stewed 267
Tomatoes, Stuffed, Baked 269
Tomatoes, Swiss Steak with 273
Tomatoes, Taco Salad with 265
Tomatoes, Tuna Stuffed 265
Tomatoes, Turkey Vegetable Soup with 263
Tomatoes, Wax Beans and 13
Tuna Stuffed Tomatoes 265
Turkey Breast Cabbage Vegetable Stuffing 51
Turkey Carrot Pea Soup 55
Turkey Minestrone with Cabbage 44
Turkey Onion Rice Soup 138
Turkey Patties with Celery 73
Turkey Vegetable Soup with Tomatoes 263
Turkey Zucchini Skillet 242
Turnip Carrot Cabbage Salad 286
Turnip Greens 290
Turnip Greens, How to Cook 290
Turnip Greens, How to Freeze 291
Turnip Pie 290
Turnip Slaw 286
Turnip Soufflé 288
Turnip Soup 285
Turnip Vegetable Soup 285
Turnips and Carrots, Cheesy 287
Turnips with Onions 287
Turnips, Baked, Stuffed 288
Turnips, Curried 287
Turnips, How to Cook 286
Turnips, How to Freeze 291
Turnips, Irish Stew with 288
Twice Baked Potatoes 177
Vegetable Cabbage Slaw 45
Vegetable Pizza with Cauliflower 66
Vegetarian Stuffed Eggplant 100
Watercress Soup 117
Watermelon Ice 131
Watermelon Popsicles 131
Watermelon Rind, Spiced 132

Watermelon Slush 131
Wax Beans and Tomatoes 13
Whipped Butternut Squash 295
Whole Fried Okra 134
Whole Stuffed Pumpkin 189
Whole Wheat Pie Crust 193
Wilted Lettuce Salad 118
Wilted Spinach Salad with
        Marinated Mushrooms 214
Winter Squash Balls 296
Winter Squash Casserole 299
Winter Squash Doughnuts 300
Winter Squash Fritters 296
Winter Squash Soup 293
Winter Squash, Deep Fried Pumpkin or 188
Winter Squash, How to Bake 294
Winter Squash, How to Can 301
Winter Squash, How to Cook 294
Winter Squash, How to Freeze 301
Yellow Squash Pie 248
Yellow Squash with Cream, Zucchini and 240
Yellow Squash with Herbed Rice 240
Zesty Tomato Sauce 265
Zucchini and Yellow Squash with Cream 240
Zucchini Boats, Stuffed 238
Zucchini Bread 246
Zucchini Bread and Butter Pickle 250
Zucchini Broccoli Potato Soup 233
Zucchini Brownies 247
Zucchini Carrot Cake 248
Zucchini Casserole, Tomato 269
Zucchini Chicken Rice Casserole 245
Zucchini Chocolate Cake 247
Zucchini Cookies with Lemon Glaze 247
Zucchini Dessert 248
Zucchini Ground Beef Casserole 245
Zucchini Ham Casserole 244
Zucchini Lasagna 242
Zucchini Meat Loaf 241
Zucchini Muffins 246
Zucchini Omelet 239
Zucchini Parmesan 234
Zucchini Pineapple Stir Fry, Pork 243
Zucchini Pineapple to Can 249
Zucchini Pita Sandwiches 234
Zucchini Pizza Casserole 245
Zucchini Potato Patties 239
Zucchini Quiche 237
Zucchini Relish 250
Zucchini Salad, Carrot and 56

Index

Zucchini Skillet, Turkey 242

Zucchini Stew 241

Zucchini Stir Fry, Sausage 242

Zucchini Tuna Casserole 244

Zucchini Vegetable Mix 250

Zucchini with Pasta 241

Zucchini with Spaghetti, Sausage and 244

Zucchini, Baked 235

Zucchini, Baked and Tomatoes 236

Zucchini, Baked and
    Tomatoes with Cheese Sauce 237

Zucchini, Beef Stir Fry with 243

Zucchini, Broiled 235

Zucchini, Grilled and other Vegetables 236

Zucchini, Stir Fried 235

Zucchini, Stuffed 238

The Practical Produce Cookbook
Ray and Elsie Hoover
EP 4230 March Rapids Ave.
Stratford, WI   54484

Phone: 715-687-4558

Please send me _____ copies of **The Practical Produce Cookbook** $14.95 each_____
Wisconsin residents add sales tax of 5.5%   _____
Include postage and handling (call for shipping rates on quantity orders) $2.50 each

Dealers, distributors and retailers call for more information.

Make checks payable to
The Practical Produce Cookbook

Name _____
(please print)

Street _____

City _____ State _____ Zip _____

The Practical Produce Cookbook
Ray and Elsie Hoover
EP 4230 March Rapids Ave.
Stratford, WI   54484

Phone: 715-687-4558

Please send me _____ copies of **The Practical Produce Cookbook** $14.95 each_____
Wisconsin residents add sales tax of 5.5%   _____
Include postage and handling (call for shipping rates on quantity orders) $2.50 each_____

Dealers, distributors and retailers call for more information.

Make checks payable to
The Practical Produce Cookbook

Name _____
(please print)

Street _____

City _____ State _____ Zip _____